BASKETBALL

BASKETBALL

Great Writing About America's Game

Alexander Wolff, EDITOR

WITH A FOREWORD BY
Kareem Abdul-Jabbar

THE LIBRARY OF AMERICA

Foreword, Introduction, headnotes, and volume compilation copyright © 2018
by Literary Classics of the United States, Inc., New York, N.Y. All rights reserved.

Published in the United States by Library of America
www.loa.org

No part of this book may be reproduced in any manner whatsoever
without the permission of the publisher, except in the case of
brief quotations embodied in critical articles and reviews.

Some of the material in this volume is reprinted with the permission of holders
of copyright and publishing rights. Acknowledgments are on page 445.

Distributed to the trade in the United States by Penguin Random
House Inc. and in Canada by Penguin Random House Canada Ltd.

Library of Congress Control Number: 2017951244

ISBN 978–1–59853–556–3

1 3 5 7 9 10 8 6 4 2

Manufactured in the United States of America

Contents

Foreword

by Kareem Abdul-Jabbar

TWO WOODEN PEACH BASKETS. A heavy leather soccer ball. Two nine-man teams. No dribbling allowed. No running with the ball.

That was the basic setup for the first basketball game played on December 21, 1891, when the game's inventor, Dr. James Naismith, asked his gym class students to try something new, a safer alternative to injury-prone football. One of Naismith's students reacted with an unenthusiastic "Huh! Another new game!" But they played their two fifteen-minute halves with a five-minute break between, finishing with a resounding 1–0 score. It was just as well that the game was low-scoring considering that the peach basket still had its bottom intact, so after a basket was made the janitor had to climb up on a ladder and get the ball down.

Huh, indeed!

An inauspicious beginning for one of the world's most popular sports. With over one billion fans worldwide, basketball is second only to soccer in having the largest number of professional teams and is the fastest growing sport in the world. One reason for its popularity is its simplicity. Basketball is one of the few major sports that you can play with a team or by yourself. All you need is a hoop and a ball. That's why there are small basketball hoops on the backs of the doors of so many bedrooms, dorm rooms, and office rooms, and so many balled-up pieces of paper around wastebaskets.

As a child, I was more interested in baseball. However, my height and encouragement from the basketball coach brought me out on the court to give it a try. At first, I was a lousy player, all arms and legs and very little coordination. I moved like a daddy longlegs spider on roller skates. But the more I played, the more the game became an integral part of me. It was no longer just something I did, it was how I saw myself as an individual and how I saw myself as part of my peers.

Growing up in Catholic schools, I was one of only two or three black kids in the entire student population. This was during the 1950s and 1960s, when America was going through a tumultuous political upheaval. Atrocities against African Americans were being broadcast on the nightly news and the black community responded with protests in the streets, some nonviolent, others descending into riots. I was just a school kid trying to figure out where I stood in all this turmoil. At school, the white kids were also trying to figure where I stood.

Playing for the school teams from middle school through high school was one way I was able to demonstrate that, while I was well aware of the social inequities and was outspoken about them, I was still a loyal part of the school itself. Being part of a team was important to me because I learned how to work with others so that we all could be successful together. It was satisfying to me as a player, but it was also satisfying to me as an African American to show us all working in harmony.

Also, the better I played as an individual, the more of a statement I was making about the negative stereotypes about blacks that were prevalent at that time. When a hook shot soared over an opponent and swished through the basket, I felt like I'd scored for all blacks. "See what we can do if given a chance?" I was saying. Sure, there were plenty of successful black athletes out there, but each addition to their ranks made the statement even bolder. I was determined to join in that statement with each game.

Basketball gave me the confidence to speak out and it gave me the platform to be heard. And, while the sport helped forge my personal and social values, it was never just about making a statement. There was also the pure joy of the game. When ten players are on the court, hustling, sweating, passing, muscling, looking for a shot, the outside world fades away to a distant thrum. There is only your training, your will, and your trust in your teammates. You feel it deep inside in a way that defies description.

That's where writers come in. Writing about basketball isn't just about showing enthusiasm for the game, it's also about understanding the elegance of the sport, the chesslike intricacies of the gameplans, the emotional impact on the fans, and what it says about the society that heralds it. This definitive collection includes some of the most famous sportswriters, players, aficionados, and enthusiasts the sport of basketball has ever known. And they get it right.

Whether you already love basketball or you're just wondering what the fuss is all about, this book will give you insights into all aspects of the game, from personal experiences playing and coaching to the joys and frustrations of being a fan to the relevance of the sport in our culture.

And you don't even have to work up a sweat.

Introduction

by Alexander Wolff

February Reconsidered

G EORGE PLIMPTON was the embodiment of the literary sports-writer, respected equally in the saloon and the salon. Perhaps that explains why his "Small Ball Theory" has hung like a shroud over writing about America's homegrown sport. "The smaller the ball, the more formidable the literature," Plimpton wrote in 1992. "There are superb books about golf, very good books about baseball, not many good books about football or soccer, very few good books about basketball and no good books about beach balls."

In his slight regard for basketball writing, Plimpton had company. There's only one basketball story among the fifty-nine pieces in the 1999 collection *The Best American Sports Writing of the Century.* (You can find it in this volume on page 150.) Decades before that, after he left sports to write novels, New York *Daily News* columnist Paul Gallico was asked why. "February," Gallico replied—not fingering basketball explicitly, but delivering an indictment by association just the same.

Consider this collection a rebuttal, as well as an updated survey of a basketball bibliography that, a quarter century after Plimpton's pronouncement, can stand unapologetically tall. His theory couldn't yet account for such books set far from the spotlight as Darcy Frey's *The Last Shot* (1994), John Edgar Wideman's *Hoop Roots* (2001), Pat Conroy's *My Losing Season* (2002), and George Dohrmann's *Play Their Hearts Out* (2010), much less work inspired by the NBA's Nineties boom or college basketball's ESPN-aided ascendancy. Attention begets fame, which begets public curiosity—in Bobby Knight, in Michael Jordan, in the Dream Team, in LeBron James. In meeting that demand, contemporary writers have backloaded the hoops canon.

To get a fix on what basketball writing is, it's worth stipulating what it isn't. It's less concerned with individual characters than boxing writing is, even if basketball also features large personalities performing outsized feats. Nor is the genre marked by the nostalgia that consumes so much baseball writing. Football writing tends to convey that sport's violent nature and steady evolution into spectacle; basketball is physical and commercialized, to be sure, but it's more balletic than brutal, with an intimacy that keeps writers from dwelling on the game as mass entertainment.

At its best, writing about basketball is likely to feature at least one of several characteristics. The first is what might be called a formalist approach. Even many non-sportswriters have been moved to examine the masters of this expressive team game that seeks to hold in balance freedom and unity, two tenets at the heart of the American experiment. That might mean celebrating conspicuous talents, like those of Julius Erving, as limned here by Mark Jacobson; or highlighting the subservient, almost imperceptible gifts of Shane Battier, a player, Michael Lewis writes, "widely regarded inside the NBA as, at best, a replaceable cog in a machine driven by superstars. And yet every team he has ever played on has acquired some magical ability to win." Another type of compelling piece sketches one of the characters the game has a knack for attracting, someone like Wilfred Hetzel, the aging trick-shot specialist profiled by Roy Blount, Jr., or Marquette coach Al McGuire, of whom Jimmy Breslin writes, in the argot of their native Queens, "I know the guy a long time." And given the game's African American inflections, as well as a lifespan that runs from *Plessy v. Ferguson* through the civil rights era to Charlottesville, good basketball writing tends to extend to themes beyond the arena or playground, race above all. Peter Goldman's ode to a Harlem Globetrotter, the dribbling wizard and certified character Leon Hillard, satisfies on each of these counts, but especially the last. When Goldman sets the scene of a terrified band of Trotters about to go on strike, holed up in a motel room and peering through the blinds as fans file into the arena across the street, we see the opening act of a stage play begging to be written.

More than anything, some of the best basketball writing can be personal in a way that writing about other games simply can't be. No other major sport so lends itself to playing alone, or is so anthropological, rife with both tribes to which the individual belongs and rites in which he participates—or to which she is subjected. "This is the way it works," writes Melissa King in "It's All in the Game," inviting us to consider what it's like to be the oddest of ducks on the courts of Chicago. Pat Conroy's book is a multisession exercise in post-traumatic psychoanalysis. Wideman suggests that basketball is so profoundly personal that it can create a parallel persona: "Read something in a newspaper about one of your basketball buddies and never know it's him. *Snobs*, inside the disguise of a whole, proper name. You'll have to hear the good news or bad news over again on the sidelines from somebody who tells the story with the court name in place. *D'you hear about Snobs, man.*"

Just as a game can turn on one play, many of the pieces here turn on one sentence or phrase. Here's Douglas Bauer, a high school bench-warmer, on his girlfriend, the star of the girls' team: "How great it would be to be so good that a bad night was the reason one's team had lost." George Dohrmann, on an adolescent casualty of the basketball-industrial complex: "Now, with his future hanging in the air like a ball on the rim, he cowered in a bathroom stall." Bryan Curtis, on the therapeutic value of sending shots *thunggg*-ing against a fiberglass backboard: "It was like shooting a silky Rabbit Angstrom jumper and committing a flagrant foul in the same motion." Brian Doyle, on a telepathic moment between brothers as they watch a pickup game: "That's a beautiful thing because it's little, and we saw it and we knew what it meant." Read these in context and you'll wind up remembering each story by its essential fragment, the same way you remember a play-off game by that moment LeBron pinned a last-minute layup as if mounting it on a wall.

Basketball's rise as popular entertainment coincided with the ascendancy of a new school of sportswriting. By the dawn of the Sixties a cohort of newspaper and magazine writers, refusing to "god up" athletes, began to focus instead on sports in their social context. The old guard called them "the Chipmunks," and these antiestablishment reporters, chattering among themselves in the press room, wore the epithet as a badge of honor. Journalists became more confident and allusive, pulling into a basketball piece not just race but also money and, at their intersection, labor relations. Another chronicler of the Sixties, David Halberstam, joined Peter Goldman in hitting those notes in the basketball work included here.

A glance at this volume's table of contents over the space of a few years highlights this revolution in sensibility. In 1965, John McPhee profiles Princeton star Bill Bradley, a Sunday School teacher and exemplar of the very muscular Christianity that motivated James Naismith, the game's inventor, to become a physical educator. Not a half dozen years later, in *The City Game*, Pete Axthelm is juxtaposing the exploits of Bradley and his New York Knicks teammates with sketches of heroin casualties in Harlem. George Kiseda is championing the lonely calvary of Vanderbilt star Perry Wallace as he integrated the Southeastern Conference. And Breslin is telling of how McGuire called time-out so his black players could raise their fists to honor Malcolm X in the middle of a game. We've come a long way from Bradley in his dorm room pregame, motivating himself by playing the warhorse from *The Sound of Music*, "Climb Ev'ry Mountain." If basketball writing has now found its stride, it helps that the Sixties happened, but that the New Journalism did, too. A hoops piece now refracts even old verities like diligence and teamwork through a lens with the warp of the modern game.

The selections here are limited to nonfiction, but the contributors include a striking number of poets—not only poets by primary vocation, like Donald Hall, James McKean, and Rowan Ricardo Phillips, but also such essayists as Bauer and Doyle, for whom poetry has been a supplemental genre, as well as Tom Meschery, who wrote verse during and after his NBA career. The critic and novelist Elizabeth Hardwick once ascribed her love for the prose of poets to "the offhand flashes, the absence of the lumber . . . the quickness, the deftness, confidence, and even the relief from spelling everything out, plank by plank." Which is to say she kindled to the very things that basketball delivers.

If poetry is the business of isolating moments in the rushing continuum of life, those drawn to writing and reading about basketball seek also to pull something memorable from the burbling that is this most fluid of games. And basketball writers keep the company of people who understand, viscerally if only subconsciously, that rhyme, meter, and poetic resonances lie in there somewhere. Ask the former English Lit professor and Los Angeles Lakers coach Paul Westhead about the jump shot of one of his players, forward Jamaal Wilkes, and the answer comes back: "It's like snow on a bamboo leaf."

Verbiage produced by the human voice is the very sign of a basketball game's vitality. In a comment to Kareem Abdul-Jabbar, who writes of his season coaching on a reservation in Arizona, a Native American colleague sees the silence with which Apache kids play the game as a virtue, approvingly calling it "ninja basketball." But Abdul-Jabbar finds the quiet troubling. To him, it's more than a matter of upholding basketball's African American oral tradition, which encourages the selling of wolf tickets to claim a seat in an opponent's head. If you play ball, you lay a rap on, for basketball demands verbal engagement as does no other sport. To play on a team, writes McKean, is to traffic in "single-word information—*left, right, switch, mine, my fault*—all directed to honing the moment to a simple edge, your two points and their absolute denial." From spoken word, it's just a short hop to vocal music: Phillips takes us beyond the simplistic assertion that "basketball is jazz," matching a player, Steph Curry, with a standard, Nina Simone's "Feeling Good."

In their introduction to the collection *Fast Break to Line Break: Poets on the Art of Basketball*, Todd Davis and J. D. Scrimgoeur note that Walt Whitman died a few months after Naismith hung up the primordial peach baskets in December 1891. "Whitman doubtless would have been pleased with Naismith's game, born of necessity and joy, requiring ego and egolessness," they write. "A game with patterns that can feel elemental, yet distinguished by improbable improvisations, full of the energy of the city and the stillness (ever taken a foul shot?) of the prairie—an American game. Indeed, one might imagine Whitman's spirit transferring from his body into this new game and the bodies that play it, their moves graceful as grasses in the wind, stunning as sunlight flashing off the East River."

Hold that image: New York City and the glint of sunlight, but off shards of glass, swept to the edge of a patch of macadam girdled by chain link. Three of the excerpts here—from Rick Telander's *Heaven Is a Playground*, as well as *The Last Shot* and *The City Game*—address basketball at street level within the city's boroughs. Each piece delivers a variation on the theme of striving in the face of racial barriers and urban poverty, from a white journalist who comes back with a handful of the naked city's eight million hard-luck stories. But each earns its place here for a distinctive emphasis—for whom it reserves its sympathy or at whom it points a finger.

It took the Knicks winning their 1969–70 NBA title for the provincial Manhattan book publishing world to fully embrace basketball, but

when it did—that team alone spawned more than a half dozen titles—
a dam broke. *Heaven Is a Playground* found its way to Hawaii, where an
African American adolescent was being raised by white grandparents
while attending an elite private school. After he enrolled at Columbia
University in Manhattan, Barack Obama recounts in his 1995 memoir *Dreams from My Father*, he made sure to visit "courts I'd once read
about."

Of course, Obama wasn't merely a reader of basketball, even as
Telander's 1976 account of a summer spent on the playgrounds of
Brooklyn helped the future president negotiate that fatherless, racially
isolated upbringing. He loved to watch and play it, Obama said during
the 2008 campaign, because the game features "improvisation within
a discipline that I find very powerful." In his memoir, Obama tells
how basketball fired him with an early sense of self-sufficiency, manhood, and racial identity. He captures its folkways and initiation rites,
and in one run-on sentence—a kind of prose poem in miniature—he
both hints at what will be a lifelong engagement with the game and
evokes its fluid nature with a writerly ambition. Basketball, he testi-
fies, offers "a way of being together when the game was tight and the
sweat broke and the best players stopped worrying about their points
and the worst players got swept up in the moment and the score only
mattered because that's how you sustained the trance."

By confining his critique to books, Plimpton failed to account for bas-
ketball's representation in magazines. *The New Yorker* editor William
Shawn greenlit both McPhee on Bradley and Herbert Warren Wind on
Bob Cousy. *Harper's* bankrolled the original reporting by Axthelm and
Frey, while the editors of *Sport* offered two moonlighting real-world
journalists, Breslin and Goldman, a chance to scratch their itch to
write on the game, and even coaxed a mash note to Earl (The Pearl)
Monroe from director Woody Allen.

But no periodical served basketball more faithfully than *Sports Illustrated*. In a thinly veiled reference in his novel *Semi-Tough*, longtime
senior writer Dan Jenkins disparaged the old *SI* as "a slick cookbook
for the two-yacht family." The Sixties changed the magazine, as they
changed so much: All nine of the selections here from *SI* were published in 1970 or afterward, six of them by some of the most distinctive

voices to grace its pages—Blount, Frank Deford, Curry Kirkpatrick, Gary Smith, Rick Reilly, and Steve Rushin. Each enjoyed stylistic freedom and as much space as he wanted, with editors essentially calling for clear-outs, as a coach would for a star player. "He wrote like he was shooting for something," *SI* copy chief Gabe Miller said of Deford, and the same might be said of those colleagues, especially Smith. All could deliver the lengthy piece that didn't feel long, and built persuasively upon some kernel of truth, like this from Deford on Bobby Knight: "It's the rabbits that are doing him in."

For the first eight years of the magazine's existence, a writer and editor named Jeremiah (Jerry) Tax had maintained a mostly lonely vigil over the sport. The colleges were especially challenging to cover, with isolated hotbeds in the Bay Area, Philadelphia, and the river valleys of the Ohio and Missouri. As Tax made his rounds, and coaches pressed him on where he had been and what he had seen, he recognized an opportunity if only the magazine would see the sport as one sprawling, national whole. In 1962, spotting Deford's six feet, four inches, and learning of his pedigree as a high school star, Tax commandeered the new hire for the basketball beat. NBA players then ate on thin-gruel per diems, and here was a guy their age and size and fortified by a Time Inc. expense account. The journalist who rarely dines alone seldom fears for an empty notebook, and the man from *SI*, whom Boston Celtics like Bill Russell and John Havlicek could glimpse in the front cabin as they languished in coach, would become a lifelong friend. Even as the Celtics won title after title through the mid-sixties, television did little beyond parachuting in for the Finals; in the aftermath of one championship, a network gofer, charged with wrangling Red Auerbach for an interview, found himself waved off by the Celtics coach's signature cigar. "Where the fuck were you in February?" Auerbach said, draping his other arm around Deford. "I'm going with my writers."

But college basketball benefited the most as *SI* expanded its coverage. Kentucky coach Adolph Rupp invited Deford into the locker room at halftime of the 1966 NCAA title game, in which his all-white Wildcats would lose to Texas Western and its all-black starting five. What Junior Johnson was to Tom Wolfe, rebel spirits like (Pistol) Pete Maravich, Johnny Neumann, and Dwight (Bo) Lamar were to Kirkpatrick, whose work turned each into a familiar name, and trafficked in scenes like that of Texas Western coach Don Haskins, on the eve of the game's *Brown v. Board of Ed* moment, throwing back beers with frat boys at the team's motel lest the students wake his sleeping players.

In 1973, when the NCAA moved its title game to prime time on Monday night, *SI* held open its cover and several front-of-the-book pages, and soon a symbiosis between the magazine and the tournament set in: *SI* got first dibs on hanging strobe lights from arena rafters; the NCAA reached seventeen million people with a words-and-pictures keepsake of an event, the Final Four, that would eventually chase the Oscars from Monday night. As pro basketball bristled with new life through the Bird-and-Magic Era, Michael Jordan's six titles, and the age of the NBA's Superteams, *SI*'s Jack McCallum and Lee Jenkins captured the league's personalities and increasing social relevance with scenes and quotes born of unusual access. "Come back, Paul Gallico!" Deford wrote in 2012. "It's a new and improved February!"

With the 2010s winding down, magazines in crisis, and *SI* scaling back from weekly publication, a counterweight of voices has already materialized on the web. When it launched in 2005, the site *FreeDarko* made the case that, to fulfill the potential of being an NBA fan, it wasn't enough to cheer for some team. You had to luxuriate in the variety of players in "the Association," each worth following and studying on his own terms. Members of the *FreeDarko* collective brought their overstuffed minds to bear on the NBA in hopes of making pro basketball, in the words of cofounder Nathaniel Friedman, aka Bethlehem Shoals, "a little more appealing to people who don't get off on X's and O's or tired macho posturing."

Although he never wrote for *FreeDarko*, Zach Lowe folded some of its spirit into his work for *ESPN.com*, as did many of the correspondents Henry Abbott assembled for the True Hoop network at the same site. Soon voice and quirkiness began leaching through online writing about the game. Readers devoured Bill Simmons's blog and his fan's manifesto, *The Book of Basketball*, but Simmons would make an even bigger impact as impresario at *Grantland* and *The Ringer*. Two highly personal pieces in this volume, by Lowe and Bryan Curtis, benefited from Simmons's midwifery. And perhaps it takes a decorated poet to deliver poetic justice: In 2015, Rowan Ricardo Phillips began blogging regularly about basketball at the website of *The Paris Review*, the literary journal founded by and still identified with George Plimpton.

When Plimpton advanced his Small Ball Theory, basketball wasn't just a less unbridled game. The kind of sports piece likely to earn acclaim as "good writing" was also much more circumscribed. Today basketball doesn't wear a straitjacket well, and writing about the game similarly resists the encumbrances of taxonomy. Consider the range of genres represented here: game account, profile, column, obituary, diary, memoir, essay, web take, and road piece, with plenty of blurring of one category into another. This collection covers the pros and colleges and high schools, to be sure, but also playground, driveway, trick-shot, summer travel team, and six-to-a-side girls basketball, as well as clowning, officiating, and analytics.

If writing about other sports fails to encompass quite so much, hold those games blameless. Instead, all credit to basketball. Hoops is broad and deep enough to lend itself to the finest deli-slicing. It's a companionable subject whether you want to pick nits with the world as you find it or excavate the achingly intimate. Today those who play the game and those who write about it find themselves empowered as never before; just as NBA free agents can plot to sign with the same team in a flurry of texts, the basketball web supplies a soapbox to anyone with something to say. Versatile, adaptable, available to all, basketball is that two-way player, comfortable on either side of the ball.

And there's no late-winter wait to see if it will emerge to glimpse its shadow. The heirs to Plimpton and Gallico can vouch that by February the game has long since been out and about, and that it will be with us through June and beyond, a muse for all seasons.

James Naismith

For a game with American origins and an unbuttoned spirit, basketball owes its invention to an unlikely figure: a teetotaling, Canadian-born, Presbyterian minister and physical educator. A devotee of the popular muscular Christianity movement, Dr. James Naismith (1861–1939) believed that "by using up our surplus energy, we invite to rest, rather than to mischief." In December 1891, while teaching at the YMCA Training School in Springfield, Massachusetts, he devised a game both challenging enough to engage a class of wintering rugby and football players and safe enough to be played indoors. Naismith went on to spend four decades running the Physical Education department at the University of Kansas, where he watched with some befuddlement as others capitalized on his invention. In the mid-1930s, shortly after his retirement, family members urged him to write about the beginnings of the game that had become a fixture in America's cities and small towns and was poised to make its Olympic debut. Naismith's oldest son tried to move the process along, taking dictation during fitful sessions one summer at the family cabin on the Kaw River outside Lawrence. Frustrated, he enlisted the help of an English composition instructor he had studied under as a Kansas undergraduate, and she helped shape, edit, and proofread the posthumously published *Basketball: Its Origins and Development* (1941). Here Naismith recalls the restless hours he spent coming up with the game. He also describes a children's pastime back in Bennie's Corners, Ontario, which inspired the precise, arching throw the world would come to know as a basketball shot.

from

Basketball: Its Origin and Development

TWO WEEKS had almost passed since I had taken over the troublesome class. The time was almost gone; in a day or two I would have to report to the faculty the success or failure of my attempts. So far they had all been failures, and it seemed to me that I had exhausted my resources. The prospect before me was, to say the least, discouraging. How I hated the thought of going back to the group and admitting that, after all my theories, I, too, had failed to hold the interest of the class. It was worse than losing a game. All the stubbornness of my Scotch ancestry was aroused, all my pride of achievement urged me on; I would not go back and admit that I had failed.

1

The day before my two weeks ended I met the class. I will always remember that meeting. I had nothing new to try and no idea of what I was going to do. The class period passed with little order, and at the end of the hour the boys left the gym. I can still see that group of fellows filing out the door. As that last pair of grey pants vanished into the locker room, I saw the end of all my ambitions and hopes.

With weary footsteps I mounted the flight of narrow stairs that led to my office directly over the locker room. I slumped down in my chair, my head in my hands and my elbows on the desk. I was a thoroughly disheartened and discouraged young instructor. Below me, I could hear the boys in the locker room having a good time; they were giving expression to the very spirit that I had tried so hard to evoke.

I had been a student the year before, and I could picture the group in that locker room. A towel would snap and some fellow would jerk erect and try to locate the guilty individual. Some of it was rough play, but it was all in fun, and each of them entered into it with that spirit. There would be talking and jesting, and I could even imagine the things that the group would be saying about my efforts. I was sure that the fellows did not dislike me, but I was just as sure that they felt that I had given them nothing better than the other instructors.

As I listened to the noise in the room below, my discouragement left me. I looked back over my attempts to see, if possible, the cause of my failures. I passed in review the gymnastic games that I had tried, and I saw that they were impossible. They were really children's games; the object that was to be obtained changed with each play, and no man could be interested in this type of game. It was necessary to have some permanent objective that would keep the minds of the participants active and interested.

As I thought of the other games that I had tried, I realized that the normal individual is strongly influenced by tradition. If he is interested in a game, any attempt to modify that game sets up an antagonism in his mind. I realized that any attempt to change the known games would necessarily result in failure. It was evident that a new principle was necessary; but how to evolve this principle was beyond my ken.

As I sat there at my desk, I began to study games from the philosophical side. I had been taking one game at a time and had failed to find what I was looking for. This time I would take games as a whole and study them.

My first generalization was that all team games used a ball of some kind; therefore, any new game must have a ball. Two kinds of balls were used at that time, one large and the other small. I noted that all games that used a small ball had some intermediate equipment with which to handle it. Cricket and baseball had bats, lacrosse and hockey had sticks, tennis and squash had rackets. In each of these games, the use of the intermediate equipment made the game more difficult to learn. The Americans were at sea with a lacrosse stick, and the Canadians could not use a baseball bat.

The game that we sought would be played by many; therefore, it must be easy to learn. Another objection to a small ball was that it could be easily hidden. It would be difficult for a group to play a game in which the ball was in sight only part of the time.

I then considered a large ball that could be easily handled and which almost anyone could catch and throw with very little practice. I decided that the ball should be large and light, one that could be easily handled and yet could not be concealed. There were two balls of this kind then in use, one the spheroid of Rugby and the other the round ball of soccer. It was not until later that I decided which one of these two I would select.

The type of a ball being settled, I turned next to the point of interest of various games. I concluded that the most interesting game at that time was American Rugby. I asked myself why this game could not be used as an indoor sport. The answer to this was easy. It was because tackling was necessary in Rugby. But why was tackling necessary? Again the answer was easy. It was because the men were allowed to run with the ball, and it was necessary to stop them. With these facts in mind, I sat erect at my desk and said aloud:

"If he can't run with the ball, we don't have to tackle; and if we don't have to tackle, the roughness will be eliminated."

I can still recall how I snapped my fingers and shouted,

"I've got it!"

This time I felt that I really had a new principle for a game, one that would not violate any tradition. On looking back, it was hard to see why I was so elated. I had as yet nothing but a single idea, but I was sure that the rest would work out correctly.

Starting with the idea that the player in possession of the ball could not run with it, the next step was to see just what he could do with it. There was little choice in this respect. It would be necessary for him to throw it or bat it with his hand. In my mind, I began to play a game and to visualize the movements of the players. Suppose that a player was running, and a teammate threw the ball to him. Realizing that it would be impossible for him to stop immediately, I made this exception: when a man was running and received the ball, he must make an honest effort to stop or else pass the ball immediately. This was the second step of the game.

In my mind I was still sticking to the traditions of the older games, especially football. In that game, the ball could be thrown in any direction except forward. In this new game, however, the player with the ball could not advance, and I saw no reason why he should not be allowed to throw or bat it in any direction. So far, I had a game that was played with a large light ball; the players could not run with the ball, but must pass it or bat it with the hands; and the pass could be made in any direction.

As I mentally played the game, I remembered that I had seen two players in a soccer game, both after the ball. One player attempted to head the ball just as the other player kicked at it. The result was a badly gashed head for the first man. I then turned this incident to the new game. I could imagine one player attempting to strike the ball with his fist and, intentionally or otherwise, coming in contact with another player's face. I then decided that the fist must not be used in striking the ball.

The game now had progressed only to the point where it was "keep away," and my experience with gymnastic games convinced me that it would not hold the interest of the players.

The next step was to devise some objective for the players. In all existing games there was some kind of a goal, and I felt that this was essential. I thought of the different games, in the hope that I might be able to use one of their goals. Football had a goal line, over which the ball must be carried, and goal posts, over which the ball might be kicked. Soccer, lacrosse, and hockey had goals into which the ball might be driven. Tennis and badminton had marks on the court inside which the ball must be kept. Thinking of all these, I mentally placed a goal like the one used in lacrosse at each end of the floor.

A lacrosse goal is simply a space six feet high and eight feet wide. The players attempt to throw the ball into this space; the harder the ball is thrown, the more chance to make a goal. I was sure that this play would lead to roughness, and I did not want that. I thought of limiting the sweep of the arms or of having the ball delivered from in front of the person, but I knew that many would resent my limiting the power of the player.

By what line of association it occurred to me I do not know, but I was back in Bennie's Corners, Ontario, playing Duck on the Rock. I could remember distinctly the large rock back of the blacksmith shop, about as high as our knees and as large around as a wash tub. Each of us would get a "duck," a stone about as large as our two doubled fists. About twenty feet from the large rock we would draw a base line, and then in various manners we would choose one of the group to be guard, or "it."

To start the game, the guard placed his duck on the rock, and we behind the base line attempted to knock it off by throwing our ducks. More often than not, when we threw our ducks we missed, and if we went to retrieve them, the guard tagged us; then one of us had to change places with him. If, however, someone knocked the guard's "duck" off the rock, he had to replace it before he could tag anyone.

It came distinctly to my mind that some of the boys threw their ducks as hard as they could; when they missed, the ducks were far from the base. When they went to retrieve them, they had farther to run and had more chance of being tagged. On the other hand, if the duck was tossed in an arc, it did not go so far. If the guard's duck was hit, it fell on the far side of the rock, whereas the one that was thrown bounced nearer the base and was easily caught up before the guard replaced his. When the duck was thrown in an arc, accuracy was more effective than force.

With this game in mind, I thought that if the goal were horizontal instead of vertical, the players would be compelled to throw the ball in an arc; and force, which made for roughness, would be of no value.

A horizontal goal, then, was what I was looking for, and I pictured it in my mind. I would place a box at either end of the floor, and each time the ball entered the box it would count as a goal. There was one thing, however, that I had overlooked. If nine men formed a defense around the goal, it would be impossible for the ball to enter it; but if I placed the goal above the players' heads, this type of defense would be useless. The only chance that the guards would have would be to go out and get the ball before the opponents had an opportunity to throw for goal.

I had a team game with equipment and an objective. My problem now was how to start it. Again I reviewed the games with which I was familiar. I found that the intent of starting any game was to give each side an equal chance to obtain the ball. I thought of water polo, where the teams were lined up at the ends of the pool and at a signal the ball was thrown into the center. There was always a mad scramble to gain possession of the ball, and it took only an instant for me to reject this plan. I could see nine men at each end of the gym, all making a rush for the ball as it was thrown into the center of the floor; and I winced as I thought of the results of that collision.

I then turned to the game of English Rugby. When the ball went out of bounds on the side line, it was taken by the umpire and thrown in between two lines of forward players. This was somewhat like polo, but the players had no chance to run at each other. As I thought of this method of starting the game, I remembered one incident that happened to me. In a game with Queen's College, the ball was thrown between the two lines of players. I took one step and went high in the air. I got the ball all right, but as I came down I landed on a shoulder that was shoved into my midriff. I decided that this method would not do. I did feel, though, that if the roughness could be eliminated, that tossing up the ball between two teams was the fairest way of starting a game. I reasoned that if I picked only one player from each team and threw the ball up between them, there would be little chance for roughness. I realize now how seriously I underestimated the ingenuity of the American boy.

When I had decided how I would start the game, I felt that I would have little trouble. I knew that there would be questions to be met; but I had the fundamental principles of a game, and I was more than willing to try to meet these problems. I continued with my day's work, and it was late in the evening before I again had a chance to think of my new scheme. I believe that I am the first person who ever played basketball; and although I used the bed for a court, I certainly played a hard game that night.

The following morning I went into my office, thinking of the new game. I had not yet decided what ball I should use. Side by side on the floor lay two balls, one a football and the other a soccer ball.

I noticed the lines of the football and realized that it was shaped so that it might be carried in the arms. There was to be no carrying of the ball in this new game, so I walked over, picked up the soccer ball, and started in search of a goal.

As I walked down the hall, I met Mr. Stebbins, the superintendent of buildings. I asked him if he had two boxes about eighteen inches square. Stebbins thought a minute, and then said:

"No, I haven't any boxes, but I'll tell you what I do have. I have two old peach baskets down in the store room, if they will do you any good."

I told him to bring them up, and a few minutes later he appeared with the two baskets tucked under his arm. They were round and somewhat larger at the top than at the bottom. I found a hammer and some nails and tacked the baskets to the lower rail of the balcony, one at either end of the gym.

I was almost ready to try the new game, but I felt that I needed a set of rules, in order that the men would have some guide. I went to my office, pulled out a scratch pad, and set to work. The rules were so clear in my mind that in less than an hour I took my copy to Miss Lyons, our stenographer, who typed the following set of thirteen rules.

The ball to be an ordinary *Association* football.

1. The ball may be thrown in any direction with one or both hands.

2. The ball may be batted in any direction with one or both hands (never with the fist).

3. A player cannot run with the ball. The player must throw it from the spot on which he catches it; allowance to be made for a man who catches the ball when running at a good speed.

4. The ball must be held in or between the hands; the arms or body must not be used for holding it.

5. No shouldering, holding, pushing, tripping, or striking, in any way the person of an opponent shall be allowed; the first infringement of this rule by any person shall count as a foul, the second shall disqualify him until the next goal is made, or, if there was evident intent to injure the person for the whole of the game, no substitute allowed.

6. A foul is striking at the ball with the fist, violation of Rules 3, 4, and such as described in Rule 5.

7. If either side makes three consecutive fouls, it shall count a goal for the opponents. (Consecutive means without the opponents in the meantime making a foul.)

8. A goal shall be made when the ball is thrown or batted from the grounds into the basket and stays there, providing those defending the goal do not touch or disturb the goal. If the ball rests on the edge and the opponent moves the basket, it shall count as a goal.

9. When the ball goes out of bounds, it shall be thrown into the field and played by the person first touching it. In case of a dispute, the umpire shall throw it straight into the field. The thrower-in is allowed five seconds. If he holds it longer it shall go to the opponent. If any side persists in delaying the game, the umpire shall call a foul on them.

10. The umpire shall be judge of the men and shall note the fouls and notify the referee when three consecutive fouls have been made. He shall have power to disqualify men according to Rule 5.

11. The referee shall be judge of the ball and shall decide when the ball is in play, in bounds, to which side it belongs, and shall keep the time. He shall decide when a goal has been made, and keep account of the goals, with any other duties that are usually performed by a referee.

12. The time shall be two fifteen minute halves, with five minutes rest between.

13. The side making the most goals in that time shall be declared the winners. In case of a draw, the game may, by agreement of the captains, be continued until another goal is made.

When Miss Lyons finished typing the rules, it was almost class time, and I was anxious to get down to the gym. I took the rules and made my way down the stairs. Just inside the door there was a bulletin board for notices. With thumb tacks I fastened the rules to this board and then walked across the gym. I was sure in my own mind that the game was good, but it needed a real test. I felt that its success or failure depended largely on the way that the class received it.

The first member of the class to arrive was Frank Mahan. He was a southerner from North Carolina, had played tackle on the football team, and was the ringleader of the group. He saw me standing with a ball in my hand and perhaps surmised that another experiment was to be tried. He looked up at the basket on one end of the gallery, and then his eyes turned to me. He gazed at me for an instant, and then looked toward the other end of the gym. Perhaps I was nervous, because his exclamation sounded like a death knell as he said,

"Huh! another new game!"

When the class arrived, I called the roll and told them that I had another game, which I felt sure would be good. I promised them that if this was a failure, I would not try any more experiments. I then read the rules from the bulletin board and proceeded to organize the game.

There were eighteen men in the class; I selected two captains and had them choose sides. When the teams were chosen, I placed the men on the floor. There were three forwards, three centers, and three backs on each team. I chose two of the center men to jump, then threw the ball between them. It was the start of the first basketball game and the finish of the trouble with that class.

As was to be expected, they made a great many fouls at first; and as a foul was penalized by putting the offender on the side lines until the next goal was made, sometimes half of a team would be in the penalty area. It was simply a case of no one knowing just what to do. There was no team work, but each man did his best. The forwards tried to make goals and the backs tried to keep the opponents from making them. The team was large, and the floor was small. Any man on the field was close enough to the basket to throw for goal, and most of them were anxious to score. We tried, however, to develop team work by having the guards pass the ball to the forwards.

The game was a success from the time that the first ball was tossed up. The players were interested and seemed to enjoy the game. Word soon got around that they were having fun in Naismith's gym class, and only a few days after the first game we began to have a gallery.

Several years ago, as I was returning from a summer trip in Colorado, I came by the way of the so-called world's highest bridge, spanning the Royal Gorge a few miles above Canyon City, Colo. At the south end of the bridge we came upon the deserted camp of the men who had built the structure. There was little to tell of the number of men and boys who had spent many months playing and working on this spot. At one end of the former camp, however, there were two basketball backstops. The goals had been removed, and they stood alone against the dark pines, a mute reminder of the activity that had once been a part of the camp life.

I am sure that no man can derive more pleasure from money or power than I do from seeing a pair of basketball goals in some out of the way place—deep in the Wisconsin woods an old barrel hoop nailed to a tree, or a weather-beaten shed on the Mexican border with a rusty iron hoop nailed to one end. These sights are constant reminders that I have in some measure accomplished the objective that I set up years ago.

Thousands of times, especially in the last few years, I have been asked whether I ever got anything out of basketball. To answer this question, I can only smile. It would be impossible for me to explain my feelings to the great mass of people who ask this question, as my pay has not been in dollars but in the satisfaction of giving something to the world that is a benefit to masses of people.

Red Smith

On the page and in person, Walter Wellesley (Red) Smith (1905–1982) was among the most graceful members of the sportswriting lodge during the broad middle of the twentieth century. It remains basketball's misfortune that Smith liked the game much less than boxing, horseracing, baseball, and golf. The columnist who in 1976 would win a Pulitzer Prize for commentary didn't care for its back-and-forth action, the advantage that fell to tall "goons," or its frequent stoppages—"whistleball," he called it. To be fair, as Smith's was becoming the most influential voice in the sports section, the pro game remained bush league, flogged by promoters in small markets, while college basketball was limited to pockets of regional interest. But in 1946, shortly after landing at the *New York Herald Tribune*, Smith filed this column from a game featuring Rhode Island State (now University of Rhode Island) and its star, Ernie Calverley, in the National Invitation Tournament, then more ballyhooed than its NCAA counterpart. The piece hints at what the future would bring. Right away Smith admits to his anti-basketball bias, only to launch into a rhapsody about Calverley and the rewards of watching the Rams' fast-breaking style with lots on the line. Smith doesn't realize that he has succumbed to an early strain of March Madness, the malady that would soon make the basketball-averse sportswriter in the springtime a very rare specimen indeed.

A Case of Malnutrition

A FEW MORE nights like the opening round of the National Invitation Basketball Tournament and the memory of Dr. Naismith, who perpetrated basketball, will cease to be a hissing and a byword around here. Indeed, get a few more guys like Rhode Island State's Ernie Calverley playing the game and some movie company is a cinch to do the life of Dr. Naismith, picturing him as a benefactor of the human race like Mme Curie, Alexander Graham Bell and Al Capone.

This is written by one who would rather drink a Bronx cocktail than speak well of basketball. Yet it must be confessed that there hasn't been another sports show in years which lifted the hackles and stirred the pulse quite so thoroughly as the performance of young Calverley leading his team to an overtime conquest of Bowling Green.

Calverley is a gaunt, pale young case of malnutrition who'd probably measure up as a fairly sizable gent in your living room, but looks like a waif among the goons who clutter up the courts. He may be, as alleged, the most detached defensive player on a team whose members seem to feel there is something sordid and unclean about defensive basketball. But when he lays hand on that ball and starts moving, he is a whole troop of Calverley, including the pretty white horses. The guy is terrific, colossal, and also very good.

Throughout the fevered match with Bowling Green, he was the man who set up Rhode Island's plays, taking the ball down the court, hiding it, passing it, shooting, dribbling, feinting, weaving, running the show with almost unbelievable dexterity and poise. He played without relief through a break-neck game that had others gasping inside the first quarter-hour and once he was knocked cold as an obsolete mackerel.

Making a pass, he tripped and hit the deck with his bony shoulder-blades. As he lay there supine, the ball came back to him out of a scramble and he reached up and caught it and passed it off, and then passed out.

But despite his elegance, Bowling Green was winning the game as long as Don Otten remained in circulation. Otten is the Bowling Green center. He measures one-half inch less than seven feet from end to end and he looks and moves more like an institution than a man, with agonizing deliberation and great grinding of gears.

Joe DiMaggio would be hard pressed to throw a baseball over the top of Otten and there aren't any DiMaggios playing for Rhode Island. He loped gawkily around the joint with his mouth open and plucked rebounds off the backboard like currants off a bush, while waves of adversaries surged around him and bounced off in a sort of spray. When a teammate missed a shot he simply reached up and palmed the ball and pushed it down through the hoop.

With three minutes, twenty seconds to go he committed his fifth personal foul and was flung out. The crowd cheered and it wasn't applause; it was the rejoicing of Rhode Island fans, who figured they now had a chance.

There would have been no chance, however, without Calverley. A minute and ten seconds before the last horn, he took aim from a point near the center stripe and fired a long shot that went through the hoop as though it had eyes, squaring the match at 72–all. A moment later he was fouled and missed the throw that might have won. With ten seconds to play, Vern Dunham scored for Bowling Green, and that looked like the business. But somehow, in the scant time remaining, a Bowling Green player contrived to squeeze in another foul, giving Rhode Island the ball out of bounds at midfloor with two seconds remaining.

The ball came in to Calverley in the back court. There was no time for a pass or a play and from where he stood a field goal was impossible. So, with appalling calm, he shot a field goal. Time was up.

Over in front of the Rhode Island bench, substitutes were leaping around in a crazed sort of war dance, flinging arms aloft and shouting, and out on the floor Calverley's playmates were shouting and pummeling him and the kid had his head flung back and was laughing at the ceiling.

Well, Rhode Island scored eight fast points in the extra period and Bowling Green scored five, and with a minute and a half left Calverley set out to freeze the ball. He did a magical job, dribbling in and out and around and back, keeping an appraising eye on the enemy, passing when necessary and then squirming loose for a return pass.

Then the game was over and there was a threshing swirl of players and spectators in a knot on the floor and Calverley was shoved up out of the pack and rode off on the others' shoulders. Which was fair enough, since the others had ridden to victory on his. They rushed him out and he broke loose barely in time to get down and avoid being skulled where the exit ramp goes under the stands. They like to bashed his brains out.

Edith Roberts

The credo alongside the senior photo of Edith Roberts (1902–1966) in her high school yearbook read, "I always say just what I mean." And say things Roberts did, particularly in seven novels, several set in small midwestern towns like Huntington, Indiana, where she grew up. Four of her books became movies, including *Reap the Whirlwind* (1938), based on time she spent in the Balkans, and which with its setting in Belgrade amid political turmoil seemed to foretell world war, and *That Hagen Girl* (1947), a vehicle for Ronald Reagan and Shirley Temple. Born Edith Elizabeth Kneipple and educated at the University of Chicago, Roberts took a staff position at *Coronet*, the Chicago-based monthly that resembled *Reader's Digest* in its trim size and mix of celebrity profiles, advice, and condensed books. In 1944 the magazine sent her to Kokomo for a report called "The Town with the Funny Name." By the 1950s, having set aside fiction entirely, Roberts returned to small-town Indiana for *Coronet*, filing this dispatch from little Milan, whose high school's defeat of mighty Muncie Central would inspire the 1987 film *Hoosiers*. Longshots though they were in 1954, the real-life forerunners of fictional Hickory High had reached the state semifinals the year before, alerting *Coronet's* editors to the story brewing to their southeast. With its color and detail, Roberts's story could pass as notes for a Hollywood set designer.

Indiana's Town of Champions

T HE DAY the Milan High School basketball team played in the state championship finals, the little Indiana whistle-stop became a ghost town. Every man, woman and child in Milan (pop. 1,200) who was fit to travel had made the pilgrimage to Indianapolis to cheer the boys on to victory.

The extraordinary support and enthusiasm of the townsfolk, which had carried an obscure high school squad to the final round of the championship in a conference of 751 schools, stood solidly behind the Milan Indians on that memorable Saturday.

By noon there was no one left in town but a few dogs, the postmaster and barber Russel (Rabbit) Hunter, who explained his odd behavior by stating he didn't deserve a ticket because he hadn't attended all of the school's games during the season. But to show his heart was with the boys, a sign in his window read: "CLIP 'EM CLOSE, INDIANS!"

14

To help out while Milan was deserted, neighbor communities stood by valiantly. Batesville sent over a fire-truck and crew so that the Milan Volunteer Fire Department might enjoy the game without worry. Madison lent part of its police force in order that town marshal Roy LaFollette could root for the Indians without fear that burglars might be busy back home.

Indianapolis, where the big basketball final was being played, had become accustomed to the delirious descent of the Milan motorcade. "Seems like they hardly go home but they're back again," commented Indianapolis motor patrolman Pat Stark. But he said it good-naturedly, for Milan was the popular choice to win.

He vowed that if its Miracle Men won the championship, he'd escort them against traffic around the city's famous Circle. And when they won the 1954 championship by beating the Central High School of Muncie, 32–30, he carried out his promise.

What Milan did in support of its Indians before the game was mild compared to what it did afterwards. Anyone seeing the 500 cars full of cheering fans escorting them home from Indianapolis would certainly have recognized it as a triumphal procession. But then, Milan's feat in reaching the finals was in itself something of a miracle. The escort was 13 miles long, and an estimated 40,000 people managed to cram themselves into a town normally holding 1,200.

"*Menus?*" cried restaurant-owner Frank Arkenberg incredulously. "Say, when our team wins, you're lucky if you get anything to *eat* here, let alone a menu!"

"Is this *heaven?*" Pete Nocks at the filling-station kept shouting after the victory, spilling half the gas he was pumping.

Some practical soul calculated that the cost of attending the tournament, plus the loss due to closing of business, had cost Milan at least $50,000 each Saturday it closed up. But someone immediately countered with: "Who cares? We won, didn't we?"

Win or lose (and it has been mostly win), Milan has been setting basketball records the like of which no community of equal size has ever matched in this basketball-crazy state.

The Milan High School has an enrollment of only 83 girls and 84 boys, which is infinitesimal compared to the hundreds of larger schools in Indiana. Yet in two successive years, this virtually unknown team reached the final tourney, winning the championship in 1954 with a victory that Hoosiers will talk about for years.

By the time the second triumph came round, Milan had proved beyond doubt that its brilliance was no fluke, but the result of a team's skill, a coach's inspiration, and a whole town's faith and enthusiasm. And all those qualities were needed to turn the kids from an obscure tank town into state champions.

Milan, now a familiar name to every Indiana basketball fan, is no more than a dot on the map. The tiny town straddles the Baltimore & Ohio Railroad, its stores and houses bunched round the main street.

Every storekeeper and householder in Milan works or roots for the Indians in some way. Drop into Frank Arkenberg's restaurant, or Emmett Lawless' drugstore, or Louis Kirschner's dry-goods emporium, and the chances are they will be discussing the basketball squad.

The same holds good for Bob Peak's law office or Red Smith's insurance agency or Chris Volz's garage. It was Volz who sent the team to the regional games in Pontiacs, to the semi-finals in Buicks, and to the state championship finals in Cadillacs.

Over on a side street lives Mrs. Anna Cross, who traditionally washes the Indians' uniforms and prays for the boys as she hangs up their jerseys. Out yonder is the Milan Furniture Company, the town's modest industry, whose general manager, Bill Thompson, had enough "LET'S GO, INDIANS!" placards printed to deck out everything on wheels in Ripley County. Up on a shady hillside stands the yellow-brick schoolhouse, no different from thousands of others all over America.

This is Milan, Indiana, the home of the champions, and it looks very much like any other country town its size. What made Milan great in the sporting sense is something you can't see. But it's there just the same, and you can find out what it is if you stay around and get acquainted.

Everyone is friendly and eager to talk, especially if it's about basketball and how the Indians got to be Champs. The townsfolk will tell you it was the kids and the coach. The coach will assure you it was the team and the town. The boys will declare it was the coach and fans. It was all of these, fired by an abiding faith and mutual confidence.

It all started two years ago with the new coach who came to Milan, one of the most remarkable figures in basketball today. No one believed young Marvin Wood was remarkable then, except perhaps in a derogatory sense—for he had taken a decided step down when he left well-known French Lick to coach unknown Milan.

"Woody" himself admits it was a kind of self-imposed demotion; but he says that when he came to Milan to look over the "material" he'd have to work with and found it averaging a good six feet, clear-eyed, wonderfully nourished and healthy, with a history of playing "barn-door" basketball all its young life, he had such a strong hunch that this could be turned into a victorious team that he couldn't resist playing that hunch.

Marv Wood, who is only 26 years old, had been trained under the veteran Tony Hinkle, coach at Butler University and now president of the American Basketball Coaches Association; and was wise enough about basketball to know that it required more than faith to make a winner. So, with characteristic thoroughness, he set about developing what sports writers have now made famous as "Woody's cat-and-mouse technique."

Disgruntled losers have been known to call it a "stall," but it is really a highly controlled slow-motion game. To see Milan's fine physical specimens carry this mental exercise in restraint and judgment to its utmost possibilities is a revelation in will power and nerve.

"We don't freeze the ball," explains Coach Wood. "We take our time and work it in for good shots. This type of game gives the boys a chance to *think*, and thinking enables them to take advantage of the breaks. It's as simple as that. But it pays off."

With this last, both his friends and his opponents agree. They'll be telling in Indiana for years to come how during the final quarter of the 1954 championship game, with Muncie Central High School leading by two points, Milan actually retained the ball for 4 minutes and 14 seconds without even attempting to shoot. Later, with only 18 seconds left to play, the crowd in pandemonium and the score tied, Milan calmly called time!

Two years of patient, incessant, endless drilling on the part of Coach Wood to be deliberate, to think, to look for the break, and then—and only then—to act, were about to pay off. With three seconds left to go, Bobby Plump of Milan, as coolly as if he were practice-shooting in his own backyard, took aim and dropped in the winning basket.

"Marv's technique," says Willard Green, Milan Superintendent of Schools, "certainly turns out some fine basketball players. And we think it contains all the elements for turning out fine men as well."

A few minutes after his dramatic final shot, Bobby Plump was singled out for the tourney's greatest individual honor—the Arthur H. Trester Award—given each year by the Indiana High School Athletic Association to the player with "the best scholastic record and mental attitude." It was the first time that this trophy had ever gone to a player on the championship team.

Bobby won it, but it might with equal justice have been awarded to the team as a whole, for the majority of the Indians are leaders and honor students. As for the team's "mental attitude," attorney Bob Peak says, "Throughout the season I noticed that a boy would forsake a chance to shine, and pass the ball to a player in a little better position. That's teamwork!"

When Wood came to Milan with his "hunch," nobody else in the town shared it. The local citizens warmly supported their boys, of course, as they had always done; but they felt their team, which had done no more in 40 years than win an occasional sectional game, had as much chance of flying to the moon as of winning a championship.

But Marv Wood began urging "heads-up" ball and firmly inculcating the conviction that defeat is never inevitable. Practice and drill were incessant, while the townsfolk watched and cheered.

A month before his first 1953 sectional tourney, the coach startled the team by drawing up a program showing how Milan could go all the way to the finals. Everyone thought he was crazy. When subsequent events proved him right, team and town got behind him.

In 1954 they knew they could win—which is one reason why they did. The solid backing of Milan's citizenry was behind the team, and every player knew it.

When the season ended, the coach folded away his lucky green necktie till next year. People began to speak again of secondary things, like politics and the weather. The boys themselves settled down to books, home life and chores.

Back to Pierceville, a stone's throw from Milan, where there are 100 inhabitants and 100 fans, trouped three of the Champs—Gene White,

Plump, and Rog Schroder. Nor were they above joining in the games at the homemade basketball court behind the Schroder residence.

"We've got lights," explained Rog proudly, "and we play every night. Our dads play, too, and our mothers are real fans. The little kids use the court afternoons."

A visiting reporter who had come to Milan to see what it had taken to make a championship team, reached this conclusion: "It all adds up to a few sweating, panting boys in the driveway, the backyard or a vacant lot somewhere in Indiana. That's where champions start—and that's where they plan to stay."

Herbert Warren Wind

Herbert Warren Wind (1916–2005) published sportswriting in *The New Yorker* from 1947 until his retirement in 1989, except for a six-year stretch beginning in 1954 when he wrote for *Sports Illustrated*. It was during that interregnum, in the fall of 1955, that Wind reported a two-part profile of Boston Celtics playmaker Bob Cousy. As the Celtics worked themselves into shape for the forthcoming season by barnstorming around the Northeast, the two men spent long stretches together on the road, a reportorial opportunity that paid off in part, Wind noted, because "basketball players are not so eternally beleaguered by their fandom, or by the press, radio, and television as are baseball and golf stars." Wind would find *SI*'s deadlines too cramped for his way of deliberately unpacking a subject, so he returned to *The New Yorker*, where he became as much that magazine's leisurely voice on golf as Roger Angell's would be on baseball. After a childhood spent in Brockton, Massachusetts, then a center of shoe manufacturing, Wind spurned his parents' wishes that he take over the family leather business. Instead he went to Yale, where he played basketball, and at Cambridge earned a master's in English Literature. This piece ran in *The New Yorker* in 1963 just before Cousy's retirement, eight years after Wind's first long *SI* interviews from that shotgun seat. Given the almost anthropological detachment with which he describes the sport and the man who had ruled it, it's hard to believe that Wind was himself once a high-level player. But that's what he brought to the stories he told: a proper think and a calm telling.

Farewell to Cousy

ONE OF the most puzzling organizations in sport—and its vagaries seem particularly strange because it has fourteen years of experience behind it—is the National Basketball Association. It would be reasonable to expect the N.B.A., as the professional-basketball equivalent of the National Football League, the National Hockey League, and the National and American Baseball Leagues, to have long ago grown up into a smoothly functioning big-time outfit, always on the *qui vive* for ways to improve the presentation of basketball at its top level. Well, hardly. It is, for instance, the rule rather than the exception for an N.B.A. game to be played in a harsh, frenzied, Hogarthian atmosphere. It is difficult to know for sure the key factors behind the chronic deterioration in discipline. Some observers feel that the continued absence of any reasonable uniformity in the officiating by the league staff of referees may well be the chief weakness, while others believe that far too much leniency has always been accorded the antics of the coaches. In any event, sooner or later the coaches are storming histrionically up and down the sidelines roaring at the referees, the referees are snarling back at the coaches, the players are volubly irritated, the crowd is sore at everyone except the home team, and the situation is threatening to get completely out of hand. The wonder, I suppose, is that it actually has on only a few occasions. In short, while professional basketball, under the N.B.A.'s stewardship, is today played in modern, gleaming arenas from coast to coast, it has come on hardly at all in certain important respects from what it was forty-odd years ago, when games were customarily held in smoky halls on the wrong side of town as the first half of a curious double-header event: After the final whistle had blown, someone spread corn meal over the floor to make it more slippery, a five-piece orchestra unlimbered its music stands and struck up "Ten Little Fingers and Ten Little Toes," and everybody danced.

Since 1949, when the N.B.A. came into existence through a merger of the Basketball Association of America (its more or less direct ancestor) and the National Basketball League, the N.B.A. has been run by Maurice Podoloff, who up till then had been primarily an arena operator and a hockey entrepreneur and who now became its president, and by a board of governors made up of the owners of the member teams (of which there have been as many as seventeen; today there are nine). It is difficult to figure out why this controlling group has been so apathetic about remedying professional basketball's obvious shortcomings, but apparently the traditional *laissez-faire* policy has reflected official conviction that a brink-of-brawl tension in the arenas sells more tickets. It sells a few, no doubt—most of them to the set that has always given cigars a bad name—but the fact is that the N.B.A. has managed to achieve its present prosperity almost in spite of itself. For this it can thank the players, especially those few extraordinary ones who have captured the imagination of the large section of the public that derives its winter sustenance from basketball. The first of these super-stars was Joe Fulks of the Philadelphia Warriors, who, strictly speaking, enjoyed his best years when the N.B.A. was still the B.A.A. A young man with tremendous spring in his legs, Fulks could get way up off the floor and stay there long enough to twist around toward the basket and fire an accurate two-hand shot. This so-called jump shot was almost impossible to guard against, and one evening in 1949 Fulks, in an especially elevated mood, scored twenty-seven field goals and nine foul shots, for sixty-three points—in those days (before the present rule requiring the team with the ball to take a shot within twenty-four seconds) an incredible individual score, since whole pro *teams* often scored less than that in a single game. At about that time, too, the Minneapolis Lakers came up with George Mikan. Mikan stood six feet ten inches tall, but, unlike most other early basketball giants, he was a sturdy, well-coördinated athlete. During his six seasons in the league, the Lakers won five championships and, with Vern Mikkelsen and Jim Pollard, two other good big men, assisting Mikan up front and with Slater Martin building the plays, established themselves as the first great pro-basketball team since the Original Celtics, of the nineteen-twenties. Halfway through Mikan's career, just when he was beginning to slow down a trifle, Bob Cousy, of the Boston Celtics (no relation to the Original Celtics, who operated out of New York), came along. A comparatively small man for a basketball player, only six feet one and a half inches tall, with a high forehead and deep-set dark eyes in a long, gaunt face that gives him the look of an old-time Spanish courtier, Cousy could handle a basketball as no one ever had before. While the magicians on the Harlem Globetrotters worked their wonders with the coöperation of "opponents" who travelled with them and were trained to be perfect foils, Cousy worked his wonders against bona-fide competition. Then, about six years ago, a whole new group of super-stars began to arrive: in the 1956–57 season Bill Russell, a lean six feet ten, the best of all the big men defensively, whose addition instantly transformed the Celtics into the second great modern team; in 1958–59 Elgin Baylor, of the Minneapolis (now the Los Angeles) Lakers, a powerful front-court man with a remarkable variety of offensive moves; the next year Wilt Chamberlain, of the Philadelphia (now the San Francisco) Warriors, an inch over seven feet in height and the tallest man in the Brobding-nag of pro basketball but a strong, sound athlete nevertheless, who started erasing previous scoring records by averaging thirty-seven points a game in his first Season; and in 1960–61 Oscar Robertson, of the Cincinnati Royals, a brilliant all-round player with a soft, spinless one-hand jump shot that was the ultimate refinement of the old two-hand jumper introduced by Fulks.

All these super-stars—and other such outstanding players as Bob Pettit, of the St. Louis Hawks, and Dolph Schayes, of the Syracuse Nationals—have consistently helped to create interest in the professional game, but the one man most responsible for keeping the crowds coming and the N.B.A. in business has been Cousy. No player in the history of basketball has been nearly as talented, and, at least since the Second World War, perhaps no performer in any sport has provided as many minutes of pleasure and excitement. During the last decade, the followers of basketball have grown thoroughly accustomed to a steady drumbeat from the provinces proclaiming this or that college star "another Cousy," but so far not one has fitted that description, and chances are none ever will.

This winter, there has been a deeper awareness than usual of Cousy's unique genius. Now, at thirty-four, in his thirteenth year as a professional and his seventh year as the Celtics' captain, he has announced that the current season will be his last. There is no likelihood of his staging a Sarah Bernhardt type of farewell, annually announcing his departure and as regularly returning to action, for he has contracted to coach the Boston College team next year and is already starting the transition from a nomadic life to a more normal one. In terms of the N.B.A.'s general health, Cousy will be taking his leave at a fortunate time. For one thing, Russell, Baylor, Chamberlain, and Robertson (Cousy's heir apparent) will still be around. For another, President Podoloff is due to hang up his sneakers at the end of the current season, and it is to be hoped that the owner-governors will presently be devising means of giving their organization the major-league class it has thus far sedulously managed to avoid. At the same time, it is hard to imagine the N.B.A., or basketball, without Cousy, so long has he been the commanding figure: a bravura individual star who was first and foremost a team man; a person of modest nature whose flair and fire nevertheless made him a majestic showman—the one athlete who treated you to something new and unexpected each time you saw him play; oddly enough, not only the league's top drawing card but its most constructive critic and the founder of the N.B.A.

players' union; all in all, an unusual sports hero, who grew with his fame and, even at closest range, was always a man to admire.

In view of the fact that Cousy has come to be the personification of professional basketball, it is interesting to recall what a minuscule splash he made when he entered the N.B.A., in 1950. As a player for Holy Cross, he had been a nearly unanimous choice for All-American—he was especially renowned for his deceptive ball-handling—and it was taken for granted that the Boston Celtics, who had territorial rights to him, would grab him as soon as he graduated. The Celtics, it turned out, were rather apathetic about Cousy. What they needed most at the time, they felt, was a big, rugged rebound specialist, so they chose to acquire instead Charley Share, a six-foot-eleven center from Bowling Green, Ohio. (Share proved to be only a journeyman player.) Cousy landed with the Tri-Cities Hawks, a team representing Davenport, Iowa, and Moline and Rock Island, Illinois, but the Hawks' management thought so little of his potential that they promptly traded him to the Chicago Stags. When the Stags folded before the start of the season, arrangements were made to distribute their players among the other teams in the league, but an impasse occurred. The Celtics, the Warriors, and the New York Knickerbockers all wanted Max Zaslofsky, the Stags' high-scoring forward. There was also a disagreement over who should get Andy Phillip, an established backcourt star, and who should get Cousy, so it was decided that the fairest solution was to let the owners of these three teams draw from a hat three slips of paper, bearing the names of Zaslofsky, Phillip, and Cousy. Walter Brown, the owner of the Celtics, to his disappointment, pulled out not Zaslofsky but Cousy. (Zaslofsky went to the Knickerbockers, for whom he played a few seasons of mediocre ball. Phillip went to the Warriors, and in 1956, at the tail end of his career, joined Cousy on the Celtics.) The stubborn reluctance of the Celtics to acquire the player who was to revive them financially, lead them to five championships between 1957 and 1962, and become the most popular athlete in New England since John L. Sullivan is a classic example of how mistaken people can be in estimating talent, and I imagine it will become, if it hasn't already, a stock item in the cheer-up talks that coaches deliver to dejected young men they are cutting from their squads.

Cousy didn't really come into his own until midway through his second season with the Celtics. During his first year, he averaged a creditable fifteen points a game, which made him the ninth-highest scorer in the league, but his all-round play was substantially less impressive than these figures might indicate. The usual explanation given nowadays is that he was simply too fast for his teammates—that his unexpected passes often ricocheted off their heads, chests, and arms—but there was more to it than that. The Celtics, an only ordinary team in those days, were attempting during Cousy's first year to adjust to a new style of play ordained by a new coach, Arnold (Red) Auerbach, and the result was that while they did some things well, a good part of the time they played rather inchoate basketball. In many games, Cousy appeared to be fretful and unhappy. He seldom got the ball when he wanted it, and when he did get it his frustration often made him try to force openings that didn't exist. One major change instituted by Auerbach the following year had the effect of unleashing Cousy; this was a new emphasis on a fast-break offense, with Cousy as the lead man. Now the moment the ball came into the Celtics' possession under their own basket it was passed up to Cousy, and he and as many teammates as possible tore down the court—the idea, of course, being that the speed of this counterattack would catch most of the men on the other team napping at the far end, and so the attackers would have to out-maneuver only one or two defenders and could sail in for a quick, closeup basket. There was nothing particularly novel about this—the fast break had been a standard part of basketball since the mid-nineteen-thirties, when the West Coast college teams introduced it—except that Cousy made it work with a speed and fluency no one had ever dreamed were possible. The moment he received the outlet pass and turned his head downcourt, he was able to take in, in a twinkling, the placement of every player in front of him and to build his play accordingly. Moreover, he accelerated at a furious clip. In three or four fast strides, he was past midcourt and was flashing in on the foul circle, forcing the defending players to commit themselves one way or the other. When they did so, and regardless of how they did so, Cousy could almost invariably spot an uncovered teammate in that instant and feed him an outlandishly deft pass that led him in for an easy layup shot. The amazing thing was that quite often the free man turned out to be a teammate who had got started late and trailed the play down the floor, and Cousy's aptitude for detecting the trailer's presence without looking gave the impression that he had not only exceptional peripheral vision but eyes in the back of his head. What he actually had was the ability, at the moment before he turned downcourt, to photograph the disposition of the players who would be following the play behind him, and once he had *that* in the back of his head, his rarefied basketball instinct enabled him to guess accurately just where and when a late-breaking teammate, whose habits he knew, would be catching up with the action.

Cousy's success in sparking the fast break affected his entire play. In the more static and cramped, conventional situation in which the offensive team, guarded man for man, tries to maneuver for an opening that will ultimately set up a good close-in shot, Cousy, having become the Celtics' acknowledged playmaker, began to direct their attack with a confidence that kept on enlarging until it bordered on audacity. By improving his outside shooting and by learning to utilize his teammates' pick-offs—stationary blocks—more adroitly, he made it necessary for the opposing defensive man to guard him very closely, and when his man did this, Cousy would drive around him with a burst of fantastic ambidextrous dribbling. The second he had daylight—and this was the heart of his skill—he could, with that wide-angle visual photography of his, pick out some Celtic who at that instant had got a step or half-step edge on *his* defensive man, and whistle the ball to him through the intervening mass of players. As his teammates—particularly Ed Macauley, a slim center with an excellent assortment of moves, and Bill Sharman, a superb jump-shooter—came to know better what they could expect from him, Cousy began embellishing his passing with all kinds of inventive variations: blind passes hooked over his shoulder, bounce passes slapped quickly in the midst of a dribble, little backward flips he dropped behind him with one hand as he went up into the air and faked a shot with the other, and the behind-the-back pass—and its baroque relative the twice-around-the-back pass, which he could execute while he was suspended in midair after driving in for an apparent layup shot and drawing the defense over to block it. These razzle-dazzle improvisations became Cousy's trademark, since no one else (with the possible exception of Dick McGuire, of the Knickerbockers, on some of his best nights) could approach either his imagination or his dexterity. Near the end of a game whose outcome was already clearly decided, Cousy occasionally trotted out a little of this special material simply because he knew that the customers had come to see it, but the true beauty of his basketball was that, with these minor exceptions, he used his fancy stuff only when it served a sound functional purpose. Plain or fancy, he could arouse his team and get it to play as a unit—the rarest and most valuable of all basketball gifts. For years, whenever he was taken out of a game for a breather the Celtics on the court became just five other guys, and in tight games he would be rushed back into action almost before he had had a chance to climb into his sweat jacket. In the same, somewhat inexplicable way that the average skier surmounts his usual frailties when he follows an expert instructor down a slope, basketball players become better basketball players when Cousy is on the court. This has been demonstrated time and again in the annual East-West All-Star Game, and it is also apparent at very much lower levels of competition. A couple of years ago, Cousy and Auerbach made a tour, under State Department auspices, through Europe and North Africa and the Middle East—areas that are becoming more and more basketball-conscious. Recently, Auerbach recollected, "In each town we hit, Cooz would put on a clinic for the kids and coaches. After that, a couple of the local teams would play each other. Most of the time, the two teams would be very evenly matched. Then Cooz would go in and play with one team for a few minutes and it would draw way ahead. He didn't try to do much, but his moves are contagious. The kids would sense what he wanted them to do, and all of a sudden they'd begin making the right moves themselves and playing pretty good ball. Then he'd shift over to the other team and *they'd* immediately start moving like a clock. Same identical thing wherever we went."

Under Cousy's direction, the Celtics' offense became the most elegant in basketball, but they did not become the league champions until Bill Russell joined them, late in 1956, and gave them the solid big man they had always lacked. Russell's most signal contribution, of course, was his great defensive skill, most notably his rebounding ability, but he also bolstered the offense in a way no one had anticipated—by making the team's fearsome fast break even faster. Ordinarily, when a man as mountainous as Russell comes down with a rebound off the backboard in his defensive zone, play stops momentarily while he unwinds himself and peers around to discover where everyone has gone. Russell is different. He has such superlative timing and balance that he has no sooner plucked a rebound out of the scramble than he is spinning around—often while still airborne—and firing it like a baseball to Cousy, whom he looks for to be breaking down the left side of the court. Nothing throws an opposing team off stride more surely than giving up a series of quick, easy baskets. When it became apparent, as it soon did, that Russell could almost always be counted on to snare the defensive rebound, the Celtics were frequently able to achieve this demoralizing effect on their opponents by adding a new wrinkle to their fast break: As soon as it looked as if the other team would be taking a shot at the Celtics' basket, a Celtic forward—Tommy Heinsohn or Frank Ramsey, say—would start to steal as unobtrusively as possible down the floor toward the opponents' basket. In one inter-esting variation on this play, which the Celtics sometimes use when a member of the opposing team is at the foul line for a single shot, Ramsey ignores his usual defensive assignment—which is to step in front of the shooter and cut off a rebound or a pass back—and heads for the far end of the court even before the ball leaves the shooter's hands. On the occasions when everything goes as calculated, what takes place next, with explosive speed, is one of the most astonish-ing sights in basketball. *Zip* goes Russell's pass out of the rebound to Cousy. *Zip* goes Cousy's long, arching lead pass to Ramsey, who is rac-ing for the basket ahead of the recovering defense. *Zip* goes Ramsey's layup. Even if the opposing player makes his foul shot, the play works almost as well. Then Russell simply grabs the ball in his left hand as it comes through the basket, wheels beyond the end line, and, in the same motion, wings his pass to Cousy. The play is characteristic of the daring, open-throttle style of the Celtics under Cousy's leadership, which provides a sanguine reminder that basketball can be a most exciting game, and not, as it so often is, merely a blurry amalgam of tall men milling under a basket while the rest of the cast lob jump shots from all over the premises.

For eight straight seasons, Cousy led the N.B.A. in "assists"—passes that directly set up baskets—and year after year he was a prolific scorer, finishing second in the league in this department one season and third in three others. I will let the statistics go at this, for there is a great deal that they don't reveal, such as Cousy's quite astounding ability to rise to the occasion and perform his most spectacular deeds when they count the most. Walter Brown, who is today perhaps the most devoted admirer of the man he originally thought he was stuck with, credits one heroic performance by Cousy with changing Boston overnight from a lukewarm basketball town into a rabid one. The occasion was a marathon battle with the Syracuse Nationals in the winter of 1953. Cousy had tied the score, 77–77, with a foul shot in the closing seconds of the regulation game time. In the first five-minute overtime period, which ended at 86–86, he scored six of Boston's nine points. After a second overtime, it was 90–90, but in the third overtime Syracuse jumped off into a sizable lead and was out in front by five points when, with only thirteen seconds remaining, Cousy, who had been fouled in the act of shooting, sank both the goal and the foul shot, and then, in the best Merriwell tradition, tied the game up once again by sinking a desperation heave from midcourt just as the buzzer sounded. Boston finally won out in the fourth overtime, in which it held Syracuse to six points while scoring twelve, nine of them by Cousy. All in all, he accounted for fifty points that evening, on ten goals and thirty successful foul shots in thirty-two attempts. I did not see that particular game, and, to be candid, when I read about it I remained unconvinced that even a Cousy could not have been contained better if given special attention in special circumstances. I learned better the following winter, when I saw him retrieve a seemingly irreparably lost game with the Knickerbockers by acrobatically intercepting two passes in the last thirty seconds. Those two last-ditch efforts tied the game, and the Celtics went on to win it in the first overtime period, when Cousy put on an almost unbelievable exhibition of dribbling. Since there was no twenty-four-second rule in those days, once Boston had moved out in front Cousy killed the clock for over three minutes, dribbling out of one pocket after another as two (and sometimes three) opponents tried to tie him up and make him get rid of the ball, whirling like a runaway top through the whole New York team, in fact, until time finally ran out. I feel compelled to cite one other example of a Cousy finish, for I regard it as the most sensational single play I have ever seen in basketball. It came in the final four seconds of a game with St. Louis some five or six years ago.

The Celtics, trailing by one point, had the ball out of bounds at mid-court after having called for a time-out. Awaiting the referee's whistle that would signal the resumption of play, Cousy stood just outside the sideline, prepared to pass the ball. During a game, his intensity is masked, for the most part, by a rather expressionless stare, and at this particular moment he seemed, if anything, a shade more detached than usual—as abstracted as a man riding an escalator. The whistle blew and before anyone could appreciate what had taken place the Celtics had scored and won the game. With the ball cradled between his right palm and wrist, Cousy, twisting into the half-overarm, half-sidearm motion with which a jai-alai player releases the pelota from his cesta, had snapped the ball, as if it *were* a pelota, through a forest of players and into the upstretched hands of Heinsohn, who had cut across from the left to leap into the air just in front of the basket. Heinsohn had simply turned and dropped the ball in.

Cousy's zest for competition has undoubtedly been a large factor in his uncommon longevity in a sport where most men are superannuated at thirty, but there have been a number of other interesting factors, too. For one thing, he has been relatively lucky in escaping serious injury. While his outsize hands are the first physical feature that everyone notices, Cousy also has an exceptionally sturdy and resilient pair of legs, and they have held up miraculously. About midway through his career, he picked up his first severe Charley horse, and he has been sidelined for a couple of weeks just about every year since with this type of injury in one thigh or the other, but until this winter he managed to avoid any other leg trouble. And, except for a problem with one of his arches last year, he has had no bother with his feet and ankles, either, which is remarkable, considering the gusto with which he plays. (Cousy is doubly fortunate in being so unbrittle, because he happens to be allergic to the zinc in adhesive-tape stickum.)

Cousy's penchant for critical self-analysis and plain hard work have also served to extend his career as a top star. Whereas most sports headliners are content to polish the special skills that have made their reputations, Cousy has continually scrutinized every aspect of his play with the aim of finding out why certain things that used to work weren't working as well any more, and of devising some counter-measure. Once, when he was in a momentary slump, he concluded that he had been trying to take the ball in too close to the basket before either shooting or passing—a diagnosis that Auerbach confirmed—and he found that the cure was to make that decision earlier, as he hit the foul line. It was typical of Cousy that on one of his days off that winter he was discovered working out by himself in a deserted gym near his home, in Worcester, perfecting his moves as he dribbled tirelessly up and down the floor from one foul line to the other. Though he has always been a more than adequate defensive player, he has become a much more proficient one in recent years. Since it is next to impossible to defend against a jump shot, Cousy expends his major energy on trying to prevent his man from getting the ball in the first place. To this end, he deliberately overplays his man on the "ball side"—the side from which a pass would be coming. This is a very risky business—a clever pass would give his man a free route to the basket—and a technique only a player with Cousy's quick reflexes can get away with. Three years ago, feeling he needed to add a running one-hand shot to his offensive repertoire, Cousy began to work on throwing such a shot as his right leg hit the floor. The orthodox method is to shoot off the left leg, but Cousy felt that his variation would be more difficult for the man guarding him to anticipate. His success with this unorthodox running one-hander helps to explain why, with a previous career average of making thirty-seven per cent of his shots, he has been making forty per cent of them this year.

Like all great athletes, Cousy takes an enormous, if quiet, pride in his skills and in the reputation they have earned him, and perhaps it is this, more than anything else, that has fired him to his brilliant performances week after week and year after year. The corollary has always been clear: He would never consent to linger on as a lesser player once he felt he was slipping. It was this concern about his ability to sustain his play at what was for him an acceptable level that in December, 1961, led him to give serious thought to retiring at the end of that season. Physically, he had slowed down very little. He had learned to pace himself in tough games, and, moreover, the Celtics had come up with two stalwart backcourt men, Sam Jones and K. C. Jones, who made it possible for the team to keep winning if Cousy played an average of only twenty-nine minutes a game instead of the full forty-eight minutes that he had been coming close to playing for more than a decade. It was the accumulating nervous strain he was encountering that put the idea of retirement into Cousy's head. Previously, year after year, despite the killing N.B.A. schedule, which frequently calls for a team to play four games in four different cities in the space of five or six days, he had nearly always managed to throw off his fatigue when he went out on the court, tap some reserve of vitality, and cut loose with the wizardry that everyone had come to expect of him. In the 1961–62 season, though, he found this harder and harder, and sometimes impossible. It wasn't the games that were wearing him down, he has said, but the constant travelling, the necessity for worrying about public relations at all hours, and the rest of what he calls "externals." In any event, the exertion of trying to maintain a high playing pitch on a dwindling supply of nervous energy had left him drained dry, and in December he was convinced that the time had come to step down.

For Cousy, the prospect of retirement held few of the financial terrors it holds for most athletes. He has for a number of years been one of three partners in the operation of a successful summer camp for boys in Pittsfield, New Hampshire, called Camp Graylag. He is also a partner in an insurance company in Worcester. Moreover, his popularity in the Massachusetts home counties is such that his participation in other reliable business ventures is frequently sought. Consequently, as he mulled matters over last winter, his first concern was his future connection with basketball. For years, it had been generally assumed that whenever Cousy was ready to retire he would take over as the coach of the Celtics, and that Auerbach would probably be moved upstairs to the post of general manager. The more Cousy pondered such an arrangement, though, the less attractive it looked, because as a coach in the N.B.A. he would still be living hectically out of a suitcase from September to April. An almost perfect solution presented itself in late February, when he was asked by Boston College if he would be interested in coaching its team. Before accepting the offer, he felt he owed it to Walter Brown, who had long looked after his interests more in the manner of a friend than in that of an employer, to talk things over with him. Everything seemed inextricably complicated when Brown, not unnaturally, asked if it was possible for Cousy to play one more year. Then everything resolved itself neatly when Boston College agreed to hold the coaching spot open until the 1962–63 season was over. After the playoffs last winter, Cousy, with his future course mapped, began, most untypically, to relax and enjoy some of the things he had been missing. For example, when the French branch of the Gillette Safety Razor Company asked him to undertake a promotional tour in May, he agreed to accept only if the company would underwrite, as a payment for his services, the travel expenses of his wife, Missie, and their two daughters, Marie Colette and Mary Patricia, then ten and nine. The Cousys motored *en famille* for six weeks around France while the star of *La Tournée Bob Cousy* (who is of French descent and fluently bilingual) directed basketball clinics in fifteen cities. During the summer months, he made only one real trip away from Camp Graylag, dropping down to Washington, D.C., to see if he could interest John Austin, an outstanding high-school basketball star who was weighing dozens of offers, in attending Boston College. Cousy was successful in this, his one recruiting expedition thus far, even though an athletic scholarship at Boston College covers only the cost of tuition, books, and room and board, making no provision for white convertibles or such blandishments. When Cousy arrived at the Celtics' training camp last September, he seemed sprier and more full of verve than he had been for several years. He was out to make his last season a memorable one.

This winter, I made it a point to watch the Celtics whenever they came to town, knowing that there were just so many chances left to see Cousy in action. In January, I arranged to make a short trip with the Celtics, picking them up in Cincinnati on the tenth, a Thursday, and returning with them to Boston, where they were scheduled for two games over the weekend. The game in Cincinnati was the fortieth of the eighty-game 1962–63 N.B.A. season, which had begun on October 20th and was to finish on March 17th, when the championship playoffs were to begin, and the Celtics, I knew, would be feeling the inevitable midseason weariness. On top of this, Cincinnati was the last stop on a long, enervating road trip involving nine games in fifteen days—in Syracuse on December 27th, in Cincinnati on December 28th, in St. Louis on December 29th, in San Francisco on January 2nd, in Los Angeles on January 4th and 5th, back in San Francisco on January 8th, in Chicago on January 9th, and back in Cincinnati again on January 10th. To make matters worse, Cousy had pulled a muscle on the inside of his right leg during the St. Louis game. He had been forced to sit out the first game in San Francisco and was able to play only briefly in the ensuing games while he waited for the injury to heal. I expected to find him in rotten spirits.

I got together with Cousy, whom I have known fairly well for some years, in the coffee shop of the Sheraton-Gibson Hotel at four in the afternoon before the Cincinnati game. A phone call I had made to his room half an hour earlier had roused him from a sound sleep, and when I apologized for this, he explained, over a bowl of vegetable soup and a grilled cheese sandwich, that he was still trying to catch up on the sleep he had lost two nights earlier. That night, the plane on which the team was travelling East from San Francisco had developed engine trouble and had not arrived in Chicago till eight in the morning, and in Chicago there had been a mixup in hotel reservations, which meant no rooms had been available for the players until noon. Cousy looked extremely tired around the eyes, but he was in a surprisingly equable mood, and I remarked on this. "I suppose the explanation is that I know I won't have to be doing this much longer," he answered. "In a way, though, it was a good thing this trip turned out to be so rough. The first couple of months this season, everything went so smoothly that I was wondering if I really wanted to retire. Well, I'm sure of it now. The schedule's just too brutal and the season's much too long. This is a game where you've got to put out your top effort every second. You're head to head with your man. In the final analysis, it's how much better you can sustain your drive, your purpose, than he can. That's what makes a man, and a team, superior. When you're a little under par physically, you think about that. I do at the start of each game now. I see some youngster coming out to play me who's so fired up that the saliva is practically drooling from his mouth. I was probably like that myself when I was a kid and went out to play Bob Davies or Bob Wanzer or one of the other stars. Anyway, when I step out on the floor now, I have to key myself up consciously. I can't wait for it to come naturally any more."

After Cousy had finished eating, we continued our talk in the hotel room occupied by the Celtics' trainer, Buddy Le Roux, while Cousy baked his injured right leg under an infrared diathermy lamp. "They say that experience minimizes pressures," he said at one point, "but I haven't found it to be so. For instance, it used to be much easier for me to relax on the road than it is now. On this particular trip, the only stop I enjoyed was Los Angeles. I've got the golf bug now, so I went out one day to watch the L.A. Open and had a real good time walking around with Ken Venturi. Also, I had a chance to talk to Bill Sharman. He's coaching the basketball team at Los Angeles State College now. We're trying to work out an arrangement for an annual game at Christmastime between Boston College and Los Angeles State—home and home, you know, alternate years." Cousy paused for a moment, and then continued, "I really miss Sharman. We roomed together on the road for ten years, I guess it was. You didn't have time to be bored when you were with Bill. He had everything scheduled down to the minute—when you were supposed to start eating, when you were supposed to stop eating, how long you were supposed to sleep before a game, the whole works. The only trouble was that after a while he had me eating when I didn't feel like eating, and sleeping when I didn't feel like sleeping. When Bill left, two years ago, I started rooming alone on the trips. Most of the time now, I just read or watch TV in my hotel room. Heinsohn says I've become a stodgy old man. He *would*, of course. If they didn't close the coffee shop, Heinsohn would stay up all night, just as long as he had one listener left with one eye open."

Cousy had time for a brief nap before the Celtics assembled in the lobby at six-thirty to leave by taxi for the Cincinnati Gardens. I rode out with Cousy, Heinsohn, and Auerbach. Heinsohn, a good-natured and companionable young giant, who followed Cousy from Holy Cross to the Celtics, and who also lives in Worcester, is perhaps his closest friend on the team now. What particularly struck me, however, was the warm relationship that had grown up between Cousy and Auerbach. Two men could hardly be less alike than the sensitive, disciplined star and the rambunctious coach. Cousy receives the loudest applause in the league and Auerbach the loudest boos. Quick-tempered, combative, and not averse to the spotlight, the coach is up and off the bench at least as often as any of his N.B.A. confreres, arguing flamboyantly with the referees and, on some nights, with anybody else who wants an argument. His fierce pride in the Celtics leads him into comically extravagant gestures designed to put detractors in their place, and his latest weapon in the constant psychological warfare is characteristic. Now, even when many minutes remain to be played in a game, he lights up a cigar, to let the opposing coach know that as far as he is concerned the game is over and the Celtics have won it. It should be noted, however, that, away from the court, Auerbach has mellowed into a very likable and fairly temperate man. On the ride out to the Cincinnati Gardens, he and Cousy (the one man who calls him "Arnold" and not "Red") quietly talked over a few changes they thought might help the Celtics to get rolling again after losing four of their eight games on the road trip (although the team was still securely in first place in the Eastern Division of the N.B.A.). Then their talk switched to Sid Borgia, the league's small and notably assertive head referee, who was to handle the game that evening. Auerbach and Borgia get along like flint and steel. Auerbach recited a long list of his grievances against the referee, whereupon Cousy, with the patience of an older brother, set out to calm him down, and apparently succeeded quite well.

The Celtics lost that evening, 130–121. Playing with immense spirit, Cousy led a Boston rally in the third period to tie the score at 98–98, but he had to leave the game shortly afterward when he pulled a muscle in his left groin. Auerbach had a grim evening. In addition to being denied the pomp of lighting his cigar, he had to suffer through a not-good performance by Borgia, a referee whose work can be singularly brilliant some evenings but on others, when he falls into what one critic has called his Alice in Wonderland style, can be merely singular. After the game, the Boston coach sought solace, as is his custom, at a Chinese restaurant (Auerbach is so hipped on Chinese food that on road trips he carries a hot plate along for warming up midnight—and sometimes breakfast—snacks of chow mein in his room). As for Cousy, immediately after the game he returned to the hotel and started to uncoil over a bottle of beer, after which he read for two hours. "It's the old story," he said stoically when I asked him about his new injury. "You try to favor one leg and you pull a muscle in the other. I'll have to take it easy for three or four days now. Then I'll be ready to go again."

The next morning, the Celtics were scheduled to fly home by jet, leaving Cincinnati at 10:15 A.M. and making connections with a noon flight out of Pittsburgh that would take them directly to Boston, where they were scheduled to play the Syracuse Nationals that evening at eight. However, what should have been a comparatively restful day for the dull-eyed troupe of travellers proved to be an exhausting one. A low-lying fog shrouded the Cincinnati airport, and all jet flights out were cancelled. At twelve-fifteen, after Auerbach and Le Roux had done some scurrying around, the Celtics boarded a Constellation (planes of that size were able to get out) and headed for Dayton, where they succeeded in finding space on a one-thirty jet for New York. They arrived at Idlewild around three o'clock, took a motor coach to LaGuardia, got on a four-o'clock shuttle plane to Boston, and eventually reached the Boston Garden at five-thirty. There had been a moment of comic relief at the Cincinnati airport when Auerbach and Borgia had elaborately pretended not to notice each other's presence in the waiting room, but after that it was just a matter of sitting back and hoping that the next airport would not be fogged in—"a typical day in the N.B.A.," as Russell glumly characterized it. Cousy spent most of his time reading "Total Empire," by Edmund A. Walsh, S.J., a book about Communist plans for world domination. Usually, his tastes are somewhat lighter, but during the past year he has read, among other things, "The Devil's Advocate," "The Tribe That Lost Its Head," "To Kill a Mockingbird," and "The Making of the President."

Being home again gave the Celtics an immense lift, and that evening, for all their bone-weariness, they outran and outhustled the fast Syracuse team and won handily, 134–117. They did this, moreover, without any help from Cousy. He had tried out his legs during the pre-game warmup, but after taking two shots concluded that he would run the risk of aggravating his injuries if he played. After the game, he spent an hour or so talking with reporters, giving autographs, and greeting old friends. He then joined his wife, who was waiting for him in the corridor outside the locker room, and they drove home to Worcester, taking me along. There was no game on Saturday, but Cousy was constantly on the go, handling problems that had accumulated during his two weeks' absence. The telephone began ringing at breakfast, while he was reacquainting himself with his daughters—the first call was from a Worcester friend, a priest named Father Ganynor, about some local charity work Cousy is interested in—and continued to ring fairly regularly from that time on. Mrs. Cousy, a comely young woman, who grew up with her future husband in St. Albans, Queens, was soon busy providing coffee for a steady parade of visitors. Joe Sharry, a Worcester attorney, who is Cousy's partner in the insurance business, stayed for five cups. The most important visitor, George Stavros, a Worcester restaurateur, stayed for three. Earlier that week, after several long-distance telephone talks with Cousy, Stavros had made an offer for a restaurant in Framingham called the Abner Wheeler House, and the two men, who had been collaborating on the deal for months, had many things to discuss. Cousy finally left home at noon, and I made the one-hour drive with him to the Celtics' office in the Boston Garden. There he answered some of the mail that had piled up for him, dictated a telegram to an out-of-town sportswriter who had sent him a batch of questions, and tape-recorded an interview to be used to promote a magazine article he had written. The main reason for his trip into town, however, was to give his legs the benefit of the whirlpool bath in the Celtics' dressing room, and he attended to that next. As we headed back to Worcester, he made one slight detour, driving up Beacon Street to a spot called Coolidge Corner, where he pointed out a new Chinese restaurant, called Anita Chue's. "I'm not the only one on the team interested in the restaurant business," he said, with a mischievous smile. "Wouldn't you know Auerbach would own a piece of a Chinese joint?"

On Sunday morning, Cousy picked up Heinsohn at his home shortly after eleven and they headed for the Garden and the afternoon game with the Chicago Zephyrs. It was a bright, crisp morning, and both men were in a merry, ragging mood. At one point, for example, when they were comparing their prowess in making speeches at banquets, Heinsohn remarked that he was having trouble with his favorite opening line: "I suppose all of you are wondering why I asked you here this evening." He said, "It's a great line and I hate to lose it, but some audiences don't get it at all and then it takes me five minutes to make a comeback."

The restaurant for which Cousy and Stavros were bidding is on Route 9, the turnpike connecting Worcester and Boston, and when we passed it that morning, Heinsohn asked Cousy if he planned to change its name. "We're still undecided," Cousy told him. "My partner wants to call it 'Bob Cousy's Abner Wheeler House,' but I'm sort of partial to 'Abner Wheeler's Bob Cousy House.' More class."

"If you're still thinking of taking up the piano next year, it might cut down your overhead," Heinsohn said. "You could be featured in the lounge. Playing 'Chopsticks.'"

Cousy fished around for a rejoinder. "That's good, clear thinking," he said after a moment. "I'll break the act in at Auerbach's place."

At game time, Cousy was, as usual, implacably earnest. He had decided, after taking a heat treatment, to see how his legs stood up to a light workout. However, being constitutionally incapable of keeping himself down in first or second gear, he was soon roaring all over the court, driving the Celtics into one fast break after another, passing superlatively, and shooting well. When he came out, at the end of the first quarter, the Celtics had an eighteen-point lead, Auerbach's cigar was already lit, and Cousy was no longer needed. Soon after the game, I left for New York. I was entirely worn out from the brief trip.

Cousy had another day off on Monday, but on Tuesday, along with Russell and Heinsohn, he was off for Los Angeles and the All-Star Game. I watched the game on television with considerable apprehension, knowing that Cousy was still not back in top physical shape, and feeling that it would be historically wrong if he did not give an excellent account of himself in his final All-Star Game. My worries were needless. He acted like the youngest man on the floor, and it was his *élan* and generalship that broke the game open for the East.

Some of Cousy's admirers contend that he has never played quite as well as he has this year. Perhaps that is going a bit too far, but the main point is that he has made his farewell season a suitably triumphant one. This does not come to pass very often in sports. All great athletes fully intend to call it a career when they are still at or near the peak of their powers, but for one reason or another few of them actually do, and the last chapters can be pathetic. When Cousy leaves the game after the playoffs, it will not be the same for quite some time. Indeed, the prospect brings to mind the wonderful line that begins William Hazlitt's tribute to John Cavanagh, the great nineteenth-century handball champion: "When a man dies who does any one thing better than anyone else in the world, which so many are trying to do well, it leaves a gap in society."

John McPhee

Few writers' beginnings argue more persuasively for the benefit of propinquity than those of John McPhee (b. 1931). He grew up in Princeton, New Jersey, the son of the physician for the sports teams at the local university, from which he graduated in 1953. By the early 1960s, having found a staff position at *Time* yet hoping to catch the eye of *The New Yorker*, McPhee accepted his father's invitation to join him at a Princeton freshman game to check out a basketball prodigy from Missouri. That was his introduction to Bill Bradley, who became the subject of McPhee's first long *New Yorker* profile and a good enough friend that the senior All-America would hide out in McPhee's Princeton home so he could finish his thesis free from the harassment of reporters and agents. *New Yorker* editor William Shawn at first turned down McPhee's proposal, believing the previous piece in this anthology, Herbert Warren Wind's "Farewell to Cousy," had filled his magazine's biennial quota of basketball stories. We're lucky that Shawn reconsidered, as was McPhee: during a half-century of turning out virtuoso nonfiction as a *New Yorker* staff writer, he would write canonically on such other sports as tennis and lacrosse, and on subjects as varied as canoe building, nuclear physics, and the cultivation of oranges. But he broke through with "A Sense of Where You Are," which became a book of the same name after Bradley took Princeton on its unlikely run to the 1965 Final Four. This excerpt showcases McPhee's ability to set a scene and deploy detail, two characteristic virtues of his work.

from

A Sense of Where You Are

THOSE who have never seen him are likely to assume that he is seven and a half feet tall—the sort of elaborate weed that once all but choked off the game. With an average like his, it would be fair to imagine him spending his forty minutes of action merely stuffing the ball into the net. But the age of the goon is over. Bradley is six feet five inches tall—the third-tallest player on the Princeton team. He is perfectly coördinated, and he is unbelievably accurate at every kind of shot in the basketball repertory. He does much of his scoring from considerable distances, and when he sends the ball toward the basket, the odds are that it is going in, since he has made more than half the shots he has attempted as a college player. With three, or even four, opponents clawing at him, he will rise in the air, hang still for a moment, and release a high parabola jump shot that almost always seems to drop into the basket with an equal margin to the rim on all sides. Against Harvard last February, his ninth long shot from the floor nicked the rim slightly on its way into the net. The first eight had gone cleanly through the center. He had missed none at all. He missed several as the evening continued, but when his coach finally took him out, he had scored fifty-one points. In a game twenty-four hours earlier, he had begun a thirty-nine point performance by hitting his first four straight. Then he missed a couple. Then he made ten consecutive shots, totally demoralizing Dartmouth.

Bradley is one of the few basketball players who have ever been appreciatively cheered by a disinterested away-from-home crowd while warming up. This curious event occurred last March, just before Princeton eliminated the Virginia Military Institute, the year's Southern Conference champion, from the N.C.A.A. championships. The game was played in Philadelphia and was the last of a tripleheader. The people there were worn out, because most of them were emotionally committed to either Villanova or Temple—two local teams that had just been involved in enervating battles with Providence and Connecticut, respectively, scrambling for a chance at the rest of the country. A group of Princeton boys shooting basketballs miscellaneously in preparation for still another game hardly promised to be a high point of the evening, but Bradley, whose routine in the warmup time is a gradual crescendo of activity, is more interesting to watch before a game than most players are in play. In Philadelphia that night, what he did was, for him, anything but unusual. As he does before all games, he began by shooting set shots close to the basket, gradually moving back until he was shooting long sets from twenty feet out, and nearly all of them dropped into the net with an almost mechanical rhythm of accuracy. Then he began a series of expandingly difficult jump shots, and one jumper after another went cleanly through the basket with so few exceptions that the crowd began to murmur. Then he started to perform whirling reverse moves before another cadence of almost steadily accurate jump shots, and the murmur increased. Then he began to sweep hook shots into the air. He moved in a semicircle around the court. First with his right hand, then with his left, he tried seven of these long, graceful shots—the most difficult ones in the orthodoxy of basketball—and ambidextrously made them all.

The game had not even begun, but the presumably unimpressible Philadelphians were applauding like an audience at an opera.

Bradley has a few unorthodox shots, too. He dislikes flamboyance, and, unlike some of basketball's greatest stars, has apparently never made a move merely to attract attention. While some players are eccentric in their shooting, his shots, with only occasional exceptions, are straightforward and unexaggerated. Nonetheless, he does make something of a spectacle of himself when he moves in rapidly parallel to the baseline, glides through the air with his back to the basket, looks for a teammate he can pass to, and, finding none, tosses the ball into the basket over one shoulder, like a pinch of salt. Only when the ball is actually dropping through the net does he look around to see what has happened, on the chance that something might have gone wrong, in which case he would have to go for the rebound. That shot has the essential characteristics of a wild accident, which is what many people stubbornly think they have witnessed until they see him do it for the third time in a row. All shots in basketball are supposed to have names—the set, the hook, the layup, the jump shot, and so on—and one weekend last July, while Bradley was in Princeton working on his senior thesis and putting in some time in the Princeton gymnasium to keep himself in form for the Olympics, I asked him what he called his over-the-shoulder shot. He said that he had never heard a name for it, but that he had seen Oscar Robertson, of the Cincinnati Royals, and Jerry West, of the Los Angeles Lakers, do it, and had worked it out for himself. He went on to say that it is a much simpler shot than it appears to be, and, to illustrate, he tossed a ball over his shoulder and into the basket while he was talking and looking me in the eye. I retrieved the ball and handed it back to him. "When you have played basketball for a while, you don't need to look at the basket when you are in close like this," he said, throwing it over his shoulder again and right through the hoop. "You develop a sense of where you are."

Roy Blount, Jr.

Roy Blount, Jr. (b. 1941) once described himself as a "humorist-novelist-journalist-dramatist-lyricist-lecturer-reviewer-performer-versifier-cruciverbalist-sportswriter-screenwriter-anthologist-columnist-philologist." To which—after looking up *cruciverbalist* and discovering that it's someone who constructs crossword puzzles—one might add radio personality, memoirist, and confirmed southerner. After growing up in Decatur, Georgia, Blount won a Grantland Rice Sportswriting Scholarship to attend Vanderbilt, where he edited the school newspaper, *The Hustler*. He broke in as a reporter and editorialist at the *Atlanta Journal*, then spent seven years at *Sports Illustrated*. There he staked out a remote position in the wide range of styles on staff during the late 1960s and early '70s, combining a conversational voice marbled with erudition (he had picked up a master's in English from Harvard) with the storytelling chops native to his home region. In 1970 *SI* sent Blount on just the kind of off-center assignment that more and more magazine editors would throw his way: a feature on the aging basketball showman Wilfred Hetzel. The trick-shot artist is basketball's version of a humorist, the tag most often attached to Blount, as well as the word he chose to lead that freight train of self-description above. "Generally," Blount wrote in his 1998 memoir *Be Sweet*, "you can find in the childhood of a significant humorist some event so absurdly traumatic that there's no way to make straightforward sense of it." Hetzel suffered through just such a trauma, which Blount confides in the reader here. His profile reminds us that pathos can be found in the life of an avowed entertainer, and that the story of someone who plays it for laughs is often best entrusted to a fellow funny man.

47 Years A Shot-Freak

W ORLD'S GREATEST (and doubtless only) Freak Shot Expert Wilfred Hetzel, who was discharged from the Army in 1943 "for nervousness," is nervous now. In the assembly program at Ladysmith (Va.) High School this morning, the kids were a little restless, and his performance a little ragged. True, he hit over 70% of his gallimaufry of shots—with eyes shut, with legs crossed, with legs downright entwined, on the bounce off the floor, from one foot, from one knee, from both knees, from behind the backboard (frontward and backward), from up on his toes, from back on his heels (toes in the air) and in various combinations of the above. The kids responded with a gleeful shout, as he says they almost always do, to his "goofy series," in which he suddenly assumes a fey, exaggeratedly knock-kneed or bowlegged stance and then lets fly.

But the days of his 60-foot and 70-foot peg shots, which he used to make off ceilings or over rafters or simply from one end of the court to the other, are gone. Now, 58 years old and weakened by an operation for TB, the man who bills himself as "Thrice Featured in *Believe It or Not* and Twice in *Strange as It Seems*" can shoot the ball only underhanded (except on his bounce shots) and seldom from farther out than the foul line. And in 14 tries at Ladysmith, his 18-foot dropkick, his most spectacular remaining shot, was in and out once but never quite swished. The kids cheered frequently and came up for autographs afterward but, as Hetzel says, "If I can't impress them as the *best*—well, that's the point."

Now, sitting in the boys' dressing room of Louisa County High School in Mineral, Va., 30 miles from Ladysmith, he is shaking, and drinking his fifth cup of coffee to counteract "spots of fatigue." He got only four hours of sleep last night because the pills he has been taking for his sciatica since 1949 keep him awake in spite of Sominex. The principal of this just-integrated 580-pupil school has consented to move Mr. Hetzel's performance up from 2:30 to 1 o'clock so he won't have to sit around getting tenser.

"Nothing terrifies me more," Hetzel says, "than for the ball to be falling just short by inches—because these students don't know, they don't realize the handicaps. And then maybe some of the students start laughing, and I try harder. What some people can't understand is that I'm governed by averages, too."

With that he sheds his suit, revealing himself in the maroon shorts, the gold shirt lettered WILFRED HETZEL on the front and FREAK SHOT SPE-CIALIST on the back, the worn black-top shoes and the straggly strips of tape on his knees (kneepads shift too much when he kneels to shoot) that constitute his working uniform. He has worn this outfit underneath his clothes on the road since 1962; he had read that Esther Williams kept her bathing suit on underneath for quick changes during her appearance tours. Distractedly, Hetzel proceeds to the gym and takes a few practice shots as the kids file in. Then he presents himself and relates, in an absorbed, recitative voice, a brief history of his involvement in freak shooting.

* * *

Not the comprehensive history, because he hasn't the time. If he were to include all the material he is more than happy to bring forth in conversation, he would go back to 1924, when, in Melrose, Minn., at the age of 12, he nailed a barrel hoop to the side of the family woodshed and took his first shot. If you start counting then, Hetzel has said, "and if you include all the times with a baseball, a kittenball, a soccer ball, a rag ball, some socks tied together in the form of a ball, a tennis ball, a football—I had to learn to shoot the football end over end so that it would nose down at just the right moment and pass through that small hoop"—if you count all those shots, along with the 30,000 hours he estimates he has spent shooting a regulation basketball through a real basket, says Hetzel—"I have probably shot more goals than any man in history."

In his backyard there by the woodshed he shot them year-round, in rain, snow, in tricky gusts of wind ("It was a thrill to have the wind pick up the ball and blow it six or seven feet through the hoop") and in temperatures down to 20° below. He pretended he was the University of Minnesota and also its opponents, which meant, since he did his best for both sides, that Minnesota lost half the time. He would plan out a complete schedule in advance, but when the Gophers had lost too many games to hope for a Big Ten crown, he would start over. When he tells audiences this, Hetzel says, it gives the coaches present a good laugh "because they wish they could start a season over. Of course, it's so much easier the way I do it, all make-believe."

The first time young Wilfred tried shooting with a real basketball, "it went straight, three feet under the basket, like a pass."

"Gee whiz," remarked an unkind neighborhood boy who was watching, "if I couldn't do any better than that, I'd quit."

"He was one of those boys," recalls Hetzel, "who move away a few years later, and you don't know what happened to them." One of those boys, in other words, who do not go on to become the world's greatest anything.

Somewhat later, Wilfred started doing a little shooting in the local gym—but it wasn't easy. "There were some boys there, after school, who were good at clever fakery, dribbling, passing and that, and they would hog the ball. I might have to wait two hours, from 3:30 to 5:30, until they went home and I could get in five minutes of shooting before the janitor locked the ball up. Or maybe he would lock it up as soon as they quit. I'd think nothing later of shooting 5,000 times, because I'd been deprived of it for so long."

There was no question of Hetzel's going after one of those clever-faking boys one-on-one and taking the ball away, because ball handling has never been his forte. It has never been even a part of his portfolio. The truth is that Wilfred Hetzel, who has made 144 straight foul shots standing on one foot, who bills himself as "One of Basketball's Immortals," has never learned to dribble.

"I realized I would never be good at the game one day in PT class when I was a freshman in high school," he says now. "We were supposed to do what they called a figure-eight drill. I'd be a forward, and the center would pass it to me, and I would pass it to the other forward and then I wouldn't know where to go. They never explained it to me in detail, never diagramed it or anything. After I fouled it up twice, I knew I'd never play. I was too slow and kind of awkward in other ways."

Hetzel did serve the high school team briefly as a scrub, and "I made a few shots against the first team, and I'd pass it pretty well, but I never did dribble. And I'd be open for a shot and very seldom would anyone pass it to me. There were cliques on the team—they'd pass it to their friends."

He got into one unofficial game against a local telephone team, didn't shoot and committed two technical fouls by neglecting to check in with the timekeeper each time he went in. The year before, his uniform was stolen twice. He decided to quit organized basketball forever (except for a brief exhibition game appearance with Western Union College in Le Mars, Iowa, many years later, when he was inserted to shoot two foul shots and hit one).

In fact, young Wilfred found that he had no great knack for any competitive sport. In baseball he could hit fungoes with precision and catch fly balls gloveless in his big, long-fingered hands, but he was too slow to play the outfield and couldn't get the bat around fast enough to hit pitching.

But that just meant more time for shooting basketballs by himself every day, including the day his father, a Bavarian immigrant and railroad man, was killed. The water tank for which the elder Hetzel was responsible was out of order, and evidently he went up to its rim to investigate. No one saw him fall in through the layer of ice, but when 16-year-old Wilfred came in for lunch, his father's hamburger was overcooking on the stove. Finally Mrs. Hetzel took it off. "The ice froze back over," as Hetzel tells it, "and they had to get special permission from division headquarters to go in and see if he was there. And he was."

It is easy enough to see a fateful symbolism in the mode of the father's death—the son doomed to act it out with a basketball over and over again—but Hetzel says he has never seen any irony in it. By the time his father died, at any rate, he had already devoted hundreds of hours to what was to become his vocation.

Pretty soon Hetzel was making 98 out of 100 from the free-throw line. But he never had any witnesses, "and people thought if I really had a talent like that I would be on the team." So one day as a high school senior, he put on an impromptu lunch-hour exhibition in the school gym. That was his first show, in 1929. "I've thought about writing Ed Sullivan," he says, "and saying they're all talking so much about the sports stars of the Golden '20s—Red Grange and so on—and here I am, out of the '20s and still performing."

But in those early days he had no tricks, just free throws, performed at no charge. Upon graduation from high school he moved with his mother, who had remarried, to nearby Sauk Centre, Minn., and began to do some sportswriting for local daily and weekly papers. In the line of duty, he would attend Sauk Centre games, and while the players were dressing he would seize the opportunity to take the floor in his street clothes and shoot before a crowd. He went so far as to write himself up in one of the papers, in the third person: "Wilfred Hetzel of Sauk Centre, in a recent practice session, hit 467 free throws out of 500."

Meanwhile, the local team was doing well to hit 40% from the foul line—and he reported that, too. "The fans in Sauk Centre were so hateful to me in those years," he says. "Maybe it was my fault because I slammed their team in the paper. Maybe I was like a prima donna. But once I made 120 of 122 before a game, 82 straight, and I walked off the floor, and there wasn't a single handclap. But you know, they've never had a bad team since? It kind of woke them up when I slammed them."

And then one night, in the visiting cheering section, someone woke up to Wilfred Hetzel. "This very beautiful girl came down and made such a fuss about me," he recalls. "The home people never made any fuss. The principal's son would take a couple of shots before throwing my ball back to me, and they would laugh at my embarrassment. But this beautiful girl raved about how good I was. Well, the next night Sauk Centre was to play at that girl's school, and I planned to ride with the team over there in hopes of seeing her again. But at the last minute they took only one car and didn't have room for me.

"So, rather than waste the day, I got in through the window of the gym in Melrose and practiced. I'd make 17 in a row several times, and then I'd miss. I got disgusted. 'I could do better than this with my eyes closed,' I told myself. So I just tried it that way. I shot 100 with my eyes closed and made 74. That was my first trick. I never did see that girl again."

Gradually Hetzel's reputation spread, and he was able to talk several area schools into letting him put on a free-throw show before a game or at the half. The Depression bore down, and he couldn't find much work, so he lived at home and kept on practicing his shots. When he was 20 he tired of pretending he was the University of Minnesota and began to work more on variety. He practiced for seven or eight years. After a few fans complained that free throws tended to grow monotonous, and after he lost a free-throw contest to an expert named Bunny Levitt who was traveling with the Harlem Globetrotters, he introduced his eyes-shut trick and a couple of other "unorthodox shots" to the public.

In 1937 Hetzel enrolled in the University of Minnesota and was able to work out in the gym and book himself, occasionally for a $2 or $5 honorarium, into shows at high schools, colleges and military bases throughout the state and beyond. He hitchhiked from place to place, persuaded 60 businesses in Sauk Centre to chip in on a sweat suit with SAUK CENTRE, MINNESOTA on the front and WILFRED HETZEL, STUNT SHOT SPECIALIST on the back, and it was not long before he was popping up in *Ripley's Believe It or Not* and in *Strange as It Seems*. "Wilfred Hetzel, Minneapolis Basketball Star, Shot 92 Baskets Out of 100 Tries with One Hand, Standing On One Leg and Blindfolded!" right alongside "Mrs. M. J. Wellman, Oklahoma City, Has Worn the Same Set of False Teeth for 45 Years." "Wilfred Hetzel Shot 66 Straight Basketball Foul Shots From His Knees!" right alongside "Musical Teeth! For 4 Months After Having Dental Work Done, Mrs. Fred Stutz, Indianapolis, *Could Hear*

Radio Programs Without Having the Radio Turned On! Her *Teeth* Formed a Receiving Set!"

Then, in the early '40s, after he mastered the long peg shot and the dropkick, Hetzel's career reached its fullest flower. In those years, aside from 10 months in the Army during which he experienced severe trouble with his teeth (though he heard no radio programs over them) as well as with his nerves, he spent September through May traveling the country, performing for around $25 a show, sometimes four or five times in a day. In 1941 he appeared at the Clair Bee Coaching Clinic at Manhattan Beach, N.Y. and was invited by Ned Irish to perform in a clown suit in Madison Square Garden, but that latter deal, to Hetzel's great regret, fell through. In the 1943–44 and '44–'45 seasons alone he traveled 42,000 miles, passed through 47 states and performed over 150 times. He remembers all his best performances from this heyday in detail, especially the ones in Oklahoma. "I've done an extraordinary amount of spectacular things there," he says. "In Davis, Okla., on Feb. 29, 1944—which I remember because I thought at the time, 'This is an unusual day, it comes along once in four years, I wonder what feat I'll accomplish that will make me remember this day?'—I hit 40-foot, 50-foot and 70-foot shots, all on the first try. All straight through. In fact, I lost the thrill of the 70-footer because the netting moved so barely, I thought at first the ball had just brushed it underneath. In Okmulgee, Okla., on a 60-footer, the ball hit the inside of the rim, bounced way back up diagonally, hit the junction of a rafter and the ceiling, rebounded right back to the goal, bounced around the rim and went in. That was for a girl's gym class. It was funny, I had told them my superduper was coming up.

"In Miami, Okla. I made a shot over two girders at once that the coach remembered there 10 years later. In Jenks, Okla. there was just a narrow opening to throw the ball through to get it over two crossbeams. I tried it eight times before I even got the ball through, and then it missed the basket by a foot. But I've always thanked my lucky stars that I had guts. I kept at it, and on the very next try the ball went through the opening and right down into the basket. Fifty feet. Unbeknown to me, Mickey Mantle was in junior high school in Commerce, just a few miles away, that very year."

During these cross-country tours, Hetzel would book himself for three weeks in advance. As he traveled he would write to other schools, advising them to address their replies to him in care of the school where he would be performing at the end of that period, and when he reached the school he would check his mail and map out another three weeks.

It was a grueling routine, traveling by bus or train at night (he had no car, and anyway he finds that driving impairs his touch), often getting too little sleep, lugging around his two bags (one containing clothes and the other his ball and pump), casting about in each town for a room "in some respectable place," struggling through snow-storms so as not to miss a date.

Albuquerque; Dodge City, Kans.; Forest Grove, Ore.; Homer, N.Y.; Ferndale, Mich.; San Luis Obispo, Calif.; Augusta, Ga.; Manassas, Va.; Muncie, Ind.; Louisville; Leechburg, Pa.; Ogden, Utah; Akron; Morgan-town, W. Va.; Hagerstown, Md.; Maywood, Ill.; Tombstone, Ariz. It was a thorough way of seeing the country, but it paid Hetzel only about enough to keep him going, and the travel took its toll on his health. Not until years later did he realize that he had contracted tuberculosis, which lingered until his operation—the removal of a rib and part of a lung in 1968—but he knew he did not feel up to any more full-time barnstorming, so when he found himself in Washington in the spring of 1945, he decided it was time he got a regular job. In 1942 he had applied for a defense-plant job in Chicago but "they watched me for awhile and then they rejected me. I asked why and they said I didn't have no coordination. Well, if they'd known that coordination was one of the things I was famous for! I've always attributed my success to the three Cs—confidence, coordination and concentration. But then, you can be coordinated in one thing and not in another. I never did learn to dance." This time, in '45, his touch qualified him as a civilian typist for the Marine Corps, a job he holds to this day.

Settling down in Arlington, Va., where he lives now as a roomer in a private home, Hetzel kept up his shooting career through the '50s and '60s by spacing out his leave time in bits and pieces of two or three days. His job has not paid enough to support a wife—or so he concluded after meeting the girl of his life, a toe dancer, on a bus. He confessed to her in a letter, "I kissed you when you were asleep on the bus," and she confessed in reply, "I wasn't asleep." They saw each other for some time and still exchange letters, but she married someone else. "I guess that's why I've never married," Hetzel says. "I didn't want anyone to replace her."

It was not until 1947 that he started taking off his sweat jacket to shoot—"before, on account I was so slender, I was afraid there would be more people laughing at me, and the jacket made me feel a little fleshier." The greater freedom of movement helped him to keep up his distance shots; but he made his last 70-footer in '54, his last 30-footer four years ago. In the '50s he began to find it hard "to get my pep up," and sometimes when that happened he got "snotty" receptions and reviews. "Those few times when maybe I wasn't in form, no one asked for autographs," he says. "They looked on me as a fake or a cheat or a has-been. I get emotional when I think about the time, in Jefferson-ville, Ind., some people were saying, 'He's not much,' and the coach there stood up and fairly exploded and said, 'I wish I could shoot half as good as that man.'"

In recent years he found that small, out-of-the-way black schools in the South were a fertile field, though once "they were envious—one of the boys came up and asked if I could spin the ball in my hands. I said if I could do those things, I'd have been a Globetrotter. But usually there's no resentment of me because I'm white. Without my saying it, the Negro kids come up to me and say, 'You're better than Alcindor.' Now that don't take no glory from him. He's still one of the greatest centers that ever lived. It's not the same competitive field."

In 1936 Hetzel heard Dr. James Naismith, the inventor of basketball, make a speech. "He said if you're doing something for humanity, don't think about getting a reward now, you'll get it later. I thought then, 'If I don't get a million dollars for it, I'll just enjoy it.' I do envy those football players. You know that commercial: 'Remember, Charley Conerly, such and such a day when you threw three TD passes,' and then they show the replay? I wish that on my best days they'd had TV cameras running. And I wish the people back in Minnesota that hated me and made fun of me and said, 'If there was money in it, somebody would be better at it'—I'd like to get all those people together in one gym and do all the greatest tricks I ever did."

But now, at Louisa County High School in Virginia, his audience is some 500 rural kids who have been charged 25¢ apiece by their student council for the benefit of a Korean orphan. And what Mr. Hetzel is saying now to the kids, in reference to all those doubters back in Minnesota, is "if they'd believed me back there in the beginning, when I tried to tell them I had made 98 out of 100, I might not be here now."

And he is advancing, in his gangly yet almost formal walk, to the foul line, where he begins to hit his underhanded shots, blim, blim, blim, coolly, crisply, now cross-legged, now on his toes, now on his heels, missing one occasionally but in command, running through his repertoire, down on his knees, up on one foot, and the kids are paying him mind. Mr. Hetzel's manner of shooting is memorable in many respects, but its most noteworthy feature is that when he releases the ball—even routinely in practice but especially when he knows he is going well—his face is lit by a proud and affectionate smile. The first time Wilfred Hetzel has ever tried a shot from behind a Louisa County backboard, over the crossed wires that raise and lower it, he scores. On his second try at that same shot backward, over his head, he scores. He scores on one more backspin bounce shot from his knees. And now, in closing: the dropkick.

Short. Short. Off to the right. Short. Off to the right. Short. Short. Off the rim. Off the rim. Off to the left. Off the rim. No, way short. A pause before the 13th try and then it is up, off the backboard, swish.

"Yaay! Aw-*right*! Sign him up!"

Pete Axthelm

The writing career of Pete Axthelm (1943–1991) made its greatest impact at the start. His undergraduate thesis at Yale on the modern confessional novel was good enough to be published by Yale University Press, but he was drawn not to academia but to journalism: immediately after graduation he joined the *New York Herald Tribune* as its turf writer. He soon stopped over at *Sports Illustrated* and then *Newsweek*, whose sports coverage he embodied as an editor and columnist through the 1970s. But it was his 1970 book, *The City Game*, that secured his reputation. He alternated stories from New York City playgrounds with scenes from Madison Square Garden, where the Knicks were on their way to their first NBA title. "Axthelm's eye is cinemascopic, his prose precise," wrote John Leonard in a *New York Times* review. "The mind is instructed while the emotions are exhausted." But by the 1980s Axthelm was writing less and less, turning instead to television, where he became NBC's answer to CBS oddsmaker Jimmy the Greek. After the NFL banned touts from pregame shows, he moved to ESPN, where he delivered mainstream commentary. At Axthelm's Manhattan saloon of choice, Runyon's, he would keep two tabs open, one with the bartender and another with his bookie. He celebrated his membership in a mythical brotherhood that he and his drinking buddies called SOFA, the Society of Functioning Alcoholics. But he eventually ceased to function, brushing off doctors' warnings that he sober up. The end came at age forty-seven, of liver failure, while awaiting a transplant at a hospital in Pittsburgh. When he wrote *The City Game*, Axthelm couldn't have known that he would find himself as shackled by substance abuse as Earl Manigault, the legendary Harlem ballplayer he calls "a wasted talent, a pathetic victim, even a tragic hero." After Axthelm's death, Hunter S. Thompson wasn't among the many friends wringing hands. Thompson called him "one of the last free spirits in journalism or anywhere else in these humorless times. . . . We will miss him, but not weep for him. Pete Axthelm was a winner, and he got out just in time."

from

The City Game

IN THE litany of quiet misfortunes that have claimed so many young athletes in the ghetto, it may seem almost impossible to select one man and give him special importance. Yet in the stories and traditions that are recounted in the Harlem parks, one figure does emerge above the rest. Asked about the finest athletes they have seen, scores of ballplayers in a dozen parks mention Connie Hawkins and Lew Alcindor and similar celebrities. But almost without exception, they speak first of one star who didn't go on: Earl Manigault.

No official scorers tabulate the results of pickup games; there are no composite box scores to prove that Manigault ranked highest among playground athletes. But in its own way, a reputation in the parks is as definable as a scoring average in the NBA. Cut off from more formal channels of media and exposure, street ballplayers develop their own elaborate word-of-mouth system. One spectacular performance or one backward, twisting stuff shot may be the seed of an athlete's reputation. If he can repeat it a few times in a park where the competition is tough, the word goes out that he may be something special. Then there will be challenges from more established players, and a man who can withstand them may earn a "neighborhood rep." The process continues in an expanding series of confrontations, until the best athletes have emerged. Perhaps a dozen men at a given time may enjoy "citywide reps," guaranteeing them attention and respect in any playground they may visit. And of those, one or two will stand alone.

A few years ago, Earl Manigault stood among the loftiest. But his reign was brief, and in order to capture some feeling of what his stature meant in the playground world, one must turn to two athletes who enjoy similar positions today. Herman "Helicopter" Knowings, now in his late twenties, is among the most remarkable playground phenomena; he was a demigod before Manigault, and he remains one after Earl's departure. Uneducated and unable to break into pro ball, the Helicopter has managed to retain the spring in his legs and the will power to remain at the summit after many of his contemporaries have faded from the basketball scene. Joe Hammond, not yet twenty, is generally recognized as the best of the young crop. Neither finished school and vaulted into the public spotlight, but both pick up money playing in a minor league, the Eastern League—and both return home between games to continue their domination of the parks.

The Helicopter got his name for obvious reasons: when he goes up to block a shot, he seems to hover endlessly in midair above his prey, daring him to shoot—and then blocking whatever shot his hapless foe attempts. Like most memorable playground moves, it is not only effective but magnetic. As Knowings goes up, the crowd shouts, "Fly, 'copter, fly," and seems to share his heady trip. When he shoves a ball down the throat of a visiting NBA star—as he often does in the Rucker Tournament—the Helicopter inflates the pride of a whole neighborhood.

Like Connie Hawkins, Knowings can send waves of electricity through a park with his mere presence. Standing by a court, watching a game in progress with intent eyes, the Helicopter doesn't have to ask to play. People quickly spot his dark, chiseled, ageless face and six-foot-four-inch frame, and they make room for him. Joe Hammond is less imposing. A shade over six feet, he is a skinny, sleepy-eyed kid who looks slow and tired, the way backcourt star Clinton Robinson appeared during his reign. But like Robinson, Hammond has proved himself, and now he stands as the descendant of Pablo Robertson and James Barlow and the other backcourt heroes of the streets.

The kings of playground ball are not expected to defend their titles every weekend, proving themselves again and again the way less exalted players must. But when a new athlete begins winning a large following, when the rumors spread that he is truly someone special, the call goes out: If he is a forward, get the Helicopter; if he's a guard, let's try him against Joe Hammond. A crowd will gather before the star arrives. It is time for a supreme test.

Jay Vaughn has been in such confrontations several times. He saw the Helicopter defend his reign, and he watched Joe Hammond win his own way to the top. He described the rituals:

"When I first met the Helicopter, I was only about seventeen, and I was playing with a lot of kids my age at Wagner Center. I was better than the guys I was playing with and I knew it, so I didn't feel I had anything to prove. I was playing lazy, lackadaisical. And one of the youth workers saw how cocky I was and decided to show me just how good I really was. He sent for the Helicopter.

"One day I was just shooting baskets, trying all kinds of wild shots, not thinking about fundamentals, and I saw this older dude come in. He had sneakers and shorts on and he was ready to play. I said, 'Who's this guy? He's too old for our games. Is he supposed to be good?'

"'The coach sent for him,' somebody told me, 'He's gonna play you.'

"I said to myself, 'Well, fine, I'll try him,' and I went out there one-on-one with Herman Knowings. Well, it was a disastrous thing. I tried lay-ups, jump shots, hooks. And everything I threw up, he blocked. The word had gone out that Herman was there, and a crowd was gathering, and I said to myself, 'You got to do something. You're getting humiliated.' But the harder I tried, the more he shoved the ball down into my face. I went home and thought about that game for a long time. Like a lot of other young athletes, I had been put in my place.

"I worked out like crazy after that. I was determined to get back. After about a month, I challenged him again. I found myself jumping higher, feeling stronger, and playing better than ever before. I wasn't humiliated again. But I was beaten. Since that time, I've played against Herman many times. He took an interest in me and gave me a lot of good advice. And now, when I see he's going to block a shot, I may be able to fake and go around him and score, and people will yell, 'The pupil showed the master.'

"Then, of course, he'll usually come back and stuff one on me. . . ."

"Joe Hammond was playing in the junior division games in the youth centers when I was in the senior games," Vaughn continued. "He was three years younger than me, and sometimes after I'd played, I'd stay and watch his game. He wasn't that exceptional. Just another young boy who was gonna play ball. In fact, at that time, I didn't even know his last name.

"Then I came home from school in the summer of 1969, and one name was on everyone's lips: Joe Hammond. I thought it must have been somebody new from out of town, but people said, no, he'd been around Harlem all the time. They described him and it sounded like the young kid I'd watched around the centers, but I couldn't believe it was the same guy. Then I saw him, and it was the same Joe, and he was killing a bunch of guys his own age. He was much improved, but I still said to myself, 'He's young. He won't do much against the older brothers. They've been in business too long.'

"But then I heard, 'Joe's up at 135th Street beating the pros. . . . Joe's doing everything to those guys.' I still didn't take it too seriously. In fact, when Joe came out to Mount Morris Park for a game against a good team I was on, I said, 'Now we'll see how you do. You won't do anything today.'

"Now I believe in him. Joe Hammond left that game with seven minutes to go. He had 40 points. Like everybody had said, Joe was the one."

Many reputations have risen and fallen in the decade between the arrival of the Helicopter and of Joe Hammond. Most have now been forgotten, but a few "reps" outlive the men who earn them. Two years ago Connie Hawkins did not show up for a single game during the Rucker Tournament. When it was time to vote for the Rucker All-Star team, the coaches voted for Hawkins. "If you're going to have an all-star game in Harlem," said Bob McCullough, the tournament director, "you vote for Connie or you don't vote." (Having been elected, The Hawk did appear for the All-Star game—and won the Most Valuable Player award.) One other reputation has endured on a similar scale. Countless kids in Harlem repeat the statement: "You want to talk about basketball in this city, you've got to talk about Earl Manigault."

Manigault played at Benjamin Franklin High School in 1962 and 1963, then spent a season at Laurinburg Institute. Earl never reached college, but when he returned to Harlem he continued to dominate the playgrounds. He was the king of his own generation of ballplayers, the idol for the generation that followed. He was a six-foot-two-inch forward who could outleap men eight inches taller, and his moves had a boldness and fluidity that transfixed opponents and spectators alike. Freewheeling, unbelievably high-jumping, and innovative, he was the image of the classic playground athlete.

But he was also a very human ghetto youth, with weaknesses and doubts that left him vulnerable. Lacking education and motivation, looking toward an empty future, he found that basketball could take him only so far. Then he veered into the escape route of the streets, and became the image of the hellish side of ghetto existence. Earl is now in his mid-twenties, a dope addict, in prison.

Earl's is more than a personal story. On the playgrounds, he was a powerful magnetic figure who carried the dreams and ideals of every kid around him as he spun and twisted and sailed over all obstacles. When he fell, he carried those aspirations down with him. Call him a wasted talent, a pathetic victim, even a tragic hero: he had symbolized all that was sublime and terrible about this city game.

"You think of him on the court and you think of so many incred-ible things that it's hard to sort them out," said Bob Spivey, who played briefly with Earl at Franklin. "But I particularly recall one all-star game in the gym at PS 113, in about 1964. Most of the best high school players in the city were there: Charlie Scott, who went on to North Carolina; Vaughn Harper, who went to Syracuse, and a lot more. But the people who were there will hardly remember the others. Earl was the whole show.

"For a few minutes, Earl seemed to move slowly, feeling his way, get-ting himself ready. Then he got the ball on a fast break. Harper, who was six feet six, and Val Reed, who was six feet eight, got back quickly to defend. You wouldn't have given Earl a chance to score. Then he accelerated, changing his step suddenly. And at the foul line he went into the air. Harper and Reed went up, too, and between them, the two big men completely surrounded the rim. But Earl just kept going higher, and finally he two-hand-dunked the ball over both of them. For a split second there was complete silence, and then the crowd exploded. They were cheering so loud that they stopped the game for five minutes. Five minutes. That was Earl Manigault."

Faces light up as Harlem veterans reminisce about Manigault. Many street players won reputations with elaborate innovations and tricks. Jackie Jackson was among the first to warm up for games by picking quarters off the top of the backboard. Willie Hall, the former St. John's leader, apparently originated the custom of jumping to the top of the board and, instead of merely blocking a shot, slamming a hand with tremendous force against the board; the fixture would vibrate for sev-eral seconds after the blow, causing an easy lay-up to bounce crazily off the rim. Other noted leapers were famous for "pinning"—blocking a lay-up, then simply holding it momentarily against the backboard in a gesture of triumph. Some players seemed to hold it for seconds, suspended in air, multiplying the humiliation of the man who had tried the futile shot. Then they could slam the ball back down at the shooter or, for special emphasis, flip it into the crowd.

Earl Manigault did all of those things and more, borrowing, inno-vating, and forming one of the most exciting styles Harlem crowds ever watched. Occasionally, he would drive past a few defenders, dunk the ball with one hand, catch it with the other—and raise it and stuff it through the hoop a second time before returning to earth.

"I was in the eighth grade when Earl was in the eleventh," said Charley Yelverton, now a star at Fordham. "I was just another young kid at the time. Like everybody else on the streets, I played some ball. But I just did it for something to do. I wasn't that excited about it. Then there happened to be a game around my block, down at 112th Street, and a lot of the top players were in it—and Earl came down to play. Well, I had never believed things like that could go on. I had never known what basketball could be like. Everybody in the game was doing something, stuffing or blocking shots or making great passes. There's only one game I've ever seen in my life to compare to it—the Knicks' last game against the Lakers.

"But among all the stars, there was no doubt who was the greatest. Passing, shooting, going up in the air, Earl just left everybody behind. No one could turn it on like he could."

Keith Edwards, who lived with Earl during the great days of the Young Life team, agreed. "I guess he had about the most natural ability that I've ever seen. Talent for talent, inch for inch, you'd have to put him on a par with Alcindor and the other superstars. To watch him was like poetry. To play with him or against him—just to be on the same court with him—was a deep experience.

"You can't really project him against an Alcindor, though, because you could never picture Earl going to UCLA or anyplace like that. He was never the type to really face his responsibilities and his future. He didn't want to think ahead. There was very little discipline about the man. . . ."

And so the decline began. "I lived with the man for about two or three years," said Edwards, "from his predrug period into the beginning of his drug period. There were six of us there, and maybe some of us would have liked to help him out. But we were all just young guys finding themselves, and when Earl and another cat named Onion started to get into the drug thing, nobody really had a right, or was in a position, to say much about it. And even as he got into the drugs, he remained a beautiful person. He just had nowhere to go. . . ."

"The athlete in Harlem," said Pat Smith, "naturally becomes a big man in the neighborhood. And if he goes on to college and makes his way out of the ghetto, he can keep being a big man, a respected figure. But if he doesn't make it, if he begins to realize that he isn't going to get out, then he looks around, and maybe he isn't so big anymore. The pusher and the pimp have more clothes than they can ever get around to wearing; when they walk down the street they get respect. But the ballplayer is broke, and he knows that in a certain number of years he won't even have his reputation left. And unless he is an unusually strong person, he may be tempted to go another way. . . ."

"You like to think of the black athlete as a leader of the community," said Jay Vaughn, "but sometimes the idea of leadership can get twisted. A lot of the young dudes on the streets will encourage a big-time ballplayer to be big-time in other ways. They expect you to know all the big pushers, where to buy drugs, how to handle street life. And if they're fooling with small-time drugs, maybe they'll expect you to mess with big-time drugs. It may sound ridiculous at first, but when you're confronted with these attitudes a lot, and you're not strong enough, well, you find yourself hooked."

It didn't happen suddenly. On the weekends, people would still find Earl Manigault at the parks, and flashes of the magnetic ability were there. Young athletes would ask his advice, and he would still be helpful; even among the ones who knew he was sinking deeper into his drug habit, he remained respected and popular. But by early 1968, he seldom came to the parks, and his old friends would find him on street corners along Eighth Avenue, nodding. "He was such a fine person," said Jay Vaughn, "you saw him and you wished you could see some hope, some bright spot in his existence. But there was no good part of his life, of course. Because drugs do ruin you."

In the summer of 1968, Bob Hunter was working on a drug rehabilitation program. He looked up Earl. They became close, building a friendship that went deeper than their mutual respect on a basketball court. "Earl was an unusual type of addict," said Hunter. "He understood that he was a hard addict, and he faced it very honestly. He wanted to help me in the drug program, and he gave me a lot of hints on how to handle younger addicts. He knew different tricks that would appeal to them and win their trust. And he also knew all the tricks they would use, to deceive me into thinking they were getting cured. Earl had used the tricks himself, and he helped me see through them, and maybe we managed to save a few young kids who might have got hooked much worse.

"But it's the most frustrating thing in the world, working with addicts. It's hard to accept the fact that a man who has been burned will go back and touch fire. But they do it. I have countless friends on drugs, and I had many more who have died from drugs. And somehow it's hard to just give up on them and forget that they ever existed. Maybe you would think that only the less talented types would let themselves get hooked—but then you'd see a guy like Earl and you couldn't understand. . . ."

Some people hoped that Earl would be cured that summer. He did so much to help Hunter work with others that people felt he could help himself. Hunter was not as optimistic. "The truth is that nobody is ever going to cure Earl," he said. "The only way he'll be cured is by himself. A lot of people come off drugs only after they've been faced with an extreme crisis. For example, if they come very close to dying and somehow escape, then they might be able to stay away from the fire. But it takes something like that, most of the time."

Earl was not cured, and as the months went on the habit grew more expensive. And then he had to steal. "Earl is such a warm person," said Vaughn, "you know that he'd never go around and mug people or anything. But let's face it: most addicts, sooner or later, have to rob in order to survive." Earl broke into a store. He is now in prison. "Maybe that will be the crisis he needs," said Hunter. "Maybe, just possibly . . . But when you're talking about addicts, it's very hard to get your hopes too high."

Harold "Funny" Kitt went to Franklin three years behind Earl Manigault. When Funny finished in 1967, he was rated the best high school player in the city—largely because he had modeled himself so closely after Earl. "We all idolized Earl in those days," Kitt said. "And when you idolize somebody, you think of the good things, not the bad. As we watched Earl play ball, we had visions of him going on to different places, visiting the whole world, becoming a great star and then maybe coming back here to see us and talk to us about it all.

"But he didn't do any of those things. He just went into his own strange world, a world I hope I'll never see. I guess there were reasons. I guess there were frustrations that only Earl knew about, and I feel sorry for what happened. But when Earl went into that world, it had an effect on all of us, all the young ballplayers. I idolized the man. And he hurt me."

Beyond the hurt, though, Earl left something more. If his career was a small dramatization of the world of Harlem basketball, then he was a fitting protagonist, in his magnitude and his frailty, a hero for his time. "Earl was quiet, he was honest," said Jay Vaughn, "and he handled the pressures of being the star very well. When you're on top, everybody is out to challenge you, to make their own reps by doing something against you. One guy after another wants to take a shot, and some stars react to all that by bragging, or by being aloof from the crowd.

"Earl was different. The game I'll never forget was in the G-Dub [George Washington High] tournament one summer, when the team that Earl's group was scheduled to play didn't show. The game was forfeited, and some guys were just looking for some kind of pickup game, when one fellow on the team that forfeited came in and said, 'Where's Manigault? I want to play Manigault.'

"Well, this guy was an unknown and he really had no right to talk like that. If he really wanted to challenge a guy like Earl, he should have been out in the parks, building up a rep of his own. But he kept yelling and bragging, and Earl quietly agreed to play him one-on-one. The word went out within minutes, and immediately there was a big crowd gathered for the drama.

"Then they started playing. Earl went over the guy and dunked. Then he blocked the guy's first shot. It was obvious that the man had nothing to offer against Earl. But he was really determined to win himself a rep. So he started pushing and shoving and fouling. Earl didn't say a word. He just kept making his moves and beating the guy, and the guy kept grabbing and jostling him to try to stop him. It got to the point where it wasn't really basketball. And suddenly Earl put down the ball and said, 'I don't need this. You're the best.' Then he just walked away.

"Well, if Earl had gone on and whipped the guy 30 to 0, he couldn't have proved any more than he did. The other cat just stood there, not knowing what to say. The crowd surrounded Earl, and some of us said things about the fouling and the shoving. But he didn't say anything about it. He didn't feel any need to argue or complain. He had everyone's respect and he knew it. The role he played that day never left anyone who saw it. This was a beautiful man."

George Kiseda

George Kiseda (1927–2007) was a young reporter for the *Pittsburgh Sun-Tele-graph* in 1957 when the Army football team was set to meet Tulane in the Sugar Bowl in New Orleans. How, he asked in print, could a branch of the U.S. military justify participating in a game where the fans would be segregated by race? Kiseda won that round after a congressman took up the cause and forced the game to be moved to West Point. But that one crusading column cost him, as the Hearst-owned *Sun-Telegraph* banned political comment from its sports pages and Kiseda went on to clash regularly with his superiors. The episode helps account for his vagabonding path—from the *Sun-Telegraph* to the *Philadelphia Daily News* to the *Philadelphia Evening Bulletin* and, after he abandoned writing at age forty-four, to the copy desks of *The New York Times* and *Los Angeles Times*. A well-meaning friend once asked Kiseda, a devout Catholic, "What's the Church's position on career suicide?" But commitment to principle made him a hero to his peers, especially "the Chipmunks," the generation of antiestablishment sportswriters to emerge at mid-century. Beginning with the 1960–61 season, Kiseda swung on to pro basketball, covering the Philadelphia Warriors, and eventually the 76ers, of Wilt Chamberlain. Over the next dozen years he established himself, in the judgment of the *Boston Globe*'s Bob Ryan, as "the greatest NBA writer of all time." A beat reporter in training camp can get away with filing little more than scrimmage summaries and news of the latest cuts, but to Kiseda that was stenography. So when a rookie from Vanderbilt named Perry Wallace came through the Sixers' camp in 1970, Kiseda filed this thundering column for the *Bulletin*. "George was the guy who made you feel like journalism was a calling," said Mark Heisler, who competed with him on the Sixers' beat for the *Philadelphia Inquirer*, yet like many professional rivals became a Kiseda acolyte and felt his hero's suffering. "If he was more cult figure than icon, he set it up that way. With George, the greatness had to be its own reward."

A Reflection of Society

SEPTEMBER 18, 1970

PERRY WALLACE didn't go to Vanderbilt to be Jackie Robinson. The first black athlete to survive four years in the Southeastern Conference went to Vanderbilt because (a) Nashville is his home town, (b) Vanderbilt is a good school and (c) it was a chance to play basketball in a major conference.

"I just wanted to go to college and get a good education and play basketball and realize my academic and athletic potential," Wallace said. "It was as simple as that, nothing much more and nothing much less.

"It was made a racial issue by the people who jeered. I found I had to accept it as a challenge and accept that those people who were jeering me were making me represent a lot of people. At first I tried to ignore it as a racial issue.

"I began to be successful when I began to accept it as a racial issue. It's odd that the people who deny it was a racial issue helped to make it a racial issue.

"The press almost never said anything about it. Cheerleaders were leading cheers against me, racial things, and the press never said much about it.

"I felt like the only justice I could have gotten was for them to mention it. A thing like that tends to produce a sort of madness, a sort of insanity. When you see a purple man and nobody else sees him, you begin to wonder . . . I was going through these things and other people were acting as if it didn't happen."

Sometimes the press has myopia. There are sports writers who pretend it is a Jack Armstrong world, all fun and games, but it isn't, it never was and a sports writer who says he has never met an abused athlete simply has not been doing his job. I could introduce him to Satchel Paige or Earl Lloyd or Carlos Alvarez.

Or Perry Wallace.

Until yesterday Wallace was a 76er rookie, a 6-5 forward who is a definite futurebook prospect. He went home to keep a commitment with the National Guard, but he promised he would be back next year.

Perry Wallace has an appointment with his potential that he has been waiting four years to keep.

An All-American at Pearl High School in Nashville, he played on a team that went 31–0 and won the state championship the first year the tournament was integrated. He was class valedictorian (and would later double-major in math and electrical engineering) and naturally there were college offers, 120 of them. When he picked Vanderbilt, there was rejoicing in Nashville.

"Everybody smiled," he was saying yesterday, "everybody spoke to me when I visited the university. Everything was fine on the home front."

Everything appeared to be fine four years later. Wallace was captain of the varsity, all-conference, the most popular student on campus according to a student poll, and at his farewell game 15,000 fans in the Vanderbilt gym gave him a five-minute standing ovation. Nashville congratulated itself for integrating the SEC smoothly.

A couple weeks later, Wallace dropped a bomb on Nashville, letting them know how it really was. The reactions were predictable. How could he do it to them?

His coach, Roy Skinner, seemed to be one of the few who understood. "I feel like he was trying to help us," Skinner said. "And I feel like we will all be better off because he has spoken his mind."

Exactly.

"Some of the other coaches didn't like it," Wallace said. "They thought I was ungrateful, but why would I mess up a good future in Nashville unless (1) I was crazy or (2) I wanted to make constructive criticism? . . . I was afraid everybody would think everything was beautiful.

". . . If I had allowed people to sit back and be fat and happy, maybe more athletes would have to go through the same hell."

Hell began in church. Wallace was attending services at a campus church until a group of good ol' Southern Christians told him his presence might hurt the collection plate.

They emphasized it had nothing to do with prejudice.

After that came the first game at Mississippi, a subdivision of hell. It was the middle of Wallace's sophomore year, and he was trying to shake a slump. The reception he got was just the thing to help him.

"As I walked into the stadium to warm up," he said, "I heard jeers, cursing, threats. They were coming from a lot of people, thousands of people.

"I started the game on the bench and when I went in, they just raised holy hell. Every time I made a mistake, everybody clapped, everybody laughed. They called me Leroy, which was a polite name for nigger."

Something—an elbow or a fist—found its way into Wallace's eye, and at halftime he was still in the dressing room getting treatment while his teammates were out on the floor warming up.

Wallace took one of the most frightening walks of his life—alone.

"I looked out the door and I saw our team warming up and I could hear the catcalls," he said. "You could hear the catcalls over the radio, people told me. They were hollering, 'Where's the nigger?' 'Where's the nigger?' 'Is he scared?' 'Did he quit?'

"I stood there and I looked out and I said, 'Who is on MY side?'"

He found it hard to understand that none of the people who recruited him could understand that at that moment he might need some moral support—even if it was only somebody walking out to the court with him.

There was more around the SEC. Mississippi and Alabama were only the worst (Kentucky and Florida, he said, were the best places to play).

"They would call you nigger, black boy, burrhead, or Leroy—that was always a favorite—or Willie or they'd say, 'We're gonna get you.'"

There was no physical violence, but there was mental anguish. Wallace's mother was dying of cancer. He would go back to his room at night wondering how he could survive the torment. He went three years with the knowledge his mother had terminal cancer.

"It was hard to face that and also be a pioneer in the Southeastern Conference," he said. ". . . I almost had a nervous breakdown."

Wallace can appreciate what is going on at Syracuse and other schools where blacks have demanded black coaches. "I didn't get the moral support and understanding from the people who recruited me," he said. "I didn't get the sort of follow through, the sort of inquisitiveness I expected."

He would not want to do it again, but he still helps Vanderbilt to recruit black athletes. He does not see it as a contradiction.

"It's not the same place it was four years ago," he said.

Perry Wallace is one of the reasons.

Jimmy Breslin

To hear Jimmy Breslin (1928–2017) tell it, a stint as a sportswriter, for the *New York Journal-American* during the early 1960s, launched his career as a chronicler of twentieth-century America, particularly its urban working class. A lesson learned from post-game protocol—"Go to the losers' dressing room," he liked to say—sent Breslin in search of stories further from the expense-account hotel room, and closer to his tabloid readers' experiences, than those filed by his broadsheet counterparts. Throughout his career he dipped in and out of sports, writing *Can't Anybody Here Play This Game?* in 1962 about the debut season of Casey Stengel's Amazin' Mets, and a 2011 biography of Branch Rickey, the executive who signed Jackie Robinson for the Brooklyn Dodgers. But Breslin found his voice and made his name with the kinds of cityside columns for which he won a Pulitzer Prize in 1986. Sent to cover the aftermath of John F. Kennedy's assassination in 1963, he famously filed on Clifton Pollard, the man who dug the president's grave, noting that for his service Pollard collected precisely $3.01 an hour. A decade later he wrote this profile of fellow Queens native and Irish Catholic Al McGuire, then coaching for the Jesuit fathers at Marquette. Breslin makes no apologies for champion-ing a guy from around the way, whose roots in the Rockaways lay only a half-dozen stops on the A train from Breslin's in Ozone Park. In this piece, which *Sport* billed with a titular homage to the author's best-selling comic mob novel *The Gang That Couldn't Shoot Straight*, you'll find the characteristic Breslin-ian virtues. There's an ear for dialogue; a palpable compassion for working people; a willingness to disclose even an old friend's cons and excesses; and, wouldn't you know it, an hourly wage, right there in the lede.

The Coach Who Couldn't Shoot Straight

T HE FATHER, J. W. Chones, after 22 years of working as a moulder in a steel plant in Racine, Wisconsin, was in bed in the house, the life going out of him in the hollow dry cough of lung cancer. The mother made salads in a restaurant for $1.75 an hour. The six kids, confused, depressed, went through the form of attending school. The oldest and largest, James B. Chones, 18, six feet, 11 inches, played on the basketball team at St. Catherine's High School. It was hard for him, the months in the snow in 1969, with his father home dying and the men coming into the high school to talk to him.

Chones can recount almost everything that was said to him by these men from American colleges and universities. The first man from a college to talk to him said, "Your father's sick, that's too bad. We'll get him a nice house. Get you a car. How would you like that, a nice new car for yourself?"

Another one thought for awhile when Jim Chones said his father was sick. "What we could do, we could get your mother a job. Real good job. Don't worry about what she'll get paid. Course, it'll really be your money, you know. You let us worry about how we give it to your mother."

"The father's sick," another one of them said, "Well, he can fly to all games. Doesn't take too much effort to get onto a plane, first class seat, and come and see your son play in the fieldhouse."

To the best of Jim Chones' recollection he heard from every college in the country that was interested in basketball. Except one. He had not received anything, a phone call, a letter even, from Marquette University in Milwaukee in his own state. The coach of Marquette was Alfred J. McGuire.

In April, when it was over, when J.W. Chones was gone, somebody from the high school asked Jim to stop into the athletic office.

"This is Al McGuire," the man said to Chones.

"I wanted to talk to you for a long time," Al McGuire said. "But we heard your father was sick and we didn't want to bother you."

He invited Chones to come down to the basketball banquet at Marquette. When Chones came to the banquet, Al McGuire spoke to him again. Spoke to him with those eyes locked on Chones. Big brown eyes that talk, question, laugh, challenge, get mad. Eyes that never leave you during a conversation.

"There is no money here," Al McGuire said. Chones mentioned some of the things he had been offered. "That's fine. You'll be just another hired hand for them. A field hand." Chones knew what that meant. Field nigger. "You listen to me, you can do it differently. You're big, you've got reactions, good speed. I think if you listen and work hard you have a chance to make big money as a pro. Big money for yourself. You can do whatever the hell you want with your life once you make it for yourself. You can be anybody you want, do anything you want. But make it on your own. You'll never get anything if you're just a hired hand for somebody. Listen to me and you'll make big money by yourself."

He also told Chones he had an important house rule at Marquette. A basketball player had to get a degree.

If you know Al McGuire for a long time, you smile when you hear about his rule. I sat with him when we were young and watching a college game at the old Madison Square Garden and during the warmup a ball bounced up to the seats and Al grabbed it and threw a shot, a two-handed set shot from his chest. It went into the flock of basketballs bouncing around the rim. "That's the first shot I ever took at the Garden," he said proudly. The shot had missed by a half-foot or so. Al would go home and tell everybody he put it right in. In college, he majored in defense. When he got out of school—rather, finished his time there—he announced that he was going for a master's degree. When he played with the New York Knickerbockers, he announced he could guard Bob Cousy so well that he owned him. Cousy used to score hundreds of points against the Knicks. The newspapers kept saying that Al McGuire owned Cousy. Al himself still was throwing up shots that were a half-foot wide. When he became coach at Belmont Abbey, a small school in North Carolina, he also had to teach history. The notion is his wife prepared the courses and Al did the talking in class. He remained approximately six pages ahead of the class. If a student asked him a question during class, Al said he would take that up with the boy immediately after class. At which point Al would flee out the front door of the classroom and hope the kid forgot what was on his mind.

Always, Al McGuire was growing. And what he didn't know he could cover with talk. His mind essentially was too quick for mere sports, which is why there is always so much more than sports going on when he talks to his players. Al McGuire wants college degrees for his players? Sure he does. It's a good show for Al, and a good show for the boy. The perfect way to obliterate these coaches who sell black basketball players on the theory that a car and three white broads is all they really want out of life. Al McGuire promotes things that last. And gets the players. See Maurice Lucas, this season's great sophomore. And then past the good show, past the fast talk, there is the knowledge that it not only looks right, but it is right. What better combination is there?

Al is Irish and Catholic, and he was behind a bar pulling beer at 108th Street in Rockaway Beach, in New York, before he was old enough to be allowed in as a customer. The background is supposed to produce conservative thinking. I sit with Al McGuire at dinner with business people from Milwaukee, and they are laughing about an open housing march led by a priest named Groppi. Al McGuire, the center of the table, said, "Fellas, you may think I'm losing my mind, but I have to tell you. I think the man is right." Silence fell. But not that sullen kind of silence. An embarrassed silence. They all seemed uneasy that they had said something stupid. I have been around people in a business called politics who try to sell unpopular ideas even to the smallest groups and all they ever receive is a grimace. I watched this guy talk. I had a small idea that Al McGuire is one of the few I know who can tell the bastards anything and make them like it. And maybe, as he thinks himself, it's time to try it out. But this is personal opinion. I know the guy a long time. See him through Jim Chones.

Chones came to Marquette in September, 1969. He found out a little bit more about his coach in the dressing room before a game with, he thinks, Creighton. He cannot remember it so well because he stayed in a corner of the dressing room in terror. One of the varsity players, Hugh McMahon, arrived late. The coach began screaming. McMahon started screaming back. Al McGuire was all over him so fast nobody knew what was happening. But Chones saw it clearly. The coach kneed McMahon in the groin. Then he hit McMahon in the face. He threw McMahon against the wall and was about to kick him in the groin. McMahon turned and started walking out of the dressing room, forever. It was one of the great goodbye scenes in sports. Then an arm came out and grabbed McMahon's collar and McMahon came yanking back into the middle of the room.

"All right, now get dressed and let's play," Al McGuire said to McMahon.

There was another afternoon when the team was practicing and McGuire decided Gary Brell, 6-6, wasn't in good enough shape. He had Brell running wind sprints from wall to wall in the gymnasium. Brell stopped in the middle of one of the sprints and stood in the middle of the gym, his long hair held out of his eyes by an Indian headband. "Why don't you make some of the black guys do some of the running too?" Brell said.

McGuire said nothing. He loped out to the middle of the court and he spoke to Brell. He spoke to Brell by hitting him in the face. Brell began running again.

The Marquette varsity, on the floor before games, consisted of Brell with his head down in mourning for the war, a clenched black fist or two in the air and a coach who stood at attention while his mind was on the game. When somebody asked him about respect or style during the National Anthem, Al McGuire waved a hand. What the hell did he care about form in a matter as small as this? His team was here to play, not to pose. Patriotic Milwaukee, patriotic Roman Catholic Milwaukee, agreed. A weakling or somebody pompous would turn it into an incident. Al McGuire regarded the topic as a pain in the ass and he made everybody else think his way.

His black players came to him one day and said they were sorry, but the afternoon game with Detroit fell on Malcolm X day. At three o'clock, no matter what was happening in the game, they were going to stop playing and stand in silence for Malcolm X.

"You don't have to stop playing, I'll call a time out," Al said. "Don't worry about it. Now let's get on with getting ready to win the game."

When the time out was called, and the Marquette blacks stood in silence, fists raised, the Detroit coach, Jim Harding, nearly exploded. Which was understandable and even allowable. All coaches in all sports are not very smart, nor should they be expected to be very smart. They are in a business of games. Al McGuire is in another year, another century, from coaches of sports.

"Raise your fist, raise your ass, what do I care? Win the game, that's the only thing that goes into the book."

In his sophomore year, Chones was slow in early practices. He was not in the shape he had to be in, but he was blaming it on the floor, the heat, a cold, anything around him. The only ones tall enough to guard him in practice happened to be white players. Chones, irritated, pushed them around. In the middle of the practice Al McGuire walked onto the floor.

"Goddamn, why don't you swing for once at a black guy? Are you afraid one of them'll pick up something and break your head?"

Chones thought about that after practice. He never had heard a white man talk like that to him before. Completely uninhibited. As the months wore on, he began to see that his coach was the fairest white man he ever had heard of.

He also began to learn about a thing known as an Al McGuire promise. "You will make big money," Al McGuire told him.

And in Chones' sophomore year, Marquette came into New York to play Fordham and before the game, Al McGuire walked the streets.

"How's the boy doing?" he was asked. His son Allie was in the starting lineup.

"Fine, it's probably better for him that he would have gone someplace else, but at the same time it was better for me that he's here with me. He isn't the problem right now. I got to do something with Chones."

"What?"

"Well, the kid got nothing. The mother's working, he's got nothing. It would be a shame if the two leagues merge and you have no competitive bidding for him. Cost him a fortune, if that happens."

"What can he do, he's only a sophomore?"

"Supposing he doesn't play?" Al said.

Chones was inside Madison Square Garden, a nervous sophomore waiting to play his first game in New York.

And his coach walked in off the street and on the way to the dressing room he bumped into a sportswriter.

"I don't know if I'm going to be able to keep Chones," Al said. "They're after him already. He's the best big man in the country. I can't stop him from doing what he has to do, either. I've looked in my refrigerator and I've looked in his."

"How imminent is this?" the sportswriter asked.

"The professional teams are crawling all over him," Al said.

At the end of the season, Jim Chones picked up the Milwaukee paper one day and he read an interview with Al McGuire. McGuire was quoted as saying, "I hope I can hang onto Chones for one more season." The words jumped out of the page at Chones. He went to see McGuire, but he couldn't find him. The season was over. Al McGuire has his own way of life. Nobody can find him unless he wants them to.

"I was looking all over for you," Chones said later.

"Maybe I didn't want to see you," McGuire said.

Throughout Chones' junior year, the practices were torture for Marquette. They had lost one game in '70–'71, and that by a point. They were perhaps the finest defensive team college ball had seen in decades. Through drill after drill, Chones worked on his pick and roll. The big man comes out and picks for a backcourt man and in the melee he hopes to wind up with the wrong man guarding him, at which point he immediately rolls to the basket. Or if his man does try to stay with him, the big man doing the picking hopes to wind up with the inside and, again, he rolls to the basket. It is the basic play of modern professional basketball. It also was the basic play for Al McGuire's big men.

In February, 1972, undefeated Marquette played Jacksonville. Marquette won by eight. Jim Chones scored 24, had 17 rebounds and blocked six shots. The next night, Chones was in his dormitory when he received a phone call from Gene Smith, a lawyer in Milwaukee. Gene Smith is Al McGuire's lawyer.

"Jim, I don't know what's going on," Smith said, "but I have some men here. They got my telephone number from Al. The men are from the Long Island Nets. They want to pay you, I don't know what it is, something like $2 million. You better come down here right away."

Chones went to the lawyer's office. Al McGuire was not there. Roy Boe of the Long Island Nets was there. Yes, he wanted to sign Chones to a three-year contract. No, he wasn't going to pay $2 million. That's way out of line. He would pay Jim Chones $1,800,000.

Chones called Al McGuire on the phone. It was midnight.

The phone was picked up on the other end.

"Uh."

"Coach?"

"Who the hell is this?"

"Jim Chones."

"Oh, yeah. Jimmy. I'm asleep. What's up?"

"Well these men are here from the pro team and they are offering me one point eight million dollars or something like that and I just wanted to. . . ."

"Well, good, Jimmy. I'll see you tomorrow. I'm going to sleep."

Marquette was undefeated, the tournaments were ahead, the coach was in line to be what the sports pages call "a basketball immortal."

When Chones hung up the phone, Gene Smith, the lawyer,

shrugged. He knew what to do now. He took out his pen and handed it to Chones.

There was, of course, no flim-flam. It was announced the next day Jim Chones had become a professional and he could not compete for Marquette anymore. The team without Chones immediately lost a couple of games and the season quickly came to an end.

Al McGuire shook hands with Chones, and Chones left Marquette. "He has his diploma," Al McGuire said. "A big diploma."

In the McGuire family, there are three brothers. There is Al, successor to Adolph Rupp, Henry Iba, Phog Allen. There is Dick, probably one of the best backcourt men the game has ever known. He was the Knick coach and now he is the chief scout. And there is the oldest brother, John, who is famous for having received the largest and undoubtedly most needed Western Union money order in the history of Hialeah race track.

I saw Chones recently. He was at Great Neck, on Long Island, after a Nets practice. He pulled up in a Cadillac car, and his sisters are in college and his mother is in a new house and she is not out making salads anymore. "She can't just stay home, she's so used to working," Jim was saying. "She's got to get a job. But a job doing something. Teacher's assistant, something like that. Not makin' any salads anymore. She can be useful."

"What money can do," he was told.

"But it's like he always told me," Chones said. "Coach McGuire always said to me, 'Jim, I want to take care of my family and live my own life. That's all that's important. I don't give a damn about anything else. I'm a happy man because I live my own life. I'm not dependent on somebody liking me or not. Now that's how I want you to be. Any hard work you do for yourself. You don't do it for me. And when you take care of yourself, you live your own life.'"

He got up to go. There was a team meeting upstairs.

"Everything he ever said to me came true," Chones said. "Everything. What else can I tell you?"

I said nothing, because what he was saying was an old story to me. I know the guy a long time.

Tom Meschery

Descendants of czarist nobility who counted Leo Tolstoy as a cousin, the family of Tom Meschery (b. 1938) fled east after the Bolshevik Revolution, through Siberia to Harbin, China, where Tom was born. His father soon immigrated to the U.S., expecting the rest of the family to follow him. But with the Japanese invasion of Manchuria, Tom, his sister, and their mother were detained and ultimately interned at a camp near Tokyo. Missionaries there taught Tom English, which served him well after the family was finally reunited in San Francisco six years later. During ten seasons in the NBA, for the Warriors in both Philadelphia and San Francisco and then the Seattle Super-Sonics, he had a knack for starting fights and once led the league in fouls. But off the court he flashed elbow patches on his sportcoats and loved to read and write. Between the Beat poets of his American hometown and Russian reverence for the genre, he came naturally to poetry, and after he agreed to coach the Carolina Cougars for the 1971–72 season, a New York publisher signed him up to keep a diary. In this excerpt from a tumultuous December, he captures the chaos of the old American Basketball Association. Big-money contracts for veteran Joe Caldwell and rookie Jim McDaniels mess with team chemistry, and owner Tedd Munchak fumes that he's not getting more victories on the dollar. Meschery can't understand why his players won't leave as much on the floor as he once had. Meanwhile, general manager Carl Scheer scrambles to mediate between owner and coach. Meschery eventually paves an off-ramp for himself, to the Iowa Writers' Workshop, from which he will go on to study with former U.S. poet laureate Mark Strand (who makes a brief cameo here), teach high-school English for two decades, and publish four volumes of poetry.

from

Caught in the Pivot

December 2

WHAT A wonderful feeling to be in Manhattan. We flew in early to play the Nets and it gave me a chance to grab a cab into town. New York City must have known I was depressed. It garlanded itself in its best late autumn fashions. The streets were mobbed with people of all kinds. Very different from the suburban atmosphere of Greensboro. Terrific psychological uplift.

Mark Strand called and wants to come to the game. I've just finished *Darker,* his new book of poetry. It was great to see him. He brought back memories of Seattle and my dreams of becoming a poet. Poetry obsesses me as much as basketball. That might be one of my problems as a coach; I don't want to give of my free time to thinking only basketball. I don't see enough of my family as it is and so far I've been unable to write a decent line of poetry.

December 3

New York beat us. The win for the Nets moved them into fourth and kept us solidly in last place. I'm getting a crick in my neck looking up from our basement spot. The team played uninspired ball. I feel like an idiot trying to explain the importance of being high for each game.

After the game I went to the bar at the Hempstead Motor Hotel where we were staying. I wanted to be alone but found half the team there. With the season going bad you would think they would find a more secluded spot to screw around. I didn't mind the drinks but I saw some "stadium lizards" hanging around. Jesus! We had a game the next night. "Grown men," I kept repeating to myself, "Grown men."

December 4

Lost again to Indiana. By the half we had been out-rebounded, 44 to 18. Incredible! I can't understand lack of hustle. I can't comprehend lack of board work and unaggressive defense. At half time I began slowly building up to the fury I felt in my stomach. There was no way to tell them how much their performance sickened me. "No guts," I yelled. "No pride." I repeated it over and over. My voice was becoming shrill. The players sat there taking it all with their heads down. There was no escape for them in that tiny dressing room.

The blindness that I have felt so often when I become enraged was beginning to cloud my eyes. I suddenly realized that soon I would become irrational. I stopped and turned my back. I took a deep breath. I grabbed a piece of chalk and began to scribble diagrams on the blackboard. I didn't care if the players were even watching. Our trainer came in to tell us there were only three minutes until the start of the second half. I motioned to the team to head out to the floor. Maybe the yelling did some good because we made a reasonable comeback in the second half. But the lead we gave Indiana was too great to overcome.

On the way home from Indiana my assistant coach, Jerry Steele, confided that he could barely sleep. Even though the pressure is off him, he takes everything personally. He told me that while he was waiting for the Cougars to decide whether he was to be the coach for this year, nine weeks, he slept about ten hours per week. From then on it was downhill. Finally, after he had been promised the coaching job, he was told that he could not trade Verga. It was all he could take. Jerry told me his nerves were shot from that day on. The Cougars were very inconsiderate of Jerry in handling the coaching job decision. I won't let them do the same thing to me.

December 6

I hardly slept all night myself, thinking about how to handle this team's future. I had promised them in Memphis after our first four games that I would be a prick if they wanted me to be. Idle threats hold no value. So today I fined every player $100 except George Stone and Wayne Hightower, who didn't play against Indiana, and placed a 12:45 curfew before a game. I guess I'm as susceptible as all coaches for thinking the worst of his players when he sees them in a bar the night before a game and later the game turns out badly. Now all things are different. I will never be able to capture the elusive dream of being both a coach and a fellow comrade. I am bringing myself closer and closer to the end of my coaching career. If all I'm able to do is sustain the belief of coaches and players being separate and the idea of a coach as a dictator, then I don't want the job. My feelings for the players run too deep.

Marvin Bell, in his book *The Escape Into You*, speaks about sports, figuratively, with the precise insight of the poet who is able to weave metaphor intricately with reality. When he speaks of the love of form being a black occasion, I am carried back in time to the endless darkness of each forty-eight minutes I played for ten years. Bits and pieces of men fell to the ground.

I want to sympathize. I want to say, "Yeah, the coach doesn't understand you. He doesn't know the talent you have." But, now I'm the coach.

December 9

Joe Caldwell is back, his marathon recovery stimulated by a short visit in Los Angeles with Dr. Kerlan. Dr. Kerlan, who is bent over at the waist with arthritis, is an expert on the subject of living with pain.

I was pleased with Joe's performance tonight against Kentucky. However, it necessitates another change in lineup. It means another set of upheavals and if I'm not mistaken it will mean a confrontation with Joe at some point in the future. Joe has too many ideas on how to run a team, on few of which we concur. Joe believes a good offense is the best defense. It's the other way around with me.

Carl was excited after the game. He said that the combination I used tonight of Denton at center, Mac at forward and Caldwell at the other forward was great. He told me we'll just have to live with a few losses until the combination begins to jell—"even ten games," Carl said. I'll bet he panics after three losses.

December 10

Caldwell is a constant griper. Today he complained about extra meal money the team was supposed to be getting. The day before it was our hotel accommodations. Before that he bitched that Buddy Taylor, our trainer, wouldn't pick up his uniform after the game.

I got a resounding boo from the crowd tonight. I have never been booed before in my life. Occasionally during my last year as a player, a few fans would ride me about being too old. Or like the time in New York after I had just published my first book of poetry, a fan yelled out of the crowd something about "How'd ya like that shot, ya fag poet!" But boos—never. I was deeply stung. I wish they knew how hard I'm trying to win. I felt like giving them the old Italian high sign. I would have as a player. But as a coach I'm supposed to accept it as "part of the game."

We lost a defensively shabby game. It was a shoot-out. We couldn't stop Pittsburgh and they couldn't stop us. Joanne's father, who flew in for a couple of days, came to the game. When Joanne tried to introduce him to Carl, all Carl could say was "This is the low point of the year." He couldn't even manage a handshake. His hands were too busy rubbing his temples. Carl is so uptight that, like Felix Unger, he has "clenched hair."

December 11

We flew to Denver and we got beaten. After the game I went to dinner at Alex Hannum's house. I was in no mood to visit but I rarely get a chance to talk to old friends. Alex told me that the wife of one of his players refuses to stand for the national anthem. He solved the problem by asking her to go out for coffee just before the anthem is played. He also had a meeting with his players and told them that as long as they played for him and took his capitalistic pig's money, they would have to conform to his standards. I don't think I could do that. A man, to my way of thinking, has the right to display his convictions. Black men have legitimate gripes and being only twelve percent of the population they have got to demonstrate where they can be seen. What better place than at a basketball game?

December 12

I had my first confrontation with Caldwell. He was arguing about our plays, particularly the "M" series. I told him that I had used the same set for ten years when I was playing and they were proven offensive patterns. I also told him that if they can work it against us (three of the teams in our league use the series), we should be able to work it against them just as easily. Joe backed down when George Lehmann took my side in the argument. George is a horse's ass in many ways but he knows his basketball. I don't like this sort of business, and I felt drained and particularly unhappy afterwards. We've cut plays to the minimum. They're simple to understand and work. There should be no confusion.

All the players at the start of practice were sullen. They were very down. The first hour was like pulling teeth to get them to work with anything resembling enthusiasm. But toward the end, they had turned around, and during the shooting drill they laughed and kibitzed in a friendly way with one another. Maybe we took a step forward. But we slid back so much this month the forward step might not be enough.

Joe told me he shouldn't practice hard so he can save himself for the game. God! What a psycho!

December 13

Just when I feel befuddled about this team—which road to take and how to take it—they turn around and play beautifully. We knocked off

Utah with Miller and Lehmann executing perfectly. Lehmann scored forty points. His three-point shooting was devastating. But you can't win consistently with your guards, so this game has to be looked upon as unusual. Our team's inconsistency is remarkable. I try to tell myself it is youth, lack of experience, some basic absence of certain skills, but always there crops up another feeling—one that strikes deeper and deeper into the soul of sports—about envy among the players. Even with the victory I can't control my foreboding.

December 14

Travel in the ABA is absolutely ridiculous. The cities are connected by some of the more notorious airlines such as Allegheny, Ozark and Piedmont. To get anywhere you must grab a "milk run" flight which departs Greensboro at 8:00 A.M. and suffer through four or five intermittent stops before reaching your destination. To top it off, the ABA flies coach, which is pretty hard on tall men. So, I'm all bundled up, my knees on my chest.

We left Utah this morning at 8:00 A.M., caught a two-stop connection to Greensboro via Chicago (with a two-hour delay in Chicago) arriving just in time to play Virginia. How we beat them I'll never know. So far we've beaten the Squires consistently. Carl was ecstatic. It was his birthday and we couldn't have given him a nicer gift.

December 15

We took off early this morning for Kentucky. Piedmont Airlines treated us to one of their special flights through fifty-mile per hour winds which kept half the passengers sick. We rocked off the airplane and we were still rocking when we went on the court against the Colonels. We were exhausted and they destroyed us. Munchak was there. I expect to have another conference called tomorrow.

December 16

Just as I expected, the conference, via the Bell System, took place at 2:45 P.M. This time Munchak was critical of my motivation of the team. He feels that if he could motivate a team of workers at his carpet factory, it should be just as simple on a basketball court. This sort of simplistic approach surprises me. I figured Munchak to be smarter than that. It's laughable to anybody who knows athletes. They're a different breed. No carpet salesman has the ego of an athlete. But at the moment I'm not laughing. Management is beginning to piss me off. They are also making me question my ability. I don't like these feelings of doubt. I never thought of myself as a genius, but I think that they expect miracles. It seems to me that coaches become geniuses when they have a combination of multitalented players.

Carl told me for the first time today that Ted McClain has certain incentive clauses in his contract that will earn him more money if he makes the All-Star Team, averages "X" amount of points or makes the playoffs. No wonder he's not happy with his lack of playing time. I wonder what else they're not telling me.

December 17

It's 5:00 P.M., three hours to go to game time. As a player I'd look forward to the game. As coach I keep saying, "Jesus Christ, only three hours to go." As a player you never feel like you'll lose; as a coach you know that one of the two teams must take the loss. Objectivity demands that you realize the possibility of defeat. You have to plan ahead for losses as well as wins.

In the Pittsburgh game tonight, we were ahead by two with seventeen seconds left and we had the ball in our front court. Joe Caldwell, holding the ball to stall out the clock, mysteriously threw a cross-court pass that was intercepted by George Carter. A cross-court pass, under normal circumstances, is a dangerous pass. In the last seconds of a game, it is never thrown. I think Joe was worried that Pittsburgh would foul him. Since he is a thirty-one percent free throw shooter I can understand his concern. Carter went on to score the tying basket and we were in overtime. We wound up beating them on the basis of superior rebounding.

In the locker room the team was happy, as it always is after winning. That's the difference between the team that has dissension and the one that doesn't. A team whose players do not get along is not even happy when it wins.

Some of the players were kidding George Stone, whose body resembles a swayback horse. "George, how come you have such a big belly?" Miller quipped. "It's not that I have a big belly," George answered. "It's because I got weak back muscles."

December 21

After a good win against Pittsburgh, we went to New York and lost to the Nets. Carl was very down about the loss. He has phoned me every day. He is thinking of addressing the team at practice.

Carl did just that. He pleaded for greater dedication. I don't believe anyone was listening. You can tell when athletes turn off; they remain very still. In contrast, if they are listening they become nervous. Their bodies move slightly. They fidget or sway back and forth. If players are listening their bodies expose them.

December 22

A lousy loss to Memphis at home. The crowd booed us all the way to the locker room. I was hit in the head and side by well-aimed wads of paper and ice-filled cups. I haven't had anyone throw stuff at me since my playing days against the Nats of Syracuse. There the fans would pelt the visiting team with everything they could lay their hands on. But those were opponents; here we're supposed to be the home team.

December 23

The New York fans could not believe the ABA doubleheader tonight. We played the Floridians, who brought along their bikini-clad ball girls. The bikinis as well as the red, white and blue striped ball, not to mention our horrible performance, was about as much as round ball fans of New York could stand. Lehmann played in a fog. He is strung out over Caldwell even though Caldwell insists that he can play with anybody.

I kept the team in the locker room until we had talked, discussed, even yelled at one another. It might have worked but Lehmann refused to say anything. His head between his legs, he was the picture of a depressed man. One of the real problems was the hostility between Joe and Lehmann. If George would have just opened up we would have certainly been able to air things. As it was, Miller, McDaniels and Caldwell voiced their grievances with each other. It was good but not good enough. I'm afraid that the only thing to do is trade some of the players. I still badly need a big rebounding forward.

I kept the dressing room locked to reporters until Jack Dolph, the ABA Commissioner, knocked on the door to get me to come out. Finally I went out to bullshit the press. The first question was not hard to guess. "What did you say to your players?" Did they really think I would tell them? But year in and year out reporters keep asking the same question.

December 24

Returned to Greensboro to find that my house had been bombarded with eggs during the night. These must be a lot of anger in this area for people to act so childishly.

I ask myself if I really have the stuff to motivate this team. I never had trouble motivating myself or my teammates as a player. Yet, how different this is from playing. How terribly alone and frustrated you feel when a team is floundering, looking for inspiration. I firmly believe a coach can only do so much and then it's up to the individual. I begin to sound so repetitious. I can imagine how tired the players are of hearing me always talking about aggressive boards and tough defense, switching and putting hands up on defense.

Joanne and I spent a quiet Christmas Eve together. We comforted each other before a warm fire listening to Dylan Thomas incant "A Child's Christmas in Wales." Afterward we felt better knowing that pro basketball, winning or losing, means so little in comparison to each other, to restful moments, to good health, and to the kind of life that cries out for peace. If success is what I'm after, I'd better forget about living a peaceful life.

December 25

We flew to Memphis today. The Cougars rented a plane, very plush. We settled down to two hours of cards to pass the time. I joined the card game because I couldn't concentrate on the book I was reading, *Zen and the Art of Archery*. There was a line from the book where the author wonders "over the effortless performance for which great strength is needed." How many times, watching players lift themselves into the air, have I wondered the same thing? Rick Barry, for example, seems totally unconcerned, even bored by the strain he places on his body. And though the fans cheer wildly with each picturesque shot, they cannot begin to realize the torture to those muscles.

I was also saddened looking across the card table at George Stone. I made a deal for him and now I will most certainly have to trade him or put him on waivers. Who would want him with almost one half of the season gone? George is the kind of player that needs playing time to be effective, something I can't afford to give him. I keep stalling, though Carl is getting pressure from Munchak to cut down to ten players. That means two players without a job.

We lost to Memphis. But the team played better. They looked like they wanted to play together, willing to lower their egos to a sensible level just enough to win games. After the game Carl was in a depressed state. Once again I told him that building a team does not happen overnight and that he'd better tell that to Munchak. I told him I was sure tonight's game was a positive performance and he could judge better by the results of our game against New York tomorrow.

December 26

I woke up this morning to read in the paper for the sixth time that my job was on the line. I wrote a letter to Marvin Bell, who teaches at the University of Iowa's Writer's Workshop, to find out about admission for next year.

In the afternoon we drove down to Raleigh for our game with the Nets. In the locker room before the game, I sensed a greater spirit of togetherness. For the first time, when I asked the players if they had any suggestions that would be helpful I received advice rather than bent heads. Maybe slowly, they are coming to realize the true cooperative spirit—a spirit in which the coach becomes merely a conductor of tempo, a spy to ferret out the opposition's patterns, and not the leader. True athletes must lead themselves.

My spirits were bolstered when we finally beat the Nets in a come-from-behind victory. It was a game in which I had felt confident throughout, even when we were down by fifteen points in the third quarter. I became so excited that I knocked over a row of chairs. It was purely unrehearsed dramatics.

December 27

I was ashamed this morning when I read the sport sheet. We had won a hell of a game, and our local reporter, Mitch Mitchell, still could not write a positive story. Our victory over the Nets was interwoven with constant references to our being "the worst team in the league." If a story like this took some of the thrill away from me, I wonder what it did for the Greensboro readers. If I were there after reading the story, I would conclude that the Cougars only won by accident.

Mitch Mitchell is a pain in the ass. At the beginning of the season I spent hours trying to explain all the nuances of the pro game. Nothing appears to have sunk in. Mitch is the Inspector Clouseau of the newspaper business. Wearing a bright red sport jacket, white shoes and a cigar tucked into the side of his mouth, he parades around the periphery of sports, writing down what he thinks he sees. As he is only a year out of journalism school it is questionable that he sees what he sees accurately. He simply has not been exposed. Down deep, however, I think he wants so very badly to win. He wants to be a cheerleader and be associated with a winner.

After reading Mitchell's article I turned the page to find that our owner had given a story to Larry Keech, one of the columnists. He is the same Larry Keech who took me apart for trading his friend, Bob Verga. The column told of Munchak's disappointment with both the teams he owns, the Cougars and the Greensboro Generals hockey team. It further said my job as coach, that of the Generals' coach, and the jobs of all the office personnel, are in jeopardy. Munchak, it seems, does not like his name associated with a loser—even for three months.

I wonder how the New York Knickerbocker owners felt all those years in the cellar. I guess Munchak's answer would be that they were not losing $10,000 per game. It all boils down to dollars and cents.

Carl called to reassure me that in order for Munchak to fire me, he would also have to fire him. I was not reassured, but grateful for Carl's words.

If I failed to mention my wife's annual "wives-drunk" I'll make up for it now. For the last four years Joanne had invited the wives of all the players to our house while we were on the road. The main purpose to get smashed. Two weeks ago Joanne had the players' wives over to plan gathering food, clothing and toys together for a family whose husband has just had a kidney transplant. Without taking anything away from the humanitarian goals of that get-together, it turned out to be a real blast. Last seen, the girls were dancing arm in arm, kicking their legs in a reasonable imitation of the Las Vegas Follies.

December 29

The coach of the hockey team was fired as predicted.

A losing coach lives looking over his shoulder.

Rick Telander

You've literally grown up in Peoria. Ever since reading *The Wind in the Willows* as a boy, you've been drawn to adventure writers and their capering characters. At age twenty-five you've found yourself, after an All-Big Ten career as a defensive back, cut by the Kansas City Chiefs and trying to convert your English degree from Northwestern into a livelihood as a writer. If you were Rick Telander (b. 1948), you too might have done what the future *Chicago Sun-Times* columnist did in 1974: spend a summer immersed in the basketball culture of Brooklyn to write a book called *Heaven Is a Playground*. A year earlier *Sports Illustrated* had asked Telander to catch up with current college stars on the courts they returned to when school let out, and he discovered a range of characters in Flatbush's Foster Park, including the mercurial Fly Williams, then a star at Austin Peay State in Tennessee. In choosing to go back a year later on his own dime, he addressed "a restlessness in my soul that bubbled like a broken water main," as he put it in the preface to one of three editions of *Heaven* issued since its first publication in 1976. In this excerpt, Telander introduces the most fascinating of that summer's *dramatis personae*. At first glance, Rodney Parker is an archetype, the well-connected hoops hanger-on who brokers opportunities for young players in his orbit. But Parker, who made a living as a ticket scalper, breaks the mold in his apparent altruism. (As he told Telander, "I like the ink, is all.") Bunking down in a sleeping bag on the living room floor of one of Parker's friends, Telander set out each day with his notebook and AM/FM cassette recorder, knowing he could flick the radio on to defuse a tense situation. Over that summer he played and coached and questioned, and he listened with an ear sympathetic enough that nearly three decades after *Heaven* was published, Barack Obama, then a senator from Telander's home state, pronounced it "the best basketball book I've ever read."

from

Heaven Is a Playground

C OMING around the corner of Foster and Nostrand at dusk, I see a ten-foot fence and the vague movements of people. Men sit on car hoods and trunks, gesturing, passing brown paper bags, laughing. Stains on the sidewalk sparkle dully like tiny oil slicks in a gray ocean. Garbage clogs the gutters. At the main entrance to Foster Park, I step quickly to the side to dodge a pack of young boys doing wheelies through the gate. When I came out of the subway, I had asked directions from an elderly woman with a massive bosom like a bushel of leaves, and while she spoke, I had involuntarily calculated the racial mix around me—10 percent white, 10 percent Latin, 80 percent black. Now, as I walk into the park I am greeted by a lull in the noise, pulling back like musicians fading out to display the rhythm section at work: a million basketballs whack-whacking on pavement.

Rodney Parker is there on the first court, standing still thirty feet from the basket, slowly cocking the ball. He is wearing red sneakers, sweatpants, and a sun visor that splits his Afro like a line between two cumulus clouds. His tongue is pointed out the side of his mouth, and as he shoots, he tilts his entire body sideways like a golfer coaxing home a putt.

The ball arcs up and through the iron hoop and Rodney bursts into laughter. "Oh my God, what a shot! Pay up, Clarence! Who's next? Who's got money?"

In 1966, Rodney, his wife, and two children moved from the East New York district of Brooklyn to the Vanderveer Estates, the housing project that cups Foster Park like a palm on the north and east sides. At that time the area was a predominantly Jewish, Irish, and Italian neighborhood of tidy shops, taverns, and flower beds. The Parkers were among the very first blacks to move into the Vanderveer and Rodney, a basketball fanatic since childhood, became one of the first blacks to hang out at Foster Park.

Never one to maintain a low profile, Rodney was soon organizing games between the white neighborhood players and his black friends from East New York and Bedford-Stuyvesant. On weekends he would preside over these frequently wild contests, usually from his vantage point as fifth man on a team that might include several college stars and pros. He would be everywhere, screaming, refereeing, betting money on his thirty-foot shots, with two hundred, three hundred or more people whooping it up on the sidelines. For identification purposes some people began referring to the playground as "Rodney's Park."

Then as now, Rodney's occupation was that of ticket scalper, a freelance bit of wheeling-dealing that took him to all the big sporting events in the New York area and put him in contact with most of the sporting stars.[1]

He already knew several basketball heroes from his neighborhood, among them pros Lenny Wilkens and Connie Hawkins, and with the connections he made through scalping, it wasn't long before Rodney was giving reports on Brooklyn players to coaches and scouts and anyone else who might be interested.

Rodney, whose education ended in ninth grade and whose basketball abilities were never better than average, derived a deep sense of personal worth from his hobby. "I can do things that nobody can," he liked to say. He helped boys get scholarships to college, he pushed them into prep schools, he got them reduced rates to basketball camps, he even arranged for two of the local white baseball players to get tryouts with the New York Mets. He became known around the park as somebody who could help out if you played ball and weren't getting anywhere on your own. Kids said that Rodney knew everybody in the world.

Now, seeing me by the fence, he comes over and demands that I play in a game immediately to help me get acquainted with "the guys." He charges into the middle of the players and throws commands left and right. This is the rabble—the young men who populate every New York City playground all summer long. Faceless, earnest, apathetic, talented, hoping, hopeless, these are the minor characters in every ghetto drama. They move, drifting in and out in response to Rodney's orders.

The ball bounces away from one of the players and is picked up by a small boy on the sidelines. He dribbles it with joy.

"Gimme that ball 'fore I inject this shoe five feet up your black ass and out your brain!" hollers a somber-looking player named Calvin Franks.

---

[1] Once, years later, I was in a traffic jam trying to get into an NFL game—I think it was a Giants game at the Meadowlands, but I'm not sure. It might have been a Patriots game in Foxboro, or an Eagles game in Philly. Anyway, I looked out the window of the car and there was Rodney scurrying up the side of the road, hawking tickets to stalled motorists. It cracked me up. I yelled at him from my unmoving car, and he came over and laughed, and we shook hands through the window and we chatted. But not for long. There was business afoot.

The boy dribbles, wriggling his hips and taunting. Franks lunges at the youth who drops the ball and sprints through a hole in the fence into the street.

Franks retrieves the ball and begins talking to himself. "Calvin Franks has the ball, oh shit, is he bad. He takes the man to the base . . . No, no, he shakes one! . . . two! . . . He's on wheels . . . and the crowd stands to watch the All-American . . ." Franks shoots and the ball rolls up and around the rim like a globe on its axis, then falls out. "He's fouled! Butchered! They gots to send him to the line . . ."

The sun is gone now, passed behind the buildings in a false, city sunset. Old women with stockings rolled to their ankles doze near the slides.

A boy locates his younger brother who had errands to do at home and pulls him from a card game. "I'll kick yo' ass!" he shouts, slapping his brother in the face. The youth runs out of the park, blood flowing from his nose. The friends at the game laugh and pick up the cards. Crashes of glass rise above the voices, forming a jagged tapestry interwoven with soul music and sirens.

I am placed on a team with four locals and the game begins. Rodney walks to the sidelines and starts coaching. He hollers at the players to pass the ball, not to be such stupid fools. Do they want to spend their whole useless lives as nobodies in the ghetto? Pass, defense. "You're hopeless! Fourteen-year-old Albert King could kill you all!" he shouts.

"Rodney, my man, my man! This is pro material," screams Calvin Franks. "Kareem Jabbar come to Foster Park!"

There are no lights in the park and vision is rapidly disappearing. The lights, I learned last summer, were removed several years ago to keep the boys from playing basketball all night long.

"What? What's happenin' here?" says a young, stocky player named Pablo Billy, his eyes wide in mock surprise as he dribbles between his legs and passes behind his back.

"Boom! She goes boom!" yells Franks.

"You done now, Skunk," answers Lloyd Hill, a skinny 6'3" forward with arms like vines and large yellowish eyes.

"Here come the street five! Jive alive. Loosey goosey."

"Look at him!" shrieks a player named Clarence, apparently

referring to himself, as he spins out of a crowd. "His body just come like this!"

The fouls become more violent now, with drive-in lay-ups being invitations for blood. I don't consider myself a bad basketball player, a short forward who at twenty-five could probably play on a few medio-cre high school teams, but out here I pass the ball each time I get it, not wanting to make a fool of myself. Players are jumping over my head.

"Gonna shake it, bake it, and take it to the—" A young player named Eddie has his shot batted angrily out to half court. "Nullify that shit!" says someone called "Muse" or "Music," I can't tell which.

The Vanderveer project rises on our left like a dark red embattle-ment against the sky, TV's flickering deep within like synchronized candles. The complex covers parts of four city blocks and houses nearly ten thousand people, a small American town. At one time—no more than ten years ago—the Vanderveer was totally white. Flatbush itself (a name coming from *Vlacke Bos*, which is Dutch for "wooden plain") was a haven for the working and middle-class whites who had fled Manhattan and inner Brooklyn, believing no city problems could reach this far.

By settling in the neighborhood, Rodney and the other first blacks started the chain reaction again. Within days, white residents began leaving. "Apartment for Rent" signs went up as fast as the rented vans carried families and belongings out farther to Canarsie, Sheepshead Bay, or Long Island. The exodus continued in an unbroken stream until by 1970 the Vanderveer and surrounding area was less than half white. By 1974, whites had become a small minority and the Vanderveer Estates had turned entirely black, the number being split fairly evenly between West Indian immigrants and "native born." Soon, the real signs of decay began to appear—the broken glass, graf-fiti, garbage, and battered buildings that had been predicted by the doomsayers all along.

If, indeed, there was any plus side to the degeneration, it showed itself on Foster Park courts where a new grade and style of basketball were developing. Premier leapers and ball handlers appeared almost overnight. Patterned play and set shots dissolved to twisting dunks and flashy moves. Black players seemed to bring more of themselves to the playground—rather than follow proven structures, they experimented and "did things" on the court. Soon they controlled the tempo on the half-block of asphalt between Foster and Farragut, and the whites, who came as visitors the way the blacks once had, seemed ponderous and mechanical in comparison.

To Rodney it was simple justice. "Blacks own the city," he said. "They should own the game, too."

But as the talent escalated, so did the problems. Almost every boy now came from a broken home and was, or had been, in some kind of trouble. The athletic potential had multiplied, but the risk had doubled.

There is almost total darkness now. Yellowish speckles from a street light fan through a tree at the other end but do not come this far. Teammates and opponents have merged and the only thing I can do is hold onto my man and not let him disappear. Rodney is still hollering. "Pass, dammit. Pass like Danny Odums. Hit the boards! Looking for another Fly! Who's gonna fly out of the ghetto?"

Passes have become dangerous, starting off as dark orbs which do not move but simply grow larger and blacker until at the last second hands must be thrown up in protection. The first ball that smacks dead into a player's face is greeted with hoots.

Lloyd Hill unleashes his "standing jump shot" and the ball disappears into the night. It reenters, followed by a sharp pop as it whacks straight down on someone's finger.

"Oooh, god day-yum! Pull this shit out, Leon! Thing's all crunched up—" The damaged joint is grabbed and yanked. There is a similar pop. "Eeeeee! Lorda . . . ahh . . . there, now she walking around a little . . ."

"Where's Franks?" shouts Lloyd Hill. "Where'd he went just when I'm shooting the rock in his eyeball."

Franks reappears from the side. "It's gone."

"What's gone?" Lloyd asks.

"The bike."

"What bike?"

"*My bike.*"

"You ain't got a bike, fool."

"Friend gave it to me. Had it right over there."

The ball is punched out of Rodney's arms as little kids appear like phantoms out of the darkness to shoot and dribble during the break.

"Shit, Franks, that ain't funny."

"It's terrible."

"Can't laugh. Heh, he-he."

"Five seconds, gone. Man walks in and rides out."

"Hee ga-heeee."

"It's terrible and I ain't laughing."

"Hooo hoo ooooohhhh . . . they steal things in the ghetto."

"Niggers . . . hoo-hooo . . . they take your shit!"

"Some little spook halfway to Fulton Street . . ."

"Hoo hahoo haaa . . . peddlin' his ass off in the mother-fuckin' *ghetto*—"

"In the for real Ghet-toe!"

Franks is now laughing hysterically, doubled up and slapping palms.

The darkness is complete. The old people have gone home. Slow-moving orange dots point out groups of boys smoking reefers under the trees. Two other basketball games are going on, but only the farthest can be heard. I start to wonder what I'm doing here, in this game, in this place, in these conditions. Playing basketball in total darkness is an act of devotion similar to fishing on land. Soon, I know, someone will rifle a pass and shatter my nose.

"Come on now, let's be serious," says Eddie. "We down, twenty-four, twenty-one."

The ball is returned and the contest starts again. Laughter fades and the bicycle is forgotten. Everything is in earnest and yet I am blind; I cannot follow the game with my ears. Rodney shouts but does not exist. Quietly, on an inbounds play, I walk off the court.

"Hey, hold it," says Lloyd. "Where's that white dude we had?"

"Yeh, we only got four men." Someone counts. "Where'd he go, Rod?"

The players look around.

"He went to get some water, I think. He's not used to this shit, he's quitting. Just get another man."

"Come on, little brother," says the tall player called "Muse" or "Music" to one of the hangers-on. "Put the weight to this dude and keep him outta the sky."

From thirty feet away on the bench, I can barely see the occasional sparkle of medallions as they catch the street lights along Foster Avenue. I'm exhausted and relish the chance to wipe my face with my shirt and rub my sore knees. I can hear the players' voices, and it sounds to me like they'll go all night.[2]

---

[2] How I remember the many basketball games I played in that summer! In fact, some of the dialogue recorded in *Heaven* came while I was in the thick of contests, memorized, and written down as soon as I could get to my notebook. I know a number of terrific stories were lost because, frankly, I didn't give a damn at certain moments about recording anything for journalistic purposes; I just wanted to make my shots, stop my man, grab some boards, and win.

Michael Novak

Michael Novak (1933–2017) wrote to put flesh to the bones of his belief that sports, like the arts, are too enmeshed in the human spirit to be left to the vulgar realms of ideology or politics. In holding that view Novak, a conservative Catholic social philosopher who would influence popes and prime ministers, helped confer on games like basketball a worth all their own. Hoops held a special place in the life of this grandson of Slovak immigrants, even if he had no remarkable talent. "Anticipation, quickness and attentiveness could make up for lack of special skills," he recalled of his childhood in western Pennsylvania. "Spirit reaps rewards in basketball." At Stonehill College in Massachusetts, later as a graduate student at Harvard, and then while training for the priesthood he ultimately chose not to join, Novak's appreciation for the game deepened, thanks in part to exposure to Bob Cousy. Even as a seminarian and daily communicant, Novak would carve out time to watch or listen whenever the Celtics engaged their great playoff rivals, the Los Angeles Lakers. Under the spell of those NBA Finals, he wrote in *The Joy of Sports* (1976), from which this excerpt comes, "sports events rivaled churchgoing in the frequency of my religious liturgies. The liturgies do not have the same worldview, of course, nor celebrate the same way of life. Yet as Aquinas said, so I found it to be true: grace exceeds, but does not cancel, nature."

from

The Joy of Sports

TEN FEET above the floor, the orange rims of the baskets wait in silence at each end. No sound in sports is sweeter than the clean *twang* and *snap* of the corded nets when the ball spins exactly through. The sexual metaphor of penetration has often been called upon; a neat, perfect, and cleanly dropped shot brings an ecstasy and inner pleasure analogous to the release of high sexual tension. The game proceeds, indeed, by rapid exchanges of "baskets"—the ball dropping through the hoop as often as 100 times a game. It is a long intercourse.

Skill makes the difficult seem easy, and at times it seems that the inherent conflict is a race against the clock—to drop in more baskets than the opposition before time expires. More than in football, the clock is vital; not occasionally, but in virtually every game, the final race is against the clock. The two teams try to stay within range of each other until the end. Then, in the last four or five minutes, perfection is in order; each error becomes a gift to the other side; only so many errors can be borne. Often enough, ecstasy or despair is decided only in the final five or ten seconds, perhaps in overtime. Standing at the foul line, or putting up the last decisive shot, a man will often drive his fist against the air, driving the ball home in exultation.

As in love, the game should not become too easy; intense and long resistance must be applied. And so *defense* has come to be the heart of the game. So practiced and skillful are the pros that shooting percentages are as near perfection as one might imagine—as high as .890 for free throws and .630 for field goals. Almost every other time the ball goes up, it goes in. Thus the emphasis in modern basketball has shifted to make each thrust for the basket as laden as possible with friction, difficulty, obstruction, and reluctance to yield. Crowds love the new pressing defenses, the sweat, the toll they take on blistering feet, the pounding up and down the floor, hawking, falling, leaping, tangling, pushing, shoving for position. Each team in basketball is like a single living body: the two organisms clinging to each other up and down the floor like giant wrestlers, locked in high-velocity and sweating contact at every point of movement. Warily, at times, the dribbling guards approach the other team's embrace; like arms, the defensive guards swing loosely right and left, circling, before clapping tightly into the foe's line of movement. Each team is a mystical body, one, united. Enormous feats of concentration, enormous bursts of energy, vast reservoirs of habit and instinct are required.

The solidarity of basketball makes it appealing in many cultures; slowly, it is beginning to spread. Europeans, with feet trained by soccer but hands and arms lacking in speed or subtlety, take a little while to reverse their development. The game is capable of many different cultural styles. The plodding, chesslike Russian juggernaut has proved successful against the individual talents of American All-Star teams; virtuoso excellence is not sufficient in this game, for solidarity is everything. But the deepest possibilities of the game are so embedded in the American experience, especially through the black experience, that it is difficult to believe that any other nation could consistently present teams that might outplay our own. A part of our deepest identity is uttered in this game. Those of us not black are taught possibilities we might otherwise have never known or emulated.

Stanley Cohen

A conversation with a stranger at a cocktail party during the 1970s led Stanley Cohen (b. 1934) to wonder what had become of the principals in college basketball's betting scandals of the 1950s. He laid out answers in his book *The Game They Played* (1977), a revisiting of that convulsive period in the game's history and the basis for the HBO documentary *City Dump*. In 1950, a City College of New York team that started three Jews and two blacks won both the NCAA tournament and the NIT. But the afterglow dimmed when seven players were implicated in taking payoffs from gamblers to shave points. "The City team represented us and our way of life—most of us locally bred sons of immigrant parents confronting a somewhat alien world," said Cohen, who during a half-century in journalism wrote newspaper and magazine stories as well as five books, and taught at Hunter College and NYU. "It was crushing when we learned of the scandal." Before he contracted with Farrar, Straus and Giroux to write the book, Cohen had secured the cooperation of several former CCNY players. But one of them, Floyd Lane, was then hired to coach at his alma mater and didn't want to revisit a painful subject. Soon the others withdrew their support for the project. Cohen offered to return his advance, but editor Roger Straus suggested he forge ahead, believing the book would be more powerful, and less susceptible to the self-interested shadings of interview subjects, if Cohen personalized it. Here, in the prologue, Cohen takes us to Creston Playground in the Bronx. It's in the neighborhood where the author himself grew up, sometimes playing with his heroes before and after their falls from grace—including the man at the center of this scene, former City College star Ed Roman. Cohen doesn't identify Roman by name, which helps give what transpires the power of a short story.

from

The Game They Played

I T WAS the big man who drew the crowd. He had been gone for a long season and now, in the first true chill of November, he was back, doing the thing he had always done best. He was playing the pivot in a schoolyard basketball game, positioned with his back to the basket and spinning left or right in the brief pirouettes of an unrehearsed choreography.

He was a big man, but he had an unorthodox shape for the game he played. His body seemed to be formed by a succession of sharp hooks and angles, except for the slightly rounded shoulders and the face, which was full and fleshy. His very presence spoke of awkwardness, but in context everything he did acquired the mysterious beauty of function. For there was to his movements the quick stuttering ease, the economy of motion, that is taught in the brightness of the big time but is refined and finally possessed in the lonely litanies of the schoolyard dusk.

The crowd had gathered slowly. They were clustered in a tight semi-circle around the back of the basket, drawn in almost directly beneath the backboard. It was late in the day, and beyond the crossed wire fence, some six feet above the playing surface, twilight figures moved like shadows in the direction of the five- and six-story tenements that lined both sides of the street. Except for this one small corner, the schoolyard was empty now, and it was quiet. The only sounds to be heard were the sounds of the game itself, the ball drumming against the concrete court, or rattling against the rim or the metal backboard.

There were five other players on the court. The big man was being guarded by a player of perhaps six feet two, who was giving away almost four inches in height. But he was quick and lean and very agile, and as one watched him the impression grew that his body had been wired together with catgut and whipcord. He wore a close-cropped crew cut, which was the fashion of the time, and his soft, almost casual jump shots were flicked lightly from the top of his head. The two had very different playing styles, one seemingly set against the other in the practiced medley of counterpoint.

The remaining four players formed the supporting cast. They had their own skills, some of them considerable, and on other days one or another might have stolen the game, but not today. This day, they all seemed to understand, was special because the big man was back. And so they played to the strength of his inside game, feeding the pivot and then cutting across, fast and tight, like spokes slicing past the hub of a wheel.

The pace of the game was swift and precise. The big man's team scored the first three baskets. He made the first two himself on two short spin shots, one to his right, the other to his left. On the next play he passed off for a driving lay-up. Then a shot was missed, and the crew-cut player answered back with two jump shots, fired in a flat trajectory that appeared to be short of the basket, but somehow just cleared the top and grazed the inside of the back rim before falling to the ground.

There were no nets on the baskets, and as the afternoon faded the rim seemed to lose itself against the green of the backboard. But schoolyard basketball is a game played on the accumulated instincts of one's own time and place. There were no markings on the court; no keyhole or foul line, and one learned to take his points of reference from anonymous landmarks—a jagged crack in the pavement, an imperceptible dip in the wall along the sideline, the subtle geography that is known and stored only in the private preserve of the body.

Three-man basketball is conceivably the most demanding game played in the schoolyards of America. It is not as sophisticated as the full-court game. It does not require the same kind of speed or versatility, the almost artistic devotion to discipline. But what it lacks in complexity is compensated by the intense quality of the game. It is pressure basketball, compacted in time and space, as if a boxing match were to be held in a ring cut to half its normal size. There is no place to hide and no clock to offer respite.

The game is played by the improvised rules of the home court. In some neighborhoods ten baskets win a game, in others the point is eight, but always a two-basket, or four-point, margin is required for victory. It is a game played to its own cadence, and without a referee to call fouls, it can be brutally tough. But the most important feature of three-man basketball is that the team that scores keeps possession of the ball, and so one plays always with the nagging knowledge that the game might be lost without his ever having had the chance to score. It is a shooter's game, a game that is won or lost quickly on the trigger of the hottest gun.

Now, from the corner of the court, the big man sent up a one-hand push shot that cut the center of the rim so cleanly that one could not be certain it had gone through. It broke a 10–10 tie, and before the defensive team could recover, another shot, as whistling clean as the first, fell through from slightly closer range, and the game was one basket short of completion. They were the first outside shots the big man had made, and now one recalled how easily he had made those shots, and how often, on brighter nights, beneath the hundred blazing suns of big-city arenas.

That was a while ago of course, and a long season had passed since those days of early spring in 1950 when time seemed to move on private clocks, and each night was a herald to the sound of trumpets. He was not yet twenty then, a college sophomore with honors for grades and a basketball talent that might earn him All-American mention. He had not played much basketball until he reached high school, and his natural gifts were modest. He had size, of course, and good hands, and a remarkably soft touch from the outside. But the rest of it was learned. It was learned while in high school, and then honed and polished in the schoolyards of the Bronx. He worked hard at it, shooting at night-darkened rims, and in winter clearing a path through the snow so that his shooting eye would not lose its edge. Basketball was a sport without season in the canyons of New York, and the big man, who had grown to love the game, worked at it through the months and years of his teens.

He was all-scholastic in high school, and in college he joined four other all-scholastic players on a freshman squad that could have taken the measure of more than a few college varsities. A year later they moved up as a unit to a team that was deep in talent. It was a team marked early for greatness, but no one, not even its most optimistic fans and alumni, suspected that by season's end this young racehorse band of schoolyard players would beat the best the country had to offer and win both of America's major college tournaments.

They had become instant celebrities, their fame of a type seldom known to professional athletes. For they were, after all, college kids, none yet old enough to vote, and they were the local property of the neighborhoods in which they lived. It was not through bubble-gum cards or the filter of the television screen that you knew them. You would see them on the block, or at the corner candy store, and of course in the schoolyard where you would watch them play in street clothes on the Sunday after a game, and on occasion, if the available talent was skimpy that day, you might even share the court with one of them in a three-man game.

The big man was a schoolyard regular. He would arrive late on a Sunday morning, sometimes carrying a basketball under his arm, and he would shoot at an open basket while waiting his turn to take the court. He was genial and unassuming, and even on the day after his team had won the National Invitation Tournament, he came to play choose-up ball, and as he entered the schoolyard he received the applause with a diffident grace.

It had all seemed right then. The days fell together with brickwork precision, and time was the filament on which success was measured. There was not the slightest intimation then that a year later his well-ordered world of campus and schoolyard would lay in ruin. Other glories waited; the NCAA championship would be added to the NIT title within the next two weeks, but further on, around the bend of the seasons, lay the wreckage of a national scandal. He and some of his teammates would be arrested for manipulating the scores of basketball games. They would be booked on charges of bribery and conspiracy, they would be arraigned, bail would be set, they would be convicted and sentenced. Some would receive jail terms. That is what lay ahead, eleven months to the day, and that was not necessarily the worst of it.

The worst of it, they would find, was that forgiveness would be slow. They would be remembered more widely as dumpers than as the celebrated grand-slam team. Careers would be broken, their educations stunted. They would never again play big-time basketball. Culture heroes in their teens, by the time they turned twenty they would be part of the dark side of American folklore. And it would not be short-lived. Twenty-five years later their telephone numbers would still be unlisted. They were to learn something soon about one of life's fundamental truths, as relentless as it is just: that the past is not neutral; it takes revenge.

Now, as you watched him again, you had to wonder what it all meant for him, you would like to know how much of it he understood now that the legalities were done, now that he was free to do anything except what he really wanted to do. You imagined the inside of his head to be a kaleidoscope of gray-green colors, of pictures that fed one into the other, whipping like wind through the tunnels of memory. And you wondered where it might stop, which frame might be frozen in view even now, as the ball snapped into the pivot, into the hands held high above the head, the ball raised like a torch against the dusk.

He stayed that way, motionless, for an instant, his back to the basket, the ball held high. Then he started to turn quickly to his right, his head and shoulders doing all of the work, and as quickly he was spinning the other way now, spinning left, the ball balanced lightly on the tips of his fingers, his arm stretching high toward the right side of the basket, and then the ball, in the air now, struck the crease between the rim and the backboard and bounced away, out of bounds.

And then something happened. It happened so quickly that it all seemed at the time to blur into the bleakness of imagination. But it would be recalled later in the finest of detail, summoned forth as if it had all taken place in slow motion to be run at will in the instant replay of the mind.

Two copper pennies were thrown out onto the court. They were tossed at the same time, in the same motion, and they hit one in back of the other with the abrupt report of two shots fired from a pistol. You heard them hit that way, and then you saw them roll briefly and fall, and then they were lying right beneath the basket, at the big man's feet.

The game stopped now, and everyone was looking in the direction of a boy of perhaps fifteen or sixteen. He was of medium build, and he was wearing a brown suede zipper jacket above faded blue jeans. He was smiling now, a tentative smile, as if to assure that no malice was intended, but he said nothing. He said nothing and you could hear the silence as the crew-cut jump shooter walked toward the youth. He was just a few steps away, and he walked up to him matter-of-factly and with his left hand he seized the kid by the front of the jacket, and without saying a word he eased him back in the direction of the wall.

Then, with a quick short motion, he punched out with his right hand and landed hard and clean against the side of the youth's face. You could hear the sound of the punch landing and then the kid's head bouncing lightly against the black metal door, and nothing else. The kid did not even cry out. All you heard was a muffled groan, almost inaudible, the type that follows a blow to the body. But the punch had landed flush, and the kid, making hardly a sound, sagged to the single step at the base of the door. He said nothing, and for a moment you could hardly believe it had happened.

But when the kid picked himself up you could see that his jaw was hanging loose. His jaw was dangling as if from a swivel, and on the left side of his face, where the blow had struck, there was a lump that jutted out and up in the direction of his ear. It was not the puffed-out swelling that comes with a bruise. It was, clearly, the sharp impression of a splintered bone pushing against the inside of his cheek.

The jump shooter had turned away, even before the youth drew himself up, and he walked slowly back to the court. He stopped beneath the basket, at the in-bounds line, and he waited.

"Your ball," the big man said.

Peter Goldman

Peter Goldman (b. 1933) "may have done more to explain America to itself, week in and week out, than any other journalist of his generation." Those words appeared in the final print issue of *Newsweek* to describe the man who spent forty-five of the magazine's eighty years contributing to its pages. Goldman wrote more than 120 cover stories on subjects ranging from civil rights to Vietnam to Watergate. After leaving the staff in 1988, he continued to contribute to the magazine for another two decades. "Knowing, insiderly, vaguely literary and yet unassuming" is how fellow *Newsweek* veteran Howard Fineman described Goldman's voice. The image of "Goldie" pacing the halls on a Friday night, searching for a narrative thread in reports from correspondents in the field, struck another colleague as looking like "a one-man funeral cortege." Yet by daybreak Goldman would rise from his Underwood, having pounded out the lead story for that week's national affairs section. Thirty-five of his covers came on what was known as "the race beat," as did his 1973 book *The Death and Life of Malcolm X*. "It occurred to me that the Harlem Globetrotters would be a good metaphor for race relations given their odd place in American lore," said Goldman, who began shopping a book proposal with the working title *The Last Minstrel Show*. But no publisher offered the advance necessary to do the job. When word reached him in 1977 that one of dozens of ex-Globetrotters he had already interviewed, Leon Hillard, had been shot dead, Goldman dusted off his notes and produced this piece for *Sport*. It's a profile of a man who was to the Trotters what Goldman was to *Newsweek*: largely anonymous, devoted to the institution, gaited for the long run.

Requiem for a Globetrotter

"You get what your hand called for."

—*The Sayings of Leon Hillard*

SOMEBODY SHOWED me in the papers a while ago where Leon got what his hand didn't call for. The headline jumped out at me first—EX-GLOBETROTTER IS KILLED BY WIFE—and then, sickeningly, the picture: the black gnome face with the eyes of a kid who knows a secret and a smile as stealthy as sunrise in the ghetto. *Leon Hillard*. The story told how he got messed up with his Sandra. Yelled at her, chased her downstairs to her mama's, kicked open the door and walked into a .38 slug coming out. There were a couple of perfunctory paragraphs about how he played and later coached for the Harlem Globetrotters for 15 of the years between 1951 and 1972, and how he was deep into youth work in Chicago when he died at 45. His whole life story took up half a column. What more is there to write about a dude who only used to be the Second Baddest Show Dribbler on The Road?

So Leon Hillard, a man of a thousand sayings, had it wrong for once: His hand called for better than what he got. His name, to be sure, has got lost down some back highway of our memory. Mention the Globetrotters and an older fan will come back at you with Goose Tatum and Sweetwater Clifton; a kid with Meadowlark Lemon and Curly Neal; both generations with the apparently ageless Marques Haynes. Leon? He played a lot of his years in Marques' shadow, and a lot more bojangling around what he called the little in-between towns with the Trotter second company while Marques and Curly played Front Street. You can hardly find him in authorized Globetrotter history now—he parted that badly with them. They didn't even send flowers.

But the old Globetrotters remember. Leon knew the Trotter thing better than practically anybody—learned it from Tatum, the moody master, in the 1950s and taught it to a new generation of schoolyard brothers in the '60s and '70s. How to read a crowd from the murmur before you even hit the floor. How to get 'em buttered by getting that ball *hot*—hopping hand-to-hand or hand-to-floor so fast it never wants to cool down. How to drag yourself out with your soul all bruised and legs all floor-burned, and still make people laugh. How to survive "The Road": The short bread, the long bus rides, the ennui of playing the same game every night, the funky phone calls home and back. "Leon had the real rhythm of it," said Bobby Hunter, his friend and Trotter protégé. "If the world had to start up again on the moon, you'd have to have somebody with the book on farming, y'know? Well, Leon would've been the one with the book on the Globetrotters."

And more; Leon had kinds of magic you can't do with a basketball. He could get streetcorner basic—*stern*, he liked to say—about issues of money and dignity; he walked out on the Trotters twice, and helped foment a player strike against them in 1971. *Leon crazy*, some of his less impudent teammates whispered. *A gangster. Got an attitude.* But once the deal was down, he greeted a day like an old friend, with a lopsided grin and a line of pavement-wise chatter. "Was never hushed-up today and ha-ha tomorrow," he told me once. "People asked me, 'Leon—how can you be happy all the time?' And I told 'em, 'I'm not really happy, man, but what the hell. You got to be out here six months on The Road, y'know. Ain't no sense in makin' it difficult.'"

When the Trotters retired him off The Road and back to the streets he came from, *that* was the attitude Leon took with him. His business was franchised fast food, but his thing was kids—most recently and promisingly with a Chicago-based foundation called Athletes For Better Education. Leon could talk a Blackstone Ranger out of gang-banging or charm a junkie off his jones. "'Cause they know I know what I'm talkin' about," he guessed. "I'm tellin' 'em what they're doin' around the corner, and they can't figure that out. 'Mr. Hillard, how you know that?' Well, I *been* around that corner when I was their age—that's how I know."

Leon's corner was on Chicago's West Side, where the northbound Chickenwing Express out of Arkansas had deposited his folks early in his boyhood. He came up poor, hungry, scrawny and, like most of the brothers on the block, "a little antiwhite"—the whites in his young experience consisting mostly of creditors and cops. He first picked up a basketball when he was 14, in some Y or Baptist gym or somewhere, and he learned to put it down as an act of survival. "Guys in the neighborhood used to muscle me around. Beat up on little guys. So I learned this dribblin' thang. Did what I saw Marques do, or what I *thought* I saw. Make that ball your trick."

He was just 18 when Abe Saperstein, the founding genius of the Trotters and still the reigning monopolist in black basketball talent, bought him straight out of high school for $350 a month. His mama had to sign the contract and see him off in his tatty backstreet clothes to catch up with the second unit in Johnson City, Tenn. Leon arrived green and scared among men old enough to be his father—"my *grand-father*, man"—and jealous enough to freeze him back to the ghetto if they wanted. So he faded into the scenery, shy, silent, grinning his sly grin. "Put myself in a *likable* way, y'know?" Worked on his game, tappy-tapping the ball in a thousand hotel room floors until the guests downstairs howled for the house detective and his own arm hurt from his fingertips to his shoulder. Heard, saw and spoke no evil. *Who, me? Don't know nothin'.*

So the old Trotters adopted him. Called him "Junior." Bunked him with Sam Wheeler, the gifted road-company clown who might have succeeded Goose except that his skin was too light and his dunking hand was missing two and a half fingers. Got him off hot dogs and onto beefsteak to flesh up his frame—a skinny 5-7½ then, a wiry 5-11 even in his prime. Tutored him in show basketball when it wasn't yet all show—when you might still roll into a town all road-weary and find a home team heavy with ringers sitting in their locker room with all the lights out just to scare you. Hipped him to the etiquette of life with Abe—call him "Skip," and laugh at his jokes, and never ever beat him at bid whist. Admitted Leon to the pleasures of life: Sipping, smoking, balling, betting, jiving away the long hours on the bus. Even saw him off to church on Sundays under the wing of a seriously religious teammate—"although," Leon told me, smiling, *"that's* really not The Road. Y'know?"

His real mentor was Tatum, a shambling clown with coal-house skin, saucer eyes, a slappy walk, and a seven-foot wingspan affixed improbably to a six-three body. Goose was two men, Leon always thought—like Pagliacci. Brooding, dark and dangerous as a thunder-head until the moment they put on "Sweet Georgia Brown"; then, a brilliant black-in-blackface anachronism masking his wounds and his rages behind a stretchy minstrelman smile. He was mostly a loner on The Road, out of his own preference and the respect of his team-mates for his violent temper. But Goose took to Leon, because Leon *was* likable and—just as important in Tatum's jealous eye—he wasn't Marques Haynes. Goose made Leon and Sam Wheeler his designated drivers, in a Fleetwood he bought from an uppity white dealer in Nashville for $9,000 in pennies. He let them tag along on his night prowls, sometimes buying out a whole nightclub for an evening just for them. He took his women in bunches, and then, when he had sent them home, kept Leon up to dawn just talking. "Teachin' me show business. Tellin' me tales of black."

Leon listened and learned. He rifled Goose's trick bag and, by imitation, mastered it. He cased entertainments from the Ice Capades to the Folies Bergère for what he could borrow. Timing. Movement. *Precision it down.* And he ripened his own game. He flung up rainbow-high two-hand setshots when Abe, a stubborn traditionalist, was around, and funky little one-hand jumpers when he wasn't. Leon set the beat for the rhythm section—the backcourt cats hopping the ball around a tight figure-eight weave and into the hole for Goose or Meadow or whoever to play with. He got his show dribble down to no worse than a bounce or two behind Marques, and good enough for Front Street when Marques cut out on his own. Different, too—streety and jazzy. "Marques was like a melody—da da da dum dee, da da da dum dee," Sam Wheeler said. "Leon was more like a rhythm piece—ditdidditdadadaditditdada."

What Leon never learned was going along. He fell into a kind of love-hate thing with Abe—tight with him and his family, but never at the expense of his own pride. He beat Abe at cards. ("Man, you ain't *supposed* to do that," his roomie Sam told him, but Leon did.) He hooted at Abe's attempts at coaching—instructing the Trotters, for example, to slow down the great George Mikan in an exhibition game by yanking on his pants. He sat stone-faced among the peals of black laughter at Abe's gags. ("Look at this oscar here," Abe would say, annoyed. "Didn't get the joke.") He kept bogarting Abe for better money, and when it wasn't forthcoming he walked away from the Trotters. Twice. In 1958, for a year with a breakaway team organized by Goose; in 1960, to start his own road club, thinking Goose's successor, Meadowlark, would follow. "Can't live without us, man," Leon said. "Cut off the head and the body will die."

Only Meadow didn't follow, and without him Leon and his partner Ducky Moore and their Harlem Ambassadors lasted maybe a year and a half. He had a time of it anyway; once, from a backwater town somewhere, he sent Abe a picture postcard of some cartoon cannibals stewing a missionary, with his own scrawled caption: "Thanks for the family recipe." But taking on the Trotters was more than Leon could manage, or afford. He had become a family man—had married Sandra, his neighborhood sweetie, and fathered the first of his three sons, and he finally had to throw in his hand. Folded the Ambassadors and drifted off with other road clubs, sometimes for shorter wages than Abe paid. What he wouldn't do was go back to the Trotters. Not until they begged him—he carried their come-back telegram around like a card of identity—and not until Abe was dead.

He had gone out smoking, a rebel kid with a Chicago rep, waggling a finger right in Abe's round-eyed face while his teammates scattered for shelter. But all the years of The Road buffed him smooth and broadened him. He would come home summers from Paris or Tokyo or someplace, a West Side brother with a bistro list and an acquaintance with good cognac, and would find the same old dudes sipping wine on the same old corner as if they had never moved. Leon discovered then the distance he had traveled from them. He saw in their eyes that they were dying there, and he didn't want to die with them.

So Leon came back to the Trotters and their mini-conglomerated new Chicago management a different man—road-wise, polished, bilingual in back street and front-office English. "Not ghettoish, y'know—sophisticated." He did a year show-dribbling, and then the new crowd with the custom leisure suits and the State Street attaché cases made him a player-coach. Handed him the second company, the International Unit, a low-dollar, low-spirited assortment of egos, cliques and attitudes, and told him to whip them into shape.

And Leon did. He got dazzling shows out of the team's veteran star, Showboat Hall, exploiting Boat's genius Trotter hands and working around his mercurial humors. He taught his own game to Pablo Robertson, a playground hero out of Harlem and Loyola, and helped make him a star at the risk of his own future as a player. He got his guys on speaking terms with the white opposition, and—almost as difficult—with each other. He put on one marvelous season, the kind old Trotters talk about like wine-sippers admiring a '62 Lafite Rothschild. "Chanting them on like a witch doctor," one teammate remembered—hop it now, down in, back out, on the money, *bang!*

He did almost too well—got himself promoted against his easy nature to the big team and the staticky company of Meadow George Lemon, by then Goose's successor as clown prince on the court and autocrat of the locker room. Leon handled the Lark Question by accepting him as given, and concentrated instead on bringing along the younger Trotters—the sassy asphalt stylists from Harlem and Brooklyn and Chicago's South Side with their superfly games and their flashpoint sensitivities. *Leon know what time it is*, they told each other, and he hipped them to it. The game and the life. The wisdom of The Road reduced to a thousand sayings:

Pack light.

Travel loose.

Send some home on payday.

Chase them messy gals all night if you want, but stay out of the papers, and save 40 good minutes for me and the customers.

If you got a game, play it. But none of that eye-rollin', Stepin' Fetchit stuff—got nothin' to do with the rest of black people and it demeans *you*.

If a dude makes a mistake, leave him alone—you think he *want* to look bad in front of 10,000 people? I made mistakes, and I *been* here.

Do it right and you won't have to do it over. What goes round comes round.

You get what your hand called for.

Nothin' from nothin' is nothin'.

Leon coached with skill and played with Indian-summer magic—well enough to bring the halftime jugglers and trampolinists back from their dressing rooms to watch him do his thing in the third quarter. What he lacked was a certain entrepreneurial regard for bottom lines, and the distance they require between boss and employee. A lifetime of short checks and tall promises had left him incurably suspicious of every management he ever played for—even when he became part of management himself. His view of proprietors was something like his rule for defensing a dude trying to shake-an-bake his way past you to the basket. "Don't look at the cat's feet, man, 'cause he'll shuffle on you and get away. Stand back and look at *him*. It's survival."

That stand-back distance, subversive for a player, was downright seditious for a coach. Leon encouraged the help to demand money for value, and hassled the front office for bonuses for them. Once, he even said no. He had just dragged into Dayton at 3 or 4 in the morning, the players bus-weary and heavy-eyed, and there in the hotel lobby was the local promoter sweating and fidgeting over his sluggish ticket sales. "Leon," he said, "you got to put five or six of the guys out on the corner at 8 in the morning and do a little clowning—I got a TV crew lined up." Leon stiffened, knowing it would get him in trouble and not caring. "'Cause, see," he said, "all the time in the years before, the promoters thought the Globetrotters was *machines*. And we had to act like machines, and I was a part of that. But this time I made a decision." He chuckled. "A *major* decision. I looked back at the guy and said, 'I can't help you.' I said, 'The men are tired.' I said, '*You* got to sell your tickets. What *we* do is come in and do your show.'"

The time finally came when Leon figured you don't even do that—when he and his main man Bobby Hunter and a couple of fellow heretics led the elves out on strike against Santa Claus. Mutinies had been tried before on the Trotters, and Abe had always got the jump on them, dispensing a hundred or so here, shuffling a roster there, once sacking practically his whole team and hiring a new one. So Leon moved stealthily. *Sophisticated.* He talked to the players, one by one, then in little midnight black caucuses. "Y'know, if we stopped tomorrow, they can't get no *white* Globetrotters." He got them a downtown white labor lawyer. He and Hunter collected their grievances and then their signatures on union pledge cards—everybody's, in the end, except Meadowlark's. And finally they dispatched the news to the management, with their ultimatum: "By this date and time, if we do not be recognized as a union, we will not be performin'."

This time, to their own surprise nearly as much as management's, the Trotters were serious—dead serious enough to fold the show one night in Port Huron, Mich., and hunker down in their motel for most of a prime-time month in the late autumn of '71. It was only that first day Leon reminisced about with any real pleasure—the guys painting up their picket signs and peeping out through the venetian blinds at the arena across the street. "People was flockin' there, and we was laughin' all up our sleeves—they thought it was a Globetrotter *joke.*" After that it was a siege, a dozen black guys in a motel spending their last checks and watching each other's eyes and wondering if they would wilt before the guys in the leisure suits.

They won, sort of—got their players association recognized, and doubled the average annual wage to something over $30,000, and pried loose some concessions, including meal money and premium pay for doubleheaders. But their victory, and their union, lasted roughly the three-year life of their first contract. Old faces started disappearing, all for reasons accepted in professional sports as sound. Showboat Hall was pronounced too old at 45; Pablo Robertson flunked his team physical; Bobby Hunter, the union president, got beat out of his job in training camp; some bad-ass city kids were cut for economy or supplanted by new recruits from the Southern black colleges. And Leon? Leon was one of the first to go. He couldn't cut it as a player any more, they told him, and the coaching jobs were taken by Meadow and Marques. They sent him home to Sandra and the boys with $14,000 in severance pay, but no pension. He never looked back. *Nothin' from nothin' is nothin'.*

But he did bring something home from The Road—a vocation for kids that he discovered on a Trotter tour a world away from home. "It was Africa—North Africa," he remembered, "and I learned a lesson there. From some kids, orphan kids, the oldest one about 12 years old. Not even brothers or sisters or anything—wasn't no parent over them. Just kids like you see dogs in the street, wanderin' around, tryin' to survive. *For each other.*" Remembering them Leon's eyes began flooding, and his voice thickened. "And it just opened my mind, y'know? 'Cause I didn't know thangs then about humanitarianism.

"'Cause, see, these kids followed us. Came up behind you and kind of touched on your elbow, and when you turned around, they'd be pointin' at their mouths, goin *ahhhh! Ahhhh!* And people had told us not to give 'em nothin'—'They're thieves, they're this, they're that.' But they followed Sam Wheeler and me to this restaurant—had an open door where you could just go in and see out on the streets. And these kids sat out there on the curb watchin' us eat, y'know, and we felt really bad.

"So when we left the restaurant, they followed us back, and we gave 'em some money anyway, spite of the fact that they told us not to. We got back to the hotel and went up, and we was watchin' them out the window." Leon sniffled loudly. "And they disappeared—we didn't see 'em for 15 or 20 minutes, and then they came back. Sittin' on the curb. They had went to the store and got bread. Meat. And they set there, and this 12-year-old, he divided that bread and that meat into seven pieces. They didn't argue—'Well, you got more than me!' Just divided it. Survivin' for each other. And I started thinkin'—those kind of kids, y'know, and if they could do that why couldn't *we* do that?" He was weeping now at the memory. "I always stay away from that," he apologized, "but it had a lot to do with my life. Made me want to have somethin' to do with kids' lives."

So Leon went back to the corner, to compete with the dope dealers, the gang-bangers and the storefront Marxist-Leninists for souls. For a while, he answered too many freelance distress calls from too many community groups and playground workers and plain messed-up families. "He was always moving 50 directions at once," Hunter remembers, "and ten minutes late for everything." It was almost as if he thought he could go one on one against death. Once, a lady with a kid on heroin called for help; Leon talked to the boy for four hours, made a few phone calls, and had him in a withdrawal clinic before the night was out. Another time, a street blood came at him with a piece, and Leon kung-fued him with words. "I mean, man, just shoot me, 'cause I'm tellin' you what's real. You done went to the movie and think you're Superfly or somebody, and I'm tellin you where you gonna end up at—one-to-five, boy, a dollar a day, and then you either *gonna* be dead or *wish* you was dead, 'cause you gonna be a vegetable walkin' around in these streets." The blood backed off.

It took Leon until his last year or so to get his act really together—to connect his streety wizardry with people organized to make it last. He tried for a while with the Abe Saperstein Foundation, but it got nearly as heavy working for Abe's ghost as it had been working for Abe. So he cut out, along with Bob Love, then Chicago's reigning black NBA hero, and Chick Sherrer, a close white pal who used to organize basketball camps for the NBA, and they started AFBE—Athletes For Better Education. The centerpiece of their year-round program was a two-week summer getaway for kids off the block, basketball plus saturation three-R academics plus Leonology 101–102—those rudimentary arts of life and survival known more formally as citizenship.

Leon didn't live long enough to get it really grooving, and his heirs at AFBE are left with their might-have-beens. Like the time at the first camp when one kid stole something from another, and the staff called all 125 campers together for a late-night meeting. Love was there, and Artis Gilmore of the Chicago Bulls, and a bunch of college All-Americans, but it was Leon who handled the problem—talked on nonstop for an hour about manhood and responsibility. *Survivin' for each other.* "And he just captured the entire audience," Sherrer remembers. "I mean, like nobody rustled, nobody made a noise, nobody got up to go to the bathroom. And at the end of the discussion, the kid who took whatever it was got up, tears in his eyes, and said, 'I took it.' And gave it back and apologized, and the whole camp just burst into applause."

Leon for the first time had it all—all, that is, except time. He lived out at the edge and knew it, going anywhere, confronting anybody, caring and not caring what happened to him. "I'm gonna go violently," he began saying. "There's too many things out here I can't control." He and his mother were close, in that bonding common to black families, and when she died last year, he dreamed one night that he was going, too. Felt a cleansing steal over him, and saw her standing in the room smiling at him, and suddenly he was face down on the floor, coming awake hollering, "Don't shoot! Don't shoot!"

What he didn't see was where death was coming from. He knew what The Road can do to a family—had seen too many of them come apart over the short bread, the long absences and the seven-day, uptown-Saturday-night atmosphere. He had come back to Sandra with a worldly estate consisting of less than $1,000 a year for all those years away and the mortgage on their two-flat in a fading South Side neighborhood. His youth work couldn't pay the bills, and even when he got his Lemmy's hotdog franchise going on a federal loan secured by his own sweat, economics remained a source of tension in the family. And so did the habits of The Road. Globetrotter men tend to spend their summer furloughs on their best behavior, Leon once told me, because Globetrotter women "know what he been doin' out there." The trouble comes when the men can't leave the life behind—and the gossip attending Leon's death was that he couldn't.

There was talk of another woman; of Leon banging the bottle, though no one who knew him well saw or believed it; of quarrels over love and money so bitter that the Hillards, once devoted, started talking about divorce. The official investigation did not scratch much deeper than the chatter. The fatal shooting of one black person by another is known in the argot of Chicago criminal justice as a nigger disorderly, and there was no evident reason to question Sandra Hillard's story. Yes, she told the police, she and Leon had argued till she walked out on him and took refuge with her mother downstairs. Leon, she said, phoned down and threatened mayhem unless she came home. She didn't, and, as she told it to the police, Leon came storming after her, splintered the door loose from its jamb, and, silhouetted in the empty frame, stopped a slug fired by his own wife from his own gun. It was, under the law, a justifiable homicide—deadly force in self-defense against deadly force.

They gave Leon Hillard a funeral, and everybody came. Or almost everybody; the Globetrotters' home office, since reconglomerated into Metromedia in Los Angeles, kept its silent distance, and only a couple of its currently employed hands showed up. But Bob Love came to help bear Leon's pall, and Ernie Banks, and Bobby Hunter, of course, and Old Sweets Clifton, now a cabbie in Chicago, and a lot of people nobody but Leon ever heard of. In his eulogy, Chick Sherrer mentioned how I had asked Hunter who was Leon's best friend; Hunter had automatically answered that *he* was—then reconsidered and guessed that there would be a lot of competition. There was. The friends of Leon Hillard overflowed the funeral and filled a hundred cars going to the graveyard, seeing Leon to the end of The Road.

Douglas Bauer

When Douglas Bauer (b. 1945) wrote this piece, he had recently returned to his hometown to take stock after a divorce, come to grips with turning thirty, and pare back his freelancing so as not to feel "like an itinerant fieldworker moving to his harvests." That homecoming led to his first book, *Prairie City, Iowa: Three Seasons at Home*. Rather than formally interview people, he would cock an ear to their conversations or casually join in, then retreat to a diner in a nearby town to find the privacy to write up his notes. Bauer went on to win National Endowment for the Arts grants in both fiction and nonfiction, and to teach—at Harvard, Ohio State, Smith, New Mexico, Rice, and Bennington. He returned to memoir with *What Happens Next*, which won the 2014 PEN/ New England Book Award in nonfiction for what the judges' citation called the "hauntingly beautiful" way he "lifts the great dome of sky that covers the American heartland and revisits interior spaces." Bauer's writing life has long been entangled with the opposite sex, from his first magazine gig after college, for which he adopted a female persona to write subscription come-ons for *Better Homes and Gardens*; to the influential maternal characters that crop up often in his fiction; to his great professional mentor, the food essayist M.F.K. Fisher. Recalling "my first true hero," Janet Wilson of the Prairie City High girls' team, and the thrill when the school bus stopped at the Wilson farm and Janet made her regal way down the aisle to her seat, Bauer pitched this story to another woman, *Sports Illustrated* articles editor Pat Ryan. It fixes the place of the six-to-a-side girls' game in the lives of Iowans, and does so through male adolescent eyes. The author's favorite diner refuge serves as the setting for the final scene in "Girls Win, Boys Lose," a piece memorable on its own terms, but even more so for the aphorism of its title.

Girls Win, Boys Lose

THE TROPHY case in the old Prairie City, Iowa, gym was of light pine, shellacked to a deep glaze. It was tucked into an alcove inside the front door, the statues and plaques crowded into it arranged in tiers like a chorus. Stylized halfbacks, forwards and sprinters, perpetually frozen in midstride, midmotion, stared through the glass. The largest trophy was in the center of the second row. Adorned with pennants and a couple of eagles, it stood at least six inches taller than the others, and it was topped with a figurine of a woman raising a basketball, about to go in for a layup. Her uniform had a lot of folds and pleats, and there was a certain timidity about the modeling, which brought to mind old anatomical drawings in health textbooks that fade to pastel blanks in certain areas. But she was clearly female, clearly moving to the basket. The base of the trophy was emblazoned:

GIRLS' DISTRICT CHAMPIONS
1948
PRAIRIE CITY HIGH SCHOOL

No Prairie City team before or after has played its sport as well. Following its 1948 district championship, Prairie City competed in the Iowa High School Girls' State Championship, one of 16 teams from rural villages with populations in the hundreds to do so that year. Prairie City was beaten in the first round by the team that became state champion and, according to enduring local belief, would have been the champion itself if its coach had not stayed with a strategy so plainly wrong that the memory of it still rankles many of those who watched the game.

"He put Mona out front where she couldn't. . . . Guy's about as smart as a board fence. . . . Couldn't rebound out there. . . . Four fouls. . . . Fellow's brains wouldn't cover the bottom of a coffee cup." That's the sort of thing you hear if you bring the subject up at the co-op filling station when Dick Zaayer or Don Sparks is there.

For those too young to have been witnesses, it has never been clear just *what* the coach did, beyond losing the championship. But what's important to know is that a powerful feeling about it has survived; that in this remote central Iowa town the idea of girls playing basketball can heat a conversation with emotions free of any condescension. One could grow up in the town in the late 1950s and early '60s, as I did, watching girls' sports without the least notion that there was anything prophetic about a custom that in small Iowa farming towns is as deeply embedded in the psyche as the suspicion of skies and the certainty that a stranger is a Democrat.

Prairie City's girls usually had better seasons than its boys. When I was in grade school and went with my father to watch Janet Wilson release her fluid hook shot, the girls' team nearly always won. The boys, playing afterward, usually lost. And so we drove home with predictable dispatches. Mother, in a cone of reading light in her living-room chair, looked up as we came into the house and said, "Well?"

"Girls won, boys lost."

Girls won, boys lost. Girls won, boys lost. Tuesday and Friday nights. Season after season.

In fact, most nights the boys had their best moment while the girls' game was still being played. Almost all the high school students sat together in a section near the southwest corner of the gym. At the end of the third quarter, those boys who played basketball rose up like suddenly blooming plants. Because the game had stopped, attention was directed to the stir in the bleachers, and the boys played to it for all it was worth, stretching to full height with elaborate indolence. There seemed to be the hard-bitten courage of soldiers in their rising: "Love to stay but the Huns are waiting." They slowly walked in single file the length of the floor, took a right, walked the width of the floor and disappeared into their dressing room.

After the girls' game was over, the boys came out and got beat 68–37. But, Lord, they walked like champions. Naturally, then, my grade school heroes were Janet Wilson; Joellen Wassenaar, a quick, knife-thin girl, her limbs milk-white stems, who faked a jumper and drove to either side; Margaret Morhauser, the powerful guard. I took notice of the way Judy Kutchin folded her sweat socks—down, then up again—so they formed snowy tufts above her shoes, and I resolved to wear, as Joellen did, only one (left) knee pad.

I was not alone in my adoration. In Iowa the girls' state championships draw better than the boys' tournament, invariably filling the 15,000 seats in Veterans' Memorial Auditorium, Des Moines, for five days in March. One could argue that the scheduling of the girls' games before the boys' in Prairie City implied the girls were a warmup act, a preview. But I have a clear memory of looking up into the balcony, its bleachers rising like a cliff wall, where the farmers and merchants, the town's strongest fans, sat in the dim, atticy light. Many of them put on their coats after the girls' game had ended. They knew they had just seen the best basketball they would watch that evening, and they were going home. Let the boys lose in front of their parents and their girl friends.

As it's played in Iowa high schools, girls' basketball differs significantly from the boys' game. There are six players to a team: three forwards who remain all evening on one half court, with the sole responsibility for the offense, and three guards who do nothing but guard the opponent's forwards.

After a score, the ball returns to midcourt, is handed to the other team, and a second half-court game begins. No one crosses the midcourt line. It is inviolable. Stepping over it or on it constitutes a turnover. With a half-court of momentum, a player must brake furiously once she reaches the line. Frantic ballets are danced all along it. A girl often looks as if she's teetering dangerously at a roof's edge as she strives to remain on her side of the court.

The other distinctive rules include one that stipulates that a girl must stop after two dribbles and pass or shoot. The game takes on a high syncopation. Bounce, bounce, pass. Bounce, pass, shoot. The two-dribble rule is the 24-second clock of the game; it accelerates it, raises its scores. Only a few seconds elapse between shots. The best teams frequently score 100 points. The best players sometimes score 100 points.

Various factors—the rules, the range of young women's accuracy—keep the game near the basket. Twelve-to-15-foot jump shots predominate and field-goal percentages are consequently high. A girl who cannot shoot 60% has a future as a guard.

But there's more, some believe, to the girls' accuracy than the short distances from which they shoot. (From the free-throw line, eight of 10 or nine of 10 is routine. A girl who expects to win the annual state free-throw contest cannot afford to miss any of her 25 attempts. After a first perfect round, she will advance to a playoff.) One of the state's most successful coaches once claimed that girls have a unique sensitivity in the tips of their fingers.

"They're born with it," he says fervently. "They have something in their fingers boys don't have. Call it a gift, a feel, a fine tuning. Look at a girl's hands—soft, delicate. They're just better shooters. That's a fact that's clear as a sparrow's dew."

The Pentagon recently issued a report that says women soldiers throw hand grenades more accurately than men. Thousands of Iowans were, no doubt, not at all surprised.

Year after year the Prairie City girls fought Colfax for the Rock Lake Conference title. Only six miles of undulating farmland separates the towns. Their teams had played each other—all sports, both sexes—for many years, and were nearly always closely matched. Colfax, which is the larger of the towns, with a couple of thousand people, had a legacy of railroads and coal mines and a reputation as a rough and mean-spirited place. Its inhabitants, many of them no further than a generation removed from the dead mines, drank and cursed and took menacing energy from the phases of the moon. And so, with the passing of genes, did the children who were the members of Colfax' teams.

Prairie City was reserved and humorless, predominantly influenced by a Dutch Reformed faith that found sin in dances, movies and playing cards. Secular happiness came from one's work, and if one hadn't felt a blood-rushing joy after lifting 80 bales of hay, then he should lift an 81st.

Three sour-faced Colfax guards, a kind of delinquent malice in their manner and expressions, remain memorable. They had sallow complexions and bags under their eyes that hinted of late hours and bad diets. Their hair was black, short, tucked behind their ears like matted wings. They had names like Flo and Martha Lynn and Irma. They were sinewy and quick, and they worked together with the precision of the machinery in a watch. It seemed to me as if they played for Colfax for about 12 years, a running presence through all the seasons of my memory. They were mean.

Here is a moment from their play, from the countless heated evenings of claustrophobic tension that Prairie City vs. Colfax inspired. Judy Kutchin stood with the ball at the top of the key, a teammate positioned on her right near the sideline. Her center, stationed beneath the basket, is swinging now parabolically toward the free-throw line. Kutchin passes to her teammate on her right and cuts for the basket. Right-sideline passes to center, ball and girl arriving simultaneously at the line. Center looks for Kutchin racing by. Give and go. A formulistic score. The classic maneuver of the game. Prairie City's fans are up to cheer, having already finished the play, having added the two points.

No! Flo springs from a crouch behind our center and roughly strips Kutchin of the ball. Martha Lynn comes rushing over like a vulture. Irma is angling upcourt, a receiver. Unanimous action against the grain. Martha Lynn sweeps up the ball and fires to Irma, who passes to one of her forwards waiting at the center line. It's done in a split second and with the timing of conspiratorial street thieves. Flo, Martha Lynn, Irma nod coolly. No doubt they'll committee-lip a cigarette after the game.

But just as often, Kutchin took the pass, deftly moved past the mugging and scored. Two for Calvinism.

When I was in high school, I sat in the student section, stood melodramatically at the end of the third quarter, walked the length of the court, took a right, walked its width and entered the dressing room. I was a bad basketball player, having neither size nor speed. Yet the school was so small that I won a uniform, a place on the 12-man squad and made the ceremonial walk with the rest of a mediocre team. I played perhaps three minutes and 12 seconds of high school varsity basketball. But I wore a knee pad, left knee only.

I was in love all the way through high school with Sue. She had a clean, petite beauty. She had a lilting laugh. She had large green eyes and soft, light-brown hair. She had breathtakingly shapely legs. She also had very quick feet and hands that could slap at a basketball like a rattler's tongue. She was an all-conference guard. When she graduated, she was given a trophy as Prairie City High School's best female athlete.

On the eve of a game, we would drive from school to her home in my 1951 semi-automatic Dodge. We would park in front and look out into the early-falling dark toward her unlit house. Sue's mother, a widow, had a job in Des Moines and did not get home until an hour or so after school was dismissed.

"Can I come in?"

"Not tonight," Sue would say, smiling. "Coach says we should rest. If we win tomorrow night, we'll be tied with Pleasantville."

"Just to talk?"

"We're talking right here." Not only her feet were quick.

"What do you want to do this weekend?"

"Depends. If we lose, Coach says we might have Saturday practice."

"Who you guarding tomorrow night?"

"Sandy Sampson. She's good. Has a good jump shot from the side of the lane. But she can't drive to her left. I'll overplay her, force her to the left, and it should be all right. Of course, if she's hot from out. . . ."

As she talked, I would gradually incline my head toward hers.

". . . it won't be as effective, and I'll have to try to keep a hand—what are you doing?" And she would execute as neat a head fake as Pete Maravich.

No one cheered louder than I did during the girls' games, not only for the good of the school but also for the hope that Sue would have Saturday night off and could journey 25 miles to the blinking neon of Des Moines. Streetlights, movies, pizza afterward. "None for me. Coach says it slows you half a step." I cheered as well for Sue's mood that followed a win, because she was not an athlete who left her game in the dressing room.

It mattered little to me who won the boys' game. We were at best a .500 team and another loss could not set back nonexistent title chances. And, as a substitute who had been given a place on the team mostly for the sake of symmetry, I became insulated from events on the floor. So after an evening's exercise that consisted of warming up twice and, if the outcome of the game was settled early, playing the final 27 seconds, I left the dressing room showered and eager for companionship.

Sue's play, however, always had an important influence on the outcome, and she was in the lineup—working, stealing, fighting through picks—every second. If Prairie City lost, she was disconsolate and exhausted. If the team won, she was thrilled and exhausted. Neither condition allowed me much companionship, except to help her ease her spent body onto her living-room couch.

One night we sat on the couch in her darkened living room, close but not touching. There was a gap between us, one as narrow and nearly as inviolate as the center line in the game she had just played. Outside, students' cars were ritualistically roaming the streets after the game, their glass-packed exhausts deafeningly resonant. Her gloom was on every surface like a dull wax.

"It's O.K. It's O.K.," I said. "You played great. It wasn't your. . . ."

"I played lousy. Sampson got 38 points. She drove on me like I was nailed to the floor."

"You couldn't hold her by yourself. You forced her to the left. You should have gotten some help from Ramona on that side."

"Coach told Ramona to stay put in the middle. Coach figured if we could keep Sampson going left, I would be able to handle her one-on-one."

Minutes passed. Outside, the engines throbbed at full volume. Finally, hoping against hope that the fog of her mood had lifted, I turned to her and whispered, "Whatcha thinking?"

"Oh, if I'd played *up* on her, nose to nose, hassled her as soon as she got the ball, then she wouldn't have had time to set up. She might have forced a shot."

There were lessons to be learned from those nights on the sagging maroon couch trying to console an all-conference guard who believed her play alone had led to a loss. Among the lessons were some first tentative feelings for the full equality of the sexes, for responsibilities. Free of any blame for the boys' team's performance, I said whatever comforting words there were to say and, mostly, listened. At the same time, I suppressed a deep wish to be able to trade the reserve's sweat-free innocence for the exhausted burden of Sue's talent. How great it would be to be so good that a bad night was the reason one's team had lost.

In the past dozen years, Prairie City has grown to a population of 1,200, an increase of 25%. New homes dot the streets, mixed in among the old ones like young buds. There is new construction everywhere, notably the new school building and its gymnasium.

The team's most recent star was a senior forward, Virginia McFadden, and her play was favorably compared by the men gathered in Harold (Hoop) Timmons' office beneath the co-op grain silos with Janet Wilson's, with Judy Kutchin's, even, hyperbolically, with Mona Van Steenbergen's. Mona was the leader of the 1948 state tournament team and is a member of the Iowa Girls' High School Basketball Hall of Fame. Virginia was shorter, smaller, one heard, but quick and tough and a shooter pure as back-porch butter.

"I'd say she's got it over Mona," said a farmer seated near a whining space heater. He placed both hands inside the bib of his overalls and his arms flapped for emphasis like a dwarf's.

Hoop thought about it. "I ain't so sure," he said. "The game's a whole lot faster now, so you think of Mona being slow, but she could move. Those long legs of hers."

"Smooth," said another farmer. "Smooth is what Mona was."

"This girl scores more points," said the first farmer.

Hoop, an air of verdict about him, said, "You could argue it till you're silly as a pet coon." He looked up and saw a tractor hauling grain heading for his silos. "You gentlemen are free to stay," he said, looking as he spoke for the Folger's coffee can, bottom-lined with kernels, on the floor near the heater. His spittoon. He found it and wet the kernels with a stream of Red Man. "I got to go to work."

Outside, Hoop waited near the deep grate-covered hole into which the grain would be unloaded. The tractor came up to him and moved past, big as a house, pulling two wagons with mountains of grain sloping above their tops. The tractor roared and then abruptly quieted as it negotiated the narrow space between the silos. Idling, it came to a stop precisely above the hole. Most farmers bringing their grain in brake too abruptly, setting their wagons into clangorous jerking, but this movement was clean, light, agile. Hoop raised the wagon doors, let loose the hissing fall of grain and waved to the driver. A broad, comradely wave, appreciative of the skill that made his own work easy: over the hole, open it up, let it drop.

From inside the tractor's cab, the driver, Virginia's mother, returned Hoop's salutation. She had shown where Virginia got her touch. "Call it a gift, a feel, a fine tuning. . . . They have something in their fingers a boy doesn't have."

Like all games, girls' basketball has become swifter and surer with the years. But all that has fundamentally changed is the size of the schools playing the game. The larger Iowa cities, some with three and four high schools, now have teams, and there is fear that these schools, with more money, better facilities, a greater pool of players, will dominate the tiny farming towns. The New York Yankee syndrome. In the face of that fear, coaches in the small schools place their belief in the enduring will of the rural athlete. "It seems to me," said the coach of a small Iowa school that almost always makes the tournament, "that a farm girl still knows how to *hurt* a little more."

At the north end of Colfax, near the junction of Highway 117 and Interstate 80, there is a diner popular with long-distance truckers and farmers. On a recent visit, I pulled in for Iowa eggs and bacon before going onto the interstate. As I walked inside I saw three women clustered around the cash register. They were huddled, as if planning some strategy. They wore the pink cotton uniforms of the diner. Sallow complexions, bags beneath their eyes. Lithe and poised for play. Flo, Martha Lynn and Irma.

"Scramble two, whole wheat, extra sausage," yelled the cook from her window at the back, placing a plate of food on a serving sill. The waitresses broke from their huddle. "Hot pork on white, mashed, extra gravy," yelled the cook, placing another plate beside the first. Flo picked up the eggs and headed for her customer on the left side of the horseshoe-shaped counter. Martha Lynn, sweeping up the hot-pork plate, fell in a step behind her. Irma, with a coffee pot, worked the right side, moving down the counter of empty cups, dipping the pot as if she were watering a row of plants.

"Hiya, Flo," said a trucker, frisky with sleep or pills to fight it. "Howya doing?" He reached a hand for Flo's hip as she swished past with the haste of a woman at work. Flo gave the trucker a quick move and left his hand pinching air. Martha Lynn, a step behind, knowing the move, did not break stride. "Watch the hand, honey," she said to the trucker, "'less you want hot pork in your ear." And she moved on swiftly with her plate, handing, as she walked, another customer's check to Irma, who had finished her coffee refills and stood up front at the register, waiting for the pass.

Girls win, boys lose. Girls win, boys lose.

Bill Russell and Taylor Branch

For its frankness, wide range, and philosophical flights, the autobiography of Bill Russell (b. 1934), *Second Wind: The Memoirs of an Opinionated Man*, reconfigured the bounds of the sports as-told-to upon its publication in 1979. In its pages, Russell tells again and again of being touched by the magical and mystical. In one episode, two-year-old Bill suffers from an ailment that doctors can't diagnose, and is saved only after the Russells, acting on the results of a prayer session led by a nun in a Louisiana hospital, hold him upside down by his feet—whereupon a piece of cornbread is dislodged from his throat. In another scene, as a junior walking down a California high school hallway, Russell experiences a life-altering moment when he's overcome by a signal serenity that he has integrity and worth, despite the norms of a mid-century America that seems determined not to see him and other African Americans as equals. In this excerpt, Russell shares one more juju-inflected confidence—a secret likely to astonish anyone who regards him as perhaps the most constitutional winner in the game's history. Journalist and historian Taylor Branch (b. 1947) midwifed *Second Wind* from Russell; Branch would go on to become a Pulitzer Prize–winning chronicler of the civil rights movement with a trilogy of books, and eventually return to sports in 2011 to write a scathing and influential critique of the NCAA for *The Atlantic*.

from

Second Wind

E VERY so often a Celtic game would heat up so that it became more than a physical or even mental game, and would be magical. That feeling is difficult to describe, and I certainly never talked about it when I was playing. When it happened I could feel my play rise to a new level. It came rarely, and would last anywhere from five minutes to a whole quarter or more. Three or four plays were not enough to get it going. It would surround not only me and the other Celtics but also the players on the other team, and even the referees. To me, the key was that *both* teams had to be playing at their peaks, and they had to be competitive. The Celtics could not do it alone. I remember the fifth and final game of the 1965 championship series, when we opened the fourth quarter ahead of the Lakers by sixteen points, playing beautifully together, and then we simply took off into unknown peaks and ran off twenty straight points to go up by thirty-six points, an astounding margin for a championship series. We were on fire, intimidating, making shots, running the break, and the Lakers just couldn't score. As much as I wanted to win that championship, I remember being disappointed that the Lakers were not playing better. We were playing well enough to attain that special level, but we couldn't do it without them.

That mystical feeling usually came with the better teams in the league that were challenging us for the championship. Over the years that the Celtics were consistently good, our rivals would change, as teams would come up to challenge and then fall off again. First it was the Hawks, then the Lakers, Royals, Warriors, 76ers and then the Lakers again, with the Knicks beginning to move. They were the teams good enough to reach that level with us some nights. It never started with a hot streak by a single player, or with a breakdown of one team's defense. It usually began when three or four of the ten guys on the floor would heat up; they would be the catalysts, and they were almost always the stars in the league. If we were playing the Lakers, for example, West and Baylor and Cousy or Sam and I would be enough. The feeling would spread to the other guys, and we'd all levitate. Then the game would just take off, and there'd be a natural ebb and flow that reminded you of how rhythmic and musical basketball is supposed to be. I'd find myself thinking, "This is it. I want this to keep going," and I'd actually be rooting for the other team. When their players made spectacular moves, I wanted their shots to go into the bucket; that's how pumped up I'd be. I'd be out there talking to the other Celtics, encouraging them and pushing myself harder, but at the same time part of me would be pulling for the other players too.

At that special level all sorts of odd things happened. The game would be in a white heat of competition, and yet somehow I wouldn't feel competitive—which is a miracle in itself. I'd be putting out the maximum effort, straining, coughing up parts of my lungs as we ran, and yet I never felt the pain. The game would move so quickly that every fake, cut and pass would be surprising, and yet nothing could surprise me. It was almost as if we were playing in slow motion. During those spells I could almost sense how the next play would develop and where the next shot would be taken. Even before the other team brought the ball in bounds, I could feel it so keenly that I'd want to shout to my teammates, "It's coming there!"—except that I knew everything would change if I did. My premonitions would be consistently correct, and I always felt then that I not only knew all the Celtics by heart but also all the opposing players, and that they all knew me. There have been many times in my career when I felt moved or joyful, but these were the moments when I had chills pulsing up and down my spine.

But these spells were fragile. An injury would break them, and so would a couple of bad plays or a bad call by a referee. Once a referee broke a run by making a bad call in my favor, which so irritated me that I protested it as I stood at the foul line to take my free throws. "You know that was a bad call, ref," I said wearily. He looked at me as if I was crazy, and then got so angry that I never again protested a call unless it went against me. Still, I always suffered a letdown when one of those spells died, because I never knew how to bring them back; all I could do was to keep playing my best and hope. They were sweet when they came, and the hope that one would come was one of my strongest motivations for walking out there.

Sometimes the feeling would last all the way to the end of the game, and when that happened I never cared who won. I can honestly say that those few times were the only ones when I did *not* care. I don't mean that I was a good sport about it—that I'd played my best and had nothing to be ashamed of. On the five or ten occasions when the game ended at that special level, I *literally* did not care who had won. If we lost, I'd still be as free and high as a sky hawk. But I had to be quiet about it. At times I'd hint around to other players about this feeling, but I never talked about it much, least of all to the other Celtics. I felt a little weird about it, and quite private. Besides, I couldn't let on to my teammates that it was ever all right to lose; I had too much influence on the team. We were the Celtics, and our reason for being was to win championships, so I had to keep those private feelings to myself. It's good I did; if I'd tried to explain, I'd never have gotten past the first two sentences. Anything I confided would sound too awkward and sincere for Celtic tastes, and I could just hear Satch and Nelson. The next time we lost an ordinary game they'd have been cackling, "That's all right, Russ. It don't matter that we lost, because we had that special feeling out there tonight. Yeah, it felt real special."

David Halberstam

Seven of the twenty-one books that David Halberstam (1934–2007) wrote focused on sports, and he had begun work on an eighth, about the 1958 NFL Championship Game, when he was killed in a traffic accident at age seventy-three. He called sportswriters Red Smith, Jimmy Cannon, and W. C. Heinz "the trinity of my early heroes," for "they were changing the rules, not accepting the bland, rigid, constricting form of journalism." And it was his admiration for a sports story—Gay Talese writing on Joe DiMaggio for *Esquire*—that moved him to leave daily newspapers for longer work, first at *Harper's* and then between hard covers. Halberstam had written two panoramic doorstops about twentieth-century America, *The Best and the Brightest* and *The Powers That Be*, when he decided to turn to the peculiar mix of entertainment, business, race, and group dynamics that is the NBA. For *The Breaks of the Game* he followed the Portland Trail Blazers over the 1979–80 season, when elsewhere in the league Magic Johnson and Larry Bird were rookies and the NBA had reached an auspicious inflection point that wouldn't be fully apparent for several years. The many rewards of that book include this set piece about Billy Ray Bates, the poor, black, Mississippi-born, minor-league call-up whose individualistic style ran up against Coach Jack Ramsay's fetish for team play. The Blazers' mercurial signee was a perfect subject for his chronicler, who broke into journalism in Mississippi with the West Point *Daily Times Leader* and covered civil rights for *The Tennessean* and *The New York Times*. Bates would go on to struggle with alcoholism and financial problems, and land in prison after a robbery gone bad. Just the same, Halberstam recalled, "I remember his sweetness. He had such a humanity to him." In the context of Bates's brief stretch of NBA glory, one of the giants of American journalism captures that quality, among others, for posterity.

from

The Breaks of the Game

THERE WAS, on that day in Portsmouth, a young black kid from Kentucky State named Billy Ray Bates, and he had been dazzling, a player of awesome, almost completely undisciplined talent. The crowd had immediately adopted him as its favorite. He seemed to go up for dunks and hang in the air, and then hang some more, and then dunk over much taller players. He touched something deep in Buckwalter, who could look at him and instantly see all the natural ability and then, with his practiced eye, see all the things the young man had never been taught, all the things other kids with better luck would have learned by their second year at Indiana or UCLA or North Carolina. Bates was to Buckwalter terribly poignant, a stepchild on the court. He felt first a sadness that so much talent was being wasted, and then, secondly, a coach's fascination; for Billy Bates was everything a coach could want in a player, at once so terribly untutored and so talented. If I were a player today, that's who I would want to be, Buckwalter thought. The next year Buckwalter was coaching in the Continental league and he saw very soon that Billy Ray Bates was the best player in the league. When in January 1980 it became clear that Kevin Kunnert was out for the season Buckwalter had started pushing Inman and Ramsay to sign Bates, who was again starring in the Continental league. With Kunnert out, Buckwalter argued, there was a place on the roster. Bates, he said, was a great raw talent, well worth a try. If Portland signed him in the normal way and he came to a rookie camp, it was likely he would be shunted aside, quickly lose confidence and fail. But if he could sign on now, in a no-fail way, the pressure would be far less, he would have a chance to learn the plays more slowly, he could practice with the team every day, and he might be able to make it. If he made it, he might become a truly great basketball player. It was almost impossible, Buckwalter said, to exaggerate how much natural talent he had, and also impossible to exaggerate how little coaching he had been given. Inman was interested but somewhat dubious. He had seen Billy Bates, agreed that he had talent but was unsure that so undisciplined a player could fit into so disciplined a system as Jack Ramsay's. Like most basketball people he doubted that Bates's head was equal to his talent. Ramsay himself seemed unconvinced. He had heard about Bates and he was not very enthusiastic about what he had heard.

Billy Ray Bates was a child of the feudal South, the son of sharecroppers, an American whose roots ran a short way back into slavery itself. He had chopped cotton, he always remembered what it did to his back and how much he disliked doing it, and he had grown up in a sharecropper's shack owned by a distant rich man of another color. Many of his teammates had grown up hearing stories similar to his but at a generation or two removed. It would be hard to imagine an American of Bates's own generation against whom the odds were so hopelessly stacked. Most of the young men and women of his time in Mississippi had little choice about life: they could remain in those small rural Mississippi towns until they died, subservient and obedient, embittered but somehow willing to swallow their resentment, and get by, or they could pack their belongings into the inevitable cardboard suitcases, take the bus to Memphis, and from there the next bus to Detroit or Cleveland, in frail hope of finding some industrial job. But even in the North, as agrarian uneducated black children in a highly industrialized and technological new world, they were, more often than not, doomed to end up lost on the cold winter streets. Billy Ray Bates was different. He had had a chance to get away because he was a surpassing athlete, so talented that colleges in his native state, once all-white, competed for his presence on their campuses. He was born in Goodman, Mississippi, a tiny village near Kosciusko, the town which had produced James Meredith, the young man who at great personal risk had integrated the University of Mississippi in the early sixties. Billy Bates did not know for whom Kosciusko was named; since there were so many Choctaw Indians in the area, he had always assumed that it was named for a Choctaw chief, not a Polish-American patriot. The farm on which the Bates family toiled was huge, a man could work all his life on that one piece of land and never see the end of it, he thought. The owner was a man named Pat Smithson. He was okay, Billy thought, in that unlike some of the other big white men he never did anything cruel to black people. Five or six families lived on Smithson's farm. Ellen Bates, Billy's mother, helped clean house for the Smithsons. His mother, he was quite sure, was part Choctaw. There was something in her face that told him. Also, she kept pet snakes, and told him that the snakes were her friends. To black people in Mississippi talking about snakes like that was a sure sign of Indian blood. There were four brothers and four sisters, and everyone worked in some way or another. Billy Bates as a boy had many jobs: he picked cotton, sometimes he broke clods of fertilizer up as he followed behind a tractor, and sometimes he hooked logs for the lumbermen. The cotton money was the best; there had been times when he worked hard and had made as much as $50 a week picking cotton. But he was not a good picker. His heart was never in it. He tended to pick a little, and sleep a little, and pick a little, and sleep a little, just like the cartoon figure of the shiftless southern black. The white people who saw him thought him shiftless. His father was Frank

Bates, known as Shack. Shack was not a good worker, nor finally, Billy came to realize, a very happy man. Billy's early memories were of him laughing and playing, but then when Billy was about five, he seemed to change. He was hot-tempered and began to work less and to get in fights more. Increasingly he would spend the day drinking, returning to his family late in the day when he was drunk. Soon Ellen Bates had to protect her children from their own father. Later Billy Bates came to understand why his father had come apart, and why he had begun to drink. For a black man in Mississippi life was nothing but farming and not even farming for yourself, but farming for the owner. Too much like slavery, he thought. His father died when he was seven. From then on everyone in the family had to contribute even more. When he was a sophomore in high school the family stopped sharecropping and started paying rent. The thing he remembered most clearly about that life was the poverty of it, the fact that they had no electricity, and no indoor plumbing, and very little food and not enough clothes. He decided when he was very young that when he grew up the first thing he would do was to buy a good house for his mother, not just so that she would have some electricity and indoor plumbing, but so that when it stormed the lightning and thunder would not seem to be right there inside the house. Of the nine children he was the next to the youngest. When he was about ten years old he told his mother what he intended. "We'll see, we'll see," she had said.

Sometime after he had reached Portland and become an instant success, reporters would wait in the locker room and ask him how it had all happened so quickly, the meteoric rise to the highest level of professional success from nowhere, and Billy Ray Bates would answer, not a bit surprised or perplexed by the question, no bravado in his voice, "I was born to play basketball." Perhaps he was. He had one of the most powerful bodies of any guard in the NBA, a huge barrel chest, immense hands, strong legs that sprang from thick thighs. He had done some hard physical work as a boy, but he believed the body had been given to him; almost everyone else in his family, uncles, aunts, cousins, had bodies something like his. The talent had always been there. No one had ever taught him to jump, he could simply do it from the first day he tried. He could dunk the ball from his sophomore year in high school and he lived for those moments, sailing above the rim, and then slamming the ball *down*; in that instant, back in Mississippi, he felt all-powerful; he was up and everyone else was down. Dunking was outlawed in Mississippi high school play, deemed illegal by white men writing white rules. But sometimes when his team was up by fifteen points he would risk a technical foul and he would take off and soar in the air, every split second to be remembered and savored.

Billy Ray Bates was in some ways much luckier than many black Mississippians of his generation. He was born in 1956, two years after the Supreme Court had ordered the nation to integrate its schools with all deliberate speed. Mississippi, the state with the highest percentage of blacks, resisted integration the most fiercely and its speed was more deliberate than anywhere else in the South. For years after the ruling, black children continued to attend the tattered rural schools which the state had deeded over to its less favored citizens. But by the time Billy Ray Bates had arrived at McAdams High School in 1970, the courts had finally pressured Mississippi into integration. He arrived at the once all-white school to find riots and signs that said NIGGERS GET OUT, NIGGERS GO HOME. Police were everywhere and no one knew which side the police were on, including themselves. Thus was he welcomed to the white world of Attala County. For a week the school shut down. When it reopened what had been a white high school had turned into a predominantly black school. Whites departed for their own new instant private schools. But they left behind for the young blacks of Mississippi something previously unattainable—first-rate facilities, gyms built by white school boards for white children, athletic budgets set by white boards for white players, and a tradition of white newspapers covering local high school sports events. That was important, it kept these same teams, now black, still a point of community focus. His coach, Wilson Jackson, then twenty-seven, was a black Mississippi native who had grown up with far less in the way of state-supplied facilities.

Even in the seventh and eighth grades he had always been hanging around the gym trying to get on the basketball team. No matter that he was smaller than the other kids and too young to be on the team. Finally, when he was a high school freshman, Jackson allowed him to join the team. "You that little boy I always used to chase out of here?" Jackson asked. Billy nodded his assent. His shooting eye was exceptional and his body was growing and filling out quickly. He loved shooting the ball and regrettably had a good deal less interest in playing defense. But whenever McAdams was behind, Jackson sent him in. Once in a game, Billy refused to look his coach in the eye in the event of a time-out—he was afraid Jackson might pull him. Jackson would see him out there, always scrupulously looking down, checking to see whether or not his sneakers were properly tied.

By the time he was a sophomore he was the strongest player on the team. He already had a powerful body and great jumping ability. Jackson sensed immediately that he was of college or pro caliber. The problem basic to the entire region was how to ward off the sense of hopelessness and defeat that destroyed so many young blacks early in their lives. Mississippi was Jackson's home and he had no great desire to go anywhere else, but he also knew what it did to young people. The signs of defeat, he knew, came early. The boys would start dropping out of class, and then slipping out of school. Then they would start drinking. The drinking was the big move. It was just a way of showing off at first, he thought, of being big men. But once a boy started, he rarely stopped. Jackson was sure Billy could play college ball. The problem was going to be getting him that far in school. The moment that basketball season was over, Billy simply disappeared. School was a gym, it had no other attraction. Billy Ray Bates, like countless other young black kids in America, was going to be a professional basketball player or he was going to be nothing. (Harry Edwards, the black sociologist who disliked the singular attraction of professional athletics for black youths, once estimated that there were some 3 million blacks between thirteen and twenty-two planning to be professional athletes; the odds, Edwards figured, were worse than 20,000 to 1 against their making it.) When Billy disappeared Wilson Jackson simply went to Billy's cousin's house, deep in the backcountry. There would be the two of them, Billy and his cousin, playing basketball. Coach and player resumed their ongoing argument.

"*Boy*, what are you going to do with yourself after school?"

"I'm going to play pro ball, Coach. I *know* I can make it."

"Boy, before you turn pro you got to turn college first, and before you go to college you got to finish this school right here."

Finally, in desperation, Jackson prevailed on the school authorities to add an extra period of gym to the school schedule, right at the end of the day. The pot sweetened, Billy stayed in school. But the pull of defeat was always there. He slept through classes, he missed others, and Jackson had to force him to study. Sometimes the hopelessness around them was so great that Jackson was afraid it was going to pull all of them down. Jackson would give the students his lectures on hard work, on staying in school, on what the future might be. But then when they were gone, he often at night had his own doubts. He knew their families, he knew how many fathers were gone, and how many fathers were not able to make a living. Above all, he knew the odds against them. Mostly he knew in his heart what they could *not* be. What could he tell them to be—doctors, lawyers, architects? Who would listen to him? Maybe if he found a few students a year with strength and character, they might be able to become teachers and nurses. In Billy's junior and senior years, Jackson, worried about the drinking, took his star home with him on the day of games so that he would not drink. Billy, Jackson believed, didn't drink all that much, it was just that he wanted people to *think* he had been drinking, and that he was a big man. In his senior year Billy stayed away from booze and averaged forty-five points and twenty-one rebounds. In the end, in his senior year, an astonishing number of once all-white colleges, including Ole Miss, applied for his services. Ole Miss would take him as a football player *or* a basketball player. Billy seemed to be gravitating towards Jackson State, which was a black sports power only sixty miles away. Wilson Jackson fought the decision. He knew what would happen if Billy went to Jackson State: it was too near McAdams and Billy would play basketball, drift back in the off-season to his old haunts, start drinking and hanging around. Wilson Jackson thought his best chance was if he got out of Mississippi and he pushed him towards Kentucky State, where he finally enrolled.

He played well at Kentucky State, a sure scorer, a powerful exciting presence on the court, but by the mid-seventies black schools like Kentucky State, once a prime producer of talent for the NBA, were no longer considered a very good source of athletic talent. The revolution had come so quickly in black athletics, so many once all-white schools had opened up to blacks, the scouts had become so much better at foraging through the high school circuit, that by the early seventies the finest black southern talent was already being spotted in high school, and the better players were now going to the best state schools in the Midwest and the South. States like Alabama and Tennessee and Kentucky, which had once allowed their indigenous blacks to play in the Big Ten, now fought to keep them in state, not at some small black school but at the main university. White fans now cheered for blacks, players they had once tried to bar from their colleges, finding in them lesser racial qualities only when they lost. The world of black colleges was now worked by the second and third tier of scouts looking for fourth-, fifth- and sixth-round draft choices. Indeed if a player was with an all-black college, there was already an unstated judgment against him: the presumption was that he would have been picked up at the high school level if he were really any good. That presumption worked against Billy Ray Bates at Kentucky State. Scouts watching him saw the powerful body and the natural instinct for the game. But they looked at his annual statistics and then they asked themselves: Why hadn't he been picked by a better college? Was he a bad kid? Was he a head problem? As for the points, who did he get them against? Above all, was he smart enough to learn plays and be part of a disciplined system? By going to a black college he had at the age of seventeen already damaged his reputation in the professional basketball world. But then he had looked good in the Portsmouth All-Star game, and he was drafted for the NBA in the fourth round by an interested but wary Houston. Given the growing odds against him, it wasn't bad. Yet since in America it is largely true that the rich get richer, the converse is surely true, that the poor get poorer, and at this juncture Billy Ray Bates, who desperately needed good advice, signed with an agent who gave him what Bates later concluded had been the worst kind of advice imaginable.

The agent, who had been brought to Billy by his college coach, told him to hold out for guaranteed money from Houston, and not to report without it. This made little sense. In the first place, fourth-round draft choices did not get guaranteed money, and even more important, Billy Ray Bates's best chance was simply to go to the camp and *play*, letting his game be his best advertisement. The last thing wanted by any team already ensnarled in tedious negotiations with its first- and second-round draft choices, as Houston was, was problems with its fourth-round picks. So he arrived late to the camp, a camp he could have dominated, and found the place filled with guards holding no-cut contracts. He immediately showed raw skill but had trouble with the plays. Tom Nissalke, the coach, was already furious with Billy's agent, and the anger reached over to Billy. Soon he was cut.

He was hurt but not yet bitter. He was sure he was better than some of the players they kept. Deciding that somehow he would be back, he went to Bangor, Maine, to play for the Maine Lumberjacks of the Continental Basketball Association.

Within limits Billy Ray Bates enjoyed playing in the Continental league. The Maine Lumberjacks were not the Boston Celtics but it *was* professional basketball, and the dream was still on, just one step away. Sometimes in those games he would go against a player who had once played in the NBA and then he turned it on; inevitably he was the stronger player, and the experience encouraged him to believe that he still had a chance. There were, of course, almost always rumors of scouts in the crowd, and when the rumors circulated, the Continental game, not very much given to structure anyway, completely degenerated. *No one* passed the ball. It wasn't just Billy Ray Bates who was desperate to get to the top, it was everyone in that league. He was Rookie of the Year in the Continental, and won a slam-dunk contest in the All-Star game. In the summer he returned to Mississippi, played some ball, worked some construction. He had a car and he often drove his mother around town. Every day he would pick her up and they would go to a cousin's house, or to a store. She bought less and less at the stores so that she would have more reason to drive back the next day, he noticed. She loved the power and the freedom that the car gave her.

While he was doing this, a young man named Don Leventhal, a Philadelphia basketball junkie who had worked as a publicity man for the Continental Association, was in his spare time trying to put together a team for Philly's summer circuit, the Baker League. Leventhal in his own way was as anxious to get into the NBA as any Continental player. He wanted to get into player personnel, and become, he hoped, the next Stu Inman. The Baker was comparable to the other outdoor summer leagues, an almost perfect showplace of black playground play. Pros, college stars, high school stars and of course playground wizards were all blended together. No one really knew on a given night which famous player might show up. It was the kind of wild, exciting game which made a purist like Jack Ramsay nervous. Individual artistry triumphed over teamwork. Nor was there a lot of defense. Almost all of the players were from the Philadelphia area. Leventhal, putting together his team, sent out letters to a number of players he knew. Then, almost as a joke, because he had handled

Billy Bates's statistics so often in his Continental league job, though of course he had never seen him play, Leventhal sent a letter to Billy Ray Bates in Goodman, Mississippi, asking if he would like to play in the Baker League. The letter included a form which asked a prospective player to check off which month he preferred to play—June, July or August. In a week Billy Bates returned the form, checking off all three months. Soon they were talking on the phone. Billy said he needed money for the bus ride to get up there, and Leventhal somewhat nervously lent him $85 for a ticket. At the same time Billy went to Wilson Jackson and borrowed bus money from him as well. Thus well-armed he set off for Philly. The Philadelphia bus station at 3 a.m. is not the most hospitable place in the world, but Leventhal was there to meet him. Out came the bus riders of America, a few elderly people, a few young people, a few servicemen and then a tall powerfully built young black man. His cream-colored pants were adorned with his own handwritten graffiti. BILLY RAY "DUNK" BATES they read. Oh my god, thought Leventhal, what kind of a cowboy have I got? Leventhal and a young lawyer named Steve Kauffman took him in, and tried to explain the complexities of a city to him, how to use a bank, how to lease an apartment. The thing that staggered Billy, Leventhal thought, was how many young women Philadelphia had. "You know," he kept saying, "Kosciusko is a *small* town, and it's only got one or two girls, but *this* town, there's *thousands*, man, *thousands*."

The night after he arrived, Billy Bates scored twenty-nine points in a game. Some of his opponents were professional players. Leventhal and Kauffman worked to get him a professional tryout. Soon Jack McMahon, a veteran white basketball man and former player-coach, now a Philly scout, showed up. "Billy, this is Mister Jack McMahon of the Sixers," Leventhal had said. "Mister McMahon, it's very nice to meet you and I'll try not to disappoint you, sir," Billy had answered. Then he had hit his first nine shots and scored thirty-eight points. McMahon, who had signed Darryl Dawkins out of high school, loved him. "I've scouted all year and that's the best game by a guard I've seen yet," he told Leventhal. Philly held a secret predraft camp where they let some of the players they were thinking of drafting work out. Billy Bates went, was the best player there and, without drafting him, Philly gave him a $10,000 bonus and a $60,000 guaranteed contract for one year. Billy Bates was sure he made it. So was Leventhal. A week later the draft was held and in the first round Philadelphia drafted Jim Spanarkel, a tall white guard from Duke. Leventhal became immediately suspicious. Billy Bates did well in the early drills and there were favorable articles about him in the Philly papers. He wrote back to Mississippi to tell Coach Jackson that he was going to make it. Could they now retire his jersey? he asked. Then he began to struggle. No one doubted his talent. Jack McMahon was for him but Chuck Daly, an assistant who had coached at Penn, was dubious. Philadelphia, an assemblage of great raw talent, was still smarting from the defeat by Portland two years earlier, and trying to change the freewheeling nature of its team. The last thing it needed was another one-on-one superstar; it had, after all, just gotten rid of Lloyd Free and no one in the league had been particularly anxious to pick Free up. In the camp Billy Bates looked at Jim Spanarkel, who was white and slow, and he thought that there was never a day that the sun had come out that he could not take Spanarkel anywhere he wanted on the court and do with him what he wanted. But Spanarkel was a first-round draft choice, he knew, and professional teams were reluctant to admit that they had made mistakes with their firsts. In the end Billy was cut. The last day he had looked long and carefully at Spanarkel, a quiet reserved young man, and he had thought, *I know I'm better than you. I know there are lots of things that you can do better than me, all kinds of things. But this is one thing I know I can do better than you.*

Cut, but still signed to a Philly contract, he went back to Bangor. He was very bitter now, he had failed twice. He had been given a chance without being given a chance. He was also shrewd enough to know that in the NBA being cut a second time was more serious, that by then it became part of your reputation, there was always a *they* in life and the *they* in professional basketball would believe now that he had had his chance. He felt terribly cheated; he knew it was not because he lacked talent. It was, he believed, because he was a poor black from Mississippi. It was as if people were telling him he was a nigger without actually using the word. The others, the ones who made it, were *blacks*, but he was still somehow because of Mississippi a *nigger*. When he had been a boy he had always thought that sports was his way out, and now he felt beaten because sports seemed to be just another dead end like everything else. His coach in Bangor was Mike Uporsky, who had spent the previous season scouting for Seattle, had tried to sell the

Sonics on Calvin Natt and had been let loose by the Sonics. He was himself unhappy about being back in the minor leagues.

"Billy, can you play here?" Uporsky asked him.

"I don't know yet," Bates had answered, "my head's so far down it hasn't caught up with my body yet. I don't know if I can spend the rest of my life in the Continental league."

Uporsky had expected Billy Bates to be a smart-ass, a difficult kid who thought he knew more than the coach, an attitude which frequently accompanied such raw skills, but the reverse turned out to be true. He was a child of Mississippi poverty, untouched and uncorrupted still, a great favorite in Bangor where he spent the entire winter wrapped in a huge sheepskin coat out of which only his eyes seemed to appear. He could, Uporsky thought, have run for mayor of Bangor, he was so good and kind with people, so much loved. At one point, wary of tampering with this natural force, Uporsky asked Billy to shoot less and go for six assists a game. "When you're on the court I want you to think only of sacrificing. We know you can score. Can you do it?" "I don't know if I can handle it," he had answered. "There's something in me that's just got to go. I don't know if I can control it." But he tried, and became a good passer.

The Continental league, Uporsky thought, with its dinky gyms and tiny $12-a-night motels and cold franchise-food hamburgers was like prison for Billy. The team traveled back and forth to games in a huge Winnebago motor home. Midway during the year there was a call from Gene Shue at San Diego. The Clippers were looking for a small forward. Billy Ray Bates went down to Philadelphia for a tryout with them. Uporsky warned him not to get his hopes up. He did not even play in a full scrimmage, just three-on-three. He never heard from the Clippers again, something which was to haunt Shue later in that same season.

By mid-February the Portland guard situation was desperate. Lionel Hollins was gone, Dave Twardzik, the other lead guard, was playing with a body exhausted by injuries. His legs, Ron Culp told Ramsay, were dead. Anytime Twardzik played more than twenty minutes in a game, he paid for it the next two or three days. Ramsay seemed to be losing confidence in T. R. Dunn. Ron Brewer, who had started the season so strongly, was apparently losing confidence in himself. Jim Paxson, the first-round draft choice from Dayton whom Inman had been so high on, was playing erratically, a disappointment to himself and to Ramsay. His court vision and intelligence were excellent, but he had been drafted as a shooter and the team needed points and he was shooting poorly. He was playing tight. Because of all the other injuries he was getting an exceptional chance to play and he was doing very little with it. Midway through the season, Ramsay had begun to wonder if Paxson, product of a secure middle-class home, son of a former professional player who had given up the sport to take over a successful life insurance business, was tough enough to play in the NBA. He never contested referees' calls on the floor, never seemed to fight back. Rather he accepted things. Ramsay was convinced that one thing common to all superior professional athletes was a certain meanness or toughness, whichever you wanted to call it, a desire to leave their mark on opponents. Possibly Paxson, so fine and intelligent and secure a young man, lacked that. He might, Culp thought, be too stable for the league. In early February, before Buckwalter began to push for Bates, Inman was scouting the Continental league looking for a big man. But he was also looking at guards. Inman, onetime star of the San Jose Spartans and a connoisseur of offbeat team nicknames, loved the idea of the Maine *Lumberjacks*. He went to Hawaii to watch the Hawaiian *Volcanoes* against the *Lumberjacks*. That way he could see Stan Eckwood, whom he had liked from the previous draft, and Billy Bates, whom Buckwalter and others had talked of. By the time Inman caught up with the Lumberjacks in Hawaii, Uporsky had been fired, replaced by the owner's son, who coached only home games. That fact, the flakiness of it, excited Inman even more. "What kind of plays do you run?" Inman had asked Bates and Eckwood before the game. "Oh, we don't run plays," Bates had answered, "we just take the ball down and shake and bake a little." "Well," said Inman, "what do you talk about before a game?" "Where we're going to go after the game," said Eckwood. Inman watched Bates and liked him, the power in the body was self-evident, the hands were huge, and Bates could, in Inman's coach-talk, "pass for profit in heavy traffic. A big plus." But there was something extra Billy Bates had, something that could neither be studied, nor taught, and that was an essential instinct for the game. It was something you were born with, and Billy Ray Bates had it. Intrigued, Inman located Uporsky in Arizona. They had similar tastes. As scouts both had wanted Calvin Natt. Uporsky had even coveted Seattle's other first-round draft pick that year, Jimmy Paxson. "Mike, is he the best in your league?" Inman asked.

"Stu, he may be the best in *your* league. Only Westphal has more natural ability. I'd get him on a plane before anyone else finds out," Uporsky said.

Inman watched two games in Honolulu and then followed the Lumberjacks to Alaska to watch them against the Anchorage Northern Knights, another perfectly delightful name. He had taken Bates to lunch. When he had arrived Bates was surrounded by kids, signing autographs, asking each of them if he was or she was going to the game that night. Inman liked that—score more points for Billy Bates. "If I were your best friend," Inman told Bates at lunch, "I would tell you that what you're in now is the worst environment I can imagine for you. No coaching, no plays, no discipline. You're blessed with great skills, Billy, and you've got a great body. No one can teach you to shoot like that or jump like that. But there's a thousand players like you all over the country in the Rucker and the Baker and a hundred other leagues. Every city has them and they're talented and they watch some pro game and they think, 'Hey, I'm better than the pros.' Maybe they can do one little thing better, go to the hoop, dunk. But that's not basketball. Can they play in a team? Can they play in harmony with four other players? I think you can but you've got to be able to want to do it. We want to sign you, Billy. Do you know who Coach Ramsay is?"

"I've seen him. Gets angry at referees a lot."

"He can teach you how to see your teammates, he can help you. Do you want to try it?"

"Yes, sir," said Billy Ray Bates. "I want to play in the NBA more than anything else in the world."

So it was that Billy Ray Bates, in February 1980, the season three-quarters gone, joined the Portland Trail Blazers. The signing was not without its acrimony. Bates was represented by Steve Kauffman, the young Philadelphia lawyer who had befriended him and was still trying to get him loose from his unfortunate first contract. Portland wanted a five-year contract, with only the first full season guaranteed. The money, if it ever came through, was acceptable but not particularly good by NBA standards. Kauffman was dubious; it put all the burden on Billy and implied little responsibility on the part of the Portland franchise. If Billy was convenient to them then they had him for a very long time. If he failed then they were out free. Kauff-man believed that it was an unfortunate pattern, that they used their maximum leverage at a player's greatest moment of vulnerability, and that there was a dangerous payback. He wanted a two-year contract if possible and a three-year one at most. "You're squeezing my kid and it's wrong," he said. Portland finally came down to four years. Kauff-man advised Billy Bates not to sign it. "We've got to sign it," Billy Bates said. "I've got to get my chance to play. I can't fail again." "Go ahead then," Kauffman said, but he did not like the contract; he wished there were more generosity of spirit shown in it.

Among those in Portland who did not seem especially elated by the arrival of Billy Ray Bates was Jack Ramsay. He had not been impressed by Buckwalter's original recommendation and he had no great yearn-ing for a player whose skills were apparently so different from those he sought. The last thing he wanted this late in the season was a raw, untutored kid who had never played in a system. When he talked of Billy Ray Bates it was as if he were talking of an outsider, someone who was not really on the team. Among other NBA coaches and general managers, most of whom knew a good deal about Billy Bates's repu-tation and even more about Jack Ramsay's system, there was a good deal of amusement at the idea of Dr. Jack Ramsay trying to coach Billy Ray Bates.

But the Blazers had already changed. The treasured Calvin Natt had come at a high price and one day he might be an exceptional player for Ramsay's system, but he was not ready yet. It was clear that Natt was in his own way a project. He was a rookie and more, a rookie with his second team in one year. He did not know the plays. There was even a question of whether he was the right man for the position. He was an immensely powerful young man, perhaps the strongest player at small forward in the league, but was he a small forward—quick, deft, good passer—for the Ramsay system? Or was he a slightly shorter power forward, a hardworking player, but not supple enough for the position? He was not as good a passer as Bobby Gross, and his game was one of power, and one-on-one moves. When the ball came to him it rarely went to anyone else; his presence altered the ball flow, some-times stopped it. Calvin Natt, it soon became clear, was not exactly the player they had needed. If he was to be effective it would be on a very different team.

When Billy Ray Bates arrived in Portland there was something touchingly innocent about him, uncorrupted. But no one knew what was just beneath the surface, and that was troubling; if he became successful, would he change? Would he start arguing with Ramsay for more minutes, talking about being traded? Would he swagger? Would he demand to renegotiate his contract? For the moment he was completely unspoiled and grateful to be there. "He still calls everyone 'sir,'" said an amused Herm Gilliam. "Young and innocent, isn't he?" In his first road game he dressed for the game Lumberjack style, that is, changing at the hotel. He arrived for the bus in his warmup clothes, while the others were still in their civilian finery. That amused them. Back in Portland he drove to practice on the first day with Ron Culp. In the background, as they drove, stood the majestic Mount Hood. "There's no snow here, right?" he said to Culp, pointing to the Portland streets they were driving through. "That's right, Billy," said Culp. Billy pointed to Mount Hood. "How come there's snow up there?" Culp began a long explanation of elevation, temperature and snow. It was not, he realized, very successful. In the end he had not just confused Billy, he had confused himself. The next day they drove by the Willamette River. "There any fish in there?" Billy asked. "Yes," said Culp. "You ever caught any?" Billy asked. "No," said Culp. "Why not?" asked Billy, absolutely perplexed, such a grand opportunity passed by. I don't know, Billy, thought Culp, I just don't know.

At first Ramsay did not use him very much. Perhaps for a few minutes late in games already gone. But word about him spread throughout the league and crowds began to gather around the baseline when the Blazers came to watch his dunks. Finally Ramsay used him because he had no one else and because his team was playing so poorly. They were struggling for the last spot in the Western conference playoffs, slightly behind San Diego, and they were playing listlessly. They went to Milwaukee with only nine games left in the season, with the competition for the last playoff spot more and more heated.

On the morning of the Milwaukee game, Jack Ramsay, physical fitness freak, devoted exerciser of the Ramsay body, went swimming in the pool of the Pfister Hotel. He tried to swim every day, some twenty laps if possible on good days, many more on bad ones, swimming on the good days to keep in shape, swimming farther on bad ones to exorcise demons and burn off the anger and frustration. On this morning Ramsay was preoccupied with the faltering nature of his own team, and with a new burden, the news that the great center Bob Lanier had managed to trade himself from Detroit, where his presence meant little because the team was so bad, to the Milwaukee Bucks, a rising and aggressively talented team, where he might help create a championship. Ramsay was dissatisfied with his own center lately; Tom Owens was, in the phrase Ramsay used to friends, playing soft. Angry about games past, worried about games to come, especially today's, he dove in and swam as hard as he could, forgetting that the Pfister did not offer an Olympic-size pool, and soon smashed his head against the far end, splitting his scalp badly. Blood began to pour out.

He called Ron Culp in his room, "Do you have something to close up a wound?" he asked.

An odd request, Culp thought, something to close up a wound. "Jack, what kind of wound?" Culp asked, slightly puzzled.

"Well, I've hurt myself, I've got a wound," Ramsay answered.

That's odd, Culp thought. Ramsay, usually so candid, was being unusually evasive. "What kind of injury, Jack?" he asked, intrigued now.

"Well, it's an injury to my head," he said. "An unusual one. You better come up here." So Culp with his kit went up to Ramsay's room where he found the coach with a bloodsoaked cloth around his head. At first Culp was alarmed: was this the denouement of all those Ramsay late-night walks? "Jack, for god's sake, what happened?" the trainer asked.

"You know," said Ramsay, "it's an old hotel and they have a very small pool here." He sounded, Culp thought, very sheepish.

Lanier's play was strong; midway into the third quarter the Bucks were up 85–59. At that point Ramsay went to Bates and Jeelani, the one a very recent veteran of the Continental league, the other of the Italian league. Both of them were, at their best, freelancers, clumsy in a system, strong in games where nothing else worked. They quickly brought Portland back. Bates had 14 points in 15 minutes, Jeelani 16 points in 15 minutes. They closed the score to 98–93 with 7:49 left. Ramsay sent in his regular lineup. The Blazers collapsed.

The next night in Chicago it was even more dramatic. It was a slow, heavy game—everyone, it seemed, worn out by the long season. Bodies moved slowly. Watching his team play against Artis Gilmore, knowing exactly what it should be doing, Ramsay was enraged to see the Blazers walking through their assignments, giving Gilmore position close to the basket again and again. His players looked like sleepwalkers. With four and a half minutes left in the third quarter, Chicago was ahead by 17 points. In came Bates and Jeelani. In the final 17 minutes, the two of them, freelancing and gunning, playing with enthusiasm and excitement, combined for 43 points. Billy more than anyone else simply took over the game. When he had the ball it was as if everyone on the court stopped to watch him. He drove to the basket and scored, then did it again. Chicago changed defensive guards and still he did it. Then they began to drop off him, conceding the jump shot to stop the drive. Immediately he started hitting jump shots. With Portland behind by two points everyone cleared out so he could drive on the immense Artis Gilmore. He took off, drove, jumped, faked, brought Gilmore up with him, pumped again, still held the ball and then, at the last second, dunked. The Chicago arena broke into spontaneous applause. In the end Portland, playing sloppy defense, let Gilmore hit two easy shots from the inside and Chicago won. As Bates walked off the court, the Chicago announcer said: "Billy Ray Bates scored points." He paused. The Chicago crowd began to roar. "Sixteen of them in the last quarter." The noise was deafening.

The locker room, except for a crowd of reporters around Billy, was grim. They had done a terrible job on Gilmore. "You don't stop Artis once he has the ball," Buckwalter was saying, "you prevent him from getting it where he wants. Otherwise he'll score all night. He's too damn strong." Gilmore had eleven of fourteen, all short, easy shots. The coaches had diagrammed exactly what they had wanted done, and nothing had happened. Ramsay was trying to deal with the Chicago reporters. He hated losing so close a game after so exceptional a comeback. Right now it didn't matter that it was an un-Ramsay-like manner of play that had brought them back.

In a corner a Chicago reporter was interviewing Billy Ray. "Billy, how would *you* play defense against *Billy Ray Bates*?" "Well, you know," said Billy, "I can go to the hoop and I can shoot outside. 'How do you play defense against me?' Hard to say, hard to say."

Bobby Gross, the last survivor of the classic team—Twardzik had flown home earlier with a sore neck—was talking about how good a passer Bates was, how he could with those huge hands and his great strength hold on to the ball until the very last split second and then still pass. "I don't know if he can play in a pattern," Gross was saying, "but he's good, isn't he? Something special." Gross felt disconnected from the new team. He was a part, he said, that no longer fit. There was no resonance, no rhythm to this team. He was sure he was going to be traded. He had become a $300,000 a year benchwarmer. Weinberg, he said, would not like that. The trade of Lionel had been the final straw. He had badly needed Lionel for his game; they had always understood each other, and knew what they were going to do as if they had their own secret radar. With Lionel on the court, said Gross, if you gave up the ball, you always knew you might get it back. On this team he tried to pass and because the others were not good passers themselves they were rarely ready to take it. The key to passing was anticipation, two men sensing that the same thing *would* happen, not that it *had* happened. Anything in the past tense, indeed the *present* tense, in this game was already too late. Ramsay was pushing Gross to take his shot. But that was alien to him, his instinct was always to look for the pass first. The night before, in Milwaukee, the Bucks had doubled a Blazer guard and the ball had come to Gross, who was wide open for a shot. He had looked at the basket, looked for a pass, hesitated that fraction of a second and by the time he was ready to shoot the defender was back. Two days later, Ramsay was still angry. *"Can you imagine that!"* he said. *"Can you imagine that! They double us, we beat the double and he waits until his man returns!"* In the Chicago game his line was dispiriting. He played eighteen minutes, shot zero for six, shot no fouls and had one assist. It was a line for a player on his way out of the league.

Several days later Ramsay was still annoyed at Gross. Gross was talking openly with other players of his discontent and the fact that he would probably be with another team the next year. He had been quoted in the *Oregonian* recently saying that basketball was not the only thing in his life, that he had a new baby daughter and that his family was also important. Ramsay, reading the story, had not liked it. That was one of the things wrong with this team. Too many interests outside of basketball. No one was single-minded enough. To Ramsay an athlete was someone consumed by his sport, who in-season during his brief career thought of virtually nothing else. The game was first.

Only later, if there was time left over, should there be anything else. Ramsay's own life was organized perilously close to that idea.

He took Gross aside and told him there would be a new team the next year. It would resemble the team of the past and would need Gross's skills. But he also said that Gross must stop living in the past. The championship season was over. There were new strong teams in the league and the accomplishments of the past quickly became meaningless. Gross, listening to Ramsay, was not so sure that he would be back, nor that he wanted to be.

Two nights later they went to Oakland for an important game with Golden State. There were only six games left in the season after this. San Diego was faltering now too. The Portland bus reached the Oakland Coliseum around 5 p.m. While the other players waited in the locker room taking their time getting dressed—there was after all always too much time before a game—Billy dressed and walked out into the empty arena and began shooting baskets. Bucky Buckwalter, walking through the arena, saw him there, a distant lonely figure practicing in a huge darkened room before empty seats. He stopped and watched Billy for a few minutes, suddenly realizing that this moment was devoted not so much to improving Billy Bates's touch but rather to reconnecting him to reality, to prove to himself that it really was all true, that he was finally playing in the NBA. That night Ramsay went to Billy much earlier than usual. He scored twenty-two points and helped send the game into overtime, which Portland won. Afterwards reporters were asking him about a key play in which he had driven to the basket and scored.

"Well, I knew I could beat the old guy," he said.

"What old guy?" a reporter asked.

"You know, the old guy who used to play for Boston," he said. Thus did Billy Ray Bates describe Jo Jo White, one of basketball's great stars, then all of thirty-three years old.

He was a star now. The NBA made him its Player of the Week. People wanted him to endorse their sneakers. Writers continued to seek him out. On the flight home from Golden State he took aside a writer who had interviewed him two weeks earlier when he had first arrived in the league. "You going to write all of that, aren't you?" he said. "Write all of what?" the reporter asked. "All of what I told you about growing up, about how we had no electricity and no indoor plumbing." The writer said yes, he was going to write it. "That means everywhere I go in the NBA and every time I'm on television, people going to look at me and think of me going to the bathroom outdoors and growing up without electricity. They're going to think about it." He thought for a moment. "They're going to think about Billy Bates out there in that old shack."

Frank Deford

During more than fifty years at *Sports Illustrated*, Frank Deford (1938–2017) smartly explored the icons and meaning of our most conventional sports with an assured voice. But he could just as confidently escort the reader on a tour of subcultural Americana, whether Soap Box Derby, bowling, or the Miss America Pageant. Deford was second-team All-City at Baltimore's Gilman School and played basketball briefly at Princeton, until Coach Cappy Cappon, having taken note of his contributions to *The Daily Princetonian*, said, "You know, Deford, you write basketball much better than you play it." At *SI* he first made his name on the hoops beat, filing during the 1960s on historic titles won by Bill Russell's Celtics and Texas Western College. By the 1970s he had an updated calling card, the profile that lit up the back of the book and featured a reliable virtue: though never hit jobs, they always had an edge to them. The edge wasn't that of some switchblade flipped out in a clinch. It came rather from Deford's ability to pull back or bore in—to see a person's life in a grander sweep or put a subject on the metaphorical couch. With the clarifying aid of a subhead ("Bobby Knight may be tremendously successful on the court, but off it, Indiana's basketball coach often stalks the insignificant"), the title of this 1981 piece, "The Rabbit Hunter," could serve as Knight's epitaph. Though events would take nearly two more decades to unspool, Deford foretold the volcanic coach's end: in 2000, several months after Indiana placed Knight on "zero-tolerance" notice for his behavior, the school fired him for grabbing a freshman on campus, a random Bugs Bunny the coach felt had been impertinent by saying, "Hey, Knight, what's up?" Decades later, what wear so well are the story's broad sensibility, authoritative voice, and refusal to treat even an exasperating subject unsympathetically.

The Rabbit Hunter

Success is feminine and like a woman; if you cringe before her, she will override you. So the way to treat her is to show her the back of your hand. Then maybe she will do the crawling.

—*William Faulkner*

I: RABBITS

A S BOBBY KNIGHT is the first to say, a considerable part of his difficulty with the world at large is the simple matter of appearance. "What do we call it?" he wonders. "Countenance. A lot of my problem is just that too many people don't go beyond countenances."

That's astute—Bobby Knight is an astute man—but it's not so much that his appearance is unappealing. No, like so much of him, his looks are merely at odds. Probably, for example, no matter how well you know Coach Knight, you have never been informed—much less noticed yourself—that he's dimpled. Well, he is, and invariably when anyone else has dimples, a great to-do is made about them. But, in Bobby's case, being dimpled just won't fly.

After all: DIMPLED COACH RAGES AGAIN. No. But then, symbolically, Knight doesn't possess dimples, plural, as one would expect. He has only the prize one, on his left side. Visualize him, standing in line, dressed like the New Year's Baby, when they were handing out dimples. He gets the one on his left side. "What the bleep is this?" says little Bobby, drawing away.

"Wait, wait!" cries the Good Fairy or the Angel Gabriel or whoever's in charge of distributing dimples. But it's too late. Bobby has no time for this extraneous crap with dimples. He's already way down the line, taking extras on bile.

"Countenances," Knight goes on, woefully. "I just don't have the personality that connotes humor. It kills me. I get castigated just for screaming at some official. And the other coach? Oh, he's perfect, he's being deified, and I know he's one of the worst cheaters in the country. It's like I tell my players: your biggest opponent isn't the other guy. It's human nature."

Knight happens to be a substance guy in a style world. Hey, he could look very good in polyester and boots and one of those teardrop haircuts that anchormen and male stewardesses wear. Very good: he's tall, 6'5", and dimpled (as we know) and handsome, and the gray hair and embryonic potbelly that have come to him as he crosses into his 41st winter are pleasant modifying effects.

In the early '60s, when Knight was a big-talking substitute on the famous Jerry Lucas teams at Ohio State, he was known as Dragon. Most people think it was in honor of his fire-snorting mien, with the bright and broken nose that wanders down his face and makes everything he says appear to have an exclamation mark. Only this was not so. He was called Dragon because when he came to Ohio State, he told everybody he was the leader of a motorcycle gang called the Dragons. This was pure fabrication, of course, but all the fresh-scrubbed crew cuts on the team lapped it up. It was easy. People

have always been charmed by him; or conned; anyway, he gets in
the last word.

It's never neat, of a piece. When Knight stands up, coaching, with
his hands in his pockets, he looks like a street-corner guy. But with
his tousled hair, the tie forever undone, there's also a childish aspect
to his appearance:

Wear your tie, Bobby.

All right, Mom, I'll put it on, but I won't tie it tight.

The boy-coach who got his first major-college head-coaching job
at 24 may be middle-aged now, but still, every day, in some way,
adolescence must be conquered again. "Listen to me," Woody Hayes
pleaded with him once. "Listen to me, Bobby, because I've made a lot
of mistakes and you don't have to repeat mine."

The real issue isn't the countenance, anyway. The real issue is the
rabbits. And Knight knows that. In the Indiana locker room before a
game earlier this season, Knight was telling his players to concentrate
on the important things. He said, "How many times I got to tell you?
Don't fight the rabbits. Because, boys, if you fight the rabbits, the elephants are going to kill you." But the coach doesn't listen to himself.
He's always chasing after the incidental; he's still a prodigy in search
of proportion. "There are too many rabbits around," he says. "I know
that. But it doesn't do me any good. Instead of fighting the elephants,
I just keep going after the rabbits." And it's the rabbits that are doing
him in, ruining such a good thing.

Pete Newell, the former Cal coach, a mentor: "There are times
Bobby comes so close to self-destructing." Edwin Cady, a Duke University professor, after the Indiana Athletics Committee he chaired
recommended Knight's hiring in 1971: "He's in a race now between
overcoming immaturity and disaster." And even the warmest, most
benign observers of the man offer variations on these themes.

Others are much more critical—especially since the sad events of
July 1979 at the Pan American Games in Puerto Rico when Knight, the
U.S. basketball coach, was arrested for aggravated assault on a police
officer (and subsequently convicted *in absentia* and sentenced to six
months in prison). "Bobby's so intelligent, but he has tunnel vision,"
says another Midwestern coach. "None of that stuff in Puerto Rico had
to happen. On the contrary, he could've come out of there a hero. But
he's a bully, always having to put people down. Someday, I'm afraid,

he's going to be a sad old man." Says an Eastern coach, "He'll get away with the bullying and the vulgarity only so long as he wins. But the shame is, he's so smart, and he's so faithful to his principles, so why can't he understand that other people have principles too?"

Such criticism doesn't necessarily affect Knight in the ways and to the extent that most people imagine. In a sense, he enjoys being mis-understood, so no one can get a fix on him. It's like the effect Indiana's good defense has on the coaches of its opponents: "The average coach wants his team to score points." Knight says. "It's his character, his machismo, whatever you want to call it, that's at stake. So if I make a coach concerned enough about my defense stopping his offense, then he'll forget about *my* offense."

Though Knight may not give a hoot whether most people like him, it genuinely upsets him that anyone might think he's impulsive, much less berserk: "Hey, I'm not dumb and too many people look at our operation as if we're all dumb here," he says. "Only people really involved here know what the hell we're doing. See, I don't think peo-ple understand what I can or can't do. They're not cognizant of my situation and *what I know about myself.* I always know what I'm doing."

Yet as intelligent as Knight is about most things, as searching as his mind is, he's also encumbered by a curious parochialism that too often brings him to grief. When all is said and done, his difficulties in Puerto Rico resulted mostly from his inability to concede that San Juan isn't just another Chicago, or that the Pan Am Games aren't another Mideast Regional—and it's their own fault that they're not. Knight's mind is too good to be wasted on a mere game—and he prob-ably recognizes that—but he's personally not comfortable away from the precisely circumscribed environment in which college basketball is played. Therein lies the great conflict in him.

Does anybody else in this universe of shifting sands still have the control of a coach? No wonder it's difficult for a person like Knight, who tends toward prepossession anyway, to be confused about the limits of his dominion. Puerto Rico, women, writers, shoe salesmen, NCAA bigwigs . . . all of them are just more Rubicons to cross. He's in command; an awful lot of what you see is a good act. Says Harold Andreas, the high school coach who first hired Bobby as an assistant: "He can be as charming as anybody in the world or he can be the big-gest horse's ass in the world. But *he* makes that decision, and he does it in a split second." Everyone identifies Knight with bad language, but the fact is that he can talk for hours, if he chooses to, using much less profanity than the average Joe. He doesn't have a foul mouth; he simply deploys bad language when it can be a weapon.

Knight is forever putting people back on their heels, testing them, making them uncomfortable in some way. Stop them from scoring points, and they won't be prepared to stop you. Although it's fashionable to say Knight rules by intimidation, he actually rules more by derision. He abuses the people he comes into contact with, taking the license to treat them as he does his players.

"O.K., it's true sometimes I intimidate a kid," Knight says. "Usually when I first get him. That sets up the best conditions for teaching. But that's only true with basketball players, not with anyone else. I don't think I'm overbearing with people, but look, that's an awfully hard thing for a man to judge of himself."

Most find him guilty. But, here, you judge. Here's five minutes of typical Bobby Knight. This isn't extreme Bobby Knight. This isn't Puerto Rico Bobby Knight. This is just some everyday stuff, the way he keeps an edge, even over people he likes.

It's practice time, and two of Knight's acquaintances are sitting at the scorer's table. One is a black man, Joby Wright, who starred on Knight's first Hoosier team in 1971–72. Six years after his athletic eligibility ran out, Wright returned to Indiana to get his degree; now he's going for a master's in counseling and guidance. All along, Knight helped Wright and encouraged him with his academics, as he has many of his players. In Knight's nine years, only one Hoosier among those who have played out their eligibility has failed sooner or later to get a degree.

The other person at the table is a white woman, Maryalyce Jeremiah, the Indiana women's basketball coach. Now it's an accepted fact of life—disputed, perhaps, only by Nancy Knight, Bobby's wife—that Knight is a misogynist, but Jeremiah he at least abides. She's a coach, after all.

Knight advances on Wright, and says, "Hey, Joby. Do me a favor."

"Sure, Coach."

"I want you to get my car and go downtown." Wright nods, taken in. Knight slams the trap: "And I want you to go to a pet shop and buy me a collar and a leash to put on that dog out there." And he points to one of his players, a kid Wright has been working with.

O.K., it's a harmless enough dig, and Wright laughs, easily. But Knight won't quit: "Because if you don't start to shape him up, I'll have to get some white guys working on him. You guys don't show any leadership, you don't show any incentive since you started getting too much welfare."

Wright smiles again, though uneasily. Now, understand, Knight isn't anti-black. Just anti-tact. That's the point. One of his former black stars once recalled a halftime against Michigan when Knight singled out two of his white regulars as gutless, and then went over as they cowered and slapped their cheeks, snarling, "Maybe this'll put some color in your faces." It isn't *racial* prejudice. Still, still. . . .

Knight walks down to the other end of the scorer's table. "Hey, Maryalyce."

Brightly: "Yes, Bobby?"

"You know what a dab is?"

"A what?"

"A dab—D-A-B."

"No, what's that?"

"It's a dumb-assed broad," he says, smirking.

"I don't know any of those," she replies—a pretty quick comeback.

But he won't leave it alone. The edge, again: "Yeah, you know one more than you think you do."

And he moves on. The white woman shrugs. It's just Bobby. The black man shrugs. It's just Bobby. But why is it just Bobby? Why does he do this to himself? He's smart enough to know that, in this instance, he isn't hurting his two friends nearly so much as he hurts himself, cumulatively, by casting this kind of bread upon the waters, day after day. Why? Why, Bobby, why?

What a setup he has. Forty years old, acknowledged to be at the top of his profession. Says the very coach who disparages Knight for being a bully, "Any coach who says Bobby's not the best is just plain jealous." Knight has already won 317 games, and nobody, not even Adolph Rupp, achieved that by his age.

Someday Knight could even surpass Rupp's record 874 wins, a seemingly insurmountable total. Knight has won one NCAA championship, in 1976, and five Big Ten titles in nine seasons; he was twice national coach of the year; he's the only man ever to both play on and coach an NCAA champion. He's the coach at one of America's great basketball schools, one that's also an academic institution of note. The state worships him; Hoosier politicians vie for his benediction. His contemporaries in coaching not only revere him for his professional gifts, but some of his esteemed predecessors—mythic men of basketball lore—see Knight as the very keeper of the game. The torch is in his hands.

He's also a clever man and delightful company when he chooses to be. Beyond all that he has an exemplary character, without any of the vices of the flesh that so often afflict men in his station and at his time of life. He's devoted to his family, Nancy and their two sons, Timothy, 16, and Patrick, 10. His supporters fall over themselves relating tales of his civic and charitable good works, a light that Knight humbly hides under a basket. In this era of athletic corruption Knight stands foursquare for the values of higher education that so many coaches and boot-lickers in the NCAA only pay lip service to. His loyalty is as unquestioned as his integrity. He is the best and brightest . . . and the most honorable, too. He has it all, every bit of it. Just lying there on the table. He has only to lean down, pick it up and let the chip fall off. But he can't. For Knight to succeed at basketball—not only to win, you understand, but to succeed because "That's much harder," he says—all the world must be in the game. All the people are players, for or against, to be scouted, tested, broken down, built back up if they matter. Life isn't lived; it's played. And the rabbits are everywhere.

II: COACHES

Perhaps the most revealing statement that Knight makes about himself is this: "You know why Havlicek became such a great pro? Just because he wanted to beat Lucas, that's why." Yes, of course, Knight hasn't even mentioned himself, but that's the trick. Obviously, if only subconsciously, he's not really talking about John Havlicek superseding Lucas; he's talking about himself superseding Havlicek and Lucas both.

The best thing that ever happened to Knight was that after high school—he's still the greatest star ever to come out of Orrville, Ohio—he didn't amount to a hill of beans as a player. Knight the failed hero has not only served as the challenge for Knight the coach, but also

Knight the disappointed hero is the model for the Everyplayer Knight coaches. That boy was limited, self-centered, frustrated, a pouter, then a bitcher, ultimately a back-biter against his coach, Fred Taylor, who once called Knight "the Brat from Orrville."

The one thing Knight could do was shoot, a strange low-trajectory shot that was deadly against zones when he had the time to get it off. To this day, no Knight team has ever set up in a zone defense. It's like Groucho Marx, who once said he didn't want to be part of any club that would have him as a member.

Although Knight only started two games in three years on the Buckeye varsity, he was a major figure on the team, something of a clubhouse lawyer and a practical joker (which he still is). Dragon and a roommate led the Buckeyes in hustling tickets, and he stunned his wide-eyed teammates with his brash high jinks. On a trip to New York he boldly swiped a couple of bottles of wine from Mamma Leone's restaurant, and not only pilfered a few ties from a midtown shop, but with the contraband under his coat, he went over to a cop who entered the store at that moment and started chatting him up.

There is little Knight's players can put over on him because he did just about all of it himself. Taylor wasn't the only coach Knight challenged, either. In his senior year at Orrville, he defied the school's new coach by refusing to leave a game for a substitute and was booted off the squad. Although subsequently reinstated, he found that season so unsatisfying that he gave up his baseball eligibility to barnstorm with an all-star basketball team in the spring. "I regret that more than anything I've ever done," he says, because he could hit a baseball and hit with power. Knight probably would've been better at baseball than he was at basketball.

Knight was also a pretty fair football end, and as he should've been a baseball player, so, by temperament, he would have made a better football coach. Wilkinson, Bryant, Hayes, Schembechler, Paterno and Royal are all friends and/or models of his, and he has a tape of Lombardi exhortations, plus a Lombardi polemic hanging on his office wall. And, like football coaches, Knight devotes himself to studying film, back and forth, over and over, like some Buddhist monk with his prayer wheel.

In the dazzle of the tight arena, basketball coaches tend to be popinjays, ruling by force of personality, glint of teeth, while football

coaches are distant, solid sorts, administrators, with scores of lieuten-
ants and troops. Being a basketball coach doesn't seem to prepare you
for anything else in life, but even football coaches who can't win get
bumped upstairs to assistant athletic director (a football coach who
wins becomes athletic director). "I've always thought there's a greater
depth to football coaches," Knight says.

But that's subsidiary to the main point: Knight loves all coaches.
He will ask people who knew Rupp well to tell him about the old
man. What made the Baron tick? Why did he do this? How? He has
spent many hours listening to Sparky Anderson. He calls in the old
basketball masters and studies at their feet. In his office, the only photographs (apart from those of his teams) are of Pete Newell and Clair
Bee. Even as a boy, he would go off on scouting trips with coaches.
Bill Shunkwiler, his football coach at Orrville, remembers that after
school, when other kids were hanging out, chasing, Bobby would
come by Shunkwiler's house and the two of them would sit and have
milk and cookies and talk coach talk. Knight still keeps in touch with
many of his old coaches, still calls them "Mister," and there is, in
Coach Knight, almost a tribal sense of heritage and tradition.

"I just love the game of basketball so," he says. "The game! I don't
need the 18,000 people screaming and all the peripheral things. To
me, what's most enjoyable is the practice and preparation."

The ultimate contradiction is that Bobby Knight, of all people,
profane as he is, seeks after purity. What troubles him is that the
game must be muddied by outlanders and apostates—the press, for
example. In fact, Knight has studied the subject, and he understands
the press better than some writers who cover him understand basketball. He even numbers several writers as friends, and sometimes he
will actually offer a grudging admiration beyond his famous institu-
tional assessment: "All of us learn to write by the second grade, then
most of us go on to other things." But his truest feelings were probably
revealed one day recently when he blurted out, "How do they know
what it's like if they've never played? How? *How?* Tell me: How can
they know?"

At the base of everything, this is it: if you're not part of basketball,
you can't really belong, you can only distort. He has taken over the
microphone at Assembly Hall, the Hoosiers' arena, and told his own

fans to back off, be good sports, even to stop using dirty words. Imagine, Knight telling people to improve their language. "It showed no bleeping class," he snapped afterward.

He just always wanted to be Coach Knight, officially expressing this desire in an autobiography he wrote when he was a junior in high school. It was entitled *It's Been A Great Life (So Far)*. Nancy Knight remembers nothing otherwise: "All Bobby ever wanted was to be a coach, in the Big Ten." Even now, when Knight deliberates on the rest of his life, he doesn't go much beyond his one love. "I hope," he says, "that when I retire I'll have enough assistants in head jobs so I can live anywhere I want and still have a place nearby where I can go over and help out and watch some films." As much as there is such a thing, he's a natural-born coach.

III: OLDER PEOPLE

Knight's father—his square name was Carroll, but everyone called him Pat—was a railroad man from Oklahoma, who came to Orrville because it was a railroad town, a division point. The main Pennsy line passed through, and the city slickers from Cleveland and Akron had to journey down on a spur to little Orrville to catch the Broadway Limited. So, despite having only about 5,000 folks when Bobby was growing up, Orrville was not quite as closed and homogeneous as you would expect of a Midwest coloring-book place, set in a dell, with a water tower.

Knight was born there, one of the last of the Depression Babies, on Oct. 25, 1940, a couple of weeks before FDR won his third term over Wendell Willkie and the objections of the Orrville electorate. He was reared in the '50s. Actually, the '50s were not much different in attitudes and values from the two decades that preceded them, but what sets the '50s apart is that they came right before the upheaval of the '60s. But just as the '60s flowered, Knight went off to coach at West Point, where his '50s just kept on going, even becoming sort of a badge of separation.

The '50s are too often disparaged for being simple, everyone in lockstep. But more accurately, what the '50s offered, in spades, was definition. In analyzing pre-'60s coaches like the unrepentant Knight, observers tend to confuse definition with discipline. Knight most of all wants to know where people stand—and that they do stand for something. Here's an example of how rigidly lines were drawn when Knight was growing up.

Shunkwiler takes out a copy of the 1958 *MemORRies*, the high school yearbook when Knight was a senior, and peruses the photographs of the boys, skipping the ones with pompadours, stopping on the ones who, like Bobby, wore crew cuts: "Athlete . . . athlete . . . athlete . . . ," he says. He comes to yet another boy with short hair. "Not an athlete." And hastily, "But a good kid." It was that easy then. More than one-third of the 200 or so boys were involved in athletics. Many of these were also involved in girls, too, but only *in their place*. If a coach so much as saw one of his players holding hands, he would bark out: "Hey, no skin-to-skin!"

The coach, you see, was a giant of a man in this well-defined culture. Shunkwiler recalls that if a coach was notified by a teacher that one of his players was causing a problem, the coach would take the boy aside and, presto, "That would be the end of the trouble." Jack Graham, another of Knight's Orrville basketball coaches, once kicked Bobby out of practice. Knight didn't head to the locker room, though; he waited patiently in the hallway so he could see Coach as soon as practice ended. "Bobby understood," Graham says. "I told him, 'There's only one man who can be the boss out there, and, Bobby, that's the coach.'"

Early this season Knight purposely overreacted one day so that he could boot his star, sophomore Guard Isiah Thomas, out of practice. He needed to show the kid, and the whole team, that there can be no exceptions. Some things don't change. Coach Knight can throw his star out at Indiana University as sure as Coach Graham could at Orrville High. On the team, on the court, time is frozen; *it's been a great life (so far)*.

What Knight didn't learn from his coaches came by example from his father, though theirs was an unusual relationship. The father and son weren't buddies, which has led some people to conclude that Knight's deep affection for older coaches is a manifestation of a perpetual search for a father figure. To some extent this analysis may be true, but the relationships in the Knight household were more complex than that analysis suggests.

Bobby was born six years into a marriage that had come late in life. Though he was an only child, he had a companion at home—his maternal grandmother, Sarah Henthorne. "A classy lady—the love of Bobby's life," says Pauline Boop, who was Knight's childhood next-door neighbor and remains his friend. No wonder he gets along so well with older people; he grew up in a house full of them.

Both of Knight's parents worked—Pat on the railroad, Hazel as an elementary school teacher—and although they were loving, they weren't enthusiastic about the thing their only son loved the most, basketball. But at least Knight always had an ally in his grandmother. She was the one who followed his basketball closely. No matter what the hour, when Bobby came home he would go and kiss her good night. "I think he was closer to his grandmother than he ever was to me or his father," says the widowed Hazel Knight, who still lives in the house on North Vine Street, across the field from the high school where Bobby starred for the Orrville Red Riders.

Knight came home for spring vacation of his sophomore year at Ohio State, right after the Buckeyes had won the national championship. One day he returned to the house in the afternoon, and his grandmother was sitting there in her favorite chair. She had gone shopping in the morning and was tired. It took a while before Bobby realized that she wasn't napping, that she was dead. He remembers it very well: "She was just sitting there. Her legs were crossed at the ankles." Knight's grandmother had been sick all winter, and there are those in Orrville who say she willed herself to stay alive until the season was over and her beloved Bobby could come home from his basketball to see her. It was during the next two seasons he had all the trouble with Fred Taylor.

Knight's father died a decade later, when Bobby was 29. In those 29 years, Pat Knight owned only three automobiles. Most places, he walked. He rarely tipped; "Nobody tips me," he would say. The only thing he ever bought on time was the house on North Vine Street. And he hated to do that. He took out a 20-year mortgage and paid it off in 4-1/2 years. He gave up golf and many other pleasures until he could square accounts. Now, you see, now we are talking about discipline. "My father was the most disciplined man I ever saw," Bobby Knight says. "Most people, they hear the word discipline, and right away they think about a whip and a chair. I've worked up my own definition. And this took a long time. Discipline: doing what you have to do, and doing it as well as you possibly can, and doing it that way all the time."

Pat Knight was very hard-of-hearing, which limited his communications with his son. He would turn off his hearing aid every night and read the evening paper, front to back. "And he believed every word he read," Knight says emphatically, explaining why he becomes so distraught when the press fails to meet his expectations. Pat also introduced his son to hunting and fishing, and to this day that's Bobby's escape. There are no outsiders to louse it up; it's as pure, God willing, as basketball should be.

"People are always surprised when they hear about my fishing," he says. "Everybody thinks I'm going to get so wound up I'm going to have to leave in five minutes. But I don't carry over that stuff you see on the court. There's nothing I enjoy more than winding down some river, floating along, watching for deer, counting the squirrels." A warm smile, a pause, and then: "And nobody knows what you've done that day except you and the guys involved."

IV: WOMEN

This particular day, he had been away, hunting down in southern Indiana with some of the guys. Nancy had a meeting to attend in the evening, but she passed it up, because Bobby was late getting back. She cooked a huge, scrumptious dinner, but apparently that's standard fare at the Knights'.

Whatever other ambiguities Knight has to deal with in these cloudy times, Nancy isn't one of them. "She's just a great coach's wife," he says. She knows her man, too, knows not to intrude on the game. When Indiana won the NCAA in Philadelphia in 1976, Knight and some old friends from basketball and Orrville went out to dinner afterward—the victory celebration, the culmination of his career. Neither Nancy nor any other woman was included.

Says Steve Green, one of Knight's better players, who graduated in 1975, "He feels women are just an obstacle that must be overcome. Players' girl friends didn't really exist for him. Just didn't exist. If he heard me talking to someone about my wedding, he'd be yelling, 'Don't do it! Don't do it!'"

It is instructive that Knight's language seldom goes beyond the anal stage. In the course of a day, he describes an incredible number of things being done to the derriere: it's burned, chewed out, kicked, frosted, blistered, chipped at, etc. Plus, almost every time he loses his temper, there is invariably a literal bottom line, involving the suggestion that the posterior be used as a depot—for money, a whistle, the Time and Life Building, what have you. But, when addressing the fairer sex, Knight has a reputation for purposely expanding his anatomical vocabulary to include graphic references to the male genitalia. This curious proclivity has offended people of both sexes and, perhaps more than anything, has tarnished his personal reputation.

One of Knight's heroes is Harry S. Truman, which is why Give-'em-hell Harry is conspicuously honored by bric-a-brac in Knight's office. But this graphic assessment of another president, Lyndon Johnson, by columnist William S. White, is eerily applicable to Knight: "His shortcomings were not the polite, pleasant little shortcomings, but the big ones—high temper, of course, too driving a personality, both of others and himself, too much of a perfectionist by far . . . Curiously enough I think one of the reasons he didn't go down better . . . was that his faults were highly masculine and that our society is becoming increasingly less masculine; that there's a certain femininity about our society that he didn't fit into."

On the subject of Bobby and women, Nancy Knight demurs: "I certainly couldn't have been married more than 17 years to a man who hates women. But I can understand how Bobby feels about some of them. I believe a woman should try and stay in the home. I've never been anything but very happy and satisfied to spend my life raising a family."

Nancy is, really, the only woman who ever came from the outside into Knight's life. She isn't pretentious, and their sprawling house, hidden in the woods just outside of Bloomington, is warm and comfortable. But those who would deal glibly in harsh housewife stereotypes must be careful. Everyone who knows the Knights well has the same one secret: Nancy influences Bobby *more than you ever would guess*.

Like many coaches, she often speaks for her husband in the first person plural—"We got the job at West Point"—but in neither a proprietary nor insecure way. He has the court, she has the home. It's defined.

Nancy acknowledges that Bobby's disputes with the press may well be exacerbated by her overreaction to criticism of him. "I read about this ogre," she says, "and he's the gentlest, kindest person to his family. He does so much good everywhere, I just can't stand to see the man I love being torn apart."

It would also seem that Bobby is equally protective of Nancy. His seemingly exaggerated responses in two major controversies may be traced in part to the fact that Nancy was involved peripherally in each. His protracted altercation with this magazine [*Sports Illustrated*] centers on disputes he has had with Senior Writer Curry Kirkpatrick, who did a piece on the Hoosiers in 1975. But Nancy was also personally wounded by a throwaway line of Kirkpatrick's, just as she had been by a passing reference another *SI* writer, Barry McDermott, made in an earlier article. In trying to humorously mock Knight's martinetism, McDermott suggested that the Hoosier players had gone over to the coach's house for a holiday meal of bread and water. Nancy, who prides herself on being a gracious hostess and accomplished cook, took the crack literally. "I cried and cried," she says.

Then there were the 1979 Pan Am Games. Puerto Rico was, in many respects, an accident waiting to happen. Those who know Knight best say the episode traumatized him, and while he's a chatterbox, he talks compulsively on this subject. And he still won't give an inch. "There is no way I was going down there and turn the other cheek," he says. "If there was trouble, I was ready to give it right back to them. The first day we were down there, they burned some American flags. There was tremendous resentment toward the United States, tremendous hostility. Listen, America means a lot to me. If the guy . . ."

What guy?

"The *Guy*. If The Guy says tomorrow, hey, this country is in trouble and it needs you in this position or that one, then I give up coaching tomorrow and go."

So, even before the officious San Juan policeman threatened him—cursing him, poking at him—Knight was simmering. Then he became concerned for the safety of Nancy and his two sons. "It was terrifying," she says. "We had to change apartments. I couldn't sit in my seat at the games. I had to stay at the press table. I feared for my life and my children's."

However Knight behaved in Puerto Rico—"You have no respect for anybody. You treat us like dirt. You are an embarrassment to America, our country. You are an Ugly American," a Puerto Rican sports official snapped at him after the Pan Am basketball final—it must be understood that Knight perceived, correctly or not, that the three things he values most in his life were being menaced—his family, his country and his team.

V: PLAYERS

Late in his senior year at Ohio State, Knight considered a job at a high school in Celina, Ohio, as the coach of basketball and an assistant in football. He liked the place, but walking back across the school's gridiron, he kicked at the turf and shook his head. "I thought, if I'm going to be a basketball coach, I can't be diverted," he says. "I wanted vertical concentration. That's still the essence of my coaching." So he took a lesser job as a basketball assistant, without any football responsibility, in Cuyahoga Falls, Ohio. In his first game as head coach of the 10th-graders, he broke a clipboard.

Intensity?

A year later, with Taylor's help, the Brat from Orrville got the assistant's post at West Point under Tates Locke, enlisting in the Army to qualify for the job. When Locke left in 1965, the brass stunned everybody by giving Pfc. Knight the job. "I've never had any apologies for being a head coach at 24," he says. "I was making $99 a month then. I have no sympathy for people who don't make progress because they won't accept the pay somewhere."

Money has never motivated Knight. He has turned down raises, preferring that the money go to his assistants, and he professes not even to know what his salary is—except that, relative to what other teachers at Indiana make, it's too much. This is not to say, of course, that Knight wears a hair shirt. He has a television show, a summer basketball camp, the free use of a car, and, he volunteers, Checkers-like, "I did take a fishing rod once." Also, it's an absolute point of pride with him that he must be paid as much as the Hoosier football coach, Lee Corso. But just as pointedly he has advised alumni and the commercial camp-followers who grubstake coaches on the side to take a wide berth. Recently, however, Knight decided he was a fool to look a gift horse in the mouth, so he solicited bids from shoe companies that were willing to pay him in the hope that his players would wear their sneakers. Adidas won, but instead of sticking this "pimp money," as he calls it, in his own pocket, Knight is turning it over to the university.

This isn't going to endear Knight to the coach who's looking to put a new Florida room on the house, just as a lot of Knight's colleagues weren't thrilled two years ago when he kicked three players off his team for abuses of training rules (drugs, obviously), and then trumpeted that he was the only coach extant with the "guts" to live up to his principles. But his honor even exceeds his smugness. "He just doesn't cheat," says Newell. "Never. Bobby doesn't even rationalize. Instead, what he does do is the single most important thing in coaching: he turns out educated kids who are ready for society."

Now Knight is on an even broader crusade, trying to impose on others, by legislation, his devotion to academics. He would like the NCAA to pass a regulation that would deny a college some of its allotment of athletic scholarships if its players don't graduate within a year after their eligibility ends. That is, if a coach has five so-called student-athletes finishing up on the team in 1981 and only two graduate by 1982, then the coach can only replace the five with two new recruits. "With this, you're making the faculty a police department for the NCAA," Knight says. "Even if you can get a few professors to pimp for a coach, you can't buy a whole damn faculty." He laughs, devilishly. "And how can a coach vote against this plan? How can anyone vote publicly against education?"

Nothing pleases Knight as much as the success his players have had off the court. Indeed, he uses their accomplishments to justify the controversial "way we operate," saying, "Look, if all our players were losing jobs, I'd have to reassess my way. And if I heard some of my old players blistering my ass for the way I run things, I'd have to reassess. But, you see, despite all the crap you read, the only ones who've ever complained are the kids who didn't play, got frustrated and quit."

But, tit for tat, it may also be true that Knight's players have a high success rate because only success-oriented types would select Indiana basketball in the first place. In other words, the twigs only grow as they were bent a long time ago.

Knight's honesty extends to his recruiting. When a recruit is brought to Bloomington, he's introduced to the whole squad, and not merely sequestered with a happy star, a Mr. Personality and a pretty cheerleader. Parents of recruits are encouraged to talk with parents of present squad members. Knight doesn't have a missionary instinct. He isn't, he says, "an animal trainer. Recruit jackasses, they play like jackasses." Instead: "We've drawn up a personality profile, and you might even say it's a narrow-minded thing."

So, black or white, rich or poor, the neatly groomed Indiana players tend to be well-intentioned young things, upwardly mobile, serious about education and so well adjusted that they can endure Coach Knight's wrath in fair exchange for the bounty of his professional genius. Calculated coach, calculated players.

The hand-picked Hoosiers are expected to speak to the press, even in defeat, the better to mature and cope. They dress in coats and ties on game days, and during the season must wear trim haircuts, without beards or mustaches.

Significantly, things have gone awry only since the national championship season, soon after which a number of players quit, some castigating Knight, and two seasons after that when the coach bounced the three players for disciplinary reasons. "All of a sudden I won, and I thought I could be a social worker, too," he says. "I thought I could take a guy off death row at Sing Sing and turn him into a basketball player." Never again. The prime result of that convulsion has been an even more careful weeding-out process. A single blackball from a team member can eliminate a prospect from consideration, and as a consequence, a sort of natural selection of the species has occurred. The system has become so inbred that, as contradictory as this sounds, rough-tough Knight's team now includes a bunch of nice Nellys. The Hoosier basketball coaches all worried about this even before this rather disappointing season—Indiana was 10–6 at the end of last week—confirmed their fears. Knight himself, like a grizzled old soldier, waxes nostalgic about the single-minded roughnecks who chopped their way to victory for him at the Point.

Had Knight never won a game at Indiana, he would have secured a lasting reputation for his work at Army, where he succeeded with little talent and no height. At Indiana, as well, the mark of Knight as coach goes far beyond his mere W–L totals. When he arrived in Bloomington, the entire Big Ten played run-and-gun, in the image of Indiana, the conference's traditional lodestar: racehorse ball, the

Hurryin' Hoosiers. It wasn't just a catchy sports nickname. It was a real statement. The Hurryin' Hoosiers. The Bronx Bombers. The Monsters of the Midway. There aren't many of them. But no matter how much the old alumni whined at the loss of tradition and hittin' a hundred, Knight went his own way. From Knight's arrival through last week, Indiana has gone 215–65, but, more significantly, the average Big Ten score has declined from 74.0 to 67.5 in that span.

His strategic axioms are firm—no zones, disciplined offense—but he exercises latitude year by year, permitting himself to be dictated to by his material and the state of the art. He has such consummate confidence in his ability as a coach that he suffers no insecurity about crediting the sources of his handiwork. It all came from other coaches, didn't it? His defense is based on the old Ohio State pressure game, which Taylor had borrowed from Newell. His offense is an amalgam of the freelancing style used at Princeton in the early '60s, by Butch van Breda Kolff ("The best college coach I ever saw"), intertwined with the passing game that the venerable Hank Iba employed at Oklahoma State.

This season Knight was willing to modify some of his most cherished tenets to permit Isiah Thomas more artistic freedom. But, ultimately, those who would survive at Indiana, much less succeed, must subjugate themselves to the one man and his one way. Incredibly, 10 of Knight's former assistants are head coaches at major colleges, but those who coach under him are strictly that: underlings. Among other things, they aren't allowed to utter so much as a word of profanity before the players. Only Bobby.

He prowls the practice court, slouched, belly out, usually with a sour, disbelieving expression upon his visage. He is dressed in Indiana red and white, but of a different mix-and-match from his assistants'. Except for a few instructions barked out by these subordinates, the place is as silent as a tomb. Only the most privileged visitors are permitted to watch this class.

The chosen few watch on two levels of consciousness: what they see before them, and what they anticipate Coach Knight might do next. If he really contrives to make a point, he will perhaps merely rage, or pick up a chair and slam it against the wall, or dismiss a hopeless athlete. It's like technical fouls—you don't ever get them, you take them. And, like every good coach, Knight knows how to deal with the unexpected. One day a few years ago Knight kicked a ball in anger. He caught it perfectly on his instep and the ball soared toward the very heavens, straight up. More miraculously, when it plummeted back to earth, it fell into a wastebasket, lodging there. It was a million-to-one shot, something from a Road Runner cartoon. But nobody dared change his expression. Finally, Knight began to grin, then to laugh, and only at that point did everyone else break up.

"I've always said, all along, that if I ever get to a point where I can't control myself, I'll quit," Knight says stoutly, though unmindful, perhaps, that he can drive things out of control even as he skirts the edge himself.

VI: MORE RABBITS

John Havlicek once said, "Bobby was quite a split personality. There were times when we were good friends and, then, like that, times when he wouldn't even talk to me." Knight says, "My manners set me apart in a little cocoon, and that's something that's very beneficial to me." Maybe, but too many people humor Knight instead of responding to him, and that may be the single real deprivation of his life.

The one group of people who can still treat him honestly are the older coaches, Dutch uncles, who have earned his respect. A few years ago he took on as an assistant Harold Andreas, the man who had first hired him as an assistant at Cuyahoga Falls. What a wonderful gesture! Andreas retired from coaching in 1977. And so, in Andreas' place as the father/grandmother figure, Knight hired Roy Bates, who used to coach one of Orrville High's rivals. Bates, who recently took a leave of absence because of poor health, is a no-nonsense fellow with a crippled left arm, whose teams were 441–82 in basketball and 476–52 in baseball. Bates adored Knight, and though Knight had three younger assistants, it was the older man he was closest to, literally and otherwise. Bates always sat next to him on the bench.

Still Bates had to be tested, like everyone else. He has had a radio show in Ohio since 1949, and one time a while ago, when he was staying at the Knights', he asked Bobby to do a five-minute tape with him. Bobby said sure, but then he put Bates off and put him off. Finally, one day Bates said, "You know, Bobby, I've had that radio show for 30 years without you on it." And with that, he put on his coat and headed for the car. By the time Bates had started up the driveway, Knight was out there, waving for him to come back, and as soon as Bates arrived back at his home in Ohio, Bobby was on the phone to him. Knight was still in control of himself. But not of events.

"Bobby has got so much," Bates says. "And nobody can ever get him. He doesn't cheat. He doesn't drink. He doesn't even chase women. But for some reason he thinks he has been a bad boy, and no matter how successful he becomes, he thinks he must be punished."

This may be the best clue of all. Certainly, Knight accepts success defensively, if not suspiciously. His office celebrates underdogs like Truman and Lombardi, who weren't expected to triumph but, given the chance, thrived on their own sweet terms. And Patton is in evidence, as you might expect. A mean-spirited quote of his hangs on the wall, keynoting a display—an anthology—of paranoid sentiments.

Patton warns ominously that if you strive for a goal, "your loyal friends [will do] their hypocritical Goddamndest to trip you, blacken you and break your spirit." A flanking prayer advises, "If man thwart you pay no heed/If man hate you have no care. . . ." And an essay entitled "The Penalty of Leadership" warns, "The reward is widespread recognition, the punishment fierce denial and detraction."

Is it really that lonely at the top?

Knight also passes out copies of *If* to visitors.

And yet, as wary as he is of the hypocritical rabbits all around him, Knight is, in many respects, even more unsparing of himself. The game, we hear so often, has passed so-and-so by. With Knight, it may be the reverse; he may have passed it by. But he loves it so, and therefore he must concoct hurdles so that he can still be challenged by it. He even talks a lot about how nobody is really capable of playing the game well. Ultimately, it may be the final irony that the players themselves must become interlopers, separating him from the game.

Already he has gone so far that at age 40 winning is no longer the goal. "Look, I know this," he says. "If you're going to play the game, you're going to get more out of it winning. I know that, sure. Now, at West Point I made up my mind to win—*gotta win*. Not at all costs. Never that. But winning was the hub of everything I was doing. And understand, I've never gotten over West Point. Winning had to be more important there, and I had a point to prove. I was just coming off a playing career during which I didn't do as well as I'd hoped. I had to win. And so, to some extent, I won't change.

"But somewhere I decided I was wrong. You could win and still not succeed, not achieve what you should. And you can lose without really failing at all. But it's harder to coach this way, with this, uh, approach. I'm sure I'd be easier on myself and on other people if just winning were my ultimate objective." He pauses; he is in his study at home, amid his books, away from all the basketball regalia. "I never said much about this before."

It was a good secret. Now, Bobby Knight is one step closer to utter control of his game. Now all those dim-witted rabbits cannot touch him. They'll be looking at the scoreboard and the AP poll, judging him by those, but they won't have a clue, not the foggiest. Nobody holds a mortgage on him. Now, you see, now we are talking about definition.

Nancy says: "People keep asking me if Bobby is mellowing. We're not mellowing. What we are, we're growing up with the game. You've got to remember that not many people get a chance to start coaching in their 20s. We're not mellowing. Growing up is still more of the word for us."

There is still so much time for the Knights to take what is theirs and enjoy it. It can be a great life (someday).

David Bradley

The son of a minister who worked as a historian and journal editor for the African Methodist Episcopal Church, David Bradley (b. 1950) counted himself among the first generation of Bradley men since slavery not to include a preacher. As a child David spent summers accompanying his dad as he drove around the South conducting Christian Ed workshops. Thanks to multiple scholarships, he then made his way from his hometown of Bedford, a largely white farming community in southwestern Pennsylvania, to the University of Pennsylvania, where he met another contributor to this volume, John Edgar Wideman, who became his first writing teacher and a lifelong mentor. After earning a master's at King's College London, Bradley published two novels, the second of which, *The Chaneysville Incident*, won the PEN/Faulkner Award in 1982. That's when *Esquire* asked him to write this profile of Kareem Abdul-Jabbar. Around the same time, Bradley largely abandoned fiction for essays and journalism, which he practiced between gigs in publishing and teaching, including twenty years on the faculty at Temple and another ten at Oregon. When Bradley writes that "the inevitability of [Abdul-Jabbar's] retirement holds more dread for me than for him," his observation is simply that of a fan identifying with his hero. But their respective lives each featured a traumatic loss. Bradley makes brief mention of the 1983 fire that destroyed Abdul-Jabbar's oriental rugs, trophies, and treasured collection of jazz albums; the author had no way of knowing that, decades later, he would be victimized by a similar incident, when a leaky toilet in Bradley's home outside San Diego led to flooding that ruined two thousand books in his library.

The Autumn of the Age of Jabbar

E ARLY DECEMBER 1982. I am seated at the bar of the Tavern on Green, which rests in a gentrified neighborhood a few blocks from the Philadelphia Museum of Art. The Tavern on Green is not normally a sports bar, but tonight there is a late-night telecast from the Coast, where the Philadelphia 76ers are doing battle with the Lakers of Los Angeles.

The last time the two teams met was in the championship series the previous June. Then the Lakers cut in the turbocharger of their Ferrari fast break and cruised over the Sixers as if they were the Pennsylvania Turnpike. The same thing had happened two years before. And so, in Philadelphia, this game is an affair of honor. Which means Philadelphia fans are out for blood.

They believe they will get it. In the off-season the Sixers agreed to pay $13.2 million over the next six years to Moses Malone, formerly of the Houston Rockets. If Malone can neutralize the Laker center, seven-foot-two Kareem Abdul-Jabbar, Philadelphia fans say, this will be the year they've been telling the Lakers to wait until.

This night Malone earns his money, outscoring Jabbar 29 to 15, out-rebounding him 14 to 2. The Sixers triumph by 10 points, and the Tavern on Green resounds with cheers and jeers, most of the latter being directed at the televised image of Jabbar, who, with his incredibly long arms and legs, his knobby knees and elbows, his balding pate, and his bulging protective goggles, looks like a meditative praying mantis.

"Look at him," one watcher snarls. "He loses and he acts like he's bored. He thinks it's a business. And those dumb goggles: What does he have to wear them for? And what is this name business anyway? It's all PR. He's the most overrated player in basketball."

I am a Lakers fan. I have been one since the late Fifties, when Kareem Abdul-Jabbar was a six-foot sixth-grader who answered to the name Ferdinand Lewis Alcindor Jr. And so I launched into a counter-argument from the Kareem Abdul-Jabbar Media Guide: high school all-America who led New York's Power Memorial Academy to a 95–6 record; three times consensus college All-America who powered the UCLA juggernaut to a three-year 88–2 record and three consecutive NCAA championships; in thirteen years as a professional a twelve-time All-Star, six-time league Most Valuable Player, who is the leading active player in points scored, second all-time in that category behind the legendary Wilt "The Stilt" Chamberlain, and almost sure to pass him in a season or two, anchor of three world champion teams, one in Milwaukee, two in L.A., one of only twelve to play on championship teams in two cities. Maybe, I say, if he looks bored it's because he has just about done it all. "What's with him," somebody whispers. "He in love with that Kareem or something?"

Not exactly. But I did hug him once.

SEPTEMBER 1968. I was a freshman in college, preoccupied with freshmen of the opposite sex. One young lady seemed especially friendly and appealing. I made inquiries. "Aw, man, forget it," I was told. "She's been dating Lew Alcindor." I let it go; the competition was overwhelming. Alcindor was athletic, militant, televised, and upsetting to the establishment; the ultimate BMOC credentials for a black in 1968. And he was tall too.

Controversy focused on his eighty-six inches (or was it eighty-eight? There was always a suspicion that he was taller than advertised). It gave him an "unfair" advantage. It would destroy the game. Bill Van Breda Kolff, then the Lakers' coach, who knew he would never get to sign Alcindor and who already had Wilt Chamberlain, suggested that rather than try to bring Alcindor into the NBA, "each team in the league should give him one hundred thousand dollars and tell him to go to the beach."

There was a lot about Alcindor that people found unfair. It was unfair that he had forsaken his high school coach, Jack Donohue, who had moved on to Holy Cross and could surely have used a seven-foot center. (What coach couldn't have used a seven-foot center in 1965?) It was even more unfair that Alcindor should go to UCLA, whose Bruins had already won two consecutive NCAA championships and whose coach, John Wooden, was already established in a Trinity with Red Auerbach and Adolph Rupp.

Of course, UCLA got its comeuppance when, in the exhibition game intended to show off the brand-new Pauley Pavilion and honor Coach Wooden, Alcindor brashly scored 31 points and hauled down 21 rebounds and piloted the freshman team to a 15-point landing on the NCAA-champion varsity. But the comeuppance did not come very far; a year later, in his varsity debut, Alcindor scored 56 points, and Wooden, speaking of the acute anxiety Alcindor must inspire in other coaches, said, "He even frightens me."

That anxiety prompted the NCAA, after Alcindor led the Bruins to an undefeated season and championship, to ban the dunk shot. Nothing was said officially about Alcindor, but unofficially they called it the Alcindor rule and Wooden at the time declared that there was "no question that the rule is designed to curtail the ability of one player." It did not work; Alcindor compensated for the lost dunk with pinpoint passing and a shot he had been using for nearly a decade—what years later would be christened the "skyhook" by sportscaster Eddie Doucette and pronounced by Bill Russell "the prettiest thing in sports." He took the Bruins to two more championships. But by the time they won the second one, he was in trouble with the media.

It was not entirely his fault. His high school coach had put him under a gag order, and the UCLA athletic department applied a similar restraint to the entire freshman team. But somehow the policy was interpreted as being Alcindor's idea, which caused resentment among reporters. And once the ban was lifted, Alcindor's behavior seemed to lend credence to the interpretation. "I hadn't come to school to spend my time buttering up the press," he later said.

Things might have been easier for him if he had. He might have gotten more sympathy during his sophomore year, when anonymous threats against his life were taken seriously enough for UCLA to hire a bodyguard. His physical problems might have been viewed with more understanding; his migraine headaches might have been presented as truly debilitating, rather than as ailments on the order of a hangnail (fortunately Wooden himself was a migraine sufferer, and understood), and the scratched eyeball from which he suffered when UCLA lost its first game in years, to Houston, might have been seen as a legitimate reason for Alcindor's subpar performance, rather than as a lame excuse.

But sometime during his sophomore year his inexperience with the media had led him to speak earnestly but incautiously about his interest in Malcolm X, the teaching of Islam, and his belief that racial hatred was destroying America. It was hardly an unusual manifesto for a college sophomore in 1966 or 1967, but athletes, particularly black college athletes, were not supposed to have such thoughts or fool around with weird foreign religions. (America was still determined to call Muhammad Ali Cassius Clay.) When, in the fall of 1967, it was learned that Alcindor had met with black militant athletes, notably San Jose State track stars Tommie Smith and Lee Evans, to discuss a possible boycott of the U.S. Olympic team, it became clear to much of the public and most of the media that Alcindor was "angry." And so UCLA's loss to Houston and Alcindor's poor performance before a prime-time TV audience satisfied a lot of people politically.

The results of the rematch did not. After UCLA's 32-point win, Alcindor strolled out of the locker room wearing a red, orange, and yellow African robe. "It was my way," he explained later, "of saying I'm black and here it is, man, you can take it or leave it."

It was months before Smith and John Carlos would commit the ultramilitant acts of wearing long black socks and hoisting black-gloved fists during the playing of "The Star-Spangled Banner" at the Mexico City Olympics; Jabbar was the first prominent college athlete to be identified as a "black militant." And by the time Smith and Carlos joined him in the militant ranks, he had gone to a Sunnite mosque on 125th Street and asked for instruction. In late August he had had his *shahada*, a kind of Muslim baptism. He returned to Los Angeles for his senior year not only an angry black but also a Muslim with a name that translated roughly as "generous powerful servant of Allah": Kareem Abdul-Jabbar.

And then, just before his first professional season, Jabbar sold his story to *Sports Illustrated*. What he told confounded the expectations of a goodly chunk of America.

His childhood had not been the mass media–produced black experience with poverty, illiteracy, unemployment, cultural deprivation, rats, roaches, and drugs as standard equipment. His father was a graduate of the Juilliard School of Music and an avid reader; Jabbar's youth had been full of music, his home crowded with a "zillion" books. That home had not been a "ghetto" railroad flat; he was raised in a predominantly white housing project in the grassy precincts of northern Manhattan—his bedroom overlooked not a garbage-strewn alley, but the cool beauty of the Cloisters museum. His was not the stereotypical saga of endless hours working just on flashy moves, dreaming only of being a professional basketball player—he had wanted to be an architect. He had lost respect for his high school coach, who exploited his name and once used the word *nigger* as a motivational device. He had "more important things" on his mind than the loss that ended Power Memorial's seventy-one-game winning streak. He had not only dated a white co-ed, *he* had broken off the relationship because it "wasn't worth having both our lives wrecked by all this pressure." His first car had been a Mercedes-Benz. He not only thought John Wooden, the "Wizard of Westwood," made occasional mistakes in coaching, he believed Wooden's midwestern morality constituted a personality flaw. And even with a professional contract that one reporter characterized as giving him "the entire eastern half of Wisconsin plus the Strategic Air Command" and while standing on the brink of what everybody who knew the sport admitted could be one of the most spectacular careers in the history of basketball, he was looking beyond to what he would do when he finished. "What I really want to do," he said, "is play ten or twelve years in the NBA, see what I can do there against the big guys. Then I'll go back to more normal things."

All of that was bad enough. But Jabbar admitted to the sin for which no black can be forgiven: once upon a time he hated white people.

LATE APRIL 1982. It is a heady time if you are a Lakers fan. The team has done a number on the Western Conference of the NBA, winning its division by five games, bettering the record of the winner of the other division by nine. The team has a few days' rest while also-rans quarrel in the preliminaries of the play-offs. The rest could be all-important. It has been a long season, and Kareem Abdul-Jabbar has just turned thirty-five.

That is a fact the media have been making much of. For Jabbar is at a dramatic point in his career. He has played his "ten or twelve" seasons, but he could play a few more. He may have lost a step or two, but then, he always had a step or two to give. And so his path lies somewhere in the strip of badlands that lies between "veteran player" and "too damned old," and the vultures are gathering above him.

To make it more dramatic, Jabbar seems to have changed, to have become willing to risk some of his austere dignity. He has appeared in a comic motion picture, *Airplane*, and engaged in a little good-natured one-on-one with his critics. He has clowned around for *Sports Illustrated*'s cameras. He has signed a contract for an autobiography. Some people say that all this Jabbarian jocularity has to do with the possibility that, after the 1982–1983 season, he may become a thirty-six-year-old free agent, in search of a team and a city, in need of all the good exposure he can get. Others say he's mellowing with age.

On April 16, his birthday, Lakers coach Pat Riley gives him a present and lets him sit out the last half of a meaningless game. Two days later, during the telecast of the season's final game, broadcasters Bill Russell and Dick Stockton make note of that, and make repeated reference to Jabbar's age. He is, they agree, still a dominant factor, which isn't bad for a thirty-five-year-old. They mean it as a gruff masculine tribute, but to me it seems patronizing, as if he were some kind of toothless senior citizen remarkable because, despite approaching senility, he can still play the kazoo. I am a little sensitive about Jabbar's age. We are of a generation.

Which accounts for my presence in Los Angeles. I see Jabbar as my representative on the court, the visible presence of the experiences of my youth, and I want to know what I should make of this change. I want to know if it is a good thing.

The next day, I drive up Sunset Boulevard, to Jabbar's home in Bel Air, hardly a mansion by anybody's standards. Jabbar opens his own front door wearing a Dodgers T-shirt. He asks me to remove my shoes in deference to the umpety-ump thousand dollars' worth of Oriental rugs that cover the floors and lie piled beside the well-used fireplace. Jabbar sits down on the couch, his knees bending to an amazingly acute angle. On one of them he balances his nineteen-month-old son, Amir. It occurs to me that Jabbar is using Amir as a shield.

Jabbar knows where I went to school and asks if I ever ran into the young woman I admired as a freshman. The only thing he can think of that his early involvement with basketball cost him was the opportunity for "dealing with the ladies while I was in high school." It is something he has said before. But when I shift the subject to something he has spoken of so often he should have gone to sleep, the glory of the dynasty and whether it could ever happen again, at UCLA or elsewhere, he adds a new element to the answer: "It could happen. There's a lot of pressure for it *not* to. When I was a senior in high school, I just took the whole southeastern part of the country and cut that off the map. And good black athletes from that part of the country either had to go to a black school or they'd leave, they'd go to the Big Ten, they'd come out here. The athletic programs in the Big Ten and out here benefited from Jim Crow a lot. Once that was over, you had those guys staying at home, and the basketball teams in that area of the country have improved."

He says it very coolly, as if it were an analysis of ancient history, rather than a force that shaped his life. I ask him about his "white hating" period, which, ironically, was at its apex years before he was branded a militant. Again he speaks of it coolly, citing as a cause the events of the civil rights movement: "Watching all those freedom rides and stuff on television, I'll never forget the people on the Pettus Bridge [outside Selma, Alabama]. I watched that. And then when they blew up that church in Birmingham, that really freaked me out." He resists the idea that there was anything more personal, even though, back in 1969, he spoke of racist slights that caused him to tell his light-skinned mother that he hated every drop of white blood in her, and in himself. Now, two decades after that incident, he dismisses the slights as minor and speaks of a bus trip he took. "When I was in high school my mother sent me down to Goldsboro, North Carolina, to be my family's representative at a graduation. And I saw it all. Black water fountains. So-and-so's white grocery. The whole thing with Jim Crow was right there for me to see, as soon as we got past Washington, D.C."

He mentions that trip not to explain his own feelings, but as part of a demonstration of his belief that things have changed. "Now," he says, "I play with a guy named Norman Nixon. He's from as far down south as you can get, as far as I'm concerned. He didn't really have to deal with that type of discrimination. So I know things have changed." Now he says that the change in his name, which seemed so crucial to everyone back in 1969, was not that big a deal, that he could have kept body and soul together as Lew Alcindor. "It wouldn't have been any problem. But at that time I really wanted to assert my own identity, not one that was dropped on me by the slave trader Alcindor." Now, although "certain aspects of American racism are very intractable," he says, "my frustration comes from dealing with black people, who could, at this point, do a lot for themselves and still don't . . . the whole idea of economic cooperation and political activism that can definitely make the system work for black people and black people don't seem to be taking advantage of it. I think survival has been the only issue; once they know they're going to survive, they slack off. That depresses me a lot." That statement, I say, could get him into trouble. He snorts disdainfully. "With who?" With almost everybody, I tell him. "It's true," he says. For him, that ends the matter.

There are similar limits on his involvement in the political and social implications of the statement. "I have a responsibility to my family," he says flatly. "The greater responsibility to the quote, black community, unquote, sometimes I don't see it. That is what all black people should shoulder."

Jabbar is shouldering other things: he is working on a book about Oriental rugs; he wants to write portions of his autobiography himself, even though he gets along well with his co-author, Peter Knobler, with whom he shares a philosophy: "Pete said we could do it well or we could do it quick. So we're going to try and do it well."

That, I realize, is a key to Jabbar; he is searching always for a kindred spirit, someone with a philosophy based on self-control, discipline, patience. It explains why, on the court, he often seems like a man doing business. He does think that part of it is business. "As soon as you come to write about it, or CBS puts it on the tube, it becomes a business." It has been so for him for a long time: "Basketball started paying bills for me early on. I got my high school tuition because I got a basketball scholarship, and that's when you really become a professional." But as far as he's concerned, "the guys that play in the Y leagues, that's the real essence of the sport."

His philosophy also explains why he was able to play for John Wooden at UCLA, despite his belief, expressed in 1969, that "whenever Coach Wooden had to deal with somebody a little different from the norm, he blew the case."

"Coach Wooden," Jabbar says now, "wasn't focused on getting us all crazy. . . . He could control the emotion and use it. . . ." The appreciation for such a disciplined approach no doubt originated in Jabbar's childhood—his father was a hardworking transit policeman who spent his free time reading and studying music—but he draws his guidance "from a lot of different sources," one of which is the seventeenth-century samurai warrior Miyamoto Musashi, author of the philosophical classic *A Book of Five Rings: A Guide to Strategy*. "In strategy," wrote Musashi, "your spiritual bearing must not be any different from normal. Both in fighting and in everyday life you should be determined though calm. . . . Be neither insufficiently spirited nor over-spirited. . . . Do not let the enemy see your spirit."

But Jabbar, a child of the eclectic Sixties, does not limit himself to one source of wisdom. He had learned from not only Musashi and, of course, the prophet Muhammad, but Hammurabi and George Patton. "I admire him a lot," Jabbar says of Patton. "He was all the way, totally committed. In order to do well at anything you have to be really committed or else have a tremendous gift that compensates for a lack of commitment. But I think he had both." That his admiration for Patton, among other things, puts him at odds with the image of him many hold is a thought he relishes: "I've messed up a lot of people's concept of image," he says happily. "It's nice being underestimated in one area and then being able to show off."

It is, I realize, a game he plays with the business about aging. He speaks of the end of his career in words so stock they seem rehearsed, albeit sincere: "I just want to finish with some dignity and try to live up to the standards I've set for myself. I've kept body and soul together and I think I can do it for another year or two. I'm testing myself to see how long I can do it as well." He grins. "I'm not losing enough to make my opponents happy."

But as I look at him I see what no grin can conceal: Jabbar is achingly tired. Tired from a long season, a long career. In 1969 he said, "I was nine years old and five feet four inches tall—the pattern of my life was set. I operated on a cycle, and the cycle was based on the basketball season. . . . All life revolves around it, like a biological clock." It has been that way, I estimate, for twenty-five or twenty-six years. "Twenty-seven," he corrects. When I suggest that he will not be playing in ten more, he says, "Let's hope not." And when he is finished with basketball he intends to get far, far away: "I've had too much of this. I've already lost enough years off my life."

MID-NOVEMBER 1982. The Lakers are world champions. Last spring they romped over all opponents, spinning out a string of play-off victories that betters the five-game streak of the 1970–1971 Milwaukee Bucks— who had a point guard named Oscar Robertson and a center named Kareem Abdul-Jabbar—and equals the longest in NBA history.

A decade after his first championship Jabbar is a dragon rampant on a hardwood field. His statistics in the play-offs put him fourth on the team in assists; third in offensive rebounds; second in defensive rebounds; first in shots blocked, with forty-five; first in scoring, with an average of 20.4 points per game. He is still, as Peter Axthelm puts it, "the lord of the sky," still, as *The New York Times* headlines it, GRAND MASTER OF THE PLAYOFFS, and still the best way to guard him, as former coach John Kerr says, is to "get real close and breathe on his goggles."

But there are things breathing down his neck, too. In the championship series migraines hampered his performance in two games. In game five he scored fewer than 10 points for the first time in 379 games. His overall scoring average was nearly 9 points below his career play-off average.

Now, in the infancy of the 1982–1983 season, that is cause for thought. The Lakers are a young team, so loaded with talent they add only one player, the number-one draft choice, James Worthy. You might speculate that they could get along without a center who is only a year or so younger than the NBA itself. In Los Angeles they are so speculating. One writer, Doug Ives, of the Long Beach *Press-Telegram*, has even found a way to blame Jabbar if the Lakers lose while he has a good game: Jabbar shoots too much. "Of all the Lakers," Ives wrote, "Kareem shows the most disappointment when he makes a move to get the ball and then it isn't passed to him." The criticism is so naive and illogical as to be insignificant. What may be significant is that it is reprinted in a Laker game program, making me wonder if perhaps the "we'd be better off without Jabbar" notion (which is nothing new) is not something the management would just as soon have floating in the backs of fans' minds.

For at the beginning of this, the final year before Jabbar becomes a free agent, the Lakers have not signed him to a new contract. That is probably shrewd business—under NBA rules, the Lakers can retain Jabbar simply by matching the best offer he gets elsewhere—but it seems a bit disrespectful. He has helped the Lakers to two championships in three years. All he wants, rumor has it, is the two-million-plus a year that Moses Malone, who has never helped anybody to a championship, is already getting. I am worried that the grueling season, the uncertainty, and the criticisms may wear him down.

And so, when the season is still young, before the showdown with the rebuilt Sixers, I go again to Los Angeles, to take Jabbar to dinner and see how he is.

He is tired. The night before I see him, after a road game, he had a shot of rum to help him sleep. He is not a drinker, and the unfamiliar alcohol propelled him to the altitude of the cheap seats and kept him in orbit there all night. Now he sits yawning in the shambles of his living room, amid a slow avalanche of leaking helium-filled balloons. Amir has had a party for his second birthday, a patented Bel Air affair complete with clowns and ponies and a choice of regular hot dogs and chicken franks, for those toddlers into modified vegetarianism.

But Jabbar's tired is a different kind than that which I detected at the end of the previous season. He is enthusiastic about the Lakers' chance to repeat as champions, something that hasn't been done in all the years he has been in the league. He is excited about his new teammate, James Worthy, and his old teammates—he is quick to point out that Worthy's is the only face that is new. He is not depressed or worried about the migraine problem; he thinks he has it cured. "Allergies," he says firmly. "I just eliminated certain things from my diet and the doctor gave me an acupuncture treatment and I haven't had any problem." Now he speculates that he could be in the game five years from now, if he still needs the challenge, citing as an example Muhammad Ali: "If Ali had stayed in shape . . . if he'd kept involved in it and fought once or twice a year, or whatever, he'd still be the best."

It is clear the off-season has invigorated him, with days of rest in Hawaii and the stimulation of a trip to China. There Jabbar found a society of a style and a philosophy close to his own. "I liked seeing how, just through sheer force of will and discipline and application, these people went from a feudal society to a twentieth-century society in like thirty-five years," he says. "The Chinese are a very self-sufficient people, and if they are going to proclaim communism—they stressed this to everybody, especially the Soviets—it's going to have to make sense to them and not to be ironclad bound to traditions. . . ."

Suddenly I hear him talking not about China but about himself. What was always important was that the thing make sense, not to anybody else, but to him, at the time. Once it made sense to change his name. And once it made sense to deal with the world as he once said he dealt with problems at UCLA: "Ever since my childhood I had this ability to draw into myself and be perfectly contented. I *had* to. I had always been such a minority of one. Very tall. Black. Catholic. I had made an adjustment to being a minority of one and now I said to myself I was going back to that."

And now it makes sense to open up even with regard to something as personal as an autobiography. For although Jabbar insists that it was important that his co-writer be black, he accepted Knobler, who is, as one of his editors put it, "the only white guy Kareem would work with." Once there would not have been one.

"I've changed my approach to people and to situations," Jabbar says. "It's time. I think I was overprotective of something . . . of my privacy, the absolute conviction that I would be misunderstood. But that's inevitable. Maybe I've acquired some wisdom and learned to be pragmatic as I've matured. My convictions are the same. But we have to learn how to deal in the world, this world, the real world."

Later I meet up with one of the reasons "it was time": Cheryl Pistono, Amir's mother and Jabbar's companion for the last few years. Cheryl, at first glance, seems to exhibit the worst qualities of the "sports wife"—pushiness, nosiness, overprotectiveness, bossiness. But a second glance reveals she's not trying to control, she is trying to take care, albeit of everything and everybody in sight. She has organized Amir's party like the Normandy invasion. ("Cheryl," Jabbar says gently, "I think we may be spoiling Amir.")

As I watch the two of them, five-foot-four-inch Cheryl playing terrier to Jabbar's greyhound, I wonder which came first, really, Cheryl or his change. It is certain that she accelerated it; she is not a woman to tolerate an excess of moody silence and she can ask questions that would make Barbara Walters envious. I do not wonder, however, at the apparent oddities in their pairing—the contrast in their sizes, and the fact that Cheryl is white, a Buddhist, nearly a decade younger, and so far removed from the world of basketball that when she met Jabbar she did not recognize him, even by name. All those things are part of her charm. Cheryl can understand Jabbar as few can, for she, too, has left Catholicism for a non-Western religion. Her youth gives her a kind of innocence; she cannot see him in light of history mostly because she doesn't remember it; with her, Jabbar can truly put it all behind. And he can know that she is not drawn to him simply by his fame or basketball abilities. She is a bridge to the "more normal things" he alluded to a dozen years ago and has never himself experienced.

In any case, she is obviously good for him. In her presence he relaxes, his voice deepens and loses some of its tension. He grins boyishly. Acts shy. Even shows his hurt that the Lakers have allowed him to go into this season unsigned. He shows his spirit, as Musashi would say.

As we leave the restaurant I reach out to shake Cheryl's hand. "I hug," she informs me, and so, of course, we do. Then she says, "Kareem hugs, too." And so Jabbar and I engage in a weird embrace, with my nose somewhere in the region of his belly button, while Cheryl beams at us like an approving parent.

NOVEMBER 1983. The beginning of another basketball season. It will be, most likely, the year Jabbar sets the NBA record for points scored. It will be his twenty-eighth season as a player, his fifteenth as a professional. I am worried that it may be his last.

The 1982–1983 season was difficult for him, both off and on the court. In January his home burned to the ground, taking with it rugs and trophies and the mementos of a career, a lifetime. In January, too, the migraines returned, forcing him to sit out the second of two regular season games against Philadelphia. The first one, back in December, proved sufficiently prophetic; in June the 76ers humiliated the Lakers, defeating them in four straight games. And through most of the months of the off-season, Jabbar remained unsigned, by the Lakers, by anyone. Philadelphia had Moses Malone, who was being touted as the league's premier center; Houston had replaced Malone with Ralph Sampson, touted as the center of the future. Jabbar floated in limbo.

Now, although the Lakers have finally re-signed him, I wonder if he can play with the same concentration, with the same desire. "Basketball," he said, "is definitely a means of personal expression." And, speaking of the immortal Robertson: "Oscar would have played a couple of more years. But whatever it was, he didn't feel he could make that commitment, and he stepped away from it." Maybe, I think, Jabbar will tell all these people playing patty-cake with his means of self-expression to go to hell, and just step away.

In any case, those thoughts have made me realize that Jabbar will step away eventually. "My days," he had said, "are numbered." And I think that the inevitability of his retirement holds more dread for me than for him. He has always thought beyond his career. "The world is bigger than all this," he had said of his sport, and, of course, he was right.

But to my mind that says only a part of it. It seems to me that Jabbar has made basketball bigger. He has altered the game. He has upset the categories into which we would like to push our athletes. He has forced some of us to deal with the reality of a seven-foot-tall black who practices Islam, reads science fiction, was rated by *Playgirl* magazine one of the ten sexiest men around, and who plays a game with the precision of a surgeon, the dignity of a statesman, and a calm that, as Bill Bradley put it, "engulfs opponents." His name on a roster, in a game program, his image on a TV screen, is a symbol of history, of the power of diversity, of the viability of alternatives, of the fact that the world is indeed bigger than all this. It may be that I have an overfondness for the values of our generation, or that I have watched so many basketball games that I am not happy unless I can see the world in passes and fast breaks, but I cannot see this same significance in other basketball players. What, I wonder, is the history of Ralph Sampson? What is the symbolism of Moses Malone?

Donald Hall

His fellow poets, Donald Hall (b. 1928) once noted, split into two camps: those bewildered by his fascination with sports, and an equal number who wished that they too could find paying work writing about the games that engross us. In 1975 Hall freed himself up to write about pretty much any thing he wanted when he quit a professorship at Michigan and decamped to a farm in New Hampshire. The short-lived *Inside Sports* published much of his sportswriting, most of it about baseball, and that sport features prominently in the essay collection *Fathers Playing Catch with Sons*, as well as in *Dock Ellis in the Country of Baseball*, which he wrote with the Pittsburgh Pirates' pitcher. Basketball claimed more and more of his attention during the 1980s, as Larry Bird and the Boston Celtics held New England in their thrall; "Basketball: The Purest Sport of Bodies" was first published in the journal *Yankee* in 1984. A former U.S. poet laureate, Hall welcomed sporting events as downbeats in the rhythms of the poet's life, and he eagerly carved out time to watch. Writing about sports transported him back to Hampden, Connecticut, where as a fifteen-year-old he had reported on his high school's games for the *New Haven Register*. Those assignments provided a recurrent thrill, he noted, making him "the proud author of a story right now multiplying itself into morning newsprint, ready to turn up on the doorstep in a few hours, large as life, BY DON HALL."

Basketball:
The Purest Sport of Bodies

P ROFESSIONAL basketball combines opposites—elegant gymnastics, ferocious ballet, gargantuan delicacy, colossal precision. . . . It is a continuous violent dream of levitating hulks. It is twist and turn, leap and fly, turn and counterturn, flick and respond, confront and evade. It is monstrous, or it would be monstrous if it were not witty.

These athletes show wit in their bodies. Watching their abrupt speed, their instant reversals of direction, I think of minnows in the pond—how the small schools slide swiftly in one direction, then reverse-flip and flash the opposite way. NBA players are quick as minnows, and with an adjustment for size great whales drive down the road. As a ball careens from a rim, huge bodies leap with legs outspread; then two high hands grasp the ball, propel it *instantly* down court to a sprinting guard, and *instantly* seven to ten enormous bodies spin and sprint on the wooden floor, pass, dribble, pass, pass, shoot—block or whoosh. . . .

Then the same bodies flip-flash back to the place they just departed from, fast as an LED display from a punched button—an intricate thrashing, a mercury-sudden pack of leviathans. . . .

In all sport, nothing requires more of a body than NBA basketball; nothing so much uses—and celebrates—bodily improvisation, invention, and imagination.

In football they measure forty-yard sprints. Nobody runs forty yards in basketball. Maybe you run the ninety-four feet of the court but more likely you sprint ten feet; then you stop, not on a dime, but on Miss Liberty's torch. In football you run over somebody's face.

When I was growing up, the winter sport was hockey. At high school, hundreds of us would stand outside at 0 degrees Fahrenheit beside a white rink puffing out white air, stamping our painful feet, our toes like frozen fishsticks. On the ice, unhelmeted shoulder-padded thick-socked blocky young men swept up and down, wedded to the moves of a black hard-rubber disk and crushing each other into boards, fighting, crashing, shooting, fighting again. Then we tromped home to unfreeze by the hot-water radiators, red-cheeked and exhausted with cold, exhilarated with pain and crowd-fight.

But basketball was a sweaty half-empty gym on a Friday afternoon, pale white legs clomping down court below billowing gym shorts; it was the two-handed set shot: pause, arch, aim, *grunt*. In the super-heated dim gymnasium, twenty-seven friends and relatives watched the desultory to-and-fro of short, slow, awkward players who were eternally pulling up twelve feet from the basket to clatter a heavy brown beachball harmlessly off a white backboard. Always we lost thirty-eight to nineteen.

It was a hockey town, and New England was hockey country.

Meantime, elsewhere—in city parks, in crepuscular gymnasiums after school with the heat turned off, or in Indiana farmyards with a basket nailed to the side of a barn—other children practiced other motions . . . and the best of these motions found their showcase, over the decades and for decades ahead, in New England's metropolis, in the leaky old ship of Boston Garden.

When I was at college, I took the subway into Boston to watch college double-headers. My Harvard team was better than the high school I went to . . . but I do not recollect that we were invited to the NIT. I watched Harvard, Boston College, Boston University—and Holy Cross. Of course I remember the astonishment of one young man's innovations: the infant Robert Cousy, who played for Holy Cross, dribbled behind his back and passed with perfect swift accuracy in a direction opposite the place toward which he gazed. Or he faked a pass, put the ball to the floor, and cut past bewildered defenders for an easy and graceful layup. As far as I am concerned, it was Robert Cousy, and not Colonel Naismith, who invented basketball.

One of the extraordinary qualities of basketball is its suddenness of change, in pace and in momentum.

Years ago, when I lived in Michigan, I frequented Cobo Hall when the Detroit Pistons played there. I watched good players on bad teams: great Bob Lanier, Big-Foot with bad knees, enormous and delicate and always hurt; Dave Bing and Chris Ford, who ended their careers with the Celtics. Once I took my young son to see the Detroit Pistons play the Boston Celtics in a play-off game. It was 1968, the first time the poor Pistons made the play-offs. It was Bill Russell's next-to-last year as player-coach of the Celtics; they went on to beat the Lakers for the championship.

I sat with my boy and his friend David, who was a Celtics fan because he had lived in Boston until he was eight months old, and watched three periods of desultory play. There were good moments from Bing and Lanier, good moments from Havlicek and White—my man Cousy retired in 1963—but Bill Russell looked half asleep even as he blocked shots. In the fourth quarter the Pistons, astonishingly, led—and I entertained notions of an upset. . . .

Then my small charges developed a desire for hot dogs; I dashed out for a few minutes, and as I returned laden, I heard a swelling of wistful applause from the knowledgeable Cobo crowd. I looked toward the floor to see Bill Russell floating through the air to sink a basket. In the space of two hot dogs, Boston had gone up by ten points—or rather, not Boston but the usually inoffensive Russell. He had waked up—and when Russell opened his eyes it was over for Detroit. . . .

"Momentum" is a cliché of the football field, but it is a habit of the wooden floor. Basketball is a game not so much of important baskets or of special plays as of violent pendulum swings. One team or another is always on a run, like a madcap gambler throwing a dozen sevens. When the Celtics are down by a dozen points in the second quarter, looking listless, hapless, helpless, we know that suddenly they can become energized—rag dolls wired with springy, reactive power. We know that twelve points down can be six points up with a crazy suddenness.

Sometimes one player does it all by himself. On a night when Cedric Maxwell has twelve thumbs and Kevin McHale three knees, when every pass hits vacant air, when the foul-shooter clanks it off the rim, suddenly Larry Bird (usually it is Larry Bird) grows five inches taller and five seconds faster. With legs outspread he leaps above the rim to take a rebound, pivots, and throws a fastball the length of the court to Gerald Henderson who lays it up. Then as the Knicks (or the Bulls, or the Bullets . . .) go into their half-court offense, he appears to fall asleep. His slack jaw sags and he does his Idiot Thing . . . only to swoop around a guard and steal the ball cleanly, like plucking a sheep-tick off a big dog, then sprint down court and float a layup. Then he steals the inbound pass and, as the power-forward fouls him, falls heavily to the floor; only while he falls, he loops the ball up with his left hand over a high head into the basket—an *impossible* three-point play. Then he fast-breaks with Maxwell and Parish, zapping the ball back and forth, and leaps as if to shoot over an immense center. But, looking straight at the basket, he passes the ball blind to Robert Parish on his left, who stuffs it behind the center's head. . . .

We have just run off nine points.

This is a game you can study on television because it is small enough to fit in the box; and, through television's slow-motion replay, we study at our leisure the learned body's performances—as when Dr. J. or George Gervin soars from the base line, ball in the right hand, appears to shoot, pauses in midair, and, when a shot-blocker hovers beside him, transfers the ball to the left hand, twists the body, and stuffs the ball through the hoop.

It is only two points. If this were gymnastics or diving from the high board at the Olympics, it would be *ten* points.

The Celtics play team ball, passing, seeking the open man when defenders double-team Bird or Parish. The ball moves so rapidly, it is like a pinball machine in which the steel ball gathers speed as it bounces off springs, rioting up and out, down and across. Zany ball, with its own wild life, always like the rabbit seeking its hole.

> Or.
> The Game.
> Slows.
> Down.

Despite the twenty-four-second clock, there are passages of sheer stasis. The point guard bounces the ball: once, twice, three times. The guard in front of him is all alert nerves, arms spread and quivering. Will he drive right? Left?

> Bounce.
> Bounce . . .
> Bounce . . . . . .

He goes right NO-he-only-seemed-to-go-right-he-is-left-around-his-man, he rises into the *air* and . . . blocked-by-a-giant-under-hands-to-his-own-giant . . . who backward-stuffs it. BANG.

Oh, my. Basketball is the purest sport of bodies.

Mark Jacobson

Before being hailed as a "street writer" and "journalistic provocateur," Mark Jacobson (b. 1948) had dropped out of both Wisconsin and Cal-Berkeley during the 1960s and done time as a cab driver, a bus-terminal baggage porter, and a producer of psychedelic light shows. Only then did he find his vocation. Jacobson has called journalism "a 24/7 job, the kind of hours I like," and all-hours entropies have long appealed to this contributor to *The Village Voice*, *Rolling Stone*, *Men's Journal*, *Esquire*, and *New York*: gang life, punk rock, urban decay. This 1985 profile of Julius Erving, the utterly composed Doctor J, would seem to be an odd fit in the Jacobson oeuvre. But as the author notes, Erving's legend began as a whisper in the demimonde of the American Basketball Association, a kind of jazz-club circuit known best to aficionados. And it was just like Jacobson to develop an ahead-of-the-curve enthusiasm for the Philadelphia 76er who, during the time they spent together for the story, would swing by 30th Street Station in his Maserati to pick Jacobson up. Here the author oscillates between unabashed fanboy and cold analyst, and for long, gratifying stretches simply lets one of the game's most eloquent figures speak for himself. As profile, it's as graceful a flight as any of Erving's toward the rim, and in the end as satisfying as a culminating dunk.

The Passion of Doctor J

I WENT for a ride through downtown Philadelphia with Julius Erving in his Maserati the other day, and with each passing block it became more apparent: Julius cannot drive very well. It wasn't a question of reckless speed or ignored signals. Rather, he seemed unsure, tentative. His huge, famous hands clutched the steering wheel a bit too tightly, his large head craned uncomfortably toward the slope of the windshield. He accelerated with a lurch; there was no smooth rush of power. Obvious openings in the flow of traffic went unseen or untried. All in all, it reflected a total absence of *feel*.

This struck me as amusing—Julius Erving, the fabulous Doctor of the court, driving a Maserati with an automatic transmission.

Just an hour before, I'd compared the act of seeing Julius play basketball to Saint Francis watching birds in flight. It was my Ultimate Compliment. When a reporter with pretensions meets an Official Legend, especially a Sports Legend, it is mandatory to concoct the

Ultimate Compliment, something beyond a plebeian "gee whiz." Something along the lines of the august Mailer's referring to Ali as a Prince of Heaven, whose very gaze caused men to look down. Or, perhaps, Liebling's mentioning that Sugar Ray Robinson had "slumberland in either hand." Saint Francis was what I'd come up with.

Viewing Doctor J move to the hoop inspired what I imagined to be an awe similar to what Saint Francis felt sitting in a field with the sparrows buzzing overhead, I told Julius. It was as if a curtain had been parted, affording a peek into the Realm of the Extraordinary, a marvelous communication that ennobled both the watcher and the watched equally. What wonders there are in the Kingdom of God! How glorious they are to behold!

"What you do affirms the supremacy of all beings," I told Julius as we sat in the offices of the Erving Group, a holding company designed to spread around the wads of capital Julius has accumulated during his career as Doctor J. Large gold-leaf plaques calling Julius things like TASTYKAKE PLAYER OF THE YEAR dot the walls. "Seeing you play basketball has enriched my life," I finished.

"Thanks, thanks a lot," Julius said politely. Then again, Julius is always polite. It was obvious, my Ultimate Compliment clearly did not knock his socks off. It was as if he were saying, "Funny thing, you're the third guy who's told me that today."

Every serious hoop fan remembers the first time he saw Julius Erving play basketball. My grandfather, a great New York Giants baseball fan, probably had the same feeling the first time he ever saw Willie Mays go back on a fly ball. There was Julius, mad-haired and scowl-faced, doing what everyone else did, rebounding, scoring, passing, but doing it with the accents shifted from the accepted but now totally humdrum position to a new, infinitely more thrilling somewhere else. Who was this man with two Jewish names who came from parts unknown with powers far greater than the mortal Trailblazer?

Flat out, there was nothing like him. No one had ever taken off from the foul line as if on a dare, cradled the ball above his head, and not come down until he crashed it through the hoop. Not like that, anyway. Julius acknowledges a debt to Elgin Baylor, whom he calls "the biggest gazelle, the first of the gliders," but, to the stunned observer, the Doctor seemed to arrive from outside the boundaries of the game itself. His body, streamlined like none before him, festooned by arms longer and hands bigger, soared with an athletic ferocity matched only by the mystical, unprecedented catapult of Bob Beamon down the Mexico City runway, or by the screaming flight of Bruce Lee.

Has any other individual in team sports radically altered the *idea* of how his particular game should be played to the degree Julius has? Jackie Robinson? Babe Ruth? Jim Brown? A more instructive comparison would be someone like Joe DiMaggio. DiMaggio was impeccable, the nonpareil. He was simply better. Yet there is something hermetic about Joe DiMaggio. He did what everyone else did, but with incomparable excellence. Joe's exemplariness is to be admired, but it doesn't offer a whole program of reform. His greatness is a dead end, specific to Joe and Joe alone. Julius, on the other hand, may not have invented the slam dunk, the finger roll, or the hanging rebound—the entire airborne game in general. But he certainly popularized it, and by doing so he announced that others could follow in his footsteps, even surpass him. Seeing Julius fly to the hoop spread the news: it can be done, so do it. Nine years ago Julius appeared alone in his ability to go pyrotechnic at any time. This past year, however, lined up against a gaggle of his poetic offspring, "human highlight film" youngbloods like Dominique Wilkins and Larry Nance, Julius was content to make his final attempt a running foul-line takeoff: the "classical" dunk, a bit of archaeology demonstrated by the father of the form.

Befitting the matter-of-factness of a legend discussing his craft, Julius is not falsely modest about his contributions to the game. In the clinical fashion he employs when delineating the *x*'s and *o*'s of his profession, he says, "I'd say I've had an effect in three main areas. First, I have taken a smaller man's game, ball-handling, passing, and the like, and brought it to the front court. Second, I've taken the big man's game, rebounding, shot-blocking, and been able to execute that even though I'm only six-foot-six. What I've tried to do is merge those two types of games, which were considered to be separate—for instance, Bill Russell does the rebounding, Cousy handles the ball—and combine them into the same player. This has more or less changed the definition of what's called the small forward position, and it creates a lot more flexibility for the individual player, and, of course, creates a lot more opportunities for the whole team. The third thing I've tried to do, and this is the most important thing, is to make this kind of basketball a winning kind of basketball, taking into account a degree of showmanship that gets people excited. My overall goal is to give people the feeling they are being entertained by an artist—and to win."

Then Julius laughs and says, "You know, the playground game . . . refined."

In Roosevelt, New York, the lower-middle-class, largely black Long Island community where he grew up, there is a playground with a sign that says THIS IS WHERE JULIUS ERVING LEARNED THE GAME OF BASKETBALL. Herein lies Julius's triumph. He successfully transmuted the black playground game and brought that cutthroat urban staple to its most sumptuous fruition. He, once and for all, no turning back, blackified pro basketball.

He did it by forcing the comparatively staid, grind-it-out, coach-dominated NBA to merge with the old ABA, a semi-outlaw league that played the run-till-you-drop "black" playground game with a garish red, white, and blue ball. Julius was in the ABA, and the older, more established NBA could not allow a phenomenon like Doctor J to exist outside its borders. Most observers feel the NBA absorbed the whole funky ABA, with its three-point shots and idiotic mascots, just to get Julius. Once they did, the entire product of pro basketball was refocused. Surprise! The ABA, comprising many performers from Podunk Junior College and some who never went to any college, had a lot more than Julius Erving. Many players long scorned by the NBA brass became stars, the incandescent "Ice," George Gervin, and Moses Malone among them. And there was a lot more running. Before the merger there was only one consistent fast-break team in the NBA, the Celtics. Now, with the ABA people around, it seemed as if the whole league was running, playing the playground game, Julius's game.

This is not to say Larry Bird isn't great, no matter where the game is, on the back lawn of Buckingham Palace or up in Harlem, but blackification was inevitable. No one will really deny that the majority of black players jump higher and run faster than the majority of white players, and that's what pro ball, as it's currently constituted, is all about—running and jumping with finesse.

Many people have wondered if all this running is such a good thing. Since the merger and the takeover by the "black" game, the pro sport has suffered reversals. Attendance is uneven and TV ratings are down; rumors of widespread social evils among the players abound. It is difficult to have any in-depth conversation about the status of the league without coming up against the Problem. A league official says, "It's race, pure and simple. No major sport comes up against it the way we do. It's just difficult to get a lot of people to watch huge, intelligent, millionaire black people on television."

When presented with the notion that by elevating his art he may have served to narrow its appeal, Julius says, "It's unfortunate, but what can be done about what is?" Well, at least the onset of the playground game has exploded several pernicious myths. If there is one thing Julius and his followers (Magic Johnson comes to mind) have proved without a doubt, it's that just because you play "flashy" doesn't mean you're not a team player. No longer is it assumed that the spectacular is really, at its root, just mindless showboating easily thwarted, in the crunch times, by the cunning of a small man chewing a cigar on the coaching lines. Julius's teams have always won.

For the hoop fan, though, likely the most treasured item concerning Julius Erving remains in that first cataclysmic moment of discovery, that first peek into the Realm of the Extraordinary. This has to do with the nature of the fan, the hoop fan in particular. All team sports have their cognoscenti, gamblers poring over the injury lists, nine-year-old boys with batting averages memorized, but somehow the variety of fan attracted to pro basketball is in a slightly more obsessive class, sweatier, seedier perhaps, but absolutely committed. This type of hoop fan I'm talking about isn't much different from the jazz buffs of the 1940s and 1950s, white people digging on an essentially black world.

How Julius, the Official Legend, comes into this is that he approached the beady consciousness as Rumor. He was a secret. He wasn't a well-publicized high school star like Kareem; he went to the University of Massachusetts (a school with no basketball reputation) and then played two years at one of the ABA's most remote outposts, the Virginia Squires. There was no hoopla surrounding him, no Brent Musburger hyping the size of his smile. The Doctor was something for the grapevine.

It cuts both ways. Probably, by somehow staying out of the limelight (that was easier in 1970) and by choosing not to go to a "big program" school where a crusty Adolph Rupp might have made it a principle to correct all that boy's strange habits, Julius was left alone to create his wholly new thing. And by virtue of this anonymity, the hoop fan was able to come upon Julius as a wondrous found object.

Magic Johnson, Sugar Ray Leonard—no one is knocking their talents, but they arrived on the scene tied in a bow, sold to anyone within eyeshot of a TV. They will always carry that stigma. Julius, however, remains eternally cool. You had to work to see Julius, seek him out. There wasn't any cable; maybe you could catch him on an independent station that had been hustled into picking up one of the numerous ABA All-Star games. Even after he came from the Squires to the Nets, then the ABA New York entry, the hoop fan had to ply the forlorn parkways to the Nassau Coliseum to sit with four thousand dour faces expressing regret that they weren't viewing a hockey game. You had to go out of your way to see Julius. But it was worth it. When you saw that Rumor was Fact, and a far more remarkable Fact than imagined, then you felt like you had your little bond with Julius, that he was in your heart.

That Julius has maintained the quality of play this long is gravy. How do you measure the benefit one gets from seeing beautiful things happen? Sometimes I find myself idly replaying some of Julius's more astounding moves inside my head. The one against the Lakers in the championship a few years back, the one where he goes behind the backboard and comes around for the reverse layup? Ones like that bring tears to my eyes. Really.

Of course, it can't last. Last season Julius's club, the Philadelphia 76ers, for whom he's played since the league merger in 1976, were mangled by the bedraggled New Jersey Nets, transplanted to the Garden State from Uniondale, New York. It was an upset. The year before the Sixers won the title in a near walkover. Of the thirteen games they played in the championship rounds, they won twelve. The Sixers didn't come close to repeating. Julius did not have a particularly good series. There were several reasons. For one, it had been a grueling season for the Doc. Numerous Sixer injuries forced him to play many more minutes than he might have wanted to at his age. He responded with perhaps his best year in the past three and had his backers for league MVP. By the playoffs, however, he was weary, worn out. In the last moments of the deciding game he made repeated turnovers and missed key shots. Had a b-ball cognoscenti arrived from Mars right then, dumb to the history of the past fifteen years, he could have watched Julius's play and pronounced it "ordinary."

So it goes. Athletes get old, and soon they're too old to play. In the variety of pro basketball Julius helped create, it happens even quicker. There is no DH in the NBA, and right now Julius, at thirty-four, is among the fifteen oldest guys in the league. If he stays another couple of seasons, as he hints he might, he could be the oldest. His Afro, once wild as a Rorschach blot and seemingly a foot high, is now demurely trimmed and flecked with gray. So it goes: a million dudes with the hot hand down in the schoolyard waiting for the Doctor to roll over so they can get their shot. No tears over that. But it's this driving that's upsetting, the way Julius is driving this Maserati with the automatic transmission. It's all so ordinary, how Julius is driving.

"Don't ask me any questions or I'll miss my turn," Julius says, smiling, as if to comment on his competence.

Then he makes this flabby, too-wide turn off Broad Street. What a deal: soon enough Julius is going to retire from basketball, but likely he'll he driving that Maserati with the automatic transmission for years to come.

"As it came it can go, as it came it most definitely *will* go," he says cheerfully, unaffected by his companion's gloom. "It won't really be that big a change for me," Julius says. "I've always thought of myself as a very ordinary guy."

This is a little tough to swallow, the Doctor an ordinary guy. This is not to say Julius Erving is not a *regular* guy. Sports-page "class"—Julius is the embodiment of it. Probably no athlete still playing has signed more autographs. His marathon sessions are spoken of with awe. Talking about it, Julius gives a look that asks, "Weren't you ever a kid?" and says, "Sometimes I ask myself, 'Should I accommodate today, or go straight ahead?' and I usually find myself accommodating." There is a limit, however. Walking through the icebound streets of Milwaukee, a fat guy accosted Julius, screaming, "Doc! Doc! Where's the other shoe?" Julius frowned. "I gave that guy one of my sneakers three years ago," he says, "and now, every time we go there, he asks for the other one. Some people are never satisfied."

As far as hoop reporters are concerned, Julius is the best. "There is no second place," says a Philly writer. This means that when deadlines are approaching and sweat is popping out on foreheads, Julius can be counted on to produce the proper verbiage, a smooth rap that, without much time-consuming translation, can be plugged into hastily written stories as "game quotes." It is something Julius works on, like any part of what he calls "my basketball function." He knows what reporters need and tries to give it to them.

"A courtesy," Julius says. Ask the right questions (nothing controversial, if you please!) and Julius will, in a voice that makes Frankie Crocker sound shrill, calmly assess the team's mood for you. He'll also say that Denver's Calvin Natt is among the toughest for him to score against, and that it is difficult to play Dallas's Mark Aguirre because "his butt is so big you can't get close to him," and that George Gervin is his favorite player, and that the Knicks' Bernard King, considered by many the best forward in the league, "will never get up to the level of the real all-timers like, say, Kareem, or myself, because he looks like he's working too hard. When you reach a level of greatness, there's a certain added element that goes into making it look easy."

Mainly, Julius keeps a low profile. He will often make inquiries about jazz—more out of educational desire than passion, for he prefers fusion. You could call him elegantly laid-back, stylish, though certainly you'd never confuse him with Walt Frazier. He is always the clean-living family man and, while sharp, displays little outward flash. He leaves the five-pound jewelry to the Darryl Dawkinses of the world, although he appears to cop no attitude toward the more flamboyant displays, sartorial or otherwise, of his fellows. He has, after all, been around, and not much raises the Doctor's eyebrow.

In Milwaukee, however, one John Matuszak, late of the Oakland Raiders football team and the movie *North Dallas Forty*, came close. The Tooz, as he has been known to call himself, appeared unannounced in the Sixers' locker room, and he was calling some attention to himself. Even in a world of large men, the Tooz stands out. He goes six-foot-eight, about three hundred pounds. In addition, he sports a mug that resembles the sort of hood ornament Screamin' Jay Hawkins might have mounted on his '55 De Soto to ward off unfriendly spirits. This is not to mention his dress on this particular night, which included a black silk coat, tuxedo pants, patent leather shoes, and a white satin tie over a leopard skin print shirt. He was also affecting a manner that would put him right up there for the Bluto part, should a remake of *Animal House* be made anytime soon.

It was the Tooz's sworn purpose to have both Julius and Moses Malone, the Sixers' famously intimidating center, join him at one of Milwaukee's more stylish wateringholes.

First he invited Moses. "Gonna win this year, Moses?" was Tooz's opener. Moses, no midget himself, was sitting on a stool stark naked. "Yeah, we're gonna win," said Moses, laying on his usual Sonny Liston–style bale.

Then, like a shot, the Tooz was down on one knee. He clasped his palms together and drove them like a hammer into Moses' thigh. "Don't say we're gonna win. Say we *gotta* win, Moses!!" the Tooz shouted, startling the few stragglers in the locker room. "Come on, Moses," the Tooz continued, "repeat after me: WE GOTTA WIN!" And, to the amazement of onlookers, Moses, who had not uttered a word in public since telling Philly reporters, "I'll be making no further comment for the rest of the season," repeated this after the Tooz. Moses, however, steadfastly refused to have a drink with the former lineman.

Thwarted, the Tooz went looking for Julius, who was in the midst of taking a shower. Unmindful of the water splashing everywhere, the Tooz confided to Julius how much he loved him. "I love you, Doctor!" the Tooz bellowed. Then he said, "Come on, Doctor. The Doctor and the Tooz must have a drink together. I got some friends, it'll be a party!"

Julius, never rude, thanked the Tooz for his offer but expressed his regrets, citing a 5:00 A.M. wake-up call the next morning.

"If you're worried about people hassling you, forget about it," the Tooz said with understanding. "No one will mess with you if you're with the Tooz!"

The football player had now stepped over the edge of the shower, his long hair dripping down over his drenched suit.

Backing into the stall, Julius, seemingly unrattled, said, "You're getting wet, you know that?"

"A drink, that's all I'm asking," Tooz repeated, reaching out to wrap his arms around the Doctor. "People love you, man," the Tooz said with sincerity, "people live to see you do your thing." Then, clearly disappointed, the Tooz left.

Several moments of silence ensued, during which Julius began to dress and Moses picked tape off his leg. Then Moses looked at Julius sleepily and said, "See those shoes?"

"What about the tie?" Julius said back.

Later Julius smiled and said, sure, it seemed like the Tooz was something of a boor, but you really had to get to know him better before you could say that unequivocally. After all, The Doc is not what you would call judgmental.

Teammates speak of him with healthy degrees of awe and camaraderie. Marc Iavaroni, a marginal forward cut by a couple of lesser NBA clubs before catching on as a "role player" in the Sixers' system, says, "Playing with the Doc? Don't pinch me, please. He looks for me. On and off the court. Can you imagine that! Doctor J looking to pass off to Marc Iavaroni? Know how that makes me feel?"

Nearly everyone close enough to Julius to have personal dealings speaks of some small kindness, a birthday remembered, an appreciated pep talk, a good laugh. League officials, always aware of the "image problem" of the sport, tell you how many young players Julius has done right by, how his example is primarily responsible for the "rehabilitation" of Chicago's troubled Quintin Dailey. Julius's community awards appear endless. Last year he got the Father Flanagan Award for Service to Youth at Boys Town; previous recipients include Mother Teresa, Danny Thomas, and Spencer Tracy's wife. The list of charities supported, youth groups spoken to (he read *Peter and the Wolf* at a special children's show of the Youth Orchestra of Greater Philadelphia), and hospital wards visited goes on and on.

"All part of my 'nice-guy image,'" Julius says with a wink. He is aware that all these good vibes add up under the economic heading of "Doctor J": is proud that the Q ratings of his numerous commercial endorsements show him rating higher in "believability" than in "popularity." "But really," he says, "I just try to be decent. I try to do the decent thing in the circumstances. Right now I happen to be a well-known professional athlete, so I attempt to be decent within that context. Being nice is pretty normal, I think. If someone was drowning in the river, you'd assume most people would throw them a life preserver. You'd figure most people would do that, under those circumstances. That would be the normal thing to do. That's what I like to believe I'd do, being a normal person."

This led to Julius's further insistence that, really, he was a very ordinary guy. An ordinary guy dealing with extraordinary circumstances, perhaps, but ordinary nevertheless.

"I've never felt particularly unique," Julius says. "Even within the context of basketball, I honestly never imagined myself as anything special. I remember, back home, when I first started playing. At nine, ten, I had a two-hand shot. Then by twelve and a half, thirteen, I got a one-hand shot. Always went to the basket, that pattern was set by then. Actually, I don't think I've changed much as a player since then. Back then, before I was physically able, I felt these different things within me, certain moves, ways to dunk. It sounds strange, being five feet tall, thinking about dunking in a clinical way, but that's how I was. I realized all I had to do was be patient and they would come. So I wasn't surprised when they did, they were part of me for so long. But I didn't find anything particularly special about it. I assumed everyone could do these things if they tried."

Julius claims the idea of being a professional basketball player didn't occur to him until he was among the country's leaders in both scoring and rebounding at UMass. He wanted to be a doctor. That's the source of his unbeatable nickname. In grammar school when the kids got up to say what they wanted to be when they grew up, Julius said, "A doctor." "Doctor!" the kids shouted, and it stuck. Later, when playing in the Rucker League, the deejay types "announcing" games were calling him the Claw, a moniker based on his large hands. Julius, always sharp to the distasteful, objected and, when asked for a substitute, said, "Oh, why don't you just call me Doctor." Doctors, after all, Julius felt, were white-haired men with soothing voices, who surrounded themselves with a great air of dignity. They also made a lot of money. These were Julius's two main concerns at the time. His father had left his mother and brother early on and wound up being run down by a car when Julius was eleven.

"I never really had a father," Julius says, "but then the possibility that I ever would was removed."

After that, security, financial and otherwise, became obsessional with Julius. Even today, with a contract that pays him more than a million each year and other lucrative interests (he refers to basketball as "my main business application"), Julius is notoriously parsimonious. Do not expect him to pick up the check. It was this desire for himself and his family (there are four children now, three boys and a girl, living in a mansion on 2.8 acres on the Main Line) that made Julius think of playing ball for money.

"That's when I started hearing all these people talking about how different I was supposed to be," Julius recounts. "When a hundred people, then a thousand people tell you you're different, you just say to yourself, 'Okay, I'm different. . . .' Don't get me wrong, I liked it, I liked what it got me. I was a young player, I was doing what came easy to me, I was having a good time, so I accepted it as a fact of life." It was only during the stresses caused by his leaving the Nets (in a protracted contract battle), the subsequent league merger, and his arrival in Philadelphia to less than knockout notices when Julius began to ponder, "Why am I different? Why, with all these great players all around, guys who play as hard as I do, guys who want to win as badly as I do, why am I Doctor J?"

Quite a picture: the angst-ridden superstar, his piston legs rocketing from the pinewood floor into the glare of the houselights, his seemingly inexorable gaze transfixed on the orange ring, yet, in reality, his leap goes nowhere, for he is lost.

That's the way Julius paints it. During his first years in Philly it became commonplace to downrate the Doc. In the ABA he'd scored 28.7 points a game and nabbed nearly a thousand rebounds each season; now he was getting 21, 22, and his 'bounds were way down. Some nodded and said it was true what they said about the old league; it was a circus, after all. In 1978 an unnamed coach was quoted in *Sports Illustrated* as saying, "[Julius] has been on vacation for three years."

For his part, Julius complained that his knees were killing him (he has had a tendinitis condition for some time) and that he'd *purposely* hidden away much of the spectacular side of the Doctor, so as to better mesh with then-teammate George McGinnis, another ABA scorer not noted for his passing skills. Yet, it wasn't fun. None of it. He let it slip that more than likely he'd be retiring when his contract ran out in 1982. Now, though, Julius says his main problem was a spiritual, not a physical, one. "I felt totally hollow," he says. "It was eating at me. I started off asking, 'Who is Doctor J? How did I get to be him? What does being Doctor J mean?' . . . then it came down to asking, 'Who, really, am I?' I became very frightened when I began to sense that I really had no idea."

One can imagine the terror Julius felt. He seems a very methodical person, someone who likes everything in its place, not one to rush into things. Perhaps due to his longtime regimen as an athlete, where every day the practice is set for a certain amount of time and the bus leaves at such-and-such o'clock, he is given to compartmentalizing his life and talking of it in terms of small, constantly repeated activities. "I admit to liking the feel of things being in context," Julius says, "the sense of the familiar waters." This extends even to the court. Julius contends, "Out of one hundred moves I make in a game, I've made ninety-nine before, at one time or another. Sure, that one new one gives me a hit, but actually I get as much or more out of doing the other ninety-nine, because when I do something I've done before it means that I've compiled this information in my mind and selected the right action for the proper situation. That gives me a lot of pleasure.

"Back then, though," Julius adds, "I felt completely alone at times. Often, after a game and a late dinner, in one of those cities, I'd be sitting up, three o'clock, four o'clock, after eating a big steak, just watching that TV, with all the phones turned off. I never felt like that before.

"It was finding my faith that pulled me through," Julius says, leaning back from the desk in his Philadelphia office. In front of him is a rectangular paperweight you'd figure would be made of copper or brass and say, in embossed letters, something like JULIUS WINFIELD ERVING JR., PRESIDENT. But it is wooden and appears to have been made in a junior high school shop class. It says JESUS.

Julius's conversion occurred during the summer of 1978, at a family get-together in South Carolina. The previous season had been his worst yet. Julius had played poorly, and he was suffering from numerous injuries. The flak was getting intense. "I was feeling a little sorry for myself," Julius says, "but when I got down there and saw all those people, people I didn't know, some of whom I didn't even know existed, yet people who were connected to me in some way, it was really something. Because I was well known, everyone sort of used me as a lightning rod, a common denominator. They used me to get closer to each other. And I felt all that love passing through me. It was a very strange and wonderful feeling."

At the meeting Julius encountered an uncle of his, Alfonso, a preacher. He told Julius about a blessing that had been laid on the family that, Alfonso said, was now being manifested through Julius. "After that," Julius says, "things fell into place for me."

When the subject of Julius-as-Christian comes up, a good portion of the cognoscenti express surprise (it is not well known) and then shake their heads. However, to the reporter with pretensions, it seemed a great boon, a fabulous opportunity. This isn't to say Julius won't go Jaycee on you at any moment; no doubt his "Dare to Be Great" speech ranks with the best. He is also given to saying things like "Did I want to open the doors to essential knowledge or did I want to remain on the merry-go-round of nondiscovery?" Primarily, though, here was an intelligent, observant man, who by the vehicle of a mysterious "blessing" had been thrust into the Realm of the Extraordinary. The hope was that he would have the presence of mind to keep his eyes and ears open while in this marvelous land, and that hope was rewarded. I mean, you could enter into a metaphysical dialogue with this man!

On a Milwaukee street we mulled over the notion of the Divine Call. On a bus in Detroit we beat around the dichotomy of true Needs and venal Wants. In a Madison Square Garden locker room we pierced the outskirts of the Spirit of Giving. But it wasn't until our discussion in his office, during a laborious spiel of mine concerning the duty of the seeker to examine the varieties of religious experience, that Julius began to get pissed.

"I just can't agree," he said, "because even if you do manage to synthesize all these systems, what good is it going to do you? Even if you're the smartest man on earth, even if you're Albert Einstein, you'll still only have a thimbleful of all the knowledge in the world. Where does that lead you? Digging and grinding on this unbelievable quest? Is there happiness in that? So it comes down to making *concessions* ... down to knowing you're not the wisest or the smartest, not the ultimate of anything, but knowing too that you have this powerful need to grasp something meaningful, something purposeful ... you want a way, a way that makes sense for you, that you can embrace."

It was clear what Julius was getting at. After all, he is a black guy in America, the son of a very religious church lady mother. He reached out to what was available to him, and it worked. He found himself capable of faith. But really, was there any other solution for the intelligent, humble man with the nice-guy image? Doctor J has not simply been a great player, he has been *the epitome* of a player, God's own fantasy of a player. If Julius meant to "deal with logic, infused by faith," as he says is his bent, was there any other conclusion but to accept the notion of the involved, controlling presence of a Higher Power? There seemed a profound sanity in Julius's belief, and the reporter with pretension found it very satisfying.

Julius says he has no fear of life A.B. (After Basketball). "The thing that frightens me is what I heard about spiritual casualties. A spiritual casualty is someone . . . say a well-known athlete who takes a spiritual stand, and then the focus shifts from looking at that person as an athlete to something else. Suddenly there are all these people who want to put this athlete in the forefront because they assume he can be as significant spiritually as he was athletically. Then this famous athlete uses this forum to talk about what he feels about this new field he's entered . . . and he doesn't know what he's talking about . . . like, say, someone might say, 'Kareem, he's a superstar ballplayer, so he should be a superstar Muslim.' A spiritual casualty is someone who falls for that."

Julius shivers at the mention of Eldridge Cleaver, who did much to make a mockery of himself in his post-Panther days, showing up on *The Hour of Power* one minute and modeling codpiece trousers the next. Julius is well aware of what went into the creation and maintenance of Doctor J, and he will do almost anything to keep that image from being defiled. "The last thing I want to be perceived as is a flake," he says warily.

Some suggest that Julius might be a little less cautious. There have been intimations that by stressing his "Christian umbrella," Julius has demonstrated a degree of naïveté concerning day-to-day life in lower-rent districts. This talk became increasingly intense after Julius's no-profile stance in the recent Philly mayoral election, which pitted liberal black W. Wilson Goode against neo-Neanderthal Frank Rizzo. Hearing this, Julius gets as close as he does to bristling. "I'm very sensitive to this type of criticism," he says, "but I'm not going to be pressured by it. My track record in the black community speaks for itself. You know, I'm not blind, I understand how things are. I remember what it was like growing up, and when we go to Boston and Chicago, there's racism there. We hear what people shout, you know. I understand the danger of getting so far from a situation that you fool yourself and say it doesn't exist, or get the illusion that because you're a well-known ballplayer it doesn't apply to me. I'm not living in a dream world, but I'll tell you I'd be a fool not to use the advantages I've earned through playing in behalf of my family. But I'm not going to invite a potentially hostile situation into my life, into the lives of my wife and children, for just anyone's idea of solidarity. If I can afford an extra layer of protection, I will exercise it.

"I've never been a political person. I've never backed a political candidate in my life. When I was with the Nets, a picture came out of me in the newspaper with a local candidate. It was just some function for the team, but this guy was there and he was running for some office, and then all these people were asking me why I was supporting the Republican candidate. I don't want that to happen again. It would threaten my livelihood. If I backed the Democratic candidate, I'd run the risk of alienating half my public, and the other way around.

"But mostly it comes down to: I've played basketball for twenty-five years, almost every situation that can come up has come up. Therefore I'm qualified to sit here and talk to you about basketball. I don't have those sort of memory cells concerning other areas."

So, Julius says, he will enter the realm of the ordinary as a businessman. "An entrepreneur," he says, professing to have always had "a deep yearning" to be such a person. Typically enough, most of his investments have reflected a stolid, blue-chippy side. He is a large stockholder in the Coca-Cola Bottling Company of New York. He makes earnest use of the products he endorses, which have included Coke, Converse, Spalding, and Chap Stick.

Don't look for Julius dancing in the back row of a Bally's Park Place Hotel Casino commercial, or any Doc's Dunkshot Bar opening in the East Sixties. Julius does, however, keep some mad money around for what he calls "risk capital ventures." One of these ventures was the now-defunct Doctor's Shoe Salon, a chic fulfillment of one of Julius's long-cherished fantasies. Throughout his life, especially since he got rich, Julius found it galling that he could not find high-fashion shoes to wrap around his size fifteens. The Doctor's Shoe Salon assumed there were many others in the same boat and sought to fill that need by offering a wide selection for the hard-to-fit dog, mostly in the two-hundred-dollar range. The shop, poshly appointed and located on Philly's South Second Street, was slated to be the prototype for a far-flung chain that would eventually take in all the NBA cities. It was not a success. "It caused me untold duress and aggravation," Julius says sheepishly. "A lot of people expected, because my name was involved, that I'd be there all the time. When I wasn't, they got mad. And when I was, I couldn't concentrate on the business. I got bombarded with all kinds of questions, basketball stuff, A to Z. Plus we had a lot of trouble with kids who thought it was a sneaker store." Kind of humorous— the great Doctor as the harried shoe salesman. But never let anyone say Doc doesn't learn from experience. Currently his "risk" project is REACH, a camp for gifted and highly motivated children. Nowhere on the brochure will you find the name Julius Erving.

Basically, though, Julius says, his business goal is "to work four hours and rest twenty, as opposed to now, when I've got to work twenty hours to rest four." Until he gets there he has other things to think about. The end of all those hotel rooms and 5:00 A.M. flights to the next city will mean a lot more time at home, a *lot* more time.

"One hundred and thirty to 140 more nights," Julius relates, admitting some anxiety about this. Now, Julius, his wife Turquoise, and their four children (Cheo, Julius III, Jazmin, and Cory) are pretty much your all-American family, as was witnessed at last season's dunk contest, during which the kids told Dad which shots to make. But 130, 140 nights. "A lot of nights," Julius predicts, "they're gonna be saying, 'Him? Again?'" Then he laughs and says, "This is all first-generation problems for all of us, my wife and I, dealing with the circumstances we find ourselves in. There's going to be a lot of trial and error, that's for sure." Then he says he's thinking of calling up John Havlicek, Jerry West, "some old-timers, people on my level," to get some pointers on the life ahead. Somehow, you figure, he'll get over.

[Editor's Note—When Jacobson included this profile in his 2005 collection *Teenage Hipster in the Modern World*, he added the following: *Michael Jordan is certainly the greatest basketball player of all time, but Julius Erving, the incomparable Doctor J, is my all-time favorite. No one ever gave me as much pleasure watching any kind of game. Since his retirement, Julius has been the subject of a number of distressing headlines, exactly the sort of stuff he sought to avoid during his career. He acknowledged the tennis player Alexandra Stevenson to be his out-of-wedlock daughter. Later, his son Cory drove his car into a lake in Florida and drowned. These are unfortunate, sad events, but even more so when connected to someone like Julius, who was once so effortlessly perfect. I've written numerous articles on sports figures, most of them basketball players, but Julius remains my number one. The fact that he used to pick me up at the Philadelphia train station in his Maserati, nearly unthinkable for a current-day player, is still one of the highlights of my career.*]

Curry Kirkpatrick

From the late 1960s until he left the *Sports Illustrated* staff two decades later, Curry Kirkpatrick (b. 1943) was college basketball's very own Tom Wolfe, the New Journalist dandy along press row whose stories—Kandy-Kolored, tangerine-flaked—leaped out for their knowing, breathless voice. During the 1960s, *SI* threw a national canopy over what had long been a regionally fractured sport, and Kirkpatrick showed readers the sweat on Pete Maravich's brow, the jowls on Guy Lewis's face, and the fibers of a UCLA song girl's sweater. He told his stories with exuberant sentences that ran with the abandon of a player for some bandit school loose on the break. He could deploy a quote like a land-mine. And he rarely failed to convey a sense of wonder, as if the game he was writing about were the first he had ever seen. In the late 1970s, Kirkpatrick briefly left the college beat for the NBA, but his caricaturist's style and mischievous sensibility inflamed professional egos, so he soon took refuge back where his heart still lay. In this 1986 account of how the Final Four vaulted into the company of the Super Bowl and World Series as a mega-event, Kirkpatrick tells how he fell hard for college basketball during his childhood in upstate New York, and found his passion further stoked at North Carolina, where as a reporter for the *Daily Tar Heel* he covered the teams of a young coach named Dean Smith. When television turned the college game and its capstone tournament into a nationwide obsession, Kirkpatrick was there to meet the demand on the page, his voice long since tuned to the siren song that had engaged him as a boy.

Memories

THERE WAS a time, long ago, when the world was young and un-complicated and comparatively drug-free, and when nobody cared about the Final Four. The thing was lowercased then rather than a registered trademark, like Xerox or Ping-Pong. It was merely an event, not a spectacular, certainly not Serious Business.

Early this basketball season, when a newspaper reporter writing about the format of the NIT–Big Apple tournament referred to its conclusion in New York City as the "final four," he received an admonitory letter from the National Collegiate Athletic Association, pointing out that the Final Four belonged to the NCAA. Well, sure it does, but it belongs to more than just the NCAA. The momentous occasion has become so popular, so national, a sort of people's park of sport, that while Ronald Reagan might not dial up the winners' locker room, he does invite the victors to the White House, same as the World Series and national spelling-bee champs.

Back when nobody cared, however, a man (then a boy) remembers the Final Four belonging only to himself. This boy appreciated baseball and football and Howdy Doody and Annette and peanut-butter sandwiches and all the other spectacular thrills of youth, but the national collegiate basketball championship was something extra special, probably because it was his alone, his secret thing. At least, that's what he thought. This was before the Weather Channel, remember, before something called "mass communications," before the global village. Though the NCAA tournament began in 1939, the very year commercial television was invented, the two didn't merge on a national basis for 15 years, and even then very few stations picked up the 1954 championship game between La Salle and Bradley. Why, a boy had to listen to the radio back then and could only *imagine* what Tom Gola looked like. (Tom Gola, by the way, was Bill Bradley before Larry Bird was a twinkle in his mama's eye.) And, too, a boy could only imagine what La Salle's uniforms with sleeves looked like.

So the boy grew up, he went to as many local college games as he could. He kept score, all the points and fouls, on the radio games, too—in anticipation of the big tournament. One March night in 1956, during the broadcast of an NCAA first-round game, he was forced to leave hearth and home and go with his family to an ice-cream parlor for dessert. Normally he would have loved this sojourn, for the parlor had the best homemade ice cream that ever had filled his chubby face. But that rainy night the boy refused to go into the parlor. He sat outside in the car and listened to the end of the game—N.C. State versus Canisius. It went four overtimes, and before it was over (Canisius, 79–78) the announcer, Bill Mazer, went completely hoarse. Sitting alone in the old family Nash, the boy thought this was all fairly amazing; that this national college basketball tournament must really be something. The best part of all was that nobody knew about it but him.

Soon the boy chose his college partly because he figured it might get him closer to the NCAA tournament. And he may even have chosen a career, a way of life, so that he could take part in it. After all, he still knew the secret of the NCAAs, something nobody else seemed to know.

In the mid-'50s the NCAA was still begging the Associated Press to move the tournament bracket on the wire, and even as late as 1972—four years after the Houston–UCLA game in the Astrodome drew 52,693 and supposedly transfixed the country—only a small portion of the nation's TV households got to see both semifinal games in the Final Four in Los Angeles. "A regional sport," the networks kept calling college basketball. Fine, the man kept thinking, they'll never figure it out, and it's still my event, to have and to hold.

But just the other day the man stumbled upon some bittersweet figures. For a long time, he was forced to admit, the secret had been out. In 1973, the championship game was moved from its traditional Saturday afternoon to Monday night prime time. By 1981, NBC was paying $10 million to televise the tournament, and a year after that, CBS swiped the package, adding far more tournament games than had ever been shown before. This year CBS is paying $32 million to the NCAA; each Final Four school will receive about $825,000.

Amid the swirl of numbers out of the 1985 Final Four, the man found these very instructive: Over the breadth of a year, the NCAA received 140,000 applications in the mail, each requesting four seats at $43 per, which meant the organization could have sold 560,000 tickets worth $2.4 million to the two sessions in Lexington. And there was also this: The 1985 *radio* broadcast drew an adult (over-18) audience of 20,280,000 listeners, roughly 12% of the entire adult population of the U.S.

Uh, oh. With that the man took himself back, metaphysically at least, to that rainy night outside the ice-cream parlor. But it wasn't the same. Never again could he sit in the car and listen to his tournament on the radio and consider himself alone with his closet passion. There was nothing to do but go in and order a banana split.

In the history of the Final Four there are as many landmark years— turning points that have helped ingrain the event in the American consciousness—as there are favorite teams, players and plays:

- 1942 Stanford–Dartmouth, the first true meeting of East and West, the one-handed shot in ascendance.
- 1946 Oklahoma A & M–North Carolina, the first time four teams converged at the finals site.

- 1951 Kentucky–Kansas State, the first expansion, a doubling of the field to 16 teams, primarily because Adolph Rupp bitched so when his Kentucky team went uninvited in '50.
- 1957 and 1963 North Carolina–Kansas and Loyola–Cincinnati, the giant-killing upsets, the audience-enhancing thriller climaxes.
- 1966 Texas Western–Kentucky, confirmation of the black player's dominance. "We could all stop counting then," says Al McGuire.
- 1969 UCLA–Purdue, the never-before, never-again, third Outstanding Player award to the great Lew Alcindor.
- 1974 North Carolina State–UCLA, the kingdom overthrown.
- 1979 Michigan State–Indiana State, Bird–Magic and Ray Meyer to boot.
- 1982 North Carolina–Georgetown, 61,612 in heaven right here on earth, the infant Jordan over the infant Ewing, the Dean finally come true.

Still and all, two years, '75 and '80, define the tremendous explosion of interest in the national tournament more accurately than any others. For fully a decade, UCLA had crystallized the event into a David-Goliath confrontation. The Bruins of coach John Wooden were a national entity: a Yankees/Cowboys/Celtics–type target to love or hate but never to neglect. Doubtless, UCLA gave the NCAAs significance and verve. But by the early '70s—in the midst of the school's 10 championships, seven in a row—the tournament seemed to be running in place; it was in danger of losing its allure. Monotony had set in.

Any teams starring Lew Alcindor and Bill Walton would have earned their keep anywhere, but it is also true that under the tournament's old and rigid regional format—West versus Midwest in one bracket, East versus Mideast in the other—UCLA had only to win the Pacific Eight (easily the toughest league west of the Mississippi), then get by an occasional Long Beach State to reach the championship game.

But in '73 the NCAA began rotating the regional matchups in the Final Four, and sure enough, in '74 UCLA had to face its Grim Reaper, North Carolina State, in the *semis*. Then in '75 the tournament fathers went a huge step further, expanding the field from 25 to 32 teams and inviting more than the standard one team per conference. By '80 the NCAA field had been enlarged to 48 and, more important, the tournament draw was balanced by a seeding system whereby any team from anywhere could be placed in any one of the four regions.

In the 1975 tournament, for the first time, UCLA had to play five games to win it all. With a last gasp—and it was a gasp—the Bruins barely escaped Montana in the second round and, Dame Fortune abounding, both Louisville and Kentucky in the Final Four at San Diego. Then Wooden, the Wizard of Westwood, finally retired. In the next four years, 16 different teams advanced to the Final Four. The NCAA's expansion balancing had done the trick. From that came other improvements. Through 1981—43 tournaments—there were but three one-point games in the final. And then: three of the next four championship games decided by a single bucket. The shocking victories by N.C. State in '83 and Villanova in '85 are vivid reminders of the inherent possibilities in sport—of the underdog factor, of surprise, bewilderment, drama. Of life itself.

What the expansionists created was not so much a newfangled Final Four as a magical Final Month. And even if there is little mystery left, there is a good side to that, too. "When we played Wilt in '57," says Tommy Kearns of North Carolina's undefeated NCAA championship squad, "he was a god, one of the most famous guys in the country. *Wilt the Stilt*, jeez. But we had never really seen him." A god like Kansas's Wilt Chamberlain could never develop in darkness today. Because of summer camps, all-star games and the dusk-to-dawn explosion of cable TV, college basketball players from coast to coast know each other as brothers, angling for a chance to show each other up in late March.

The very first national collegiate championship was won by Oregon in 1939 when Howard Hobson's Tall Firs—who towered an outrageous 6'4", 6'9", 6'4" across the tree line—cut down Ohio State 46–33 at Patten Gym in Evanston, Ill. Buckeye captain James Hull later said his team had simply been "not interested in playing in this tournament. It was just so new . . . unheard of." The Buckeyes themselves had not even heard of it until after they had won the Big Ten because their coach, Harold (Oley) Olsen, whose idea the national tournament was, did not bother to tell them. Oley, Oley in free. The Firs, meanwhile, had earlier in the season barnstormed across the country, all the way to New York City, where *The New York Times* took one look at center Urgel (Slim) Wintermute and labeled the team the "Giants from the Far West." Wintermute is believed to be the charter member of the charter all-name team.

For the first seven years of the tournament there was no such thing as a Final Four, or even a final four; only two teams advanced to the final game from a pair of four-team regions. Oregon won that first final but nearly lost the championship trophy when 5'8" Bobby Anet, a fern among the firs, dived for a loose ball over the top of a courtside table and clipped the basketball player figurine off the top of the trophy. "When they presented the trophy to us . . . they had to hold the figure on top. It was a two-handed presentation," said John Dick, who had led the winners with 15 points. Wintermute was mostly mute, finishing with four.

Last April, Hull, now an orthodontist in Columbus, received a call at his office from a bar in New Jersey. "Thersh not much differensh between then and now in thish NCAA basketball shtuff, ish there?" the caller slurred. "Thish guy Ewing got 14 points in the finalsh and losht and you got 14 in the finalsh and losht. No differensh."

Hull was kind enough not to tell the drunk that there was a difference. Hull scored 12 points in the 1939 championship game.

Contradictions. In the 1974 semifinals at Greensboro, UCLA had blown an 11-point lead over N.C. State not once but twice in regulation and a seven-point lead in the second overtime. The Wolfpack had an insurmountable 80–75 lead when Bill Walton scored his final college basket of championship play. As he loped down the floor with four seconds left—the string of seven straight championships broken, the Bruin dynasty crumbling—Walton nodded to teammate Greg Lee, as if to say, "It's over . . . yeah . . . but it's O.K."

Nearly 12 years later, Walton said of such moments, "Those are the ones that really kill you. . . . At UCLA you didn't play to win a conference or to come in second. Your goal was the championship. [The defeat] really stays with you. I was really down that day. When I think about it—like now—I get down."

In the 1979 Final Four in Salt Lake City, Larry Bird of Indiana State, who had not talked much all season, was chirping like a canary about his 33–0 Sycamores. "The Final Four means more to my teammates than it does to me," he said. "I thought we should have been here last year. If we win or lose it don't make no difference to me. I'm gonna get my money anyway."

When it was over, 75–64 to Magic Johnson and Michigan State, Bird sat on the bench sobbing into a towel.

Doggie Julian, the Holy Cross coach, in the locker room before the 1947 NCAA championship game: "Dermy, you start, and George, you start, and Kaftan, you start, and O'Connell, you start, and Greek, you start." Both Dermy and O'Connell were one Dermott O'Connell while George, Kaftan and Greek were all George Kaftan. But the Cross figured it out, put five men on the court (freshman Bob Cousy came off the bench) and beat Oklahoma 58–47.

Trivia. Who is the only man from a fourth-place team to win the Outstanding Player award in the Final Four? Answer: Jerry Chambers of Utah in 1966.

The Coach. Don Haskins was 36 years old when his Texas Western Miners won the national championship. That was 20 years ago, and Haskins—his school is now known as Texas–El Paso—hasn't been back. Hasn't been close.

It was a different era then—a line from the 1966 Final Four preview in this magazine read: "All seven of the Texas Western regulars are Negroes. . . ." The victory, over Kentucky's all-white squad (Rupp's last of six Final Four teams, and one of only two to lose), shocked the nation but, as Haskins says, "It was surprising to everyone but us. Our team simply thought they'd never lose."

The thing was, Haskins seemed to recognize every nuance of his team's opportunity. He says now, "I should have enjoyed it more." But back then he was an unknown coach from an unknown school, venturing into the vast unknown. Aspirin and cigarettes were his staples at the team motel in College Park, Md., the Final Four site, and Haskins constantly mused over the once-in-a-lifetime experience. He called himself "a young punk" and explained how it was "a thrill just playing against Mr. Rupp, let alone beating him." More than once he concluded, "This may never happen to me again."

Observers were no less stunned at the shrill way he treated his crew—among them Nevil (The Shadow) Shed and David (Big Daddy D) Lattin—than at the players' meek obeisance. "Isn't this the laziest bunch you've ever seen?" the coach yelled at a practice after benching Bobby Joe Hill, the little guard who would steal the title right away from Kentucky All-America Louie Dampier.

At a team meeting before the semifinal game with Utah, everyone was sitting around a motel room when Haskins looked over in the corner, and there was Hill . . . fast asleep, a toothpick hanging out of his mouth.

Of Rupp, Haskins said, "I really wonder whether he knows who I am yet." Then, on championship eve, his thoughts were disrupted by something else: a gang of Maryland students carousing in the motel parking lot. Haskins was afraid they would wake his players, so he invited the besotted collegians into his room. And then, through the early hours of the day he would win the national championship, he drank beer and shot the breeze with a group of kids he had never seen before.

Finally, Haskins offered them some brews to get them to go, and they did, quietly. "Once in a lifetime," he said, leaning back with a last beer. "You know, this is once in a lifetime." A friend pointed out that Haskins was young and that there would be other Final Four teams for him to coach. "No chance," he said. "Mr. Rupp is 64 and he made it a lot, but it's probably going to be just once in a lifetime for me."

Student athletes. In 1942, three members of Stanford's NCAA title-winning squad were sent final exams, to be administered by coach Everett Dean at the championship site in Kansas City. In 1980, Louisville's Wiley Brown left his artificial thumb on the breakfast table the morning of the championship game in Indianapolis; it was later retrieved from a garbage dumpster. In 1974, Marquette's Bo Ellis tapped the grotesque and enormous cardboard head of the female member of UCLA's mascot tandem, Josephine Bruin, and inquired, "Hey, if you be cute, how 'bout a date?"

Was Cinderella a Mormon? In 1944, Utah was led by freshman Arnie Ferrin, the great-grandson of a pioneer who had struggled across the mountains with Brigham Young to found Salt Lake City. Initially, the Utes had turned down the NCAA tournament—the Final Four was to be held at New York City's Madison Square Garden that year—to accept a berth in the more lucrative NIT, also at the Garden. But they were beaten in the first round of that tournament. Because an auto accident had caused the Arkansas squad to withdraw from the NCAAs, however, Utah was once again invited to fill the NCAA field. This time Utah accepted, and the Utes went on to win the NCAAs. Ferrin, dazzling blond hair flashing through the Garden haze, scored 22 points in the 42–40 overtime championship victory over Dartmouth. Then the Utes beat NIT winner St. John's in the annual Red Cross "Champion of Champions" face-off in the Garden.

The Utes' victory was the second of three straight for the NCAA champ over the NIT champ. By the following season, after Oklahoma A & M's 7-foot Bob (Foothills) Kurland outsmarted DePaul's 6'10" George Mikan in history's first Duel of Titans and the Aggies completed the trifecta, the NCAA tournament had achieved runaway dominance.

Contrasts. 1983: North Carolina State coach Jim Valvano on reaching the Final Four: "Awesome . . . the promised land. . . . It's akin to a religious experience. . . . Just saying it, the alliteration, the Final Four, is great. . . . Ring the doorbell at my house and you hear the last 44 seconds of our championship game. . . . If anybody enjoyed it more than I did, everything about it, it had to be sinful."

1982: Eric Smith of Georgetown, whose team was quartered in Biloxi, Miss., 85 miles from the Final Four site, was asked if he missed being in New Orleans. "I don't know what I've missed. Can't you see? I ain't here."

Trivia. Name the two players who participated in the Final Four for two different schools. Answer: Bob Bender, Indiana ('76) and Duke ('78), and Steve Krafcisin, North Carolina ('77) and Iowa ('80).

The Referee. Hank Nichols, chairman of the education department at Villanova in civilian life, has worked in six Final Fours and was a standby in three others. "I don't know if the phenomenon of the tournament can be explained," he says. "In 1974—the first time I was a standby—I remember the look of disbelief on the faces of the UCLA players. They couldn't believe anybody could beat them. In 1975 the semifinal between UCLA and Louisville was a smooth-flowing game, maybe one of the best I've ever officiated. It came down to the end and the Louisville kid [Terry Howard] hadn't missed a foul shot all season long. A lefthanded kid, he was in to dribble, pass and get fouled. But he missed the front end of a one-and-one that would have given Louisville the game. It was kind of sad.

"In the final that year, UCLA-Kentucky, I reported a technical foul on Dave Meyers, and John Wooden got up hollering. I couldn't believe it. I turned to one of my partners and said, 'I always thought he was a real gentleman.' But his eyes were rolling and he wanted to get me. [Wooden screamed at Nichols, 'You crook!'] That was kind of a shocker.

"Then there was 1982, North Carolina–Georgetown. I remember calling goaltending on Ewing on the first five or six North Carolina shots. I turned to my partners and said, 'I wonder how long he's going to do that? I wonder if he thinks we're not going to see it?' Then I called a foul that John Thompson didn't like and I knew he was going to give me guff, so when the Georgetown cheerleaders came on court, I got right in the middle of the biggest guys and hid so he couldn't find me.

"And 1983, Houston-Louisville, the semis. When Houston had a pass intercepted, Guy Lewis got up and threw a towel right in front of me. 'Hank, I didn't mean it, I swear,' he said. I said, 'Coach, I don't mean this personally either, but that's a T.' But what a dunking show! The guys on both teams were congratulating each other as they ran upcourt, saying, 'Helluva dunk, helluva dunk!' It was so devastating I ran right out of the way after being underneath the basket on the first one. I got out of there fast, right back in with the band."

It was Saturday evening, March 22, 1969, and Alcindor lay on his motel bed in Louisville, the three straight NCAA championships won, the three MOP awards received, the quest resolved. How many men, athletes or otherwise, ever achieve their full potential? "I'll just say it feels nice," he said. "Everything was up in my throat all week. I could see ahead to the end, but there was apprehension and fear. Fear of losing. I don't know why, but it was there. Before the other two, it didn't feel that way. But this one did. Wow, I was excited! We just had to bring this thing down in front again, where it belongs."

The annual convention of the National Association of Basketball Coaches is nearly as important a part of the Final Four as the games. Question: What is the easiest way to get one of the most coveted tickets in the universe? Answer: Join the NABC. Just convince the association you're a coach—even if you're not. An associate membership costs $15 a year and might entitle you to purchase a ticket to all Final Four games.

Nowadays exhibitions, displays, free meals—a cornucopia of basketball commerce—envelop the coaches' hotel headquarters. But in antiquity, a floor-finishing company known as Hillyard's supplied a lively hospitality room, a veritable den of crusty immortals, where Rupp and Henry Iba, for two, would debate strategy, yaw and growl and move chairs around the room as X's and O's while younger coaches packed around them 10-deep, enthralled. Much of the action now takes place in the lobby, where younger bucks swap recruiting information and other lies, seek out patsy schedules and knife each other for the open jobs.

One observer's Coaches' All-Lobby team: Pete Newell, former USF and Cal coach, now guru emeritus, the captain of the Dawn Patrol.

George Raveling, Iowa coach and basketball's Liz Smith of gossip. He beat every reporter in America to the John Wooden Retires scoop.

Joe Dean of Converse Rubber Company and "String Music" telecaster fame. Not really a coach, but don't tell him. Hires and fires and knows more coaches than the NCAA thought existed.

Abe Lemons, Oklahoma City coach, the delightful hoopsologist who once said of the Final Four: "It's just another UCLA bullfight. You gore the matador all night. In the end, he sticks it in you and the donkeys come on and drag you out."

Jim Valvano, before he went high-toned, not to mention off his rocker. "O.K., O.K., I was one of the guys who didn't even need a room," says V. "The best way to attract attention in a crowd of coaches is to stand up and say, 'I'm looking for two road games.' Gets them every time."

Final Four as recruiting tool? Between the 1981 semifinal games, Dartmouth coach Tim Cohane stood in the lobby of the Spectrum in

Philadelphia, pumping quarters into a telephone and calling every prospect he knew. Holding up the receiver so the clamor of crowd noise could be heard at the other end, he bellowed something like, "With you, we could be here next year!" The following season, Dartmouth won 10 games. Cohane is now a stockbroker in New York.

In the 1952 NCAA championship game, St. John's strongman, Solly Walker, stuck a finger in the eye of Cumulus Clyde Lovellette, the massive 6'9" Kansas center who was in the process of scoring 33 points, establishing seven individual tournament records and offensively dominating a Final Four as no other player has ever done. As the enraged Lovellette came to the bench, he blurted to KU coach Phog Allen, "Dammit, Doc, I'm going to kill the ———." Lovellette's mother, sitting nearby, stepped in and reminded Clyde as to how she'd raised him to be "a good Christian."

"O.K., Mom," Lovellette answered meekly. "I won't kill him, but I'm sure going to mark him up."

On the night of March 30, 1981, with the President of the U.S. lying wounded in a hospital bed, Indiana's Bob Knight, North Carolina's Dean Smith and tournament committeeman Dave Gavitt—America's last three Olympic coaches—huddled in a broom closet in the bowels of Philadelphia's Spectrum, awaiting word on whether the championship game would proceed. At one point the three men just stared at each other, whereupon Smith said, "Co-champions?"

The Siege of the King's Inn began tamely enough when several hundred Marquette fans arrived in Greensboro for the 1974 Final Four. Compared to Wisconsin winters, the weather in Carolina was moderate, which still didn't help the police understand why 25 lawn chairs, two chaise lounges, one soda machine and 14 forms of human life were found floating in the inn's swimming pool at different times. On three occasions Greensboro's tactical squadrons were called to the King's Inn, once in response to a complaint that Marquette coeds were roaming naked through the halls, carrying television sets.

This behavior ultimately ceased following negotiations with the motel's management, for which occasion a Marquette student committee purchased several more cases of beer. It was not exactly the

Treaty of Ghent. The King's Inn representative, who, alas, found himself drinking one-on-seven, finally said, "Awwww, yew gahs are awwwwright," and went to sleep.

Later the Marquettes encountered a couple of ACC fans who had innocently wandered in upon the carnage. "We're glad you boys aren't in the league," one of the locals said. "Nobody down here'd be alive."

Basketball was five years young when Nat Holman was born on the Lower East Side of New York in 1896. One of 10 children of Russian-Jewish immigrants, Holman's first basketball was a sack stuffed with rags. Holman once estimated that in 53 years as player, coach and spectator, he had been involved in more than 7,000 games, the most notable of which were those played by his team at City College of New York in 1949–50. That team—C'mon, let's hear it: *"Allagaroo, garoo, garah. Allagaroo, garoo, garah. Ee-yah, ee-yah, Sis, boom, bah!"*—became the first, last and only one to win both the NIT and NCAA championships in the same season.

What were the effects of such an accomplishment? When CCNY crushed Kentucky in the NIT final by 39 points—weep some more, my ladies—the Cats' Rupp told his team, "Thanks, boys, you bring me up here and then you embarrass the hell out of me." A member of the Kentucky state legislature proposed that state flags fly at half-staff.

But that was nothing compared to the emotional distress suffered in Peoria. For, you see, with 15 seconds left in the NCAA final at Madison Square Garden and CCNY ahead 69–68, Bradley's Squeaky Melchiorre picked off a pass and drove the opposite way for the winning basket. By all accounts, what happened next wouldn't play in Iwo Jima, much less Peoria. Melchiorre's drive was cut off by the entire CCNY team, which converged upon poor Squeaky, smacked him around and knocked his shot "actually sideways," according to Pete Newell, who was there. "Squeaky was hammered so hard, the ball looked like a horrible golf shank. It was the most flagrant non-call of all time." CCNY intercepted the shank, sped the other way, scored again and had its coveted double, 71–68.

Weeks later, local theaters in Peoria still ran newsreels of the alleged assassination, the marquee of the downtown Madison reading: WAS SQUEAKY FOULED? YOU BE THE JUDGE.

What CCNY had fouled, it turned out, was all of sport. Within a year of the grand slam, some of the Beavers were convicted of shaving points during the golden season. A spiritually broken Holman—and the college game—would never be the same.

Trivia. The Defender of the Faith Award goes to what poor soul who held Jerry West to 38 points and Oscar Robertson to 39 on successive nights in the Final Four of 1959? Answer: John Turner of Louisville.

The Fan. Since 1978, Merrill Lamb, the president of Cozzoli's pizza parlors in Miami, has traveled to the Final Four with a group of friends and business associates. "It's like real therapy," he says. "We play cards, we laugh. We feel like we're back in college again." Tickets? "We wait till we get there and deal with the students," says Lamb. "See, the television network wants a lot of them downstairs to generate excitement so the students get the best seats. We see where loyalty to the school parts company with the dollar. We try to get the business majors. I'd say it's usually at the $100 per ticket level that he hands over his girlfriend's ticket.

"The easiest ticket in America is the one to the Monday night final because the losing teams want to get the hell out of town. You've never seen anything as depressing as the two schools that lose on Saturday afternoon."

So Lamb cases the stands where the losers are sitting as the semifinal games near conclusion. "If you want the good seats, you have to move fast," he says. "I've bought tickets from kids as the buzzer sounded and their team just lost in overtime and they had tears running down their faces."

Would you buy a pizza from this man?

At halftime of the 1960 NCAA championship game, Ohio State had made 16 of 19 shots and taken a 37–19 lead over defending champion California. Cal coach Pete Newell slammed the door to his locker room. "Men," he said, "we have to get more defensive rebounds."

"Coach," center Darrall Imhoff said, "there've been only three, and I got 'em all."

Tribute. Iowa's Bob Hansen on Darrell Griffith of Louisville, the Outstanding Player of the 1980 Final Four: "I've guarded guys who could leap high before. But all of them came down."

Non-tribute. North Carolina's Bones McKinney, while guarding and woofing at Bob Kurland of Oklahoma A & M, the Outstanding Player of the 1946 Final Four: "All-America? You're not even all–Madison Square Garden!"

Trivia. What father of a famous 1984 U.S. Olympian made two free throws in an NCAA championship game? Answer: Ron Retton (Mary Lou's dad) for West Virginia in 1959.

By the time UCLA's Walton had made 21 of 22 shots and scored 44 points against Memphis State in the championship game of 1973, it had already been forgotten that the best individual 12 minutes of that or any other Final Four might have been played in an earlier game and in defeat. In the first half of Memphis State's semifinal victory over Providence, the Friars' 6-foot Ernie DiGregorio was simply the greatest guard who ever lived. With an assortment of exquisite shots, whiplash dribbling, lob bomb passes and between-the-limbs playmaking, DiGregorio blew the helpless Tigers out of the St. Louis Arena. He sent an 80-foot behind-the-back bounce pass to Marvin Barnes for a layup; then a 60-foot chest pass to Kevin Stacom for another; and again a 40-foot behind-the-backer to Barnes for a third. This marvelous athlete had astonished witnesses roaring and itching to see what Walton and mighty UCLA could possibly do against his brilliant legerdemain.

At halftime, Providence led 49–40; DiGregorio had scored 17 points and was responsible for 15 of the team's 22 baskets. But Ernie D did not step inside that Friar locker room. At the 12½-minute mark of the opening period Barnes had gone to the bench with a knee injury, and so DiGregorio paced furiously in the corridor, pounding his fist against the wall, seething with frustration and hurt. He knew that with Bad Marvin down, the Friars were out. And he was right.

Pete Blackman played for UCLA in 1962, Wooden's first Final Four team, the Bruin club that finished fourth. In January 1963, while he was serving in the Navy in Hawaii, Blackman received a letter from Wooden, which included a bit of free verse:

However, Pete, there's optimism
Beneath my valid criticism
I want to say—yes, I'll foretell
Eventually this team will jell,
And when they do, they will be great,
A championship could be their fate,
With every starter coming back
Yes, Walt and Gail and Keith and Jack
And Fred and Freddie and some more
We could be champs in sixty-four.

Twelve years and three months later, the Bruins had been NCAA champions 10 times over.

The Player. Benny Anders was something of a mythic figure *before* he reached the Final Four. Hip, flashy, and bright, Benny already had learned how to act and talk on his feet and look like a movie star. At Houston, however, he got the reputation of being the puerile Akeem Olajuwon's walk-around guy. In reality, Akeem was Anders's foil. "All I get is some vicious pine," said sixth-man Anders in a memorable State-of-the-Phi Slamma Jamma message, "but I got the utensils. I drop a dime on the big Swahili, he got to put it in the hole."

In the 1983 semifinals against Louisville, Akeem did just that and so did Benny and the rest of the Houston fraternity, 14 phenomenal dunks' worth, in as electrifying an athletic performance as has ever been seen in a Final Four.

Anders was in full, glorious cry, once fashioning the most spellbinding slammer of them all: a quarter-court leap over a flock of taller Cardinals followed by a dive across Albuquerque's "Pit" in which, he said in another classic line, "I took it to the rack and I stuck it." He arose from this incomprehensible play to stomp and parade in front of the enraptured Houston rooting section, clapping and crowing while some of his awestruck teammates rushed from the bench to watch the replay on a nearby TV monitor.

In the championship game, Houston met sudden doom at the hand of N.C. State. But even with that, Benny almost won it. Barely an inch more, and the lunging Anders would have intercepted a shaky Wolfpack pass and gone the distance for the winning jam.

The following year Houston and Olajuwon and Anders were back in the Final Four but trouble was abrewing. Benny had temporarily quit the team and now he was at the far end of the vicious pine. Still, he arrived in Seattle duded out in a tuxedo with a smashing pink bow tie and cummerbund. What Anders wore to the semis, however, was, he claimed, "the wrong brand of sneakers," and that's why coach Guy Lewis did not put him in against Virginia.

In Houston's championship-game loss to Georgetown, Anders played briefly (10 minutes) and rallied the Cougars with his quickness, smarts and zest for combat. But, as he said, "This was a battle of the benches. How can the man [Lewis] forget the athletes he has on the bench? I could have scored at will."

Nonetheless, as Benny lolled around the huddles, a banner was unfurled in the Kingdome stands, reading: BENNY ANDERS FOR PRESIDENT. Back at the hotel Anders met his constituency: two guys from Jackson, Ky.

A week later, one of the Kentuckians, John Gambill, received a package in the mail. Inside was Benny Anders's Phi Slamma Jamma warmup. "I'll never let it go," Gambill says. "But the best part was Benny in the flesh. We met the man behind the legend."

Anders sat out the '84–85 season at Houston with a knee injury. Then, in May, things took a turn for the worse. One day at Jeppesen Fieldhouse on the UH campus, he got into an argument with a fellow student "because the guy wanted to play basketball with Benny," according to prosecuting attorney Cheryl Turner, "and Benny didn't want to play. The argument got heated, and the other guy threw a [sprinter's] starting block at him." Anders went outside to his car, got a gun, returned and aimed the pistol at the guy who wanted to play basketball with him.

A university police officer arrived, and Anders ran off. Eventually, Benny returned and took the police to the weapon. Fully loaded and cocked, it lay in a gymnasium shower. Anders, sentenced to three years' probation, is still enrolled at Houston, and once in a while he showed up at a basketball game. "Finishing school, that's my main priority," he says. He is majoring in sociology and intends to graduate even if he doesn't play basketball, which he won't.

It is a shame, but wonders do cease. Benny Anders has sat on the vicious pine and taken it to the rack and worn a tuxedo with a pink bow tie and cummerbund and run for President at his last Final Four.

Bob Ryan and Terry Pluto

Though you could hardly tell from his longtime base in Boston, the sports beginnings of Bob Ryan (b. 1946) go back to a childhood in central New Jersey and college basketball, including Big Five tripleheaders at the Palestra in Philadelphia. After his graduation from Boston College in 1968, Ryan took an internship and soon a full-time job at the *Boston Globe*, auspiciously while the Boston Celtics' dynasty remained enthroned. For nearly a half-century he filed knowing copy on a range of sports and enjoyed a high public profile with frequent appearances on television. But nothing brought Ryan to life quite like a writing assignment on basketball, on deadline. Terry Pluto (b. 1955), when not working the Cleveland Cavaliers' beat for the *Akron Beacon-Journal*, has proved to be one of the great listeners in the profession, honing his ear with two oral histories, *Loose Balls*, an account of the old ABA, and *Tall Tales*, in which he debriefed NBA characters of the 1950s and 1960s. Inspiration for Ryan and Pluto's collaboration, *Forty-Eight Minutes: A Night in the Life of the NBA* (1987), came from *Nine Innings* (1985), Daniel Okrent's deep dive into a Major League Baseball game. Before and during the Cavs' visit to Boston Garden on January 16, 1987, each reporter gathered all he could from the vantage point of his respective team. Then, using follow-up interviews and breakdown of videotape, they deconstructed and reconstructed critical moments, folding digressions on NBA culture and conventions into their narrative. This excerpt is pegged to a call late in the third quarter, when referee Mel Whitworth whistles Boston's Kevin McHale for a three-seconds violation. Lesser players in the microdrama include Cleveland trainer Gary Briggs and Cavs' rookie John (Hot Rod) Williams.

from

Forty-Eight Minutes

2:45 McHALE CALLED FOR THREE SECONDS.

MCHALE POSTED Hot Rod in the lane. "Three seconds," yelled Gary Briggs. Mel Whitworth agreed. "About time they called it. It was more like six seconds. Why don't they just let McHale lease an apartment in the lane?" asked Briggs.

NBA referees are much like the Motion Picture Academy of Arts and Sciences in that they sometimes make cumulative calls rather than actual calls. To wit, the 1987 Oscar for Best Actor went to Paul Newman

227

for his performance in *The Color of Money*. He was a heavy favorite for the honor, not because he had threatened the best of Olivier when he reprised the role of Fast Eddie Felson (although he was certainly very good), but because the Academy was known to feel it was Newman's "time" to win the award. Though one of the most respected and well-liked men in Hollywood, Newman was a perennial also-ran when it came to Oscar nominations. He was good enough in *The Color of Money* that a guilt-ridden Academy saw fit to give him what amounted to a meritorious service Oscar. Nobody complained.

We turn now to Kevin McHale and his overstay in the three-second zone. All night long Gary Briggs has been badgering Earl Strom and Mel Whitworth to call three seconds on Kevin McHale. This is one of the things trainers do best. It seems to be what they were put on this earth to do, at least once the game starts. Former Knicks trainer Danny Whelan started shrieking "Three! Three!" from the opening tap-off in a voice that could have alerted the beleaguered citizens of London to take to the shelters in 1940, had the sirens suddenly ceased to function.

This scenario is repeated every night in the NBA. At the exact moment Briggs was hollering at Strom and Whitworth to call three seconds on McHale, for example, Detroit trainer Mike Abdenour was probably screaming at Ed Middleton and Mike Laverman to call three seconds on Houston's Akeem Olajuwon in the Pontiac Silverdome. Once the game starts, trainers do three things. They keep track of fouls, both personal and team; they keep track of timeouts; and they yell at the officials to call three-second violations on the other team's inside people.

Referees are not deaf. They can absorb information during the course of a game, and they certainly want to get things straight. Kevin McHale does continually set up shop on the edge of the foul lane. He does stray into the forbidden three-second area on occasion, and logic dictates that if this game has progressed through thirty-three minutes and fifteen seconds of playing time it's entirely possible McHale has been guilty of a three-second violation, at least once.

It is, furthermore, entirely possible that Mel Whitworth had decided to monitor the three-second situation a little more closely. Gary Briggs's incessant carping on the subject was impossible to ignore. There certainly *could* be some validity to the charge.

The Celtics had come into possession of the basketball when Williams attempted a hook and Parish rebounded. The Celtics came upcourt at a moderate pace, and McHale went to work on the left hand side of the lane. Time, perhaps, to take John Williams back into the Torture Chamber.

He moved into the lane. Mel Whitworth was on that side of the court, standing a few feet out of bounds. Gary Briggs was there to remind him about McHale's affinity for the real estate inside the foul lane. McHale was in there and Whitworth started his count. *One thousand one*—McHale is still in there—*one thousand two*—McHale is still in there—*one thousand thr*—McHale is now exiting the lane—*eee*. McHale is now out. This may have been a two and seven-eighths second violation. It may have been a two and nine-tenths second violation. It may have been a two and ninety-nine one-hundredths second violation. But it was *not* a three-second violation.

But Whitworth has decided that it is time to cite McHale. Now we know who Mel Whitworth would have voted for in 1987 had he been a member of the Academy.

Dave Kindred

He would go on to be a columnist at the *Washington Post*, the *Atlanta Journal-Constitution*, and *The Sporting News*, respected for his lapidary prose and untrimmed point of view. But a formative experience for Dave Kindred (b. 1941) came in a smaller market, during eleven years as Kentucky basketball beat reporter and then a columnist for the *Louisville Courier-Journal*. Even to a former point guard at Atlanta (Illinois) High School, that Bluegrass stopover revealed how deep the game could run. Every year Kindred would take two weeks to drive around the state in search of basketball stories, listening to Kentuckians like the proprietor of a general store in Letcher County who told him, "If a lump of coal ain't Jesus Christ, basketball is." Much of that reporting turned up in his 1976 book, *Basketball: The Dream Game in Kentucky*. By 2010, in semi-retirement and having found his way back to downstate Illinois, Kindred also brought his career full circle: he sat in the stands at the games of a girls' team near his home, the Morton High Lady Potters, and faithfully posted dispatches to Facebook and the web, his compensation nothing more than a box of Milk Duds slipped to him by the coach. "It feels right," he said. "It's where I started, in little gyms around Illinois. It's a game I love, and the Lady Potters play it with class, elegance, and grace." Those three virtues show up in this 1988 column from Kindred's big-time period, written after Pete Maravich's death. It's as lean and simple as the deceased was showy and complex. With his opening sentence, Kindred invites readers to see his subject. Throughout, he's faithful to the writer's oath to *show, don't tell*. And the final sentence offers one last look at Maravich doing what he did best. All told, it's a newsreel elegy put to the page.

Pete Maravich

JANUARY 6, 1988

YOU'D BE afraid to take your eyes off Pete Maravich. You'd be afraid that the moment you looked anywhere else, he'd do something you'd never seen before and would never see again. Creative genius works that way. The deed would spring full-blown before the thought occurred to anyone, even Maravich.

Many players moved with greater grace, Earl Monroe for one, but none moved with more purpose than Peter Press Maravich. An inelegant collection of bones, the skinny 6-foot-5 Maravich flailed his way downcourt, all elbows and knees, sharp angles rearranging themselves, that mop of hair flopping in antic rhythm to his gallop, an Ichabod Crane on the fast break, and you dared not blink.

Only Wilt Chamberlain commanded more attention on a basketball court. And even Chamberlain didn't have the ball *all* the time. Maravich holds the NCAA career scoring record of 44.2 points a game. He scored more than 50 points 28 times. In a decade as a pro, he scored 25 a game. Yet he was only secondarily a shooter. Maravich was a ballhandler, nonpareil.

As if telekinesis were one of Maravich's gifts, the basketball did his bidding. We see it spin on his fingertips. We see it move behind his back and over his shoulder. In reports of his death yesterday, we saw a film of Maravich on a fast break, the ball floating ahead of him, untouched, and what does he do? He moves his right hand around the ball, a blur he does it so quickly, making a circle around the ball until he slaps it to a man on the left wing, not so much a pass as a deflection, not a deflection as much as imagination made real.

The basketball was part of Maravich, soulmates. Five years old, he could dribble through his house blindfolded. He took the end seat at movies so he could bounce the ball in the aisle. He dribbled the ball on the street from inside a moving car. A Maravich fan called WSB radio and read a poem he'd written on Pete's death, a line of which said, "At night he went to bed with a basketball in his hand."

It couldn't have been easy to be Pete Maravich. His father, Press, was a failed pro player who became a coach. After his father's games at North Carolina State, Pete practiced alone for hours. At LSU, the father now coaching the son, Press Maravich told reporters who compared Pete to Bob Cousy, "Cousy never saw the day he had moves like Pete."

Their obsession exacted a high price in pain. As good as Pete Maravich was, his teams were never good. Many people blamed Maravich, said he needed the ball too much, wouldn't share it. Off the court, it was worse. His mother, an alcoholic, committed suicide. He had only basketball to comfort him, and it was no answer. Too many mornings in too many cities, Maravich woke up lost in an alcohol fog. He would come to say, "The only thing that ever mattered to me was basketball. I sold my soul to the game."

After retiring from the NBA at age 33, a burnt-out case, Maravich began a search for himself. It took odd turns to meditation, vegetarianism, astrology. He painted a sign on a barn roof inviting extraterrestrials to capture him. In time he married and had two children. He said he met Jesus Christ. He preached alongside Billy Graham. He ran basketball camps with religion a part of the daily routine; as deep as the wounds of basketball had been, he loved the game too much to blame it for his failings.

It has been said that Maravich was a white man playing black man's basketball. That wasn't so. Maravich's work was distinctly and only Maravich's. No one, not even Cousy, ever had such hand-eye skills. And certainly no one without such skills could have dared ask that all eyes be on him all the time.

"One of these nights," he said as a senior at LSU, "I'm going to hit all my shots."

A listener said, "Come on."

"Yes, if I take 40, I'll make 40," Maravich said. "I don't know when it's going to happen—in college or where—but it'll happen."

Maravich redefined basketball. His genius stretched the boundaries of the acceptable. In the late '60s only Maravich dribbled between his legs on the fast break; only Maravich threw behind-the-back passes across the court; only Maravich put up odd-angled, off-balance shots, hook shots, bank shots, shots from downtown, thrown from the shoulder, shots from the hip, "Pistol Pete" blazing away.

He died during a pickup game on a basketball court at age 40. Friends said he had become a happy man, the circle closed in peace, "and now," to finish the Maravich fan's poem, "he's gone to heaven with a basketball in his hand." The television news shows ran a film clip of that last pickup game, guys walking through the motions, laughing. The last we saw of Pete, he banked one in from 17 feet.

Alexander Wolff

Alexander Wolff (b. 1957) pushed at basketball's boundaries with *Big Game, Small World*, his 2002 travelogue about the sport's global spread, which appeared just as U.S. dominance was diminishing internationally and non-Americans were injecting new life into the NBA. Several years later, after moving to Vermont, he explored the opposite extreme, ginning up a wholly local story by founding the minor-league Vermont Frost Heaves and writing about their brief life and two ABA titles for *Sports Illustrated* and its fledgling website. Wolff primarily covered the colleges during thirty-six years on the *SI* staff, writing from NCAA title games on a tight Monday night deadline over nearly two decades. In 1989 he got a tip that legendary UCLA coach John Wooden hadn't slept beneath the covers of his bed since the death of his wife, Nell, four years earlier. Wolff honored Wooden's wish that the public be spared that intimate detail, and it was left to others to divulge it later. But its truth added a layer of poignancy to everything the old coach did choose to share about their marriage. "I can't think of anything more presumptuous than suggesting someone get over the death of a spouse," Wolff said. "But I felt I'd been drafted into the role of messenger by his former players and other coaches, who desperately wanted him engaged in the game again." Wooden eventually did emerge from his despondency, living a strikingly public life until his death in 2010 at age 99.

The Coach and His Champion

JOHN WOODEN will not be in Seattle this weekend. Instead, the greatest basketball coach ever—the man who so completely made the Final Four his private reserve that the fans and the press and the rest of the college game couldn't get in on the fun until he retired—will be at home, in Encino, Calif., in what is called the Valley.

He will not stay home because he is unwelcome in Seattle. Men like Bob Knight and Dean Smith have implored him to come, to grace with his presence the annual meeting of the National Association of Basketball Coaches, which is held at the Final Four. But their entreaties have been unavailing. "We need him at our convention," says current UCLA coach Jim Harrick, who is the sixth man in 14 years to try to wear Wooden's whistle. "He is a shining light. My wife and I have offered to take him. I hounded him so much that he finally told me to lay off. The more you badger him, the more stubborn he gets. But I can see his point. The memories would be really difficult."

To most coaches, memories of 10 NCAA championships in 12 years, including seven in a row, would be sweet and easy. Indeed, this spring marks the 25th anniversary of Wooden's first title, the championship won by UCLA's tiny Hazzard-Goodrich-Erickson team, the one he likens to his first child. But beginning in 1947, when he was coaching at Indiana State, and continuing for 37 consecutive years, Wooden attended the coaches' convention and the Final Four in the company of his late wife, Nell. At 78 he's not about to start going alone, not now.

Nell was perennial, consensus All-Lobby. She knew the names that went with the faces, and she would whisper cues to her husband as well-wishers approached. He needed her with him, for she was as outgoing as he was reserved. A few coaches didn't cotton to Nell's presence, for they had left their own wives at home and knew that the usual boys-will-be-boys shenanigans would never pass unnoticed before Nell's Irish eyes. But her husband wasn't for an instant to be talked out of bringing her, just as today he isn't to be talked into going without her.

So Wooden will spend college basketball's premier weekend in much the same way he passes all his days now. The games on TV will be mere divertissements. He will take his early-morning walk, past the park, the eucalyptus trees and the preschool his great-granddaughter attends. Each evening he will speak to Nell in apostrophe before retiring. He may whisper the lines from Wordsworth that he finds so felicitous: "She lived unknown, and few could know/When Lucy ceased to be;/But she is in her grave, and, oh,/The difference to me!"

Sunday will be for church, for the long drive to Nell's grave in Glendale and for their children, their children's children, and their children's children's children. At night he will repair to the bedroom of the condominium he and Nell shared, in which virtually nothing has been altered since her death four years ago. Wooden sleeps fitfully these days, as if expecting a call. He talks often of death but does not fear it. "No fear at all, absolutely none," he says. "I'll confess that prior to losing Nellie I had some."

Upon finishing his morning constitutional—a doctor prescribed it in 1972 because of heart trouble—he often will sit down in his study, underneath the pictures of the 10 national championship teams that were hung, at Nell's suggestion, to form a pyramid, and a poem or aphorism will take shape. He remarks on how effortlessly this one flowed from him one morning:

The years have left their imprint on my hands and on my face;
Erect no longer is my walk, and slower is my pace.
But there is no fear within my heart because I'm growing old;
I only wish I had more time to better serve my Lord.
When I've gone to Him in prayer He's brought me inner peace,
And soon my cares and worries and other problems cease;
He's helped me in so many ways, He's never let me down;
Why should I fear the future, when soon I could be near His crown?
Though I know down here my time is short, there is endless time up there,
And He will forgive and keep me ever in His loving care.

And how did you imagine John Wooden spending his later years? The mind, the values, the spring in his step—they're all still in place. He could probably take over a misbegotten college varsity, demonstrate the reverse pivot, intone a few homilies and have the team whipped into Top 20 shape in, oh, six weeks. He continues to stage summer basketball camps in which you won't necessarily meet famous players but you may actually learn the game. He answers his own mail, in a hand that you'll remember from grammar school as "cursive writing."

He books most of his own speaking engagements, although several outfits have solicited his services. Audiences rarely ask about Nell, but he tends to bring her up anyway. He usually refers to her as "my sweetheart of 60 years, my wife of 53, till I lost her." The cards he sends to family and the checks he makes out for the children's trusts, he signs in both their names. "That pleases Nellie," he says.

His life is lived to that end. "I won't ever leave here, because I see her everywhere," he says in his—their—living room. "I miss her as much now as I ever have. It never gets easier. There are friends who would like to see me find another woman for the companionship. I wouldn't do it. It would never work."

He takes the morning walk in part because she insisted he take it. He has continued to participate in the camps because his share of the profits goes into the trusts, and family was so important to her. He gives the speeches, usually on his Pyramid of Success—a homespun collection of life principles—because, if you riffle back through the Norman Rockwell scenes of their life together, back to high school in Martinsville, Ind., you'll see it was Nell who persuaded taciturn Johnny Wooden to take a speech class to help him out of his shell. He struggled until the teacher, Mabel Hinds, who knew of his fondness for poetry, gave him a copy of Thomas Gray's *Elegy Written in a Country Churchyard*, which made the speaking easier.

He still knows Gray's *Elegy* cold, and in Martinsville in January, at a banquet on the eve of ceremonies to dedicate the 12-year-old high school gym in his name, he recited it. With all manner of acclaim being slung at him, he intoned this stanza as if raising a shield to protect himself:

> *The boast of heraldry, the pomp of pow'r,*
> *And all that beauty, all that wealth e're gave;*
> *Awaits alike th' inevitable hour.*
> *The paths of glory lead but to the grave.*

"And they do," he added from the dais. "We're all going to go someday."

"As a coach, did you ever lose your temper?"

The postprandial question comes from the audience in Martinsville. Wooden's answer provides a lesson about self-control: "I always told my players to control their tempers, and I couldn't very well expect them to if I wasn't setting a good example myself. I lost my temper once in a while. But I never lost control. I never threw anything. I never threw a chair."

Not 20 miles from Bloomington, within the pale of Bob Knight, the banquet hall erupts with approval.

The sphinx of the Pyramid of Success rests his left forearm against his stomach, parallel to the ground. His left hand is a socket for his right elbow. His right forearm forms a hypotenuse leading to his chin, where the index finger sticks upright, hovering just over his mouth. When speaking, Wooden strikes this pose frequently and unconsciously. A photograph of him in the same pose—Nell's favorite—hangs in their bedroom.

It is an enigma, that finger to the mouth. Is it the stern Midwestern schoolteacher, meting out discipline, admonishing the class? Or is it the kindly grandfather, guiding the wayward and confused young, giving them assurances that everything will be all right?

Or is it both? Wooden's greatest achievement isn't the 10 in 12, or seven in a row, although such a feat will surely never be accomplished again. It is rather that he did all this during the roily years from 1964 to '75—an era in which 18 to 22-year-old males were at their most contrary—at UCLA, a big-city campus awash in the prevailing freedoms.

Your star player lies down in rush-hour traffic to protest the Vietnam War. (Stand up for what you believe, Bill Walton's coach always said, but be willing to accept the consequences.)

Four of your players ask to use your office after practice to conduct meditation sessions. (You let them.) One asks your permission to smoke marijuana, saying he'd heard it would relieve the pain in his knees. (I am not a doctor, you tell Walton. All I know is it's against the law.)

College players still take drugs, but none today go in to discuss it with the coach beforehand. What was it about Wooden that caused Walton to broach this subject? "Decisions are more apt to be accepted when you've listened to suggestions first," says Wooden. "I wanted them to see the reason behind what I asked of them, not to do things just because I said so."

Yet Wooden threw down the clipboard when he had to. Former UCLA center Steve Patterson remembers the day, in the fall of 1970, that he and forward Sidney Wicks asked to be excused from practice to show solidarity with a nationwide rally protesting the Vietnam War. "He asked us if this reflected our convictions, and we told him it did," says Patterson. "He told us he had his convictions, too, and if we missed practice it would be the end of our careers at UCLA.

"We blinked. I don't think he was necessarily unsympathetic to the statement we wanted to make. He may even have agreed with us. But I see the connection. I didn't at the time, but I do now. He continually challenged you about your attitude toward the team as a whole. He set the standards. He didn't let us set the standards, even though we wanted to."

Wooden's practice gym was a sort of one-room schoolhouse, transported from the Indiana plains. For two hours in the afternoon his pupils listened to material that seemed to have emerged from a time warp. They listened because they knew they would win if they learned their lessons. The fundamentals came complete with hoary precepts: Failure to prepare is preparing to fail. Be quick, but don't be in a hurry. Don't mistake activity for achievement. The purpose of discipline isn't to punish but to correct. Things turn out best for those who make the best of the way things turn out.

One sentiment is so dear to Wooden that he has mined the anthologies for two renderings of it. "The journey is better than the end" comes from Cervantes. And Robert Louis Stevenson said, "To travel hopefully is a better thing than to arrive." Says Wooden, "I appreciated that notion more later, after we started to win championships. The saying that it's tougher to stay on top than to get there—I don't believe it. It's very tough to get there. And along the way you learn, as Lincoln would say, not just what to do, but what not to do.

"People say we could never win those championships again, what with parity. But I'm not so sure it couldn't happen today. Winning breeds winning. If we had had freshman eligibility during the 1960s, we would have won another one [with Lew Alcindor, now Kareem Abdul-Jabbar, in 1965–66]. When everyone has good players, teaching will be a telling difference."

Wooden taught basketball according to the simplest pedagogical principles. He used what he calls the whole-part method. Show the whole and then break it down, "just like parsing a sentence," he says, "or solving a math problem." He followed his four laws of learning: explanation, demonstration, correction and repetition. For 16 years there was talk of a new gym, and when UCLA finally opened Pauley Pavilion in 1965, Wooden made sure he didn't get just an arena, but a classroom with bleachers that roll back.

Wooden taught English at South Bend Central High before heading to Indiana State for two seasons and then to Westwood for the rest of his coaching life. He always preferred the practices to the games. The games were just exams, when the teacher's work was done. "There again," he says, "the journey's better than the end."

Piggie Lambert, Wooden's coach at Purdue, preached that the team making the most mistakes would win, for good things come to those who risk error by taking the initiative. Thus, initiative is part of Wooden's Pyramid. You would think, given his success, that someone might still coach his way today. But rare is the coach who doesn't have a tight rein, a hard derriere or both. How can a real teacher not indulge mistakes? "George Patton is not my idol," Wooden says. "I prefer Omar Bradley."

As he sees all the games the networks satellite-dish out, Wooden concludes that, besides turning the young men into dogs and ponies, television has transformed the coaches into showmen. Coaches today overcontrol. Instead, they should teach players the game and let them play it. Goodness gracious sakes alive—you may hear that truncated to Gracious sakes, but from Wooden you'll hear no stronger oath— coaches nowadays haven't even hit their forties before they're writing books with titles like *A Coach's World* and *Born to Coach*.

Wooden's first book is still in print. Published in 1966, it's called *Practical Modern Basketball*. Read it and you'll learn that basketball is a game of threes: forward, center, guard; shoot, drive, pass; ball, you, man; conditioning, skill, teamwork. These last three elements made up Lambert's hoops trinity, and they are the three blocks at the heart of the Pyramid. The Wooden text also holds that the way to play the game—soundly, and with balance—isn't a bad way to live your life.

"You might have thought of that as a golden time, when you've climbed to the top of the mountain. But we were at the top of the mountain when we showed up." Greg Lee is talking about the Walton era, the three seasons Lee played at guard, between 1971 and '74. "Half the time we didn't even know who our opponent would be," he says. "Winning 88 straight games—that's not normal. It would have been better if we'd have struggled."

When Lee and his classmates were precocious sophomores, Wooden warned them that, as seniors, they would be intolerable. Headstrong young men like Walton, guard Tommy Curtis and Lee—"I'd like to be able to say I didn't contribute to the problems," Wooden says, "but I did"—didn't prove him wrong. But Wooden bent too much, and his normally steady hand seemed to waver. He relaxed some of the inviolable principles on which he had always insisted. He excused Walton from practice on Mondays and Tuesdays because of the center's aching knees. Detecting inconsistency, the team took advantage.

That March, as if to vindicate 25 years' worth of strictures suddenly allowed to go flaccid, UCLA squandered a seven-point lead in the second overtime of the NCAA semifinals and lost to North Carolina State. "Bill was such a megastar he probably didn't need to practice," says Lee. "But maybe the team needed him to practice."

Lee, now coach at a high school near San Diego, has learned that lesson in discipline in retrospect. But Wooden, even if he denies it today, relearned it then and there. The next season, with the Bruins again playing on his exacting terms, they became champions once more.

Since his retirement, the catty strains of Wooden revisionism have made their way through the coaching fraternity. Unlikely as it may seem, between 1948 and 1963 Wooden did not win an NCAA crown at UCLA, and during this period the critics accused him of being a jockey of referees and opposing players. They said that he overheated the old "B.O. Barn," the Bruins' second-floor gym, because he knew his teams could stand it. They said that he had two sets of standards, one for stars and another for everybody else. But the most persistent whisper has always been that the cornerstone of the Pyramid was no middle-American verity, not conditioning or skill or teamwork, but a Los Angeles contractor and UCLA booster named Sam Gilbert.

Gilbert was everything Wooden wasn't. Worldly and wealthy, he offered players advice and, in violation of NCAA rules, gave them gifts and paid for their girlfriends' abortions. Black players, in particular, received healthy doses of his street wisdom and regular invitations to the lavish spreads at his house on Sunday mornings. "I remember we were on a road trip in Chicago, and five guys all got on the bus together wearing matching coats with fur-lined collars," says Lee. "It was pretty conspicuous. It's not like Coach was an ostrich about Sam, but he wouldn't confront the problem."

Wooden insists that no one enrolled at UCLA because of Gilbert. But once a player became a Bruin, few were denied his largess. With the inertia born of a successful program, and with Wooden's lack of interest in matters outside the gym or the classroom, Gilbert went unchallenged. After becoming the UCLA coach in the late '70s, Larry Brown, who resented Gilbert's sway with his players, tried to run him off. Gilbert responded by threatening not only to cut off Brown's testicles but also to do it "without him even knowing it." In 1987 a Florida grand jury, unaware of Gilbert's death four days earlier, indicted him in a drug-money-laundering scheme.

In the simplistic analogy, Gilbert is the hoodlum on the fringe of the school yard, and Wooden is the teacher who can only tell his pupils to Just Say No. "I warned them, but I couldn't pick their friends," says Wooden. Today Wooden owns up to breaking NCAA rules himself. He invited players to have meals with him and Nell during in-season school vacations so they would not be alone in dormitories on campus. He helped pay the rent of a player with a child and a sick wife. He bailed out of jail another player who had been picked up for delinquent parking violations. These transgressions all conformed to Wooden's higher rules.

"I honestly feel Sam meant well," says Wooden. "He felt whatever he did was right, even if it was against the rules." As different as he and Gilbert were, Wooden felt much the same way.

"I never had a smarter player than Mike Warren," Wooden frequently says. He also says, "I never had a better athlete than Keith Erickson." This is a salutary lesson about race, from a man who grew up in Indiana, then a hotbed of the Ku Klux Klan. Warren, who later starred in *Hill Street Blues,* is black; Erickson, white. In a sport infected with racial code phrases like "heady ballplayer" and "great athlete," Wooden's comments are March on Washington stuff. But he says he isn't the slightest bit aware of their stereotype-busting implications. Wisdom subdues bigotry. With the experience to judge, one need not prejudge.

By her husband's count, Nell was twice at death's door before she finally succumbed. A heart attack, which she suffered while undergoing a hip-replacement operation in 1982, put her in a coma. Friends and family took turns visiting St. Vincent's Hospital in downtown Los Angeles, not to see Nell in her quiet as much as to succor her husband. He spent 10- and 12-hour days at her bedside, and he might not have found time to eat were it not for their solicitude.

"The doctors told me to talk to her," says Wooden. "They said that I might not see any signs, but in her subconscious she might be hearing me." Three months after Nell entered the coma, as her body lay suctioned and plugged with intravenous tubing, he took her hand and squeezed it, and he felt a squeeze back. There are no nets to cut down when something like that happens.

But shortly thereafter Nell had to go back into the hospital to have her gallbladder removed, and that, the doctors said, was a no-hoper. No way she could weather the trauma. Yet she survived the surgery, recovering enough to live life rather than just muddle through it. She even made one last Final Four—Seattle, in fact, in 1984. She was in a wheelchair but was still alert and vivacious, still matching the names with the faces. "It was," the coach says, "the last enjoyable thing she did."

That is why this weekend in Seattle would have been so difficult. Early on Christmas morning in 1984, Nell had to be rushed to the hospital. By then a number of ailments, including cancer and emphysema, had gotten ornery. At 73 she just wasn't going to pull off any more miracles. Nell fought on through the rest of the winter, playing out the season. She died on the first day of spring.

Before every tip-off back at Martinsville High, Wooden had looked up from his guard position and caught her eye in the stands, where she played the cornet in the band. She would give him the O.K. sign and he would wave back. They kept up that ritual even as Johnny Wooden (Hall of Fame, inducted as a player in 1960) became John R. Wooden (Hall of Fame, inducted as a coach in 1972). He's the only person with the old one-two combo. Few knew that he clutched a cross in his hand. Fewer knew that she clutched an identical one in hers. She took it with her to the grave.

The reclusiveness that ruled Wooden's first year as a widower alarmed doctors, family and friends alike. Former players and assistant coaches conspired to telephone regularly until Wooden's granddaughter, Caryn, gave birth to a girl, Cori, and he brightened somewhat. "I try to be thankful for the time Nellie and I had together," says Wooden. "But sometimes you wonder what you could have done. There's a certain amount of second-guessing that goes on."

He never went off to scout opponents, never brought the practices home and didn't make more than a dozen recruiting trips in his entire career. What could so faithful and doting a husband possibly regret? "We did things because I wanted to, not because she did," he says. "We never went to Ireland. Nellie always wanted to go to Ireland. We had planned to, too. But something would always come up. And Nellie loved to dance. I was not a dancer, you know."

He averts his eyes, betraying his small-town bashfulness. That's what Nell, at 13, had to crack; that's what she and her friend Mary Schnaiter would talk about when they repaired to the quarries outside town. Of course, Johnny was already smitten. "She was as cute as can be," says Mary. "Little, with a turned-up nose. She could do just about anything she wanted."

And my, the life John and Nell spent together. You can almost hear Alistair Cooke in the voice-over: Johnny, born in Hall, Ind., in 1910, one of four sons of a simple and devout couple, spent much of his youth in a farmhouse with a three-holer outhouse out back. His father forged the iron goal he learned to shoot at. John and Nell waited out his four years at Purdue, only to have their savings—$909 and a nickel—wiped out in a bank failure on the eve of their wedding.

So rock-solid a couple was grossly misplaced amid the shifting-sand values of Los Angeles. When John and Nell left Indiana State for UCLA, they found the support of two familiar Midwestern pillars. Wales Smith, the minister at the church they joined in Santa Monica, had been in Wooden's class at Martinsville High. Ralph Irwin, the doctor they chose, had performed an emergency appendectomy on Wooden in Iowa City. With a pastor and a doctor they could trust, John and Nell needed little more. "Oh, you're from back East!" people would say. Crossly, Nell would correct them.

She would speak up at times when John wouldn't. She upbraided the fans who she thought were too greedy. She threw withering looks at the caviling men along press row. She badgered J. D. Morgan, UCLA's shrewd and parsimonious athletic director, about her husband's insulting salary and the anemic retirement package awaiting them. "I know John Wooden never lies," one coach said during the early '70s, "but he can't be making twenty-nine-five." At the time he was. And he never made more than $32,500.

He had no shoe contracts or courtesy cars, either. In the early days, before all the titles, before Pauley was built, Wooden's Bruins practiced amid the gymnasts and wrestlers and shared a locker room with the other men's sports. The dust from all the gym classes would build up by practice time, and Wooden and his managers had to mop the floor themselves. The undisciplined circumstances under which he was asked to teach ate away at him, but he and Nell never really considered going elsewhere, even as offers from NBA teams and several schools in the Big Ten came his way. Their son, Jim, had fallen for surfing; their daughter, Nan, for Hollywood, where she and her girlfriends staked out the stars, autograph books clutched to their breasts. Soon enough Wooden made peace with the broken promises and his chaotic classroom. "I whipped it," he says, "by recognizing it."

Some people think Wooden was too deferential to Morgan. Certainly, the same couldn't be said of Nell. "She really thought they were taking advantage of him," says Nan. "And Daddy never wanted to complain, because he never wanted for anything. But Daddy didn't have to get mad. He could stay very serene, because his other half was getting it out. Nobody was his champion the way Mother was."

Championing a champion took its toll. During his early days as a coach, Wooden would stop smoking the day practice began and forswear cigarettes for the balance of the season. In 1955, he quit entirely. But it wasn't so easy for Nell. From the time she first acquired a taste for cigarettes, Nell had relied on smoking to help her cope with the stress. Her husband desperately wanted her to give up the habit that would hasten her departure from him, but she played games with him, stashing butts in her purse, retiring to her daughter's house to get a fix.

As the dynasty pushed into the '70s, success was spoiling what should have been glorious times and edging Wooden toward retirement. "Sometimes I'm very slow making up my mind," he says. "But once I make it up, I'm very slow to change it."

On the floor of the San Diego Sports Arena in 1975, after Wooden had won his last NCAA title, a booster sought him out and said, "Great victory, John. It makes up for your letting us down last year." The attitude implicit in that statement disgusted him. There would be no second thoughts, no regrets, about retiring. He didn't want to step down. He had to. "Daddy's job wasn't fun for us," says Nan. "It really wasn't."

Here is a lesson about learning. Back in the late '60s, when he was in the midst of winning those seven straight titles and had little reason to question himself about anything, Wooden attended a press conference at which the Los Angeles Lakers announced that they had traded for Wilt Chamberlain. A reporter asked Wilt about his reputation for being hard to handle. Would the Laker coach have problems handling him? "I am not a thing," Chamberlain said. "You handle things. You work with people."

Upon returning home that day, Wooden opened a copy of *Practical Modern Basketball*. He turned to the section titled "Handling Your Players," crossed out "Handling" and wrote in "Working With." He phoned his publisher and asked that the change be made in all subsequent printings.

"John was a better coach at 55 than he was at 50," says Pete Newell, the former coach at Cal and San Francisco, who has known Wooden for more than 40 years. "He was a better coach at 60 than at 55. He's a true example of a man who learned from day one to day last."

In the outer lobby of the old Martinsville High gym hangs a picture of the Artesians' 1927 state championship team. "Gone," says Wooden, pointing to the player in the top left-hand corner. "Gone, gone, gone, gone," he continues, moving his finger from teammate to teammate. "Almost gone," he says, his finger finally coming to rest on his likeness.

When speaking engagements take him east, he'll route himself through Indianapolis, rent a car, drive the highway south and slip into the various graveyards around Martinsville, where his and Nell's forebears are buried. At each one he'll say a prayer. The neighboring gravestones are graced with names like Way and Byroad and Schoolcraft, names that sound as if they came from a novel about Puritans.

His preoccupation with death lifts only when Cori, 3, and her cousin, John, who's pushing three, come by to visit. Cori is the philosophical one, and little John is the instigator. It was John who got Papa, as they call their great-grandfather, to turn off all the lights and play a flashlight game that the kids call Ghostbusters. Nell must have been cackling from behind the credenza.

Meanwhile, over the hill in Westwood, a variation of the same game goes on. "The problem we're having is John Wooden," a Bruin named Kenny Fields said a few years ago. "He won too much. Now our fans can't accept anything less."

Wooden has scrupulously avoided commenting on the performance of any of his many successors. Indeed, Harrick says he has to crowbar advice out of him. Watch Wooden watching the Bruins, from his second-row seat across from the UCLA bench, occasionally with

Cori and John scrambling around him: He claps rhythmically to the pep band during timeouts, but otherwise he betrays little reaction to the basketball before him.

Wooden won't say this explicitly, but the man UCLA should have hired back in 1975, the man the old coach praises whenever he has a chance, is Louisville's Denny Crum. That single move might have forestalled all the Bruins' recent travails. But Morgan refused to consider him as Wooden's replacement simply because Crum, a former UCLA player and assistant coach, had been divorced. Such were the impossible standards of John and Nell's legacy.

So we come to the lesson of the peaks and the valleys. If you should catch one of those Final Four historical shows on late-night cable, be sure to study Wooden's Bruins in victory. They're happy campers, storming the floor and cutting down the nets, but always they hold something back. "Of course, I will have reminded them in a timeout," says Wooden, "for every artificial peak you create there is a valley. I don't like valleys. Games can be lost in them."

He had seen Phil Woolpert win back-to-back national championships at San Francisco in 1955 and '56 and then struggle in the crucible of trying to keep winning. Then he saw Ed Jucker also win two in a row, at Cincinnati in '61 and '62, only to leave coaching because of similar pressure. That's when he resolved never to exult unduly in victory or to languish in defeat. "One's life," he says, "should be the same."

But with Nell's death his very faith wavered. Never mind that a favorite plaque of theirs hangs in his study and reads GOD NEVER CLOSES ONE DOOR WITHOUT OPENING ANOTHER. "He did not want to live," says Gary Cunningham, his old assistant. "A lot of us were worried, and disappointed, too. What he had instilled in our lives he wasn't practicing in his own." All that winning, and look what one loss did.

A few weeks ago Cori and Papa looked up as an airplane passed overhead. "See that airplane, Papa?" said Cori. "I'm going to take that airplane and fly all the way to heaven and get Mama and bring her back, so Papa won't be lonely anymore."

Gracious sakes, Cori, no. Stay right here with Papa. For later, there, he'll have Mama. For now, here, he has you and John, two previous generations of Woodens, and—should he ever change that mind that's so hard to change once it's made up—a convention full of rudderless coaches of basketball, who desperately need to learn how to teach the game.

Before this extraordinary life gets played out, before the buzzer sounds, won't someone please call timeout to remind him? He has taught so many of us such wonderful lessons. He has one more lesson, his own, to study up on.

Charles P. Pierce

A sports story by Charlie Pierce (b. 1953) will spill beyond the length and breadth of any playing surface. It ranges far afield, alighting here and burrowing there, with history, politics, and culture as its lodestars. Yet there's always that distinctive voice, earnest in its curiosity, firm in its convictions, sometimes fired by indignation, usually leavened with compassion. Rare is the Pierce story that fails to betray his real-world pedigree: he studied under former LBJ press secretary George Reedy at Marquette and covered presidential campaigns for alt weeklies. Pierce served up some of his most memorable basketball profiles—on players like Magic Johnson and Shaquille O'Neal, and such coaches as Abe Lemons and Ben Jobe—in carefully set layers. This portrait of Larry Bird doubles as an explication of the Boston Celtics forward's place in the Venn overlap of race and basketball in a city that has had intense engagements with both. Pierce made his bones in that town, at the *Boston Phoenix* and *Boston Herald*, before reaching a wider audience with the *National Sports Daily*, *GQ*, *Esquire*, *Grantland*, and *Sports Illustrated*, and as a regular on such NPR shows as *Wait, Wait . . . Don't Tell Me* and *Only a Game*. Devoted fans who reach for a Pierce piece know he'll pull at multiple threads and somehow tie them together—and won't underestimate his readers along the way.

The Brother from Another Planet

THIS IS some pale stuff out there on the wing. All the other basketball players, Celtics and Pacers alike, have cleared the side, and they have left two of their own all alone. This is the isolation play, an offensive maneuver as simple as milk, yet responsible in large part for the wild and unruly success that has overtaken professional basketball in the past decade. It is out of this alignment that Michael Jordan is cleared for takeoff, and it was out of this alignment that Magic Johnson ground up the hapless on his way to the low post, and it is out of this alignment that Charles Barkley is freed to do both, often on the same play. It is a wonderful set piece—a scorer and a defender, alone with each other, the center of all focus. It is a prideful moment for both players—the Ur-matchup of the American game. One-on-one.

Anyway, this is some pale stuff out there. Larry Bird has the ball cocked high and waiting. He is guarded by an Indiana Pacer named

Detlef Schrempf, a blond German with a brush cut who makes Larry Bird look like Sam Cooke. Bird has Schrempf on a string now, moving the ball just slightly, faking with his fingertips. Other Celtics heckle the Pacer forward from the bench. More tiny fakes, and Schrempf is hearing imaginary cutters thundering behind him toward the hoop. His eyes cheat a bit over his shoulders. Finally, with Schrempf utterly discombobulated, Bird dips the ball all the way around his opponent's hip. Schrempf half-turns to help defensively on the man to whom he's sure Bird has just passed the ball. Bird pulls the ball back, looking very much like a dip who's just plucked a rube's gold watch from his vest pocket. He throws up that smooth hay-baler of a jump shot from just above his right ear, and it whispers through the net. The play draws cheers and laughter, and even Bird is smiling a little as the two teams head down the court again.

A few days earlier, Connie Hawkins was nominated for the Basketball Hall of Fame, the final vindication of what poet Jim Carroll has written about basketball, "a game where you can correct all your mistakes instantly, and in midair." Hawkins was a glider and a soarer. A legend in Brooklyn long before he was twenty, he fits snugly between Elgin Baylor and Julius Erving on the path of the game that continues upward to (for the moment) Michael Jordan.

Hawkins's best years were wasted in exile on the game's fringes; his innocent involvement in the point-shaving investigation of 1961 truncated his college career and put him on an NBA blacklist until 1969. He will go into the Hall of Fame only because some people saw him do something wondrous and they told the tale. It is a triumph for the game's oral history, for its living tradition. There is a transcendence about Connie Hawkins and about his legend. It resides out of time and place, floating sweetly there in the air above all convention and cavil.

In large part, of course, this living tradition is an African-American tradition. In reaction to it, basketball's overwhelmingly white establishment assailed the skills of legends like Connie Hawkins, deriding their game as "playground basketball," the result of some atavistic superiority that must be controlled by (predominantly white) coaches for the greater good. Black players were innately talented, of course, but they were lacking in the Fundamentals, which virtually always were defined in a way that brought the game back to earth and removed it from the largely black custodians of its living tradition.

Withal, both sides were talking past each other. The game's white establishment was talking about strategy and tactics. Black players were talking about the psychology of defining oneself as a person by what one did on the court. From this emphasis on psyche came the concept of Face—a philosophy of glorious retribution by which you dunk unto others as they have already dunked unto you, only higher and harder. It's this competitive attitude that makes the Fundamentals interesting. And it's this guilty knowledge that made basketball's white establishment so determined to minimize its obvious importance. Soon, these views ossified into the attitudes by which black players are praised for their "athletic ability"—code for the Super Negro not far removed from William Shockley's laboratory—while white players are usually commended for their "intelligence" and their "work ethic." Both sides internalized these notions, and they were irreconcilable.

By the late 1970s, the NBA, having expanded far too quickly and recklessly for its own good, was floundering. Competition had vanished. So had most of the fans. There were some drug busts, common enough in all sports. At the same time, the league was perceived as becoming blacker; by 1979, 70 percent of the players were African American. People made the usual foul connections. There were the nods and the winks in the executive suites. Disillusioned fans drifted away, and pretty soon the NBA found its championship series being broadcast on tape delay.

In 1979, Larry Bird and Magic Johnson began their careers with the Boston Celtics and the Los Angeles Lakers, respectively. There was a frisson of expectation as soon as they went around the league. By season's end, Bird had been named the NBA Rookie of the Year, and Johnson had propelled the Lakers to the title, scoring forty-two points against the Philadelphia 76ers in the seventh game of the final series. Over the next decade, the two of them played so well and drew so many fans that they are now given undisputed credit for saving professional basketball. Neither one ever evinced eye-popping athletic skills; Bird may be the only great player in history more earthbound than Magic. Their importance lies in the fact that the two irreconcilable halves of the game found in them—and, especially, in Bird—a common ground.

The most fundamental of the traditional Fundamentals is that a great player must make his team greater. Thus does a whirling dunk count only the same two points as a simple layup. Both Bird and Magic pass this test easily. However, the game's living tradition demands that this be accomplished in a way that ups the psychic ante, that forces the cycle of payback onto the opposition. Neither man has ever shrunk from this imperative. What Bird did to Schrempf, he did not do merely to score two points for the Celtics but to break his opponent's will, just as once in a championship game, he looked down to see where the three-point line was, took a conspicuous step back behind it, and then sunk a coup de grace through the Houston Rockets.

In short, the NBA has succeeded because it has become the world's premier athletic show. Playground ball has triumphed completely. It's hard to imagine now that college basketball once thought it was a good idea to ban the dunk, or that former UCLA coach John Wooden *still* thinks it's a good idea. Wooden, supreme guru of the Funda-mentals, now sounds like a hopeless crank. What Bird and Magic did was difficult, and damned-near revolutionary—they made the Fundamentals part of the show. They did it by infusing the simple act of throwing a pass with the same splendid arrogance that so vividly illuminated Connie Hawkins midflight.

"What you've got to understand about Larry is that he plays a white game with a black head," says Atlanta's Dominique Wilkins. "If he could do a three-sixty dunk and laugh at you, he'd do it. Instead, he hits that three, and then he laughs at you."

"There's no doubt about it," adds Indiana's Chuck Person, who has enjoyed a spirited rivalry with Bird. "Larry's a street kid."

It comes from his life—a lost, lonely kid whose father was an ami-able drunk who one day called Larry's mother on the phone and, with her listening, blew his brains out. There was grinding poverty. There was hopelessness. Compared to this life, Magic Johnson had it easy, as did Michael Jordan. Compared to this life, Spike Lee, who uses Bird as a cartoon foil, was one of the Cleavers. Instinctively, Larry Bird under-stands the country's most pernicious division as one of class and not of race—a distinction that a decade of public demagoguery has done its damnedest to obscure.

"The poorer person," he muses, "the person who don't have much will spend more time playing sports to get rid of the energy he has." And anger and desperation? "Yeah, them too. Why go home when you got nothing to go home to?"

All his life, he has resisted the notion of being anyone's great white hope, because it never seemed logical to him. "I've always thought of basketball as a black man's game," Bird says. "I just tried to do everything I could to fit in."

Long ago, Indiana was a demographic fluke. Unlike the other midwestern states, it was settled from south to north rather than from east to west. It was flooded with refugees from Tennessee and the Carolinas. They brought with them so much of the Old South that, by 1922, the Ku Klux Klan was virtually running the state. An Indiana town called Martinsville is famous for being the home of two institutions—John Wooden and the modern Klan. When Jerry Sichting, a former NBA player and now the Celtics' radio commentator, left Martinsville to go to Purdue, his black teammates shied away from him. "I said I was from Martinsville, and I got that look," Sichting says. "It's still out there, no question." Larry Bird is from French Lick, which is thirty miles down Highway 37 from Martinsville. Thirty miles south.

Bird seems to have grown up remarkably free of prejudice. Throughout his career, he has managed to stay admirably clear of those who would make him a symbol through which to act out their own fears and bigotry. He has called Magic Johnson his role model, and he referred to former teammate Dennis Johnson as "the greatest player I ever saw." He even delighted in bringing NBA pal Quinn Buckner home to French Lick and into the worst redneck joints in town. "Yeah," recalls Buckner. "He took me to some places that I might not have gotten out of in less than three pieces if I went in alone. But Larry truly doesn't look at it that way. He doesn't want any part of that great white hope stuff. He never did."

"Just the other day," Bird says, "a guy come up to me and says, 'Here, sign this. Put on it that you're the greatest white player to ever play the game.' To me, that don't mean nothing. The greatest player ever to play the game. That means a helluva lot more."

Unfortunately, Bird has been a lightning rod. The Celtics, whose historical record on racial matters is positively revolutionary, have been forced to carry the weight of Boston's abysmal history in the matter of race relations. They were criticized for lightening up their roster in the early Eighties, although it's difficult to make the case that it's immoral to draft Bird and Kevin McHale, or to concoct a roster that won the NBA title three times in the decade. However, on a larger scale, the Eighties were generally a decade of reaction in racial matters. Bird's first season coincided with the ascendancy in culture and politics of the shibboleth of the Oppressed White Male. A society that could straight-facedly equate Allan Bakke with Rosa Parks evolved easily to one that could see no metaphorical distance between Clarence Thomas and the Scottsboro Boys.

Those comforted by the prevailing reactionary zeitgeist were looking for a hero, and Larry Bird and the Celtics qualified. Those revolted by it were looking for a villain, and Bird and the Celtics qualified there too. Thus, when it became fashionable to make Larry Bird into the greatest player of all time—certainly an arguable proposition, particularly up until about 1986—few people were objective about it anymore.

In 1987, after losing to the Celtics in a conference playoff series, Isiah Thomas blurted out the problem. Defending statements made by rookie Dennis Rodman, he said, "If Bird were black, he'd be just another good guy." The comment was graceless and ill-timed, but it was also the truth. Had Bird been black, his physical abilities would've been emphasized at the expense of his intelligence and his diligence at practice. Thomas's statement was excoriated for being racist, which it certainly was not. To identify a racial problem is not racist. One might as well call a black man racist who points out that white people are rather heavily involved in redlining his neighborhood.

By downplaying the comments and refusing to respond, Bird got Thomas out of the situation so deftly that Thomas later credited Bird with saving his public career. Bird would not have been able to do that had he not effectively defused the issue among his peers by connecting with the game's psychology. While he passed and rebounded and got praised for his mastery of the Fundamentals, he exhibited such cutthroat competitive flair that the dunkers sensed a kindred spirit.

"I always said that Larry was one of the most creative players I ever saw," says Celtic center Robert Parish. "That same kind of thing that makes people do a dunk makes Larry throw that touch pass over his shoulder."

Neither was Bird blind to what was happening elsewhere. Just last fall, Celtic rookie Dee Brown was thrown to the ground by police in the chichi suburb of Wellesley because some clerk thought Brown "looked like" the man who had recently robbed the bank.

"It's still a scar," Bird says. "You hear that Boston is a tough town for blacks. I don't know. I can't speak for them because I'm not black. I've seen some incidents, though. Dee Brown. Robert Parish got stopped a couple of times. Just for being black, you know."

Joe Bird's son never talked about him. It was part of a past buried so deeply that when a writer from *Sports Illustrated* mentioned Joe's suicide in an article, some of the boys from French Lick were said to have gone looking for him. But the son talked about Joe Bird this year. Talked freely, if not easily. Talked because a black man, a friend in L.A., was threatened by a fatal disease, and suddenly there was a connection between an amiable and self-destructive white man in a hard little town in Indiana and an amiable and doomed black man in the fastest lane of all. The son of the first saw the connection there between his father and his friend, and he saw it clearly, far beyond the cold balm of convenient banality.

"I thought about when my Dad passed away," said Larry Bird on the night after Magic Johnson announced that he had tested positive for HIV. "I thought about how I wandered around for a week, just numb. That's what this is like."

He said it in that light little twang, the one that the people in southern Indiana brought with them from Tennessee, the one that made even Elvis sound modest in conversation. In truth, Bird has grown up remarkably unmarked by the benefits of his celebrity. "Larry doesn't care about being a famous white player," says Dave Gavitt, the Celtics CEO, "because Larry doesn't care about being famous, period." Indeed, as far as commercial endorsements are concerned, he falls well behind Johnson and Jordan. He has, however, consciously worked to change the racial debate in a way not easily done. He has proven himself in his way on someone else's terms.

It would have been easy for him to grow up hard in the native bigotry of his place. Once grown, he could have easily sensed in his bones that that bigotry is general throughout the land and exploited it shamelessly. If there are people who would make him the best player ever simply because he is white, then that's their problem. If the Celtics became white America's team, then that's white America's fault. Larry Bird, as an individual basketball player, has defined his enormous abilities in an African-American context, and he has triumphed within it.

In his play—and, therefore, in his life, because the two are inextricably bound—he has declined to profit from the advantages that spring from the worst in our common culture. There are politicians, men infinitely more powerful than Larry Bird, who have proven unable to resist this same impulse. One of them plays horseshoes in the White House now.

They say that basketball's greatness is in its ability to bring people together, but that's a lie. Glib and facile people say that about every sport, and yet sports are as riven by class and race as any other major institution of this culture. Those people are closer to being right in basketball, though, than they are in any other sport. Basketball, much more than baseball or football, unites and makes whole two cultures, and it obliterates the artificial divisions created by faceless, fearful men who cling to their own pathetic advantages. Those who would turn Larry Bird into a symbol useful to that vicious endeavor—and those who would use him as a straw man against whom they could fight back—are all blind to his true genius. They are frightened of the best possibilities of America.

On this night, before he talked about his father and Magic, Larry Bird began the game by throwing a floor-length, behind-the-back pass that nobody could recall having seen Bird ever throw. But everyone on the floor knew it for what it was—an homage, extended in high style and in the game's truest and most precious currency. Everyone who ever had dunked on a man, or had defied both aerodynamics and orthopedics to drop a shot full of life and music, identified it immediately. Dominique Wilkins, trailing the play, saw it for what it was—an entertainer's play, but a bounce pass sure enough, with the arm extended right through to the fingertips, following through just the way that Clair Bee and Nat Holman and all those other guys wrote it down years ago, before the game moved into the air for good. The Fundamentals, but Showtime, too, beyond all measure.

"Larry," said one of his coaches, "was just saying goodbye."

Darcy Frey

When he showed up on Brooklyn's Coney Island in the fall of 1991 to follow the fortunes of the Lincoln High School team, Darcy Frey (b. 1961) was a freelancer with a rattletrap Toyota and enough time on his hands to simply hang around. He thought he'd be telling the story of young men who use talent and pluck to bootstrap their way out of a bleak environment. Instead, after a nine-month gestation, Frey realized he had a larger and darker story to tell—about a system where kids with dreams of stardom are set up to lose, and quickly learn, as he puts it at the end of *The Last Shot* (the title of the magazine article and the book that grew out of it), "that in this particular game failure is commonplace, like a shrug, and heartbreak the order of the day." *The New York Times* hailed the book on its publication in 1994 for "elegance, economy and just the right amount of outrage." For the article, published in *Harper's* the year before, Frey won both a National Magazine Award and a Livingston Award. Before he landed at Harvard as a lecturer in English, Frey filed stories for *The New York Times Magazine* that would find their way into other media: a piece about airtraffic controllers led to the movie *Pushing Tin*, and the National Theatre of Great Britain adapted his profile of environmental scientist George Divoky into the stage production *Greenland*. *The Last Shot* could easily be repurposed for a theatre audience too, with its cinematic ensemble of compassionately drawn characters. The book opens with this excerpt, set at "the Garden," the outdoor court in the middle of Coney Island's largest housing project. There's an early glimpse of fourteen-year-old Stephon Marbury, who went on to become an NBA All-Star and New York Knick in the big-time Garden. But the other Lincoln Railsplitters encountered disappointment, or worse. Tchaka Shipp met the NCAA's standardized test score requirement and found his way to the Big East, only to watch his career spiral downward after an auto accident. Corey Johnson's back-up plan to become a writer was scuttled in classrooms where learning isn't taken seriously. As for Russell Thomas, Frey's pseudonym for Darryle Flicking, his life ended at age twenty-six in California where, homeless, he was struck and killed by an Amtrak train.

from

The Last Shot

R USSELL THOMAS places the toe of his right sneaker one inch behind the three-point line. Inspecting the basket with a level gaze, he bends twice at the knees, raises the ball to shoot, then suddenly looks around. What is it? Has he spotted me, watching from the opposite end of the playground? No, something else is up. He's lifting his nose to the wind like a spaniel; he appears to be gauging air currents. Russell waits until the wind settles, bits of trash feathering lightly to the ground. Then he sends a twenty-five-foot jump shot arcing through the soft summer twilight. It drops without a sound through the dead center of the bare iron rim. So does the next one. So does the one after that. Alone in the gathering dusk, Russell begins to work the perimeter against imaginary defenders, unspooling jump shots from all points.

It's the summer of 1991, and Russell has just finished his junior year at Abraham Lincoln High School in Coney Island, New York. Eighteen years old, he stands six feet two, weighs a hundred and eighty pounds, and is the proud owner of a newly shaved scalp and a small goatee. When he practices at this court, everything between his shiny bald top and his jutting, bearded chin goes blank, and he moves over the asphalt as if in a trance—silent, monklike, in a galaxy of his own. Most summer evenings I come by this court to watch Russell and his friends play ball, and I have found few sights quite as stirring as that of Russell's jumper, tracing a meteor curve in the still, expectant air. But the shot, I realize tonight, is merely the final gesture, the public flourish of a private regimen that brings Russell to this court day and night. Avoiding pickup games, he gets down to work: an hour of three-point shooting, then wind sprints up the fourteen flights in his project stairwell, then back to this court where, much to his friends' amusement, he shoots one-handers ten feet from the basket while sitting in a chair.

At this hour Russell usually has the court to himself. Lately New York City has been slogging through one of its enervating heat waves, a string of 95-degree days, and most of Coney Island's other players won't come out until after dark, when the thick, humid air begins to stir with night breezes and the court lights come on. But tonight is turning out to be a fine one—cool and foggy. The low, slanting sun sheds a pink light over the silvery Atlantic just a block away, and milky sheets of fog roll off the ocean and drift in tatters along the project walkways. The air smells of sewage and salt water. At the far end of the court, where someone has torn a hole in the chain-link fence, other players climb in and begin warming up.

"Just do it, right?" I glance to my left, and there is Corey Johnson, smiling mischievously, eyes alight. He nods toward the court—Russell at one end, a group of players stretching out and taking lay-ups at the other—and it does, in fact, resemble a sneaker commercial. "Work hard, play hard, buy yourself a pair of Nikes, young man," Corey intones. Corey, who is known throughout Coney Island for a variety of talents, practices some deft mimicry, and his rendition of a white, stentorian-voiced TV announcer is easily among his best. "They get you where you want to go, which is out of the ghet-to!" He laughs, we shake hands, and he takes up an observation post by my side.

I am always pleased, though somewhat surprised, when Corey comes by this court. Corey is Russell's best friend and one of Lincoln High's other star juniors. But he specializes in ironic detachment and normally shows up courtside, carrying his Walkman, merely to watch for girls with his handsome, hooded eyes. That may be his intention yet. Tonight he is wearing a fresh white T-shirt, expertly ripped along the back and sleeves to reveal glimpses of his sculpted physique, denim shorts that reach to his knees, and a pair of orange sneakers that go splendidly with his lid—a tan baseball cap with orange piping, which he wears with the bill pointing skyward. From his headphones come the sounds of Color Me Badd, and Corey sings along: *I-wanna-sex-you-up* . . . He loops his fingers around the chain-link fence and says, "I tell you, Coney Island is like a disease—of the mind. It makes you lazy. You relax too much. 'Cause all you ever see is other guys relaxing."

There was a time, of course, when Coney Island inspired among its residents more sanguine remarks—when the neighborhood was home to three world-renowned amusement parks, and its streets were lined with three-story homes, filled to the eaves with Jewish, Irish, and Italian families who proclaimed Coney Island the most welcoming place in America for a newly arrived immigrant—a latter-day Plymouth Rock. Now, however, all but a few scattered rides have been dismantled; most of the cottages and triple-deckers have succumbed to the bulldozers of urban renewal; and in their place the city has erected a vast tract of housing projects, home to Coney Island's newest arrivals—African-Americans—and packed so densely along a twenty-block stretch that a new skyline has risen at land's end by the beach and the boardwalk.

The experiment of public housing, which has worked throughout the country to isolate its impoverished and predominantly black tenants from the hearts of their cities, may have succeeded here with even greater efficiency because of Coney Island's utter remoteness. On this peninsula, at the southern tip of Brooklyn, there are almost no stores, no trees, no police; nothing, in fact, but block after block of gray-cement projects—hulking, prisonlike, and jutting straight into the sea. Most summer nights now, an amorphous unease settles over Coney Island, as apartments become stifling and the streets fall prey to the gangs and drug dealers. Options are limited: to the south is the stiff gray meringue of the Atlantic; to the north, more than ten miles away, one can just make out the Statue of Liberty and the glass-and-steel spires of Manhattan's financial district. Officially, Coney Island is part of the endless phantasmagoria that is New York City. But on a night like this, as the dealers set up their drug marts in the streets and alleyways, and the sounds of sirens and gunfire keep pace with the darkening sky, it feels like the end of the world.

Yet even in Coney Island there is a use to which a young man's talent, ambition, and desire to stay out of harm's way may be put: there is basketball. Hidden behind the projects are dozens of courts, and every night they fill with restless teenagers, who remain there for hours until exhaustion or the hoodlums take over. The high school dropouts and the aging players who never made it to college usually show up for a physical game at a barren strip of courts by the water known as Chop-Chop Land, where bruises and minutes played are accrued at a one-to-one ratio. The younger kids congregate for rowdy games at Run-and-Gun Land. The court there is short and the rims are low, so everyone can dunk, and the only pass ever made is the one inbounding the ball. At Run-and-Gun, players stay on the move for another reason: the court sits just below one of the most dreaded projects, where Coney Island's worst hoodlums sometimes pass a summer evening "getting hectic," as they say—shooting at each other or tossing batteries and beer bottles onto the court from apartment windows fifteen stories above.

The neighborhood's best players—Russell, Corey, and their brethren on the Lincoln varsity—practice a disciplined, team-driven style of basketball at the court where I am standing tonight, which has been dubbed the Garden, after the New York Knicks' arena. In a neighborhood ravaged by the commerce of drugs, the Garden offers a cherished sanctuary. A few years ago community activists petitioned the housing authority to install night lights. And the players themselves resurfaced the court and put up regulation-height rims that snap back after a player dunks. Russell may be the only kid at the Garden who shoots one-handers from a chair or practices his defensive footwork with a ten-pound brick in each hand, but no one here treats the game as child's play. Even the dealers and hoodlums refrain from vandalizing the Garden, because in Coney Island the possibility of transcendence through basketball—in this case, an athletic scholarship to a four-year Division I college—is an article of faith.

Although a pickup game has begun at the basket nearest Corey and me, Russell still commands the other. As the last light drains from the summer sky, he finishes with three-pointers and moves on to baby hooks: fifteen with the left hand, fifteen with the right; miss one and start all over again. It is not too much to say that basketball has saved Russell. The Thomases—Russell, his mother, and his two younger sisters—live in one of the neighborhood's toughest projects, just a block from this court; and in earlier days Russell often caused his family considerable grief, sometimes leaving home for long stretches to hang out on the streets with his friends. Every teenager does this to some extent, but the custom posed a greater threat in Russell's case since certain of his friends back then liked to wander over to neighboring Brighton Beach in order to hold up pensioners at gunpoint. But having watched so many of his contemporaries fall into gangs or prison or an early grave, Russell has developed new ambitions for himself. A few months ago, he led the team at Lincoln High to the New York City public school championship, which was played at Madison Square Garden and broadcast citywide on cable TV. For most of his teammates, it was a moment to savor; Russell hardly broke stride to celebrate. Until he wins his college scholarship, sometime in the months ahead, all else in his life seems to dwindle to the vanishing point—everything besides the ball, this basket, and his conviction that, by practicing each day and playing by all the rules, he has set himself on a path that will change his life. "Man, I *hate* Coney Island," Russell has told me several times. "Maybe after I finish college I'll come back to get my mom. But that's it. I'm leaving. And I'm *never* coming back."

Soon the orange court lights at the Garden come on, displacing the encroaching darkness, and two players on either end of the court climb the fence and sit atop the backboards, hanging nets—a sign that a serious game is about to begin. A few minutes later, a uniformed referee actually shows up to officiate. Suddenly a ferocious grinding noise fills the air. It gets louder and louder, and then a teenage kid riding a Big Wheel careers onto the court. He darts through the playground crowd, leaving a wake of pissed-off players, hops off his ride, and watches it crash kamikaze-style into the fence. "Ah, yes, Stephon Marbury," Corey remarks dryly. "Future of the neighborhood."

Stephon is barely fourteen, has yet to begin his freshman year at Lincoln High, but is already considered the most gifted young New York City guard since Kenny Anderson came out of the Lefrak City projects in Queens two years ago on his way to becoming the star of the New Jersey Nets. Last summer, as an eighth-grader, Stephon snuck into a basketball camp for high-schoolers and would have been kicked out, except that he played with such consummate brilliance that his stunt was written up in the sports pages of the *New York Daily News*. Fourteen years old, and his college recruiting has already begun. Coaches send him letters (in violation of NCAA rules), requesting the pleasure of his company during his years of college eligibility; street agents, paid under the table by colleges to bring top players to their programs, are cultivating Stephon; and practically every high school coach in the city heaps him with free gear—sneakers, caps, bags—in an attempt to lure him to his school.

At first glance, Stephon doesn't look like the future of anything. He's diminutive, barely five feet nine, with the rounded forehead and delicate features of an infant. He sports a stylish razor cut and a newly pierced ear, and the huge gold stud seems to tilt his tiny bald head off its axis. Caught somewhere between puberty and superstardom, he walks around with his sneakers untied, the ends of his belt drooping suggestively from his pants, and half a Snickers bar extruding from his mouth. But what on earth is this? Dribbling by himself in a corner of the court, Stephon has raised a ball with one hand directly over his head and threaded it through his legs. From back to front. Without interrupting his dribble. Now he's doing it with *two* balls!

With Stephon here, Corey hands me his Walkman and strolls onto the court. Russell, too, is persuaded to give up his solo regimen and puts his gold chain around my neck for safekeeping. In fact, every star from Lincoln High has come out tonight except the team's center, Tchaka Shipp, but the game won't be delayed on his account. Tchaka lives miles away in the more working-class environs of Jamaica, Queens; and although at six feet seven he towers above all his team-mates, he has been leery of hanging around the Coney Island courts ever since he came here to play, spent the night at Corey's apartment, and someone blew up a car right outside Corey's window. Not long ago Tchaka ventured to the Garden, knowing he'd get the best run in all five boroughs here, but after he surveyed the mangy dogs and ragged street people lingering around the court's edges, he concluded, "Too many low-life, rowdy-ass Brooklyn niggers. I'm heading back to Queens. *Now.*"

Tonight, however, darkness brings only a cool, vaporous sea breeze and nothing to distract the players from their game. Basketball, it is commonly said, is a sport of pure instinct, but the five-on-five contest that begins here is something else. Corey and Stephon are cousins, and Russell is as good as family—the three of them have played together since they were in grade school. They seem to move as if the spontane-ous, magical geometry of the game has all been rehearsed in advance. Stephon, the smallest by far, is doing tricks with the ball as though it were dangling from his hand by a string, then gunning it to his older teammates with a series of virtuoso no-look passes: behind-the-back passes, sidearm passes, shovel passes. Corey is lulling defenders with his sleepy eyes, then exploding to the basket, where he casually tosses the ball through the hoop. Russell is sinking twenty-footers as if they were six-inch putts.

The game has just begun when a crowd starts to form: sidelined players, three deep, waiting their turn. A prostitute trolling for clients. A drunk yelling maniacally, "I played with Jordan, I played with Jab-bar. They ain't *shit*. And neither are *you!*" A buffed-out guy in a silk suit and alligator shoes arrives, swigging from a bottle of Courvoisier. An agent? A scout? The crowd gives him elbow room. A couple of teenage mothers with strollers come by. There are many of them in Coney Island; they get significantly less elbow room.

It's past midnight now, and the ambient glow of Manhattan's remote skyscrapers has turned the sky a metallic blue. Standing court-side, we can see only the darkened outlines of the projects, looming in every direction, and the shirtless players streaking back and forth, drenched in orange light. Now and then the ref steps out from the darkness onto center court and his official stripes glow incongruously beneath the court lights as the Doppler wail of police sirens drifts in from the nearby streets. Corey, sprinting downcourt, calls out, "Homeboy! Homeboy!" Standing under his own basket, Stephon lets fly with a long, improbable pass that Corey, running full speed, somehow manages to catch and dunk in one balletic leap. The game is called on account of total pandemonium: players and spectators are screaming and staggering around the court—knees buckling, heads held in astonishment. Even Mr. Courvoisier loses his cool. Stephon laughs and points to the rim, still shuddering from its run-in with Corey's fists. "Yo, cuz!" he yells. "Make it bleed!" Then he raises his arms jubilantly and dances a little jig, rendered momentarily insane by the sheer, giddy pleasure of playing this game to perfection.

Gary Smith

By the late 1970s, more than a year before he graduated with an English degree from LaSalle, Gary Smith (b. 1953) was already working full-time at the *Philadelphia Daily News*. It was "a great place to hatch," he said—a sports department where "creativity and unusual storytelling were prized." Smith took that license and went on to essentially turn himself into a nonfiction short story writer, at *Inside Sports* from 1979 to '82, and for thirty years after that at *Sports Illustrated*, winning an unprecedented four National Magazine Awards and ten finalist nominations along the way. Smith would call subjects back multiple times to press them on what they were thinking—reportorial grunt work that gave him the credibility to "get inside heads" on the page. When he turned to this 1998 piece about Tennessee women's coach Pat Summitt, Smith had already profiled several demanding coaches, including college basketball's John Chaney and pro football's Dick Vermeil, and in a fit of restlessness tried a different tack: "I wanted to use more of a cinematographic eye, to see if where you set up 'the camera' on a long narrative story could affect its emotional impact." He collected several anecdotes about Summitt's relationship with her headstrong point guard, Michelle Marciniak, and later, in the Marciniak family living room, discovered that he was sitting on the very couch where a pregnant Summitt, determined to land her recruit, had once nearly given birth. "I realized the Michelle lens was the one I'd be keeping my eye pressed to until the finish line," Smith said. "Which meant bouncing virtually everything vital about Pat's story off Michelle, so it could all be strained through her." The result is the kind of profile that the writer made his specialty—"the article that eloquently and dramatically inhabits the consciousness of its subject," as editor and critic Ben Yagoda wrote of Smith's storytelling, "and whose momentum takes us toward the kind of artistic and emotional payoff we expect from the best literary art."

Eyes of the Storm

HERE COMES this lady into your life. You don't know that she has been up all night peeing, racked with pain in her lower back. You don't know how many people told her she was nuts to get on an airplane and fly to your hometown at a time like this. You don't know that an hour ago, when her water broke, she was crouched in an eight-seat King Air blotting her legs with paper towels. Hell, you're *16*. You don't know that she's spitting Nature in the eye and kicking Time in the teeth.

She's sitting on your sofa as you come through the door from school on a September day in 1990, and she grins and grinds her teeth against the contractions. How could you know that it's already too late—that Pat Summitt's got you, she's got you forever?

Michelle Marciniak takes a seat and looks around her living room. She's a senior at Allentown (Pennsylvania) Central Catholic High, an hour north of Philadelphia, a guard who in six months will become the Naismith and Gatorade player of the year. But that's not enough for Michelle. In her dream she has both the acclaim that goes to the best player in the land *and* the championship that her high school team keeps falling short of. She would love to put her dream in Pat's hands, but in Pat's hands already rests the *other* player of the year candidate, the *other* All-America who plays Michelle's position.

Michelle knows something weird is going on the minute she walks in the door . . . but what is it? Her mom, Betsy, and her older brother, Steve, are wearing the same nervous, crooked little smile. Michelle's cocker spaniel, Frosty, is yip-yapping laps around the premier coach in the history of women's basketball. Pat's bouncing from the sofa to the bathroom to the telephone and back. Her assistant coach, Mickie DeMoss, is whipping through Tennessee's recruiting scrapbook as if she's sitting on a mound of fire ants: *Here's the arena, here's the library, here's the '89 national championship—O.K., Michelle, any questions?* Michelle's dad, Whitey, is sitting across the room jingling coins manically in his pocket. You try it. It's not easy to jingle coins while you're sitting down.

Suddenly Nature mounts a furious comeback, Time starts kicking Pat in the teeth. "Mickie," she blurts, "we have to go. *Now.*" Suddenly they're babbling to the teenage girl that Pat's baby is coming, and Steve and Michelle are racing to his car to lead the Tennessee coaches to—to the hospital, right?—heck no, to the airport, because Patricia Head Summitt is going to have this baby when and where she wants it. Suddenly Steve and Michelle are swerving around curves, blowing through red lights and stop signs and DO NOT ENTER signs, swiveling their heads to look back at Mickie, who's freaking out at the wheel of the rental car, and Pat, who has her feet on the dashboard and is groaning. They all screech to a halt near the airport's private hangars. Mickie runs up the steps into an airplane. Wrong airplane. She pops back out. "I'll call you!" Pat shouts to Michelle. She strides into the King Air, and off she roars into the sky.

There are a hundred ways to write a story about a hurricane. We could watch it gathering shape and strength from afar and chronicle its course. We could follow at its heels and document its wake, or attempt to speak to all who experienced it and make a mosaic of their impressions. But perhaps the most direct and true way is to see and smell and feel it through one person—one girl who ran both from it and straight at it; one girl sucked into its eye and then set down on its other side; one girl, now a woman, who has had time to sort out what it did to her life.

Those who are playing for Pat Summitt now at Tennessee—members of the 1997–98 team, which finished the regular season 30–0 and is favored to win an astonishing third consecutive national title, the sixth in 12 years—cannot see the hurricane clearly because they're still inside it. They're hugging a tree for dear life, waiting for the wind and water to recede. Someone else, on a dry, sunny day a few years from now, can ask them to describe what it was like to play for this woman whose five national championships are surpassed in NCAA basketball history only by John Wooden's ten; whose .814 winning percentage in 23 seasons ranks fifth among all coaches in the history of men's and women's college basketball; whose number of trips to the Final Four, 14 and counting, will most likely never be matched, seeing how she's only 45. This woman who never raised a placard or a peep for women's rights, who never filed a suit or overturned a statute or gave a flying hoot about *isms* or *movements*, this unconscious revolutionary who's tearing up the terrain of sexual stereotypes and seeding it with young women who have an altered vision of what a female can be.

So we'll leave her for now, we who can't grasp yet what women like her will mean to the rest of us. We'll leave her doubled over in pain on an airplane, clenching every muscle she's got, trying to recall everything her mother told her about birthing babies so she can do the *opposite* until she's back on the ground in Tennessee. And we'll return to the teenage girl by the phone, awaiting Pat's call, trying to fathom what this strange day portends.

It's so hard, when so much air has leaked out of your dream, to inflate it again. For the previous two years, whenever Michelle was frustrated or angry on the court, whenever her high school coach yanked her midway through the third quarter because he didn't believe in stars or 40-point scoring nights, all she had to do was look up in the stands and see her mother forming that little T with her forefingers. It meant Tennessee, but it really meant Pat. It meant NCAA championships and All-America honors and Olympic gold medals, because that's what girls got when they were handpicked by Pat.

Ever since that day in December '87, during her freshman year, when Michelle persuaded her mom to take her on an unofficial visit to Knoxville and she watched this tall, handsome, crisply dressed woman coach a game and a practice, Michelle's aim in life had been to play for Pat. That practice had blown her mind; never had Michelle met a woman—hell, a *human being*—so intense, so authoritative, so certain and yet so caring. Pat walked into a room, and everything about her—her ramrod posture, her confident smile, her piercing blue eyes and her direct manner of speaking—said, "I love what I'm doing and this is what I'm here to talk about, and you'll pay attention while I'm talking or you'll leave the room." Michelle could picture her as president—no, not of the university but of the country! And imagine this: Coach Summitt told her girls to call her *Pat*!

For hours the teenager would thumb through her bible, a scrapbook full of photographs of Tennessee women's basketball and of warm notes from Pat. To heck with rival recruiters who warned her that Pat would snuff out her flamboyance on the court—envy, pure poison envy. She was going to play for the lady, case closed . . . until that afternoon in the spring of 1990, the end of her junior year. It was the day after Michelle's second unofficial visit to Knoxville, and on the way home she stopped in Hampton, Virginia, to play in an AAU tournament. She had decided it was time to announce her decision to the world when . . .

"Did you hear about Tiffany?" It was her AAU coach, Michael Flynn, addressing Michelle just before she took the court.

"No, what about her?" said Michelle.

"She committed to Tennessee."

"That *can't* be true! I was just there yesterday!"

"Well, it is. She committed today."

Michelle felt as if she were choking, as if she might faint. Tiffany Woosley was the girl who would vie with Michelle for every player of the year award during their senior seasons. A Tennessee girl, for crying out loud, who played point guard, the same position as Michelle; no way there would be playing time for two freshman guards! Pat must have betrayed her! Pat must have tipped off Tiffany that Michelle was about to commit, and now Tiffany was the first one, the special one, the local hero with the inside track, and Michelle's dream was up in smoke!

She cried her way up I-95 on the journey home. Bitterly she studied the list of 200 other universities offering her scholarships and searched for a team with no dictator, no system to submit to, somewhere she could play the splashy, spinning, behind-the-back-and-between-the-legs game she loved, light it up for 30 a night and stick it to that cruel lady who . . .

Who now, six months later, has just hopelessly muddled Michelle by nearly dropping a baby in her lap! "If she didn't really want me, why did she go through all *that*, Mom?" Michelle asks as the two sit up past midnight, waiting for Pat to call. Michelle has always believed in omens, in signals from God. "Maybe this means I was *meant* to go with her," she says. "I almost feel like I'm the godmother of this baby."

At 1 a.m. the phone jangles. It's Pat, calling a 16-year-old player a half hour after giving birth to a boy. It's Pat, whose doctor has just told her that it was only because the baby's head was turned sideways in the womb that she didn't deliver him into the hands of an assistant coach at 20,000 feet.

"Congratulations!" cries Michelle. "I can't believe this! Thanks so much for calling me! Good-bye! Congratulations, Pat!"

So Michelle signs with Pat and becomes an All-America guard at Tennessee, correct?

No. When Pat pictures Michelle, she sees so much of herself—the girl who would challenge boys to races and arm-wrestling matches and tackle football. That's why Pat can't bear to disappoint Michelle, why she tells her that she wants her very much, but she can't promise her playing time or stardom. So Michelle agonizes, Michelle flip-flops, Michelle visits Tennessee a third time, hugs Pat, kisses the new baby

. . . and signs with Notre Dame. And waits all of two weeks into her freshman season to break NCAA rules by calling Pat to tell her she has made the biggest mistake of her life, and how unfulfilling it is to be the star of a confused and divided 1–5 team, and how she wants to transfer right this very minute.

Pat reports the violation, but Michelle, stubborn as fungus, calls her again, and . . . well, almost everything between this lady and this girl is going to be complicated and racked with labor pains, so let's jump forward a year and a half, leap over Michelle's transfer to Tennessee and the season that, in keeping with NCAA rules, she has to sit out as penance for the switch.

It's the fall of 1993, and Michelle finally is living her dream, and here is how the dream begins: It begins with 4:30 a.m. wakeups, with relentless wind sprints through the dark on the Tennessee track. It begins with the frightening realization that there is no excuse, none, a fact that team manager Todd Dooley learns the morning he awakens crumpled by stomach cramps and forces himself out of bed to show up at 6:30 and tries to explain to Pat why he's a half hour late, only to hear her shout, "You don't *ever* be late! Next time you just bring that toilet with you!"

It begins with Michelle walking into the Lady Vols' locker room complex and stopping to stare at all the framed photographs on the National Championship Wall and the White House Visits Wall and the Final Four Wall and the All-Americas and Olympians Wall. It begins with Pat reminding her, sometimes even testing her, about who it is up there on the walls, whom it is she *owes* excellence to. It begins with Michelle knowing that Pat kicked the 1989–90 Lady Vols out of their palatial locker room for five weeks and squeezed them into a tiny visitors' dressing room. They hadn't deserved the palace. They hadn't worked hard enough.

It begins with Michelle looking over her shoulder as she dribbles in a scrimmage and wondering what in blazes this woman is doing, three feet behind her, down on one knee and squatting lower and lower as if the view at sneaker level might reveal some hidden flaw, slapping the floor with her palm at her latest find, hanging on Michelle's next decision as if life itself were riding on it, leaning right with her as she cuts and leans in for a layup, and then, *daggone* it, the anguished squinch of Pat's cheeks and punch of her fist if Michelle misses, the disappointment even sharper than Michelle's. And the thing is, that intensity never flags, not for a day or an hour or a minute. Suddenly, in the midst of a seemingly splendid practice, Pat might shout "Hold it! Stop! Everyone stop!" and stride toward Michelle, the way she strode one day toward forward Lisa Harrison.

"Lisa!"

"Yes, Pat?"

"What have you done for your team today?"

"Well, uh . . . I . . . I don't know."

"That's *exactly* my point!"

Whoo boy. Who else demands that her players sit in the first three rows of their classes and forbids them a single unexcused absence? Who else finds out about every visit they make to the mall for a new pair of jeans, every trip to a restaurant or a movie, and always mentions it the next day, so that it seems they can do nothing without her knowing it? Who else, at the end of a three-hour practice, times the suicide sprints on the big scoreboard clock? Who else films every practice and then sits through it all over again, so that if a player is fool enough to question a single one of her criticisms, Pat takes her right to the videotape in her office and stops the dang thing so often to prove she's right that it takes an hour to cover the first 10 minutes? Who carries *five* VCRs on road trips and watches tape of her opponents while she works out on the treadmill while she scribbles POINTS OF EMPHASIS on a notepad while she talks on the phone with an assistant—all after she has read a book to her son, Tyler, and put him to bed?

Imagine living with that. For the longest time even Pat couldn't imagine who could imagine it, until she found R. B. Summitt, whom she married in 1980, her sixth season at Tennessee. A man secure in his own profession as vice president of his family's bank, a man born to the first female pilot in Monroe County, Tennessee, a man unthreatened by a woman with a life all her own. Sure, sometimes he goes off the deep end in the heat of action and yells things at opposing teams that she wouldn't, but Pat can live with that. She knows what it is to enter another realm during a game. For her, it's the one time when Time lets go of her, when it even seems to stop.

Yes, Michelle could almost smell what the pair of Vanderbilt researchers found when they hooked up some visiting coaches to a cardiac monitor one year back in the '80s. Pat's heartbeat and blood pressure, the fastest and highest of all the coaches' during the action on the court, plummeted when a timeout was called, to the lowest of them all. There's no huddle you would rather be in with 20 ticks left in a tie game. First, Pat would tap the 60-plus years of coaching experience with which she surrounds herself, consulting swiftly with her staff: DeMoss, with her uncanny ability to see what all 10 players were doing on the floor; Holly Warlick, who had the game seared into her soul as Pat's point guard in the late '70s; and Al Brown, who could study video and spot the neck twitch that indicated that the opposing team's forward was about to drive left. Then Pat would make her decision, kneel on a stool in front of her players and pull them into her dead-sure eyes. The Lady Vols would drink in this calm assurance and intensity. Ten players would walk back onto the court. Five of them knew that their coach had just given them the way to win.

Michelle is determined to be one of those five, to let Pat jump down her throat and pull out her dream. To nod and chirp "Rebound!"—as every Lady Vol is expected to do when she's corrected—louder than anyone. To look Pat flush in the eye because there's nothing that makes the lady crazier than a player who looks away from The Look, who tries to evade those two blue drill bits digging into her skull. Pat actually dips her knees, lowers herself to catch the girl's yellow-belly eyeballs, locks in on them and lifts them, and if that fails, she barks, "Look me in the eyes!" She wants to see the girl's eyes blaze right back at her, to say, "All right, lady, I'll show you!" To blaze like hers did back when Daddy would inspect the tobacco plants from which she had been pulling suckers for eight hours under a 90-degree sun and find the one damn sucker she had missed—that's what Pat wants to see. In a critical moment, if she doesn't get what she wants, her neck goes blotchy red, and a vein pops out, and you can look at it and see her heart kicking.

Michelle will do anything to appease that heart. She'll go over, under, through any obstacle and come up pumping her fist. Crash, her teammates start calling her, and the Tennessee basketball fans love her. She'll hang out at Pat's office like a faithful puppy, write Pat birthday and Christmas and Mother's Day cards. She'll stick a note on the windshield of Pat's car a week before practice saying EIGHT MORE

DAYS! I CAN'T WAIT! and make Pat grin for an hour—heck, sounds exactly like something Pat would say! She'll do anything for Pat . . . except give up her game.

It drives Pat bonkers. She leaves her office and jogs across campus, wondering, What is it with this girl? You keep telling her to slow down, to make better decisions, to forget the spin move, to throw the simple 10-foot chest pass instead of the blind 40-foot bounce pass, and she keeps nodding her head, but 30 seconds later, there's the dang thing again! Never met a girl so strong-willed in my life.

One day a man named Bill Rodgers, a Knoxville car dealer whose passion and part-time occupation he calls "performance enhancing," looks at the results of the Predictive Index personality test he's administered to Michelle and Pat. "It's amazing," he tells Pat. "It's like looking at a young *you*. Michelle's more concerned with image, with wanting to be loved, but as for almost everything else—ambitious, competitive, outgoing, leadership, stubbornness, willingness to take on all the responsibility under extreme pressure—you could literally be mother and daughter!"

The bond between them keeps deepening. Pat just smiles. If Michelle is just like her—well, then, Pat knows just what to do. She'll ride her harder still, harder than she's ridden anyone before. *"Defense?"* Pat hollers. "You call that defense, Michelle? I thought you wanted to be a leader. How can I take you to war with me? *Don't* try to tell me! I've been coaching longer than you've been *alive!*

"You're gold-digging again, Michelle! Are you going to be the show-boat or be *on* the showboat? Well, I'll just sit you, Michelle. Because I know you love to play and *hate* to sit—right, Michelle? That *kills* you, doesn't it, Michelle?"

In front of anyone, this could happen. In front of 10 strangers, Knoxville business leaders and their spouses invited into the Lady Vols' locker room as "guest coaches" on game nights, most of them staring at the floor and praying Pat doesn't suddenly turn on *them*.

She half kills Michelle that first year. Makes her sit for half of every game as a backup shooting guard, sit and watch Tiffany Woosley run the team at point guard. Michelle's determined not to cry in front of Pat, because Pat would never cry; when she did, her daddy only spanked her harder. Michelle digs her top teeth into her bottom lip when Pat tears into her. It's the same thing Pat has done so many times in her life that there's a little indent on the right side of her lower lip. Michelle turns away and grinds her teeth—how could this be happening to the girl who won the Greg Tatum Award in eighth grade as her school's most Christlike child? She holds everything in until she gets home, then cries her eyes out. She drives her red Honda to a stream in the Great Smoky Mountains near Gatlinburg, sits and listens to the water and thinks, What is it with this crazy woman? I'm giving everything I have, but everything's not enough for her. There's something driving her, bigger than what drives anybody in the world. What is it?

It's growing mutually, magnetically, their frustration with and affection for each other. If Michelle could just pigeonhole Pat as the tyrant, it would be so much easier. But Pat's the woman you wish you could cook like and water-ski like and chat up the cashier like and toss off one-liners like. Pat's the life of the party.

How does she do it? How could she turn your name into an obscenity on the court, then walk off it and become your mom? How could a woman be transformed that completely, so that when you sit in her office, she leans toward you to connect with you, the flesh around those piercing eyes wrinkling in concentration, and invariably asks what *you* think the team needs and then, as you're getting ready to leave, asks if *you* think her beige shoes go with her white skirt. Not to con you or charm you, because you would eventually sniff that out. She asks so intently that it seems the two of you are the only ones in the universe, so honestly that you smell the unsure girl beneath the awe-inducing coach.

Then, bang, you and she are done, and her eyes are flashing to her day planner, the one she keeps gorging with duties, 10:25 appointments crowbarred between 10:15s and 10:30s. All etched in perfect calligraphy, this hand-to-hand combat with Time, with neat arrows pointing to peripheral obligations that she can attend to simultaneously, without assigning them a minute of their own, with key meetings underlined and *very important* appointments blinking exclamation points!!!! Soon Michelle and all her teammates are carrying day planners, opening them together at Pat's command to fill up a stray half hour here, a vagrant hour there, even to transcribe her annual reminder in late October: *Don't forget to turn back your clocks one hour!* Soon it's an epidemic, this guilt over a moment lost.

Where's she from, this woman? What incubated her? Manhattan or Chicago? A surgeon daddy and a mama lawyer? No, people tell you. She's a *farm girl*. A farm girl from middle Tennessee, where the sun is the clock, Nature calls the rhythm, and women know their place. How can that be? "Take me there," Michelle asks Pat one day. "I want to meet your family and see where you grew up." Michelle's changing her major to psychology. She has to figure this lady out.

"Can't," says Pat. "NCAA won't let me take you. Someday we'll do it, Michelle. When all this is done."

So Michelle must play detective, cobble together scraps. The memories of Pat's former players, an anecdote from a newspaper article, the reply to a brave question she might throw at Pat. Little clues, like that scar on Pat's left knee. Slowly—it takes years—a picture begins to appear. A fuzzy, grainy picture . . .

. . . of a face, a young woman's face, hair sweat-plastered around its edges. A young woman alone at night in a gym. She's running 15 more suicides because she missed a foul shot at the end of her two-hour workout. Pat has flung off her knee brace; it's a crutch, she tells herself, and she's never going to wear it again. Now you can see that scar, blazing red.

A year has passed since she tore her anterior cruciate ligament during her senior season at Tennessee-Martin. A year since the orthopedic surgeon examined the knee and told Pat, "Forget it." It's 1974, and many men playing big-time sports are finished after tearing an ACL. A woman? Just forget it.

Fix it, Tall Man told the surgeon. Tall Man is what the hired help called her father, Richard. Fix it right, he said, because Pat's *going* to play for the U.S. in Montreal in 1976, when women will play basketball for the first time in Olympic history. Pat swallowed hard because until Daddy said it, she didn't know she was going to do that. When her best friend, Jane Brown, walked into the hospital room a few minutes later, Pat blurted, "That doctor's crazy as heck if he thinks I'm not going to play ball again!" Then everyone left her room, and she hobbled to the window, drew the curtains and cried herself to sleep.

Now she has to make Tall Man's prediction come true. She has to lose 15 pounds, rehabilitate her knee and work out twice a day to make the Olympics . . . while she's teaching four phys-ed courses at Tennessee, while she's taking four courses to get her master's degree, while she's coaching the women's basketball team. Three-mile run at 6 a.m., weights at 6:30, shower, rush to the gym to teach, dash to the lecture hall to take the exercise-physiology and sports-administration classes, sprint back to the gym to coach a two-and-a-half-hour practice, hop in the car to go scout a local high school player, burn rubber back to the gym for two hours of basketball training and sprints, shower again and hightail it home by midnight to study for the biomechanics midterm.

She's 22. She was hired to be the women's assistant basketball coach, only to learn a few weeks later that the head coach had resigned to pursue her doctorate, so the head job's hers. She has no assistant. She has never coached a game. She's scared, the way she was that day when she was 12 and Tall Man dropped her off in the middle of miles of hay, pointed to the tractor and the hay rake and said, "Do it," then drove away. What's she going to do now, 10 years later? The only thing she knows. She'll be her father. Her players can be her.

At first it's glorified intramurals, a tryout sheet posted on a bulletin board inviting women to play in front of four or five dozen fans on a shadowy floor crisscrossed by badminton, volleyball and basketball lines. Pat digs in. She sweeps floors, tapes ankles, sets out the chairs and towels, washes the uniforms on road trips. She drives the team to road games in a van, her head poked out the window to keep her awake on the drive home at 2 a.m. Behind her, her players glance at each other when the rain stops and the windshield dries and the wipers keep squeaking, squeaking, squeaking. No one musters the courage to utter a word.

She doesn't lose 15 pounds. She loses 27. She sits on the edge of a table, pokes her foot through the handles of a sack full of bricks and lifts till her knee screams, but never when her players are around to see her. She makes the '76 Olympic team—a cocaptain and the oldest player, at 24, on the U.S. roster that shocks the field and comes home with a silver medal. She takes the Lady Vols to the Final Four seven months later, in her third year as coach. She gets her master's degree in physical education. She has learned she can do it: She can overpower Nature and outmuscle Time—at least for a while, just like men do. She has learned, thanks to her father, about human will. How can she settle for filling her players with *want* . . . now that she knows the psychic power of *expect*?

You think she's tough *now*, Michelle? Oh, please, the Lady Vols with crow's feet tell her at the annual alumnae reunions. You should've seen Pat back *then*! How about that time she found out we had that all-night party, and she set up trash cans at each corner of the court and ran us till we puked in them? How about that all-night, eight-and-a-half-hour drive home after we lost in Cleveland, Mississippi—no stops, bladders and bellies be damned? What about the 2 a.m. practice after we drove three hours back from the loss at Vandy, the game Pat's father saw and told her he'd seen a better game the night before between sixth-graders? Yeah, ever notice how quick she was, after the games her father attended, to ask people, "What did my dad say?" What about that time we fell apart in the second half at South Carolina, went straight to the locker room when we got back the next day and had to put on those smelly uniforms that had been locked in the trunk all night, and Pat hollered, "Now you're going to play the half you didn't play last night!"

Pat leads the Lady Vols to the Final Four six more times over the next nine years—and wins none of them, her teams always just a little short on talent. Forget the first Olympic gold medal in U.S. women's basketball history, the one won by Pat's '84 team—heck, a half hour later Pat forgets it. Just imagine what all those fruitless Final Fours do to Tall Man's daughter. If you're Pat's roommate during the early years in Knoxville, before Pat has a husband at age 28 and a child at 38, before there are videos of opponents to watch until she's cross-eyed, you love it when another big game's approaching. Because when you wake up, the white tornado has struck again—the whole apartment's gleaming!

Price tag? Oh, you bet. Don't you think there are times, when the grease stain on the baseboard has her on her knees at 1 a.m., that she wants this thing that's got hold of her to let go? "Times," as Pat's brother Charles puts it, "when you want to knock Daddy's head off." Times when the pain from tension in Pat's left shoulder grows so sharp that she must schedule a deep massage—like, five hours before every game. Times when she's sitting on an airplane next to two women who are solemnly weighing the floral pattern against the plaid for the master-bathroom drapes, and their relationship to Time is so dramatically different from Pat's that she feels as if she's from another planet. Times when people talk about her as if she's a freak, as if she's a man.

As if she's, say, Bobby Knight. That's what they say when she seizes Michelle by the front of her jersey, twists it and snarls at her during the game against Louisiana Tech in the NCAA regionals in Michelle's sophomore year. The photograph runs in newspapers all over the country. "Spinderella and her wicked stepmother," the Knoxville press calls Michelle and Pat. From all over the country friends and relatives send the picture to Michelle and her parents, demanding, *What is this woman doing to Michelle?*

Pat flinches. Why, she wonders, can't people look at the photograph in context, why can't they understand that she's as swift to drop her whole life and rush to her players' sides when they have problems as she is to drop the roof on them when they screw up? That she's Miss Hazel's daughter every inch as much as she is Tall Man's? That she grew up watching and imitating her mother, who was the first to visit the sick or the dying, first to pick, pluck, prepare and deliver a meal of butter beans and fried chicken and mashed potatoes and homemade ice cream to the worried or the grieving?

Pat calls Michelle's mother to try to explain. "She's all yours, Pat," says Betsy, but privately she and her husband are aching for their child and wondering about Pat, too. Doesn't Pat understand that Michelle isn't just like her? Doesn't she know that Michelle's father is tough too, an old college fullback, but that every night he gave his girl a good-night kiss?

Life's funny, though, and something else happens in that 1994 NCAA tournament game after Pat grabs Michelle's jersey: Michelle grabs Pat's heart. She comes in at point guard when the Lady Vols are gagging in the second half, down by 18, and nearly saves them single-handedly before they lose by 3. Furious drives to the basket, long jumpers, brilliant passes, knee-burning steals.

Pat sits there shaking her head, the truth moving from her mind into her gut. Michelle is the only one out there refusing to lose; the only one just like her! Pat can't wait. She tells Michelle right after the game: Tiffany's out. You're in. You're my starting point guard next year. "But remember," Pat says, "the point guard's an extension of me on the court. You've never been through anything like what you're about to go through."

Michelle goes home. She places one large framed picture of Pat twisting her jersey and snarling at her on her bedroom wall, and one small framed picture of the same scene on the dashboard of her car. Now Pat's everywhere Michelle goes, everywhere Michelle hides.

We've got an appointment, so let's break into a trot. Let's dash right past another year and a half; let's bully Time, the way Pat does. Let's fly by the day Pat throws her starting point guard out of practice in her junior year, past the day when Michelle finally crumbles and sobs in front of everyone. Let's jump clean over the last day of that same junior year, when Michelle comes within a whisker of her dream but loses in the NCAA title game to Connecticut—still unsure of herself on the floor in critical moments, still whirling between Pat's way and her way, no longer the All-America guard nor even the all-conference one.

There it goes—did you see it?—the day midway through Michelle's senior season when Pat makes her sit on a chair at midcourt, like a bad schoolgirl, and watch practice, then makes her move the chair to the far end of the floor after she whispers to a teammate.

We've got an appointment to keep, an appointment with an ice storm in Mississippi, coldest night of Michelle's life. It's February 1996. Time's not ticking now for Pat and Michelle. It's hammering. Pat has fixed that problem she had of making it to the Final Four and los- ing, fixed it mostly by persuading the best recruiter in the country, DeMoss, to leave Auburn in 1985 and be her assistant. Pat has won national titles in '87, '89 and '91, but four years have elapsed since her last one, way too long, and she needs her team leader, Michelle, as much as Michelle needs her.

Michelle's desperate. It's her last shot at the title, her last shot to make all this pain pay off. Her last chance to regain the kind of national acclaim that vanished for her after high school, to become a player whom the two fledgling women's pro leagues will come looking for. But how can she? The Lady Vols are 17–3, but they look nothing like a title team—and guess whose fault that is?

Now Pat's team has gotten skunked a fourth time, by Mississippi, and Michelle has gone 0 for 7 from the field and fouled out, having played as if she could feel Pat's eyes burning through her back. The bus is crawling toward the airport, across the ice, through the dark- ness; crawling as Michelle listens to Pat, a few seats away, ridicule her; crawling as Pat rises and takes a seat next to Michelle and tells her that unless something drastic happens, she doesn't think the Lady Vols can win a championship with Michelle as their point guard. It's hopeless—no lip-biting can possibly dam it now that the gates are open, now that Pat has already brought Michelle to tears twice that day, at halftime and just after the game, and . . . here it . . . here it comes . . . the third wave of sobs.

Michelle doesn't sleep that night. She's terrified. For the first time she has gone past anger and frustration and the hunger to show Pat she's wrong. The girl with the brightest flame is dead inside. She cannot. Take this. Anymore.

At 6:45 a.m. she calls Pat's home. Only fear and despair could make her speak to Pat Summitt this way: "You don't think we can win it all with me playing like I am," she says, "but I . . . I don't think we can win it all with you coaching like you are. You've got to back off me now, especially in front of other people. You can't do that to me anymore." Her breath catches.

Maybe it's because Pat has won so many championships that she can be more flexible now. Maybe it's impossible not to soften a little, stop choking each minute quite so hard, when there's a five-year-old boy in bed breathing the night in and out while you listen and then wrapping you in a hug when morning comes. Maybe Pat has no real choice this late in the season. She and Michelle speak for a while, and then there's silence. Well? "Doesn't mean I won't criticize you anymore, do you understand?" Pat says. "But I'll try it."

With that, everything changes. "As if we were two people in a room with boxing gloves," Michelle will say a few years later, "who finally both come out with our hands up." Pat gives Michelle more rope. Michelle quits trying to tie a triple knot when a single will do just fine. Tennessee reels off 15 straight wins, beating UConn in overtime in the NCAA semifinals behind Michelle's 21 points and then blowing out Georgia to win the crown.

Pat goes up into the stands and gets the first hug and kiss from her father that she can remember. Michelle is chosen the Final Four MVP. Her flying leap into Pat's arms nearly knocks Pat off her feet.

If this were a TV movie, it would end there. You would never get a chance to watch Michelle go home with Pat and finally understand the force, or to gaze down the road and peek around the bend to where the story really ends. But it's not a TV movie. It's summer, four months after the title, and the two women are in Pat's car busting 90 through middle Tennessee, heading to Henrietta. It's O.K. with the NCAA because Michelle has just graduated, and it's O.K. with the state police because Pat Summitt can go as fast as she wants in Tennessee, and it's O.K. between Pat and Michelle, who cried together at the senior banquet a few months before.

From this new place, from this last ledge before Michelle leaps into the pros and adulthood, then maybe marriage and children, she looks over at Pat. The championship glow is still emanating from both of them, but it's no longer blinding. It's good light in which to look at Pat and assess. . . .

Does Michelle want to be like Pat? Does she want to make herself go cold and hard inside when she needs to, or is the cost too steep? Can she have children and sweep them along with her, the way Pat does with Tyler, showering him with love and attention on airplanes and bus rides, taking him and his nanny on road trips whenever he can go . . . then steeling herself and walking out the door alone when he can't? Can Michelle dress like the First Lady, give goosebump-raising speeches, spearhead $7 million United Way fund drives, be competent in *everything*—can she be, does she *want* to be, the woman who's trying to do it all and pulling it off, as Pat is?

They climb out of the car, and Michelle stares across the hayfields and the tobacco barns and the silence. She gazes at the old homestead where Pat grew up, no girls her age within five miles. She sees the hayloft behind the house, blown off its 10-foot cinder-block legs by a tornado. It's where Pat climbed a ladder nearly every evening when chores were done and played two-on-two basketball under a low tin roof and two floodlights, on a tongue-and-groove pine floor surrounded by bales of hay, with three older brothers, two of whom would go on to play college sports on scholarship.

Michelle sees Pat's mother limp toward her on ankles worn to the bone by all the years of stocking shelves on a cement floor in the family grocery store, all the years of tucking her foot beneath the old 10-gallon milk cans, hoisting them off the ground and into the coolers with a thrust of her leg. All the years of milking cows before sunrise, picking butter beans all day in summer, laying down linoleum floors on the houses her husband was building to sell, never resting from the moment she woke till the moment she dropped into bed.

Michelle sees the three farms that Pat's father ran along with the feed store and the grocery store and the hardware store and the tobacco warehouse and the beauty salon, all while he was a school-board member and the county water commissioner. She sees the field where he once disked an entire night, through dawn, and then hitched up the mules and began a day of planting corn . . . until his head jerked up from sleep and he saw that his rows were running together. She sees the white-haired man coming home from his tractor, on which he still spends 10 hours a day after two knee replacements, prostate surgery, two ministrokes and quintuple-bypass surgery. She sees all the command and authority leak out of her coach as Tall Man draws near. . . . *Deference . . . Pat?* In a funny way, it's what Michelle needs to see: Pat's vulnerable. Pat's a regular person. Michelle does what Pat can't do. She walks up to Pat's dad and throws a hug around him.

She sees the schools where Pat never missed a day, not one, from grades one through twelve, because illnesses were like birthdays— her father didn't believe in them. She sees the high school to whose district Tall Man moved the family just so Pat could play basketball, because he never separated what a girl ought to be able to do from what a boy ought to. Michelle sits at the table where the family still gathers often because only Pat, of the five Head children, has moved on. She sees how bare-boned and basic the family's life is, and how silly a spin move can seem.

She gazes across the dirt and asphalt roads where Pat used to take the family car, killing the dashboard lights so her kid sister, Linda, couldn't see the needle nosing 95, and it begins to dawn on Michelle that the wind that has been at her own back for the last three years is really the wind that has been at Pat's back all of her life. And that maybe you don't have as much choice as you like to think—after you've lived that long and that close to a force that strong—about the kind of woman you would like to be. Maybe the wind just sends you flying.

But the significant moment in Pat's story isn't back there, in the past, or even in all those traumatic and giddy moments that she and her point guard shared. The story doesn't end with Michelle—it goes through her, and on to people that Pat will never know, because Michelle is now the carrier of a spore.

A year after she leaves Tennessee and a few months before she joins the Philadelphia Rage of the American Basketball League, Michelle meets a 15-year-old girl named Amanda Spengler, who plays basketball at a high school a few miles from Allentown, where Michelle grew up. Michelle takes Amanda under her wing—plays ball with her, lifts weights with her, talks about life with her and tells her all about Pat.

"She makes you feel there's nothing to be afraid of in life," Michelle tells Amanda. "If you want something, you go after it as hard as you can, and you make no excuses."

She tells Amanda how much she misses that lady now, how much she misses that sense of mission all around her—the urgency of 12 young women trying to be the best they can, every day, every moment. Sometimes in practice with her Philadelphia team, Michelle pretends Pat has just walked in to watch her, and she practices harder and harder. She tells Amanda how she dreams of being a coach someday, maybe even Pat's assistant.

"Let's run," she says to Amanda one day, but she doesn't run alongside the girl. She just takes off, barely conscious that she has already joined the legions of Pat's former players all over America who are spreading the urgency, breathing into thousands of teenage girls a new relationship with Time. She's barely aware that she's part of a capillary action, like the one that men have had with boys for generations, whose power is too vast to measure. She just takes off, determined to run seven-minute miles for 45 minutes, and Amanda gasps, running farther and harder than she ever dreamed she could, just trying to keep Michelle in sight.

A few weeks later Amanda goes to a high school track with a watch. We're talking about one girl now, remember, but we're *not*. We're talking about a wave. It's midday in the dead of summer. Amanda starts running and realizes after three laps that she has almost nothing left, and there's only one way to come close to Michelle's seven-minute mile. Her face turns scarlet, her body boils, her stomach turns; Nature screams at her to stop. Instead, she sprints. She sprints the entire last lap.

The watch says 7:05 as she crosses the line. Amanda can't believe she ran that fast, and she laughs as she reels and vomits near the flagpole. She laughs.

Rick Reilly

The sportswriter whose byline would become as widely sought as any of his time can point to beginnings in a tidy patch of space. Rick Reilly (b. 1958) went to college in his hometown of Boulder, Colorado, and during his sophomore year at the University of Colorado began working in the sports department of the city's *Daily Camera*. After graduation he spent two years at the *Denver Post* and another two at the *Los Angeles Times* before joining the staff of *Sports Illustrated* in 1985. He would leave for ESPN in 2007, but not before his "Life of Reilly" column had graced the final editorial page of each week's issue for a decade, commanding a handsome premium from advertisers placed next to it. Before that columnist's gig, Reilly wrote features for *SI* off the news, including this bittersweet look at Michael Jordan and the Chicago Bulls. He takes the measure of the team at the height of its fame during the 1990s, a decade when, as Reilly writes, Jordan "never started a basketball season that didn't end in a parade." At the same time, he correctly warns readers that this will be the band's last tour. The story is characteristically Reilly in how it tumbles breezily and knowingly along, with a humanizing thread laid through the narrative. The Bulls would indeed finish that 1997–98 season with another NBA title, the last of six that their star would win; Gus Lett, Jordan's friend and bodyguard, would live another two-and-a-half years before his death at age 64.

Last Call?

IT'S JUST a bus, yet kids hug it. Grown men pat it as it passes by. Women buss this bus. A kid jumped on the bumper once, trying to serve as a human hood ornament. Caravans of cars chase this bus wherever it goes. In Phoenix one night this season, about 15 cars, led by a Chevette filled with screaming teenagers, followed the bus onto the tarmac of a private airport. Hey, kids, can you spell *trespassing*?

This bus is the leading cause of bad snapshots in America. Right now, somebody somewhere is opening a pack of prints to find a dozen pictures of an unmarked chartered bus and not a famous face to be seen. Even pros do it. In Paris, paparazzi on motorcycles chased the bus, madly snapping away at blackened windows.

There is a kind of rolling panic about this bus, on account of the Chicago Bulls are inside it. If the end is coming, if the greatest sports dynasty of the 1990s is unraveling, people want to reach out and tear off its muffler before the whole thing comes unglued. In Indianapolis on March 17, so many fans gathered outside the Canterbury Hotel to witness the Bulls walk four feet—*four feet*—from the hotel's secured lobby onto the magic bus that police had to close off the street. For an hour. At times like that, Michael Jordan, the center of the madness, sits in the back of the bus, smiles and says, "O.K., we love you, but it's time to go home now."

What Americans are afraid of is that their Babe Ruth will go home before they've seen him in person. And so, this season has been the bonfire of an obsession that has been smoldering for years. In New York City last year, hundreds of people stood 10 deep outside the Plaza Hotel for a chance to see these 12 tall Beatles. Pressed into the front row were three businessmen in fine Italian suits and $300 shoes. Jammed next to them were three cross-dressers in size-20 Donna Karans and spiked heels. Shoulder-to-shoulder-pad, sideburn-to-earring, they were six guys who wanted only one thing: to be flies on the wall of history. Out came Jordan, dressed in a $3,500 tailor-made suit. As he hopped aboard the bus, the three businessmen high-fived. Then came Dennis Rodman, in bright purple bone-tight pants, an aquamarine silk blouse open to the navel, Nancy Sinatra boots and a throw pillow for a hat. As he hopped aboard, the transvestites hugged.

In one stretch of three road games in late March, the Bulls drew more than 98,000 paying fans. In Atlanta on one of those nights they set a one-game NBA attendance record of 62,046. Eight thousand of those seats had *no view of the floor*. "I think the feeling people have this year is that it's going to end," says Jordan. "And I think they should enjoy it, because you never know when it's all going to be taken away."

Is that how you feel, Michael?

"Yes," Jordan says. "Yes. Exactly."

As the world reaches out for Michael Jordan one last time, he recoils further and further into the corners of his life. He used to come out two hours early and shoot, but he doesn't now. He used to hang in the locker room with his teammates before games, but he doesn't now. Instead, until visitors and reporters are barred from the premises 45 minutes before tip-off, Jordan retreats beyond the locker room, down the corridor, past the ankle-taping tables, to a little office with a desk, a small TV and a sign on the door that says DOCTOR'S, TRAINER'S OFFICE.

It's the emperor's bedroom now. To be granted entry, you've got to be huge (Tiger Woods, Joe Montana, Muhammad Ali) or, sometimes, just small enough: The winner of last October's Chicago Marathon, 5'4" Khalid Khannouchi of Morocco, asked meekly if he could meet Mike and, miraculously, word came back that he could. Mostly, though, the answer is N-O-period. One night recently an Iowa congressman, who kept showing his congressional badge and insisting that Jordan would want to see him, had to be ushered away from the locker room. Supermodel Valeria Mazza's handlers were flabbergasted recently to learn that Jordan didn't want to meet her. Johnnie Cochran got bubkes, too.

Yet the one guy Jordan would most love to see walk through that office door hasn't been able to do it lately. He's a 61-year-old former Chicago narcotics cop named Gus Lett, and Jordan says, "He's like my second father." That sort of figures, considering that Lett and James Jordan, who was murdered in 1992, were born two months apart, both Air Force vets and both as straightforward as a left jab. Gus even looks like James did—5'10", balding, hard face around soft eyes.

Gus is one of six former or off-duty Chicago cops who can come into the office anytime they want, as far as Jordan's concerned. They look like guys you might see in a barbershop, and they spend more time with Jordan than his wife does. They're Jordan's security force, and you'll find them in the office with him, on the bus with him, in crowds with him, in his hotel suite with him, behind the bench with him. They watch his back, his front, his side and, especially, his cash, because they play *a lot* of liar's poker with him. Jordan loves the game. Chicago cops are a bitch to bluff. In the same way a hostage learns to love his captors, Jordan has made them his best friends. What choice did he have?

There's Joe Rokas, 49, a detective in the city's organized-crime unit. There's Clarence Travis, 63, Gus's old partner, retired from narcotics. There's detective John Wozniak, 45, narcotics. There's special agent Calvin Holliday, 49, internal affairs. There's Sgt. Tom West, 49, who supervises a tactical unit. And there's Gus, the man in charge, the one who's been with Jordan the longest, the former DEA undercover agent from the South Side. "Where's Gus?" Jordan would constantly bellow. "Where's Gus?"

They became friends during Jordan's second year with the Bulls, the season he spent with a cast on his broken foot. Gus was working security at the old Chicago Stadium. He noticed how hard it was for Jordan to get up and down the stairs, so he would carry Jordan's bag, give him a shoulder to lean on as he climbed. Something about the two of them just worked. Gus never asks anything of Jordan, not even an autograph. When you've taken a bullet, worked the riots in Marquette Park after Martin Luther King's assassination, worked the riots at the '68 Democratic Convention, made some of the biggest narcotics busts in Chicago in the '70s, sat in a room full of drug dealers with your cover blown, you do not worry about some scratchings on a napkin.

"We just became close," Gus says. "I don't know why. Maybe because I talk to him the way I talk to my own two sons." Gus stopped being just a guard to Jordan a dozen crises ago. "We've never lied to each other," Gus says, "and we always listen to each other."

"His wisdom is always welcome," says Jordan. "Rarely do I come to any big decision without talking to him first."

Gus knows that. "Michael loved his father very much," he says. "You know, sometimes I see him staring into space, I can tell he's thinking of him."

So when everybody—Jordan, Gus, the other guards—got the flu in Utah in February, just before the All-Star Game, nobody worried. Why shouldn't Gus and Jordan be sick at the same time? They're never much farther than a gin hand from each other. But when Jordan recovered and Gus never did, never got rid of the cough and the weakness, Jordan wouldn't stop bugging him to go to the doctor.

"It's nothin', Jumper," Gus kept saying.

"Don't make me take you," Jordan kept saying. So he went.

The news wasn't good.

When Jordan is finished, the Bulls will be finished, we all know that. Jordan tells friends he is probably finished. He says he's not playing for anybody but coach Phil Jackson or for any team but Chicago. Jackson acts as if *he's* gone, too, says he's gone and routinely and publicly rips Bulls vice president Jerry Krause. If he's staying, he's going to need a lot of Wite-Out. Jackson says he might coach some other team, might just stay home and read, might work on a possible presidential run by Bill Bradley. "People come up to me all the time and say, 'I can't believe they won't bring you back,'" Jackson says. "I tell 'em, 'Believe it.'"

The center is not holding. Scottie Pippen says he wouldn't be surprised if the Bulls just cut him. Rodman figures he'll be with the Los Angeles Lakers next season. "And it's gonna be just as crazy there, bro, lemme tell you," he says.

Jordan has always said he wants to go out "right at the peak" of his career, not on the way down, and, in a wonderful and strange way, this season may be it. He helped wring 62 wins out of a team that was without Pippen for three months and that has little bench to speak of. True, Jordan doesn't go to the hole the way he used to, and gravity has finally begun to figure him out, but watching him this year has still been like staring at a winter sun. He's so brilliant, it hurts the eyes. He was unguardable in the air as a young man, and he is just as unguardable on earth now. Nobody ever toyed with the double team the way Jordan has this season. Nobody ever hit the big shot night in and night out. Few players in the NBA's history have won the way Jordan does. Do you realize that in the 1990s Jordan has never started a basketball season that didn't end in a parade?

Yet this year there have been tiny glimpses of the end. Against the New Jersey Nets on a March night, long before the Bulls dispatched the Nets in last week's playoffs, Jordan opened the game by throwing a pass into the stands. Then he threw one into the scorer's table. In one 89-second span he missed one dunk and had another chumped by a nobody named David Vaughn. A kind of hush came over the United Center, a giant whisper, the kind heard at Sinatra concerts near the end. Of course, Sinatra didn't come back the next night with 35 points on the road against the Indiana Pacers.

"I know I will be forgotten as soon as this is over," says Jackson. "All of us will. Except Michael. Michael will be remembered forever."

As Camelot closes down, even the Bulls are finding their own ways to remember. Jackson calls this season "the last dance" and has been taking photos on the road. Center Bill Wennington takes along his video camera, making tapes to show to the grandkids. Routinely, Bulls ball boy Chris Mott brings something in for Jordan to sign—for the refs.

The rest of the world would love to get that close. The Bulls have been sold out at home for more than 10 years. The waiting list for season tickets has 23,000 names. One doctor calls ticket official Joe O'Neil every year with a standing bribe. "If I get him one season ticket," O'Neil says, "he'll give me a free nose job." Yet people still show up at the United Center, hundreds a day, hoping to find a freak ticket, begging to see the court, wanting just to be *part of it*. Lobby receptionist Michelle Danaher has to turn them away, but they're desperate, so they get *her* autograph and picture. Hey, it's something.

When Jordan eats at his own restaurant, Michael Jordan's, near the Loop, people stand vigil around his red-and-black Range Rover with the TWO TREY plates. *Well, no, Tommy, I never got to see him play. But I made sure nobody messed with his wheels.* It took only a few months for the restaurant's managers to realize that if they didn't take the Jordan logo off the dishes, they'd go broke. So, on logoless plates, Jordan eats his standard pregame meal—medium-well 23-ounce steak, mashed potatoes, a salad he rarely touches and two ginger ales, only one of which he drinks—in a private room with the shades drawn. Still, people wait patiently with cameras down a nearby hallway. Why? Because that's the way to the men's room. *See those shoes under there? Those are Michael's!*

How would you like to have a job in which your entire year's schedule is printed in the paper? In which the world knows which city you'll be in on what day, in which hotel and at what time? Outside the Ritz-Carlton Pentagon City in Arlington, Va., last November, a dozen security people had to be marshaled to hold back more than 500 people who'd left a nearby mall and gathered around the Bulls' bus. They stood, enthralled, as it idled for more than an hour. When, at last, they saw Jordan inside the lobby, they surged forward, cameras raised, pens readied, toes tipped. The path the players had been using to get to the bus narrowed by half. When Jordan saw the crowd, his shoulders hunched up. Somehow he made it onto the bus, but he looked scared. "I was," he says.

In Atlanta this season there has been such a last-day-of-Saigon thing going on that the Bulls' bus has often left without Jordan, dissolving the crowd. Jordan has then snuck out in a special car, which has pulled off the highway at a certain exit to let him rejoin the bus.

For most business travelers the hotel is a refuge, but not for Jordan. Sometimes he checks in under the name of Leonard Smith, sometimes

Lawrence Welk. One night Tom Smithburg, the Bulls' manager of media services, accidentally got Jordan's room and Jordan got Smithburg's. Smithburg hardly slept because of all the people knocking at the door. Oh, sure, the hotel was completely secured. The people knocking were hotel employees. *Everything's still fine, Mr. Jordan. Say, could you just sign a quick one for my brother?*

Sometimes fans call a hotel months in advance to get a room the night the Bulls are there. Then it's just a matter of knocking on every door until they've got their favorite player. Usually, that's Jordan. When you're Michael Jordan, the line between *fan* and *stalker* is very thin. "I really feel sorry for him sometimes," says George Kohler, Jordan's longtime assistant. "People tell me they want to be rich and famous? I tell 'em, 'Just be rich.' Michael's had 14 years of this nonsense. I wouldn't blame him for wanting to retire."

No wonder Jordan likes hanging out with the old cops who never want anything more than a locked hotel room and a rousing game of bid whist. No wonder he likes the bull sessions and the kidding, even if he's pinned into a tiny back office. No wonder it tears Jordan up not to be able to protect an old guy who has spent 14 years protecting him.

Jordan pulled up to a side entrance at Northwestern Memorial Hospital, in downtown Chicago, and was taken up a service elevator. He knew he wouldn't have a lot of time, maybe a half hour. It's the 30 Minute Rule. If Jordan stays anywhere in public longer than 30 minutes without a good exit route, it may take him hours to get out.

Gus had always been good at finding a route. "We're not above going through a few kitchens," he would say. That was the funny thing about this visit. The guy who could best get Jordan out of this kind of jam was the reason he was in it.

When Jordan got the news in late February from Gus's wife, Tisher, it hit him like a roundhouse right. *Two tumors. One in the brain and one in a lung.* The doctors said the cancer had metastasized. If that isn't the worst word in the language. *Metastasized*. Spread.

The worst thing about being John Elway or Ken Griffey Jr. or Michael Jordan is that you learn more about deadly diseases than you ever hoped to. If there's a sick or dying kid in North America, chances are good that he's written to Jordan. Twice a year Jordan fills the third floor of his restaurant with dying kids for the Make-A-Wish and Starlight foundations. He sits down with them, one by one, and talks with them, signs for them, tells them he'll see them next year, even though he knows it's a lie. He doesn't cry, though. Neither do the kids. The parents do.

But now cancer is working on a man he loves like a father. "He's got my plane, my staff, whatever," Michael told his agent after speaking to Tisher. "The best doctors, the best hospitals, whatever. I want him to have nothing but the best." That's how Gus got moved from the South Side hospital he was in to Northwestern. Hey, everybody needs a shoulder to lean on when he's got some stairs to climb, right?

After visiting Gus in the hospital, Jordan played indifferently in a win over Toronto. There was no joy in it. He refused to speak to the press, a rarity. He looked wrung out. "Bad day," he said as he left. "Very bad day."

Every home game beat writers, columnists, radio guys, cameramen and television reporters bolt from their courtside seats with a minute or so to go, scramble down the hall and jump in line outside the Bulls' locker room. They carry stepladders, stools, boom mikes. They want a good spot in line, because in about 10 minutes the locker room door will swing open, and they'll burst in, and in 20 manic seconds they'll construct a human amphitheater around Jordan's locker. We're talking about 40 to 50 people, many of them in designer dresses and silk ties, all pushing, slinking and elbowing into a perfect semicircle around a locker that isn't three feet wide.

"Seriously! Seriously! That's my foot!" a woman yells.

"Well, I can't move! If I move, this guy's gonna fall on top of us!"

"Wait! Ow! Wait! That's good!"

Finally everybody is jammed into a solid, mangled mass, some up high on chairs, some down low on their knees, arms stuck under armpits, legs akimbo. Everybody's ready. Except Jordan, of course. It'll be another half hour before he comes. Pippen, named one of the NBA's top 50 players of all time, comes and goes, and the human jigsaw puzzle doesn't budge. Rodman, wearing pajama bottoms, leaves without a bother. It would be nice to talk to them, sure, but if you do, you give up your spot, and you're toast. A lot of the newspaper writers are forced to stand in the opposite corner of the locker room and wait for the TV to show Jordan's mini press conference, which is almost always broadcast live in Chicago. It will be a bizarre scene: grown men and women taking notes off a TV set while the live, three-dimensional Jordan is standing 15 feet behind them.

Someday soon Jordan will stop coming altogether. "It's going to be quick," says Jackson. "And it's going to be painful." What then? Will the Bulls go back to what they were the season *before* Jordan—attendance of 6,365 a night, one fourth of the games televised, two photographers on the apron instead of 40? Will we all be a little like those 50 journalists, our cameras focused on an empty locker, wondering what in the *world* we're going to do now?

What in the world will they do at Chicago's Lakeview High, where, nine times a day, they use the Bulls' theme music to get kids to class fast? Who will be the big hero in Toronto, where the Raptors' mascot stomped on a Jordan jersey one night this season and was roundly booed for it? What will fans do for a team in Denver, where the crowd for the Chicago game this season wore four times as many Bulls jerseys as Nuggets jerseys? What will they write about at *The Philadelphia Daily News*, which recently put out a 52-page section to commemorate the career of an athlete who never played for a Philly team?

"People are getting desperate," says Jackie Banks, who handles Jordan's 6,000 pieces of mail a month. "They're desperate to get to him before he retires." They send letters. And cards. And packages. And flowers. And crocheting. Somebody sent the Bulls a box of Ben & Jerry's ice cream. What the sender didn't realize is that mail that arrives for the team today is opened in three months. Ice cream doesn't do three months in a hot warehouse very well. "Oh, lord," groans Banks. "That was a mess."

People send Jordan money. Do people send Dolly Parton Wonderbras? Occasional letters from Japan contain $20 or $50 for a picture or a ticket. Banks sends the money back. People write in Chinese, Polish and Swahili. "We get letters from countries I never heard of," she says. People send Bibles. Lots and lots of Bibles. People send wooden shoes and hand-sewn curtains and specially designed bathrobes and giant oil portraits of Jordan. "Tell everybody," Banks says, "Michael Jordan does *not* need another portrait of himself."

She opens the door to the warehouse. There must be 100 portraits in there. Jordan comes by every now and then and pokes his head in, sees himself in 100 poses, half smiles and closes the door. One lady knitted him a sweater with arms that are six feet long. No kidding. It's still in the warehouse. "That sweater is not going to fit anybody on this planet," says Banks.

But mostly people send their fondest wishes to be *part of it*. The weird thing is, finding out that they *aren't* really part of it makes them feel like they are. Banks is sent photos all the time of people in their backyards, squinting into the sun, proudly holding up a letter from her that reads: "Thank you for your letter to Michael Jordan. Unfortunately. . . ." Hey, it's *something*.

"It's really kind of wonderful," Banks has decided. "I constantly read, 'Dear Michael, thank you for entertaining me, thank you for entertaining my mom or my sister when they were so terribly sick. They never missed a Bulls game.'

"I don't understand sports, really. I've never been a fan. But sports seem to be such an uplifting thing for these people. It's like, for that hour and a half, people step away from all the pain and tribulation of their lives and look forward to these games and to Michael playing in them. They're overjoyed."

But who comforts Jordan?

What was it Jordan said? *Enjoy it, because you never know when it's all going to be taken away.*

Where *is* Gus?

Gus Lett had brain surgery, chemotherapy and radiation in the last month, and he's still laughing. "Good news!" he told one hospital visitor, even though he looked 20 pounds lighter and 20 years older than when he checked in. "The doctors tell me that unless I fall down the stairs or get caught in a drive-by, I'm not gonna die today."

As the free world frets about Jordan's future, Jordan's got something real to worry about. He calls Gus and goes by the hospital, keeps wanting to spend the day with him. Maybe the two of them will leave the NBA together next month, the second father and the third son. Leave the tray table and the hotel rooms and the cramped office behind, spread out in a great big room and play some *real* cards.

"Give me a coupla months, Jumper," Gus says, "and I'll be back on the job."

Only one problem with that: Gus is so damned good at liar's poker.

Melissa King

When Melissa King (b. 1966) turned twenty-seven she didn't know what she wanted from life, though she knew that northwest Arkansas wasn't supplying it. She left a job writing sell copy for plots of land in the Ozarks and moved to Chicago, renting an apartment on the Near West Side and taking a position with a mom-and-pop natural foods company. To construct a community and prove her urban bona fides, she returned to the game she had played at Vilonia High School, hoping it might provide "that old clarity . . . those blessed moments pulled from the chaos when you see what matters and nothing else." White, southern, and female, King was usually an interloper three times over as she migrated from court to inner-city court. But even as she knew she was an object of curiosity, she not only returned the gazes but also took mental notes. After a few hours on the courts, often still in her gym clothes, King would write up her most recent engagement with the game she has called "a dive into forgetting." These entries toggle between the confessional and the dismissive, and, as she has put it in her self-deprecating way, "walk the line between sage and doofus." But they come from a generous, curious, and earnest place. "It's All in the Game" was published in the *Chicago Reader* in 1998 and became the germ of her 2005 book *She's Got Next*. King eventually made her way back to her home state, where she worked for the University of Arkansas Press.

It's All in the Game

ECKHART PARK, NOBLE AND CHICAGO

I LIKE MY husband, but I love my snowmobile. That's what his T-shirt said. He didn't speak English too well, and I bet he bought the shirt at a thrift store because he liked the color—an appealing purple, actually. Somebody must have told him what "husband" meant, because he had obviously tried to eradicate the word with white shoe polish. You could still see it, but I guess he succeeded in changing the message. Yo soy heterosexual.

I don't know his name. I played basketball with him, his brother, and their roommate today. They were new to the game, but they played hard. The most experienced player (also the tallest and the best English speaker) was the one who asked me to play. I had been at the other end of the court shooting baskets, stealing glances at them, knowing they were returning the favor. When you're a 30-year-old white woman shooting around by yourself in a park populated largely by Latinos, everybody looks at you.

This is the way it works. I shoot around, make a point to have them notice me clandestinely checking them out. I stand tall and swagger a little, as if to say, "I got skills. I play all the time. I know what you're thinking. The question is, are you good enough to play with me?" I can't actually say "I got skills," or "My bad" or "I got next" or any of that stuff. I hate it when white people try to talk street. But that's how I feel.

So I did my little routine and the tall good-English-speaking guy asked me to play two-on-two. My team won both games. And I played some more after that, with another group of guys; the teams just kept melding and interchanging, with new groups of people coming to play. The sun was beating down and a slightly sickening chocolate smell wafted west from the Blommer factory on Kinzie. I played for hours.

HORNER PARK, MONTROSE AND CALIFORNIA

Tori, Melinda, and I got into a discussion tonight about whether or not the person we'd all seen as we walked into the gym was a teenage boy or a woman in her 20s.

Tori was changing into her basketball clothes right there on the side of the court. It was a little brazen, but people hadn't started arriving yet for the Monday-night women's open gym.

"It's a guy," Tori said, standing there in her bra.

"She has breasts," Melinda argued.

"He's not wearing a bra."

"So?"

There's a television commercial where Sheryl Swoopes is talking about what she likes to buy with her Discover card. "I'm very prissy," she says, and then you see her playing playground ball with a bunch of men, screaming like a crazed warrior *put up or shut up*! as she drives the lane.

"I love to get my hair done, get manicures, pedicures, but my greatest weakness is shoes," she says in the next cut, walking through a mall in a trendy outfit.

We never did decide.

John, who for some reason plays with us at the women's open gym, was there; it was just the four of us because it was really too hot to play and no one else showed up. John's not quite as good as he looks like he would be, but he looks like he would be good. A guy I used to date has a poster in his house captioned "Shirts and Skins." It's a drawing of a bunch of black men going up for a rebound, stretched out all long limbed and elegantly gangly toward the sky, everyone moving in what looks from a distance to be a synchronized unit, like a flock of geese falling in instinctually for flight. John looks like one of those guys.

John likes us. He's there almost every Monday, and I always notice him listening to what everybody's saying, even though he never says anything. So I said, "John, do you think that person out front is a man or a woman?" He was shooting around, looking like he was in his own world (he's a little cross-eyed). "Boy," he said.

"This guy walked by me once," Melinda said, taking a shot, "and he goes, 'Hey dude.' I told him, I said, 'Hey, I'm a woman.'"

Then Tori said she was in a car wreck once, and while waiting for the ambulance to arrive she was laid out on the floor of a convenience store. People kept coming up to her and looking over her and saying, "What's up with dude?" She said she kept fading in and out of consciousness saying, "Hey, I'm a woman."

I've never been mistaken for a man that I know of, but when I'm going for rebounds, screaming like a karate master, wringing the sweat from my shirt, making faces I probably wouldn't want to see, I feel kind of weird. Sometimes it occurs to me that I'm aggressive. Not "assertive"—aggressive.

Tori said to me once, "Girl, you're like a Reebok commercial. This is your world. You go."

It's a good way to feel.

WICKER PARK, DAMEN AND WICKER PARK

Sometimes I really like white people. Not always, and you might say not even very often, but sometimes I really like them. Today I rode over to Wicker Park on my bike and got stuck in the rain, waited it out under an awning. Afterward three white guys came over and played with me. We played two on two, and they were so without egos.

As they should have been—they sucked. They were fouling the hell out of each other, totally laughing, having a good time. I think they were a little drunk. This guy, Vince, who had been the first one to come over and shoot around with me, was my teammate. After one particularly good play he stuck both hands behind his back, palms up, while he was running backward down the court, for me to slap him ten. It was stupid, but he knew it was stupid. That's kind of fun. In fact, I think it's pretty evolved.

Another time in this same park I was shooting around with a kid called Orlando. His three friends rode up on two bicycles to watch us. The Gap can only dream of capturing the urban slouch of these kids in their baggy jeans, sitting on two-thirds enough bicycle.

They kept saying, "Yeah, she's going to the WNBA next week. She got a right, she got a left, she got a shot, got some D." Orlando was teasing me too, pretending he was shoving me around and laughing, saying stuff like "All right, it's on now" and "You know I'm mad now." I was kidding him back, saying, Thanks for the warning, Orlando. I like that kid.

I tried to tell Orlando about how, when you're playing defense, you need to look at someone's belly. How you don't look at his face, because he can fake you out with his face but he can't fake you out with his belly. I wanted Orlando to be good. He liked it that I was telling him something, but I think he already knew about the belly.

A group of older guys started playing on the other end of the court. They were playing 21. I hate that game sometimes, because it's so rebound oriented. I love to get rebounds, but I can't get any rebounds against those guys. "Orlando," I said, "do you think those guys would let me play with them?" Orlando looked at me funny. "I don't think so. They're kind of rough," he said.

Orlando left with his friends. I did my thing, hoping the older guys would ask me to play. They never did, even though I know they saw me wanting to get in the game. I rode home thinking those sons of bitches made me sick. They didn't know if I could play or not.

Vince had written his phone number on my arm with a felt-tip pen after we finished playing. I wrote it down somewhere else when I got home, but I don't know what I did with it now.

ECKHART PARK

Snowmobile wasn't there today, but his two compadres were. The court was so crowded I couldn't get out there. The other Snowmobiles were having the same problem, so I sat down on the ground next to them.

It makes me so mad that I can't speak Spanish. I had three semesters of it in college, for God's sake. And I made As all three times.

So I chatted in English with Snowmobile #2 and Snowmobile #3. They told me they were both taking English classes four times a week. They kept saying they still couldn't speak English. I told them yes they could.

I couldn't understand why they weren't getting in the game. I mean, for me, being a woman, sometimes you just get the sense that a court is not exactly an equal opportunity situation, but they're guys. It seemed like any guy should be able to play.

They said they weren't good enough. I told them yes they were.

When I was in college taking those Spanish classes, I used to have dreams where I could really speak Spanish. In my dreams the words would just be flying out in whole sentences with a perfect accent.

A young black guy was bouncing his ball around on the side of the court, screaming at the players in the game: "I'm gonna kick ya'll's tired asses when I get in there!"

Snowmobile #2 was telling me I could come to play with them next weekend at this park they play at sometimes where there's always plenty of room. "They have sodas," he said.

I have those same kind of dreams about basketball. That I'm making every shot, flying toward the basket, never tired, no one can stop me. When I wake up I feel like those dogs too old to run anymore. You can see them chasing rabbits in their sleep, their legs twitching.

WICKER PARK

"What's up kittycat?" That's what this old park dude was saying to me as I sat on my bike scanning the court, seeing if I wanted to play.

"What's up kittycat you gonna shoot some hoops you gonna play me some one-on-one can you dunk it?"

Damn. I almost turned around and rode off, because I knew this guy was gonna stick to me the whole time I was there, but there was an empty hoop and I all of a sudden felt irritated about having to leave a court because of this old park dude.

The guy I told you about earlier that I used to date, the one with the poster, used to say I should stay away from the criminal element. He thought I was reckless. He won't ride the el, and he never gives money to homeless people on the street. But he volunteers at homeless shelters around the holidays and sits on the boards of several charitable organizations.

Park Dude was walking away, so I shot for a while. Then he came back and started shooting around with me. There's a certain etiquette when two people shoot around. One person shoots from the outside and the other stands under the hoop and rebounds. When the shooter misses he goes in for a layup, and it's the other guy's turn. Everybody knows that.

Park Dude was not so great to shoot around with. He kept throwing the ball back to me too hard, or over my head or off to the side so that I had to jump or make a quick move to catch it. Every once in a while it got past me and I would have to run after it, trying to stop it before it went onto the other court or rolled into the middle of the softball game going on 20 feet away. It was really pissing me off. If I were a male or truly urban I would have said, "Man, would you watch that shit? What's the matter with you? Damn." But I'm not.

The thing about Park Dude was that he could really shoot a hook shot. Who the hell shoots a hook shot?

A bunch of kids trickled onto the court. At this particular park I sometimes find myself in a game with kids of all shapes and sizes. It's my ball and no one else has one, and I know they want to play, so I play.

A little white girl asked me how old I was. She nearly fell over when I told her I was 30. "How old are you?" I asked her. "Ten."

Park Dude let fly with one of his hook shots, missing the hoop completely this time. "He's weird," the girl said. "He smells like beer." He was, he did, I thought, but far as I could tell there was nothing wrong with his hearing.

Park Dude said he was getting hot, and he took his shirt off. He had a long, vertical scar running down his rib cage and stomach.

There's a sign in the park that says WARNING YOU ARE IN A SAFETY ZONE PENALTIES FOR SELLING DRUGS OR OTHER CRIMINAL ACTIVITY IN THIS PARK ARE SEVERELY INCREASED. I've seen guys walk past each other making secretive handoffs, or drive up in separate cars, walk off together, then come back a few minutes later and go their separate ways. The park is segregated, with the park dudes sticking to the Damen side and the hipsters playing Frisbee with their dogs in the back corner. All over, savvy little independent kids are running around.

I worry about what happens to a harmless park dude's brain when he's treated like dirt by arrogant white girls. My personal opinion is that inclusion is safer than exclusion, but I'm not positive about that.

All of a sudden I did feel a little reckless, not for being there myself but for being the thing that brought the park dude and the little girl together. After the game petered out, I hung around for a while, making sure everyone had scattered before I rode home.

WICKER PARK

I wanted to play so bad today. This morning I couldn't get up to save myself. I hit the snooze alarm for an hour.

I muddled through work, came straight home, got on my bicycle, and went looking for a game. I ended up at Wicker Park, shooting around with a little kid, another little kid, and his toddler brother, killing time until a game developed.

I kept grinning at the toddler because he was cute, but his brother didn't grin; he included him. He expected him to play, but he wasn't too rough on him. The toddler just ran around with the ball, happy as could be. He could dribble pretty good for a three-year-old.

All of a sudden a commotion broke out on the other court and we all got still, watching.

"Why you testin' me, nigga? Why don't you test summa these other niggas!" one kid was saying to a shorter kid, pushing him in his face. Two middle-aged guys were standing on the side of the court. They were Park District employees; I could tell because they were wearing those plastic ID holders on their shirts. One of the other boys got between the kids, and then one of the Park District guys walked over and said something. It was about damn time.

"Gentlemen, gentlemen," he said. "Let's just play ball. Gentlemen." But those two kids didn't care about some middle-aged white guy with a pot belly and an ID tag. They just kept on. "Man if you ever touch my shit again, I'll kill you. Come on, nigga, swing! Do it!"

I don't know why it ended, but it did. The taller kid stalked off, daring the other kid to follow and fight him. The older brother on my court looked over at the toddler and said gently, "Boo, wanna go see a fight?" The toddler just laughed, running around in his stiff-legged toddler way, holding the ball.

After a while the game on the other court disintegrated and an older guy asked me if I'd like to play with him and some other guys. I said sure. I was the only woman and the only white person. I played the best I've ever played, only erring a few times, when I misjudged how fast these young guys were and how high they could jump. I'm not that great a shooter, but that night I was. They kept yelling at each other, looking for someone to blame every time I made a shot. "Who's guarding that girl?" They started calling me "little Larry Bird."

We all have our moments.

The guy who asked me to play was an adult; everyone else was a teen. He was intense, and the kids were kind of laughing at him until we started kicking their butts. The guy who asked me to play kept saying to the scoffing teens, "You know I play hard." The rest of them got into it in spite of themselves, though nobody could ever remember the score.

Riding home, I remembered how I used to sit around the house waiting for something to happen. It was good not to be doing that.

ECKHART PARK

My friend Laurie used to tell me how she couldn't go to church without about three guys asking her out. It was the biggest pickup situation you ever saw, evidently, because everyone there wanted to meet somebody at church. She would joke that all the single people at her church were "datin' for Jesus!"

Well, the same thing happens in basketball. I met a guy on the court today. Let's call him Peter. I saw Peter looking at me all intense from the other end of the court. He made sure he got in the game I was in, and then he hung around afterward and asked if I wanted to go have a drink later. I said I did; he was very cute, and he was a good player. A guy doesn't have to be that good for me to like him, but it doesn't hurt.

The thing about some guys is, the most important thing about you is where they met you. For instance, I met a guy at a dog party once. It was a dog party because it was a party everyone brought a dog to, and it was supposed to help you mingle and meet other dog owners. The dogs kept fighting with each other and trying to get at each other's butts, which was potentially embarrassing for strangers trying to chat, but people just kept acting like they didn't notice and trying to meet one another.

I went to the party with this girl I worked with, who kind of talked me into it. Neither of us actually had a dog, so we borrowed one, that's how hot she was to go. Single women in their 30s are always latching on to me to do stuff like this. We don't even really like each other, necessarily, but they need someone to go do these man-meeting things with. It's incredibly depressing, and usually I run the other way when I smell these situations coming, but this time I went, mostly because I was always telling this woman no.

So at this dog party, this guy, Ed, decided he liked me. And he did everything right. He asked me out for a polite date, and I went, and it wasn't too terrible so I said I'd go out with him again. He introduced me to his friends, always asked me for the next date before he left. He was sweatin' me, as they say.

But there was no connection. The only reason he wanted to go out with me was that he could just imagine telling everybody how we met at a dog party. The story was all the cuter because I didn't even have a dog. It was very *That Girl*.

People don't want to say they met in a bar or through the personal ads. There's always got to be some damn cute story or you don't have a chance.

Peter was all over me because he met me the way he always envisioned meeting the woman: on the basketball court. That's what he said, "I always wanted to meet a woman on the basketball court." Me personally, I don't really care how I meet someone, so long as one of us doesn't bore the other half to death.

HORNER PARK

There's this other guy that keeps asking me out too. He plays with our coed group on Wednesday nights. Lucky me, he prefers my butt to all the other Wednesday night butts. I should write him a thank you note, I guess. But I already heard him say he has a girlfriend, the dumbass. Oh, and guess what; the girlfriend lives in another city.

The thing about men is, they'll ruin every last thing you like if you let them.

Peter and I went out for a week. We rode our bikes to the lake, played basketball, sat on park benches kissing. All very romantic.

He was funny, although he wasn't the kind of funny where he knew he was funny. The day we went riding I met him at his house, and he came out carrying a bottle of wine, some plastic cups, a corkscrew, and two sheets to sit on, all in a white plastic garbage bag. That kind of stuff can be kind of funny.

When he kissed me he was always pulling the back of my hair. I have short hair, and I kept thinking he was wishing I had longer hair so he could really grab on and pull. I really wanted to say, Hey what the hellareya doin', but I didn't.

One night he asked me to come to his house and watch a Bears game. I was a little late getting there, and when he answered his door he just looked at me kind of sternly and said, "You're late."

I think he was drunk, and there were two joints sitting on the kitchen counter. He was talking a mile a minute. In fact, I was starting to notice, Peter was the sort of person who didn't let you get a word in edgewise. And, if he didn't think you were listening closely enough, he would move closer and talk louder.

We sat down to watch the game, and he lit up one of the joints. I hate to admit it, but I smoked some. I used to smoke in college, but I don't anymore. I used to get too paranoid. I'm kind of self-conscious already and pot just makes it worse.

All of a sudden I couldn't tell if Peter was really stupid or just pretended to be as a joke. And I hadn't really noticed he was stupid before. I mean, he wasn't by any means the smartest guy I had ever run into, but I just thought he was really physical, that he related to the world in a physical way. If I think a guy is kind of cute, and he entertains me at all, and if he seems to like me, I can kind of make excuses for him and overlook a lot of rude and just plain stupid behavior. A lot of women do that. Decent men without girlfriends must really get sickened by it.

So I was sitting on this chair, really stoned, trying to sit up straight. Peter sat down beside me in the chair and put his arm around me, and he was kind of absentmindedly digging his fingers into my arm, hard. It seemed compulsive. It was like he couldn't help himself, it felt so good to him. And then, and this is really embarrassing, Peter got up and started gyrating around like a Chippendale dancer, saying, "So, what should I do . . . do you want me to dance for you?" I just kept hoping he meant to be cheesy to make me laugh. But I didn't laugh, because I was afraid he was serious. All I could think of to say was, "Man, I'm stoned."

All of a sudden, Peter picked me up and carried me over to an open window. I never like it when guys physically pick me up. I know it's supposed to be all romantic, but I just think it's embarrassing. It's too dramatic unless they're going to laugh and maybe act like you're so heavy they're gonna throw their back out or something.

Then I started to worry that he was going to sort of chuck me out the window. I squirmed to get down without saying why, and then Peter said, "I wouldn't throw you out the window."

That's when I really got scared. Peter's face looked really brutish to me, and when he moved anywhere near me it felt like he was trying to dominate me, not just get close. After I got out of his King Kong-like grasp, he tried to pick me up on his back, like we were going to play piggyback. And his movements were slow and, I don't know, just slow, like a dumb animal's. I got the distinct impression that he wanted to hurt me. That even if I said I would have sex with him he would still want to hurt me. I kept thinking about that postracquetball scene in *Cape Fear*, the new version, with Robert De Niro. If you saw the movie, you know what I'm talking about.

Peter kept saying, "Why are you so afraid of me, try to have a little self-confidence, why don'tcha . . . I know I can make you feel good," and other creepy stuff like that. I got the hell out of there. I was afraid to drive but I drove home anyway, thinking I was going to go mad the whole time if I had to drive that car one more inch.

But like I said, I quit smoking pot because it makes me paranoid.

WICKER PARK

These three girls I had seen before came running over, saying, "There's that girl again!"

They looked like a female version of the Fat Albert gang. I asked them if they wanted to shoot around, and the youngest one, who wore about 25 colored barrettes in her hair and jeans about three sizes too big, took the ball.

"I can't do it," she said every time she missed a shot.

"Yes you can, you just need to practice some. Nobody makes it every time."

"Why aren't you shootin'?" she asked me.

"I'm all right, go ahead."

These girls, you had to draw them in. I've never seen any boy worry about if he was keeping you from playing.

One girl wouldn't play at all. We tried to play two-on-two, but she just wouldn't play. She kept saying she didn't know how, and she couldn't make it, and all that stuff. The youngest one's younger brother came up and tried to play. He was running all over the court, never dribbling, a big grin on his face, saying "almost" every time he shot the ball.

The girls didn't play long, but they didn't leave, either. They hung around at the edge of the court, watching. You could see them kind of whispering together and looking at different boys.

"Where's you girls' boyfriends?" I asked them, just to see what they'd say.

"Twanisha got her a man," the little one said.

"Where's Twanisha's boyfriend?"

"He over there with his boys."

"That why you won't play basketball, Twanisha? What's his name?"

She shrugged her shoulders.

They were doing it already, waiting around for something to happen. Damn, it made me sad. It reminded me of this story I saw on TV, on *20/20* maybe, about whether or not little girls could learn as well when they had boys in their class. They couldn't, some researchers had decided, because the boys just got in there first, talking faster and talking louder. I wanted to shake Twanisha and say, "Listen here, young lady, you're gonna spend your life falling for arrogant men and sitting around a dirty apartment waiting for them to call if you don't start taking an interest in some things."

If I ever have a daughter, she'll have to learn how not to be stupid about men. I don't know how I'll teach her, because I don't entirely know myself. But somehow she's got to know early on it's OK to miss some shots on your own, that you can't let other people always do your shooting for you.

I started playing with some adults, so I told a bunch of adolescents who had walked up that they could play with my ball if they took care of it. They had a big game going before long.

One of the guys on their court was mad because one of his peers had defected to play with us. Leon was on my team. He was two feet shorter than almost everyone else out there, but he could play. He was smart and serious about it. This other kid was screaming at him: "Oh, yeah, I see how it is. You wanna play over there with them. Man, I hate people like you!" He was joined by a glaring fellow malcontent who ran up to us and said, "Can I play," really sarcastic. Suddenly the tension was racial, because most of the adults were white.

Once our ball flew over onto their court, and the loud kid shot it into their hoop like he thought it was the ball from their game, or I should say my ball. He looked over at us and went, "Oh, is that your ball?"

Leon ignored them. He wouldn't even look at them. We just kept playing. I kept looking over to make sure my ball was still there, and sure enough, the next time I looked up, all the kids and my ball were gone.

So as our game was winding down I asked Leon, "Hey, do you know those kids that were over there?"

"Which ones?"

"Those ones that were playing with my ball over there."

"Your ball? What's it look like?"

"Orange. Rubber."

"Man, I think they took off with it," Leon said, kind of laughing.

At the tender age of 12, Leon knew he was glad he wasn't a thief or an idiot.

Lewis, another kid about Leon's size who was playing with us, said, "There they are. Hey, Thomas, you got that girl's ball!" There they were, standing about 100 yards away with my ball. I wondered if Leon had seen them.

"Come on man, you got that girl's ball! Bring it back! Bring it back now!"

Thomas threw it across the playground at us, and we went back to our game.

WICKER PARK

Oh my God, David. That child is pure love. He comes to the park with his mom on Saturdays. She's a good player; you can tell she was really good in high school. She coaches a bunch of girls in the gym at Wicker Park.

I played with her in a pickup game once, and after it was over I shot around and David came over to talk to me.

"Where's your friend?" he asked me.

"What friend?"

"Your friend. She wears black shoes too."

David thought he remembered me from somewhere, I guess, so I told him I didn't know who he meant, was he sure it was me he had seen before, and he said yes, he was sure.

I asked him how old he was. He's five.

"I play with my mama."

"You do? Was she the one who was playing with me a little earlier? She's pretty good."

She came over to shoot around with us.

"She made me in her stomach," David informed me. I said, Really, how 'bout that.

He said something quietly to his mom. "Well, she's pretty good too," his mom said.

A few months later I was playing a two-on-two game and saw David's mom again. She told us to come inside the gym and play if we wanted. After the game, David came running over to me, shouting, "Hi Melissa!"

I couldn't remember his name. What an asshole I am, I thought as I talked to him, said it looked like his front teeth were growing in and asked what he had been doing. Then he ran around all over the gym with kids his age while his mom and I and a bunch of teens played a game.

In the middle of the game David came over and said, "Maaama . . . maaama . . . maaaaaaama!" His mom, the point guard, picked up her dribble and said, "What!"

David hesitated, caught off guard by her attention. "Do you want me?" he asked. He looked at his mom expectantly.

"I want you," she said, "but not right this minute."

Satisfied, David resumed running around, and we went on with our game.

Kareem Abdul-Jabbar

In his 1983 profile of Kareem Abdul-Jabbar (b. 1947) included in this volume, David Bradley notes that, even as the longtime Los Angeles Lakers captain became the most prolific scorer in NBA history, "he was looking beyond to what he could do when he finished." Soon after his retirement in 1989 we learned what that would be. Following years of resentment that the public saw him only as a one-dimensional athlete, Abdul-Jabbar reinvented himself—or more accurately, revealed himself—as a cultural omnivore and man of letters. He built a body of work that would be impressive for someone who had started in his twenties, much less his forties: more than a half-dozen books, including works of memoir, history, detective fiction, and juvenile literature; magazine pieces for outlets running the gamut from *Jacobin* to *Time* to *Rotarian*; online commentaries on the news; two autobiographical documentaries, including HBO's *Kareem: A Minority of One*; and numerous television and radio appearances, where he weighed in on issues of the day. In fact, as a teenager, when he was known as Lew Alcindor, he had served on his high school debate team and, through a summer program for Harlem youth, had worked as an apprentice journalist, reporting on the 1964 riots and interviewing Martin Luther King. In 1998, eager to prove his desire to hook on as an assistant coach with some NBA team, he moved to Arizona to volunteer with the Alchesay High School Falcons on the White Mountain Apache Reservation. But that longing to return to a professional bench turned out to be at odds with his nature. The lasting result of Abdul-Jabbar's desert sojourn is *A Season on the Reservation* (2000), the diary from which this selection comes. An account of the team's first practice, it hints at the rocky patches he will navigate in his role as visiting coach. It edges into history, anthropology, and culture, subjects that will mark much of his writing to come. And it offers a taste of Kareem the public intellectual, the elevated mind that fans had little interest in learning about until he had hung up his goggles for good.

from

A Season on the Reservation

As I kept watching the three-on-three drill, I realized that there were obvious reasons why the boys liked to run so much on the court. For one thing, they were going to be shorter than most of the opponents they played who were not Native American. (One of their most bitter rivals, as I would soon find out, was San Carlos, which was to the south of Whiteriver; it had its own Apache squad on the

307

San Carlos Reservation, and in the half-serious parlance of the sports world, these two teams didn't like each other.) Because the Falcons were smaller than other squads, they tried to wear down their opponents with this running style of basketball and win late in the game. They were playing at 5,300 feet above sea level, and if they could sprint like this throughout all four quarters, the other guys would probably collapse.

The Falcons were carrying on a long tradition of running from things that were chasing them or standing in their way. There were legendary stories from the Apache past of their warriors being pursued by enemies and simply riding their horses to death. There were stories of the warriors crossing sixty miles a day on foot over rough terrain and high-country mesas while the U.S. Cavalry aggressively pursued them on horseback, but still weren't able to catch up. There were stories of the Apache covering a hundred miles a day when they had to. A book written about the Apache exploits during the nineteenth-century Indian wars was called *Once They Moved Like the Wind*. Standing in the activity center, watching the boys run up and down the court that first afternoon, I knew that I really hadn't understood that title until now.

The players made a lot of mistakes on the floor. They didn't dribble well, especially with their weak hands (for the right-handed player that's the left hand, and vice versa). Their passes were often amiss. They didn't know how to position themselves under the basket for a rebound or how to use their hips, legs, shoulders, backs, or buttocks to keep other players away from the goal. They didn't shoot layups well with either their weak or strong hands. They tried to grab rebounds with one hand instead of two. (You can reach higher with one hand but have much more control over the ball when you use both.) They weren't physical with one another when playing defense and seemed reluctant to put their hands or arms on their opponents. They shot the ball off the palms of their hands rather than their fingertips. They didn't give the ball the spin needed to keep it on course.

None of this surprised me. Basketball's fundamentals are no longer being taught the way they used to be—at any level of the game. This is why today you see even pro players who can't do some of the basic things mentioned above. I stayed in college for four years and had the fundamentals of the sport driven into me at every practice.

Coach Wooden made every player on the team do every single thing involved in the game. He correctly believed that basketball is such a fluid sport that a player could never know when he would be called upon to dribble or shoot or pass or rebound or play defense or do any of a hundred other things, so he always had to be prepared, no matter what happened next.

Those days are past. College stars are not only failing to learn all the fundamentals of the game, as players my age once did, but they are leaving their schools after one or two years to turn professional; the money offered them now is simply too great to refuse. If you can get a $50 million guaranteed contract for having half a game, how can anyone turn that down? What's the incentive to keep expanding your skills? What's the monetary payoff for achieving more success?

Competition in the NBA has suffered throughout the past decade, with virtually no one able even to challenge the supremacy of the Chicago Bulls. Very few impact players, who can carry their team through the playoffs and toward a championship, have entered the league in the Nineties. The young guys just aren't getting the seasoning and apprenticeship they need at the university level before climbing up the higher rungs of the sport. Ironically, the country is now full of basketball clinics put on by renowned coaches, clinics that hardly existed when I was starting my career. But these events are mostly just celebrity get-togethers, where you pay your money and can shake a star's hand, but avoid the real task of learning how to play the game.

Big men have suffered the most from all this. The college game is no longer dominated by centers, the way it was for much of basketball's history, and the pro game is now largely a perimeter-shooting contest. Kids love to watch pro stars toss up long-range, three-point jump shots or throw down spectacular, rim-shaking dunks, and that's what they now aspire to imitate. But how many Michael Jordans are there out there? The hard and sometimes dirty work of taking the ball inside and putting up a high-percentage shot near the basket is still the most efficient way of scoring, but it's becoming a lost art.

For a decade, I've watched this trend and been increasingly bothered by it. In the 1990s, only two big men—Shaquille O'Neal and Tim Duncan—have come into pro basketball and made a real impact, but Shaq hasn't developed into a complete player. In addition to that, he hasn't shown much respect for the kind of basketball that was around long before he arrived on the scene. He's publicly referred to the way I used to play as "old man's basketball," which it may have been, but it earned me six more rings than he's got so far.

If the fundamentals were missing from the college or pro game, how could I possibly expect to find them here on the reservation? Trends filter down through the layers of a sport, and the kids out on the floor watched the same ESPN highlights of the three-point-shooting superstars that the rest of us did. What did surprise me about this first practice was not just the nonstop running or that the boys hadn't mastered or even seemed aware of many aspects of the game. What struck me was that they played the game virtually without speaking to one another. Nobody talked to anybody about anything.

Earlier in the day, the junior varsity coach, Rich Sanchez, had told me, "At Alchesay, we play ninja basketball. It's silent but deadly. The guys play very quietly and the ball should never touch the floor. Just pass it and run and pass it and run some more. All you should hear is the pitter-patter of tennis shoes as they move down the court together and then the sound of the ball laying off the glass as it goes through the net. Run and play defense and wear the other team down with our quickness and stamina. That's our style."

What I was seeing in front of me was silent all right, but it only looked deadly to their own team.

Communication with your teammates is critical during a game. When I was playing for UCLA Coach John Wooden—who won ten NCAA titles in his last twelve years on the job, a record that most likely will never be challenged—he drilled into us the need to talk to one another throughout the game. If our opponent committed a turnover and one of our players got the ball, he had to let the others know immediately so they could all react at once and switch from playing defense to offense as a group. To signal this switch, we yelled "Ball!" and then everyone knew what to do next. On defense, our players were taught to talk as much as possible, about whom we were guarding and what was happening with the ball. Talking like this was an essential part of the game where I grew up in New York City, and in most other places, and the best teams usually have the best communication skills.

The Apache kids were almost mute on the court. No joking, no ribbing, no verbal horsing around, no telling one another what had just occurred or what to expect next. They shunned talking when they were in motion.

Yet once again, when I took a few moments and thought about it, I realized there were historical reasons behind their actions, things rooted deeply in the story of their own survival for many centuries in a harsh landscape. In order to ambush people or escape from their enemies, in order to stalk food while hunting, their ancestors had mastered the art of silence. That had helped feed them and protect them from their mortal enemies.

Silence had worked well enough in those situations, but this was basketball, and they were hurting themselves (at times, literally) on the floor by not speaking up. Anyone who had ever played street basketball in a big city knew that talking and sometimes "trash talking" to your opponent were as much a part of the action as a good jump shot or a pair of tennis shoes. If your game was good enough, you could get away with saying just about anything.

That custom didn't apply here. I hadn't heard one negative word all practice—almost no words of any kind. During one of my earlier trips to the reservation, I'd been given a sheet of paper that spells out the dos and don'ts of Apache culture. It's shown to the tribe's youngsters as behavioral guidelines and sometimes passed out to non-Apache visitors who travel to Whiteriver and drop by the White Mountain Apache headquarters. Under the title of "Etiquette of Apache Dos," these things were listed: "Rise early with the sun and pray. Share. Be friendly and courteous. Respect people—the elderly, in-laws, ceremonies, Mother Nature, and the deceased. Tell stories during the winter. Keep home clean. Advise children about life. Learn about clans. Marry outside your clan. Forgive. Stay sober."

Under the title of "Etiquette of Apache Don'ts," it mentioned some things that may have explained the boys' reluctance to talk to one another or bang each other with their bodies on the court. It said not to: "Stare. Point. Whistle at night. Gossip. Be destructive. Misuse words when angry. Waste food. Panic. Make fun of people. Make fun of deer. Push another person. Spit on people. Bump people on purpose. Step over people. Marry into the same clan. Act smart and snobbish. Use makeup [facial]. Chew on fingernails. Get drunk. Lie. Steal. Touch physically unnecessarily. Plan ahead. Make fun of traditions. Pull another person's hair. Be jealous. Kick. Count the stars. Make faces. Be lazy. Bother with things you don't know about, especially Crown Dancers."

And finally it said: "Apache females do NOT participate in sweat hut ceremonies."

I watched the practice, gradually absorbing what I was seeing. It looked like a free-for-all instead of a drill, but I didn't point this out to others or say anything else. It was my first day on the job and I didn't even have a whistle around my neck, because I had forgotten to take care of this detail. I didn't feel in charge without one, but tomorrow that would change, because I would bring a whistle with me.

John Edgar Wideman

There's almost no genre that MacArthur Fellowship recipient John Edgar Wideman (b. 1941) has failed to explore: novel, short story, microfiction, poetry, review, magazine profile, historical narrative. His 2001 memoir, *Hoop Roots*, is where he undertakes his deepest and most resonant drilling down into the sport that has been a lifelong passion. A professor emeritus of Africana Studies and Literary Arts at Brown, Wideman was an All-Ivy forward at the University of Pennsylvania during the early 1960s and played with Bill Bradley when both studied at Oxford as Rhodes Scholars. His daughter Jamila exceeded his distinction as a basketball player, starring at Stanford and spending four seasons in the WNBA. In this excerpt from *Hoop Roots*, a pulsating, adapted-for-basketball prose style hurtles his sentences forward. Wideman often dispenses with the verb *to be* and delivers interrogatories as declaratives, sending words zigging and zagging like ballplayers inside a chain-link fence. He takes us to Pittsburgh's East End, to a funeral home in the Homewood neighborhood where he grew up, for the wake of a nephew who has been the victim of a gang killing. There he runs into Ed Fleming, a 6'3" former NBA center who has tested two generations of Wideman men on the local courts. The encounter prompts a meditation on several of the author's touchstone themes—race, inheritance, manhood, history—as well as on the game that, as Wideman has said, "can give us a kind of mystical awareness."

from

Hoop Roots

E D FLEMING whom I'd seen last . . . when . . . where . . . now here in Warden's in his charcoal gray, fashionable, gangster-shouldered suit in the midst of a crowd of mourners congregated just inside the entrance of Parlor A.

After we'd talked a minute or so and he had to go back inside and I needed to return to Omar, he said, Uh-huh. My mom lived on Finance. For a good long while before she passed. Heard her speak highly of Mrs. French. And Mrs. French your grandmother, huh. Hmmm. I never knew that. Heard my mother praise Mrs. French many times. Good to see you, man. You take care of yourself now, John. Don't be a stranger. Holler next time you're in town.

John. I don't believe I'd ever heard Ed Fleming say my first name. A baptism of sorts, in Warden's of all places. He'd always called me

Wideman on the court. The surname detached, objectified, like when it's entered in a scorebook. *Wideman*. A clean slate for each new game. Every game you're obligated, challenged to fill the line of empty slots following your name with field goals attempted and made, foul shots hit or missed, personal fouls, rebounds, steals, turnovers, assists, blocked shots. Who Wideman *is* is drastically simplified. You are the numbers, period. Nothing else matters—where you came from, who your daddy or grandmammy might be—you're just a player. *Wideman*. The numbers—over the course of a game, over the course of a season, a career—accumulate or not, may resonate or not when another player says your name, an announcer or fan says your name. You get used to people observing the last-name-only convention until *Wideman*'s a tag that doesn't exactly belong to you anymore. *Wideman* only signifies the numbers racked up, then wiped clean so your name's a question mark each time a game begins. And unfair though it may be, the sole numbers really mattering always the ones in progress—when they're skimpy, they peg you as a chump, forget how you kicked ass the game before or the last dozen games.

On the playground no uniforms and numbers identify you. A single name's enough on Homewood court, and if it's your surname, *Wideman*, it's said with a little intentional chill of depersonalization, the way a referee calls you by your uniform number, foul on *Ten* in high school or college games. Strictly business on the playground too, when somebody chooses you in the meat-market picking of teams for the first serious run of the day. Alternating choices till a limit of ten spots filled, the two guys choosing—they earn the privilege by being the first two to hit a foul shot—call you by your last name or maybe a nickname: Got Smith—Gimme Pooky—Got Jones—Take Sky. You can go years, a lifetime, playing alongside guys and know them only by their court handles. Read something in a newspaper about one of your basketball buddies and never know it's him. *Snobs*, inside the disguise of a whole, proper name. You'll have to hear the good news or bad news over again on the sidelines from somebody who tells the story with the court name in place. *D'you hear about Snobs, man.*

Ed Fleming had always called me Wideman in my coming-up days. For him to acknowledge a life for me off the court would have been highly improbable back then. Why would he care who I was. Or who I thought I was. He was a legend. He ruled. He was a grown man, born into a different age set, with different running buddies who'd come up hooping together, getting in and out of trouble together, and obviously no outsider could enter that cohort, just like nobody could leave it. Because I was precocious on the court, my age-group friends seldom accompanied me when I played ball. In some ways it meant I stuck out like a sore thumb. I didn't mind being a special case, didn't like the loneliness. No crew to hang with on walks to the court or back home again. No chance to replay games in our words, from our rookies' perspective. No opportunity to boast or tease each other or badmouth some old head turkey who thought he was god's gift. Over time I'd discover half the fun of playground ball resided in these rituals that extended the game, the imagined recreations like a good preacher retelling Adam and Eve, jazzing up his version with parables and homilies and metaphor not only to stitch together a way to live in the world but exemplify a style of doing it with his words. No crew meant I had no one to watch my back unless an older player chose to look out for me. Literally a look. One look all it took to dissuade a bully from coming down too hard on the youngblood. Rules, consequences communicated in a single glance from one of the enforcers like Ed Fleming nobody's hardly going to the mat to challenge.

To some of his peers he was *Ed* or *Fleming*. Always *Ed Fleming* in my mind. Both names necessary, three inseparable syllables, more incantation or open-sesame mantra than a name. A mini-sound bite like those heroic epithets identifying characters—Ox-eyed Hera, Swift-heeled Achilles—whose adventures I followed in the *Golden Book of Greek Myth* or in Classics Illustrated comic versions of the *Iliad* and *Odyssey*. See the guy down low, backing into the key, *pat, pat, pat,* demanding inch by inch the space he needs. That's not just any old Ed or Fleming. He's *the* Ed Fleming. Implacable. Irresistible. Each dribble a hammerstroke staking out his claim. *Pat. Pat.* Both names, all three syllables spoken internally, honored, even when I don't say them aloud. Even now, forty years later in Warden's, when I call him *Ed*, the single, naked sound coming out of my mouth almost as surprising for me to hear as hearing *John* pass through Ed Fleming's lips.

To my father, Edgar, he would have been *Fleming*, one of a vintage crop of good young players rising up behind him. Fleming, Stokes, and their teammates, winners at Homewood's Westinghouse High of the state title, kids good enough to groom and be wary of simultaneously, especially the Fleming boy since one day soon he might also encroach upon *Eddie*, my father's court name. My father, Edgar Wideman, would have taken a prodigy like Ed Fleming under his wing, tested him, whipped on him unmercifully, protected him with hard stares if anybody got too close to actually damaging the precious talent, the fragile ego and vulnerable physique of a large, scrappy, tough kid just about but not quite ready to handle the weight and anger of adult males who used the court to certify their deepest resources of skill, determination, heart, resources they could publicly exhibit and hone few other places in a Jim Crow society. Homewood court a threshing ground, and the weak better not stray too close to the blades. The men could find release for some of the best things in themselves, and of course that included dangerous stuff too. Play not exactly play. No-no-no. Winning and losing cut deep. Very, very deep. Yet ability, a refined repertoire of hoop skill enabling you to win more often than lose, not the thing that gave you a passing or failing grade on the court. The real examination results, the score that counts so much it keeps the play, for all its ferocity, about more than winning or losing, registers inside each player. When you step on or off the court, how do other players look at you and you at them. What name do they call you by, how is the saying of your name inflected. Among the infinitely nuanced possibilities a particular pronunciation might suggest, which one is communicated to you, to others when you're greeted, when you are picked for a squad, when players talk about you and you're not around, when they are not around and you talk to yourself about the court, about the game, replaying the action in your mind on that private, private screen at home, at night, in bed, recalling a whole hot afternoon and you have to fill in the slots, the blanks, where your name goes into the imagining. What is it, how is it said.

To Ed Fleming, *Wideman* would be the respected name of one of the old heads who broke him in and also the name of a kid coming up behind him. Wideman *père*. Wideman *fils*. Did he ever have trouble distinguishing us, keeping us straight. Did he concern himself with policing such a fine line. Something he once said to me indicated he didn't always differentiate. In Great Time what goes round comes round. After hip-checking me *blam* into the fence just behind the poles and backboard when we were both after a loose ball, or maybe it was when he lifted me off my feet and tossed me a yard or so from the sweet spot I thought I was strong enough to deny him, bodying him away from it for a couple of seconds till he decided to show me that day what he could bring to bear if he really needed a spot as much as I needed him out of it, Ed Fleming whispered words to this effect: Your daddy was extra rough on me, and boy, I'm sure gonna return the favor. Gonna give you a hard row to hoe, son, and don't start crybaby-ing or calling fouls neither, not today, youngblood. If you can't stand the heat, get out the kitchen.

So Ed Fleming's hoop war with my father not over in one genera-tion. He revisited it through me. Hard truths imprinted on Edgar Wide-man's will and flesh by some anonymous bunch of old guys hooping, then imprinted by my father on Ed Fleming, coming home to roost in my bruised feelings and meat, in the knobby-boned body I prayed daily would hurry up and get padded by muscle like Ed Fleming's.

What my father had reaped and sown would sprout up again when the weather turned warm enough for outdoor runs to commence at Homewood court. The game, its lore and lessons. For instance, *Never forget*—not where you came from nor what's coming up behind you, a lesson concretely applied when you're dribbling the ball, leading a fast break attack on the opponent's basket, when it's a matter of peripheral vision, of the Janus look backward and forward so you're aware of who's in front of you and behind, also mapping 360 degrees all the other players' positions on the court, the kaleidoscoping shifts, the evolving opportunities and hazards your rush to the hoop engen-ders. More abstractly applied, the lesson reminds you to take seriously your place in time, in tradition, within the community of players. Ed Fleming and the other vets teaching me to take my time, no mat-ter the speed I'm traveling. Teaching me to be, not to underreach or overreach myself. Either way you cheated the game, cheated your name, the name in progress, the unfolding narrative, told and retold, backward, forward, sideways, inside out, of who you would turn out to be as you played.

I learned, among other things, to recognize and be grateful for a helping hand, learned it might not be exactly the kind of hand I thought I wanted, maybe it would be a rough hand, a bitter pill, but I was learning to appreciate different hands on their different terms. Above all learning not to be so intent on moving forward I turned my back on the ones behind who might need my hand or have one to offer.

Learned about time as I was learning the game. Because the game is time. Not time out from the real business of life. Not simply play time. Time. Like good gospel music, the game brings time, tells time, announces the good news that there is Great Time beyond clock time and this superabundance, this sphere where you can be larger than you are, belongs to nobody. It's too vast. Everlasting. *Elsewhere*. Yet you can go there. It's in your hands. White people nor nobody else owns it. It's waiting for you to claim it. The game conjures Great Time, gives it and takes it away. Clock time, linear time irrelevant while the game's on—two teams might battle fifteen minutes to complete a run or twice as long or till dark hides the court forever if neither side pushes ahead by two baskets in a deuce (win by two) contest. The game trumps time, supersedes it. Good hoop, like good rhythm-and-blues music, alerts you to what's always there, abiding, presiding, master of ceremonies ready to empower your spirit and body, the beat lurking, dancing in all things whether you're conscious of its presence or not. Great Time your chance to be. To get down. Out. To do it right. Right on time. The game, again like gospel music, propagates rhythm, a flow and go, a back beat you can tune into so time's lonely, featureless stretch feels as charged, as sensuous, as accessible a medium as wind or water. You don't really own game time, but the fit feels so close to perfect you can't help believing on occasion it belongs to you.

Playing the game is not counting time nor translating, reducing, calculating it in arbitrary material measures, not turning it into something else, possessing it or hoarding it or exchanging it for money. In other words not alienating time, not following the dictates of the workaday world that would orphan our bodies from time. In the game nothing counts about time except its nonstop, swift passing and the way that passage beating inside you is so deep, so sweet and quick like a longed-for, unexpected kiss over before you know you've been kissed but the thrill isn't gone, gets stronger and stronger when time allows you to stand back from it, remember it, it lingers because you're still there as well as here, riding Great Time, what you were and are and will be as long as you're in the air, the game.

Synchronicity. You and time in synch. In touch. Rhythm one name for how the touch feels, how it registers, how you can let go and find yourself part of time's flow. Dancing with an invisible partner who's so good at dancing you forget who's leading, who's following, aware instead only of the rhythm, on time, stepping, and your body free, mind free, dancing the steps. You're large, large and tiny too. Time a co-conspirator as you *break* from clock time. Everything happening simultaneously so you don't have to hurry or slow down. The game in its own good time comes to you as you come to understand its rhythms. You're not counting but the count's inside you, heard and unheard. Disciplined by years of experiencing the action, your body responds to the measures, frees your playing mind. You let yourself go where the game flows. Gametime opens like your mouth when you drew your first breath.

Pat Conroy

Basketball makes the occasional cameo in the novels of Pat Conroy (1945–2016), most memorably as staging ground for the fraught relationship between the author and his father in the autobiographical *The Great Santini*. But it took running into a former college teammate—at a book signing in Dayton, Ohio, while on tour to promote his 1995 novel *Beach Music*—for Conroy to fully explore his lifelong engagement with the game he called "the only thing that granted me a complete and sublime congruence and oneness with the world." After talking late into the night with that old backcourt mate, John DeBrosse, Conroy was inspired to chase down every other member of The Citadel's 1966–67 varsity, as well as Coach Mel Thompson, whose job became a casualty of the team's futility. Conroy pronounced the result, his 2002 memoir *My Losing Season*, "an act of recovery," and he meant that in the therapeutic sense, to be sure. But it's also a nod to the defining characteristic of the southern writer, even an adoptive one like Conroy—a punctiliousness about keeping appointments with demons from one's past. "My losing season still haunts me and resides within me," he wrote, "a time of shadows now, but a time still endowed with a mysterious power to both hurt and enlarge me." In this chapter, "Auburn," Conroy revisits the first game of that snakebit, 8–17 senior season, in which he plays the point for "a team that spent a year perfecting the art of falling to pieces."

from

My Losing Season

A s I stare at The Citadel's schedule for the 1966–67 varsity basketball team, I mourn for the quicksilvery racehorse passage of time. Its swiftness has caught me with the same ineffable start that comes to every man and woman who lives long enough. It remains as the single great surprise of any life.

In the locker room, I got dressed for the game that would be the first game of the last year I would play organized basketball with real uniforms and real crowds and coaches who received paychecks because of their knowledge of the game. The tension in the locker room was almost electrical, special—like the atmosphere might be on Mercury, able to sustain only certain rare forms of organisms. Outside, the crowd was beginning to form and the parking lots were filling up with the makes of automobiles I now see only in period movies. The voices of strangers streaming down the sidewalk outside our locker room came to us through the cinderblock wall, barely audible, unformed, but brimming with excitement. What a good thing it is to go to games. What strange joy is felt as you leave the flatness of your daily life, the fatigue of routine, and the killing sameness of jobs to move among thousands toward a brightly lit field house at night. They passed by us in the darkness, their expectations risen by our first game with Auburn University, hope cresting that our team would prove memorable, and if we were lucky, legendary.

Auburn. It sounded so Big Time to a boy like me. "Good luck against Auburn, Pat," my mother had said on the phone, and just hearing her invoke the great name made me feel the weight of my own self-worth. I thought the entire universe would be watching me and my teammates take on the War Eagles that day in 1966. Auburn was in the Southeastern Conference, one of the proudest and showiest in the country, and recruited big-name athletes for a big-time program. I loved it whenever little Citadel invoked the myth and story of Goliath and scheduled us to play the great schools. Whenever people ask me about the teams I played against in college, I always say, "Florida State, Auburn, West Virginia, Virginia Tech, and Clemson." Never do I reply with "Erskine, Wofford, Newberry, and Presbyterian," who were the patsies and sacrificial lambs of our schedule.

In the big games The Citadel's corps always showed up in force, and that day there were nearly eighteen hundred of them on hand to offer their lionesque, full-throated allegiance to their team as we took the court. No one could rock a gymnasium like the Corps of Cadets in full ecstatic cry. When the Corps unleashed itself during the passionate fury of games, the energy was both intemperate and unforgettable to visiting teams. For us, it was like having an extra man under the boards, a sullen, mean-spirited one that could be worth six to eight points in a closely fought game.

In the locker room we heard the thunder of our violent tribe, and we felt the butterflies hatched in our stomachs. Danny Mohr sat at the first locker, the farthest away from the entrance; Jimmy Halpin sat next to me painfully putting on his knee brace; I laced up my Converse All Stars next to Mohr and regarded my image in the full-length mirror across the room.

Coach Thompson arranged us according to a strict class system: the juniors came next with DeBrosse sitting next to Halpin, followed by Bridges, Bornhorst, and Cauthen. Everyone on the team knew to keep Bob Cauthen and Doug Bridges separated. There was always a dangerous chemistry produced when those two scraped against one another.

Then came our dazzling collection of sophomores: Bill Zinsky, whose game was finished and mature; Tee Hooper, the tall slashing guard who had beaten me out for a starting position; Al Kroboth, the relentless rebounder; Greg Connor, the ex–football player whose intensity was a burning thing; and Brian Kennedy, irrepressible, clumsy, a little too loud for a sophomore.

I made my way up and down the line of dressing teammates, trying to relax the sophomores. I remembered the terror I felt before and during my first varsity game two years earlier when The Citadel had played West Virginia in Morgantown. "Last year the upperclassmen tortured you and tried to run you out of school," I said. "This year they'll treat you like gods."

"Like they treat you, right, Conroy?" Cauthen asked.

"It's my third straight year as I stride this campus like a god," I replied. "I consider myself a Zeus-like figure."

"More like a leprechaun," Bob added.

"That was a racist reference to my Irish heritage and my diminutive size," I told the sophomores. "But know this—Bob fears my rapier wit."

"Say what, Conroy?" Bob asked.

"And my vast vocabulary," I said, returning to my locker.

"Hey, Conroy," Danny Mohr said as I pulled on my warmups.

Rat warned us of our coach's arrival. "Fifteen minutes, guys."

"Who's gonna be captain this year?" Danny asked me. "Muleface say anything to you?"

"Not a word," I said. "Maybe he'll make you, me, and Jimmy tri-captains, since we're the only survivors of our fabulous freshman team."

"God, we'd've been great if we could've stayed together," Jimmy said.

"He wouldn't make just you captain? Would he, Conroy? You're just a fucking Green Weenie."

"Don't worry about my feelings, Root," I said, and Jimmy Halpin almost fell off the bench laughing.

"We don't know what he's going to do," I said. "But he's got these three charismatic, Patton-like leaders to choose from."

Bob Cauthen, who made a habit of teasing me before practice and games, yelled from the middle of the locker room, "Hey, Conroy, how are you and the other homos getting along down in the English department? I hear the English profs are one hundred percent faggots."

"I lost my Maidenform bra, Bob. Could you help me find it?"

"At least I know how to take one off. Unlike you, Conroy."

"Get ready for the game, Cauthen," DeBrosse said.

"Eat me, DeBrosse," Bob said. "Anyone who thinks we can actually beat Auburn is full of shit."

Doug Bridges laughed as though he had just been told the funniest joke in the world, and Halpin joined him, then Bridges shouted, "Hey, Conroy. Our *team*, man. You can feel it coming together, can't you?"

Bob, wilted a bit in the glare of the sophomores, said, "If we were worth a shit, we wouldn't be playing at The Citadel."

"Hey, sophomores," I shouted. "It's the positive attitude in this locker room that'll lead us from victory to victory to victory this year."

My remark brought a strange, troubled laughter from the sophomores. Always, in the time I played for Mel Thompson, there was this unsettled, lunatic disjointedness to the atmosphere. In the locker room, you felt everything except what it was like to be part of a team. Year after year, the sophomores were cast adrift in the cynical laughter in an atmosphere that should have been joyous.

I tried once again to help them relax. "Best sophomore class in the history of this school," I said to them, then leaned down to Bill Zinsky. "This school isn't gonna believe this good a basketball player got through the plebe system."

"Quit the rah-rah shit, Conroy," Cauthen said. "That bullshit don't work. Especially not here."

Then Coach Thompson entered the locker room, wearing his game face, a midwestern scowl that looked like cloud covering, and moving with that loping shambling walk that had become a trademark to us, his face exuded no light, just various textures of darkness. Everything Mel did was studied and habitual, and he allowed no accidents or hazards to disrupt the afternoons and evenings of his life.

Al Beiner worked in the equipment room getting the balls ready for the warmup drills as Rat Eubanks put fresh towels in our lockers. Rat went behind me and massaged my neck with a towel still warm from the dryer. I put my hand behind my head and squeezed his thin wrist. Before every game during the year, this was our secret, unnoticed ritual.

Coach Thompson walked by us silently. He smoked his cigarette with deliberate slowness, then went into the shower room to urinate.

I offered a prayer to the God I was afraid of losing: "O Lord, I ask that something good come to me from this basketball season. My career, so far, has been an embarrassment to me. All I ask is for something good to come to me."

Coach Thompson returned from washing his hands, threw his cigarette on the cement floor, and crushed it beneath his polished, tasseled black loafers. Our coach was a fastidious man and a sharp dresser. Other teams might outplay the Citadel basketball team, but none of the other coaches in the Southern Conference could outdress Mel Thompson.

"Conroy," he said, "you'll be captain for tonight's game." This declaration caught me and my teammates by complete surprise. If he had asked me to put on a wedding dress to play the game it would not have astonished me more since second-stringers rarely had bestowed on them the mantle of captaincy. One minute before we took the floor against the strongest team on our schedule, Coach Thompson surprised us by humiliating our highest scorer and top rebounder from last season, Danny Mohr, and giving over the leadership role to me, who had demonstrated very little of it. We said the Lord's Prayer and then gathered in the center of the room, placing our hands over the hands of our fiery-eyed coach. His dark eyes smoldered with a malefic competitiveness as he screamed, "The SEC. The SEC. Let's see if we can play with the big boys."

Al Beiner flipped me a basketball as we lined up to enter the field house for the warmup drills. I handed the ball to Danny, but he gave it back to me and murmured, "You heard what the man said. You're the fucking captain."

Though Danny would not look at me, his hurt passed through the heart of my entire team. But then Rat threw open the door, and I led the way as my team burst out into the light and the sounds of "Dixie" (played better by the Citadel band than by any band in the world). The Corps rose and roared its praise, its validation of our oneness, our uniqueness—as we took the first steps into the mysteries of time and the reality of the season that would tear us in all the soft places of our young manhoods before it was over.

But I led my team to the center of the court, then broke for the basket and laid the ball in off the glass, taking care that I made the first layup of the new season that had turned suddenly real.

One of the referees came up behind me as I was shooting jumpers from the top of the key and said, "Captain Conroy, would you join us at center court?" It was one of the sweetest sentences in the English language ever directed at me, but I saw a wounded grimace cross Danny Mohr's face as I ran to meet with the Auburn men. Though I remember shaking hands with the Auburn captain, Bobby Buisson, and noticed that he and I shared the same number, 22, I held on to little of that momentous occasion because I kept saying to myself, "I'm the captain of the Citadel basketball team and we're about to play Auburn University." Since Coach Thompson had told me every day of my life at The Citadel that I did not have enough talent to play college basketball, that doctrine had assumed a form of catechism, and became one of my most deeply held beliefs. I had never dreamed that I would be in this place and time, under these lights, and with almost three thousand people watching me represent my school and my team.

The referees went over the rules with Bobby Buisson and me, but their voices blurred when I heard a cry of "Conroy, Conroy, Conroy" go up in the raucous cadet section, and I could see my roommates, Bo Marks and Mike Devito, leading the Romeo Company knobs in chanting my name. Bobby and I shook hands and wished each other good luck and I went back to join my teammates.

Unknown to me, I had just shaken hands with the best point guard I would ever play against. My wife Sandra's favorite saying is, "When the pupil is ready, a teacher appears." Bobby Buisson had appeared in my life at the perfect moment.

Because I was a senior, Mel Thompson started me at guard with John DeBrosse. Danny Mohr would jump center against the Auburn center, the aptly named Ronnie Quick, who was two inches shorter than Danny. It struck Doug Bridges as an oddity that The Citadel had a taller center than Auburn University. Doug himself and Bill Zinsky were both taller than the Auburn forwards, Wallace Tinker, who was six three, and Tom Perry, who was an undersized six two.

Danny Mohr crouched at center court against Ronnie Quick and the ref threw up the ball. As a portent of what lay ahead, Auburn took that tip and flew down the court at breakneck speed, establishing a racehorse pace they would keep up for a solid forty minutes.

I picked up Bobby Buisson, who carried himself on the court with a brashness and a gambler's instinct that delighted me. His greatness shone in the first moments when we stopped their fast break and he dribbled back out to the top of the key to set up their offense. I was Citadel bred and Citadel trained and I knew a natural-born leader when I saw one. The great engines of the Auburn offense started and ended with this radiant and handsome young man. Bobby threw a beautiful pass to the small forward, Tinker, who taught Doug Bridges that he was not the only pure shooter on the floor.

After Auburn scored, DeBrosse took the ball out of bounds and tossed it to me. John did not like bringing it up if he didn't have to. He would simply entrust the ball to me to bring it past their guards.

I ran the ball upcourt, but on the way past the bench I heard Mel yelling at me, "Don't shoot, Conroy. Don't shoot it."

As I crossed midcourt, Buisson was waiting for me as though I were a pizza he had ordered by phone. He played me too close and he felt like wrapping paper when I went by him. Even with the noise of the crowd, I heard my coach screaming, "Don't shoot." I threw the ball to Doug on the right side of the court and I ran my route into the corner, bringing Bobby with me. Mohr set a pick for Bill Zinsky on the other side of the court.

"Swing it," Coach Thompson yelled.

Doug threw it to DeBrosse at the top of the key who swung the ball to Zinsky on the left side of the lane, then John took his man into the far left corner. Mohr picked for Bridges on the other side of the court as I moved to the top of the key, Buisson covering me like a silk glove. I had to fake a backdoor move toward the basket to open up the passing lane between me and Zinsky when I saw Mohr break toward me as I shuffled him a pass. Danny dribbled Ronnie Quick deep into the lane, then spun and shot his lovely jumper down low. Mohr actually was taller than the Auburn center, but when Danny extended his long willowy arms, he played like he was six nine or better. For a big man, Danny had the softest, supplest hands, and his shots passed through the cords as if they were trying to nest there.

Auburn played a fast-paced game but Bobby Buisson controlled the tempo and action of everything the War Eagles did. His bursts toward the basket were rabbit-swift and I started to give him some room. In the first five minutes, Bobby had proven that he could drive the lane better than I could, an accolade I did not hand out often, and always grudgingly. So I played off of him, giving him some daylight to maneuver, and hoping he would take the opportunity for jump shots. He radiated with all the dangers of the penetrator, the kind that loves to kill defenses by attacking the dead center of their engines.

"Get in his face, Conroy!" Coach Thompson yelled over the noise of the crowd, but I had all I could handle with this kid. I was a Southern Conference guard trying to hold my own with a Southeastern Conference guard, and the difference was glaringly apparent. Bobby took in the whole floor in a glance, and he got the ball to the player who was open with crisp, split-second passes that landed in his teammates' hands soft as biscuits, and at that exact moment they were ready to shoot.

Bill Zinsky scored his first college goal on a short jumper he took after grabbing a long rebound. Thirty seconds later Bridges hit a long jump shot, pulling up while trailing on a fast break, his body already glistening with sweat from the frantic pace.

"Slow it down," Mel Thompson commanded. As he shouted this, Bobby Buisson swarmed all over me, his arms snake-striking all around me, trying to flick the ball away, but Bobby was operating too close, and I passed him in a flash. We raced for the basket, he closing the gap slowly with every step we took, as Auburn's center, Quick, slipped off of Danny Mohr to intercept my drive. I do not remember if Bobby fouled me or Quick or if it was Tom Perry, but whoever fouled me did it hard and made sure I did not score on the play.

I stood on the free throw line, made a sign of the cross because it irritated the Protestant boys I played against, and threw up my underhanded free throw and scored my first point of the season. When I made the next free throw, the buzzer sounded and Tee Hooper came in to replace me at guard. My role as The Citadel's starting point guard had lasted five full minutes, and we were tied 10–10 with Auburn

University. The Green Weenies all stood and cheered as I took my place at the end of the bench, trying to hide my shame over having been pulled from the game so early. "I told you not to shoot, Conroy," Coach Thompson said.

I simply did not think I could endure one more season of riding the bench and watching a game that I loved more than anything in the world pass me by. My mediocrity at the game of basketball festered in me, tumored my normally buoyant spirit, tortured me into a kind of resigned submission as I considered the humiliation of spending my last season as a reserve guard. But I was not the kind of boy who would allow himself to fret or mope—that had not been my training. My teammates required my loyalty and enthusiastic championing of their play. And for the night of December 2, 1966, I was their captain, their leader on and off the floor, and I knew the power and necessity of being a team player.

So I fought the colossal disappointment of being replaced by a far more talented sophomore and got on with the business of cheering the Blue Team to victory. As Green Weenies, we never got to play much because in Mel Thompson's theories of coaching, you put your best athletes on the floor and let them win your basketball games with their superior skills. My coach did not believe in resting his best players because he never once asked to rest in his career as a center for North Carolina State. Fatigue was a form of moral cowardice to Mel, and all of his players understood that.

When Tee took my place, Bobby Buisson started to guard John DeBrosse, and the taller of the Auburn guards, Alex Howell, took on the rangy Hooper. Only when I returned to the bench did I realize how small Auburn's forwards were.

"Hell, we're bigger than those guys," I said.

"You ain't bigger than anybody, duck butt," Bob Cauthen said.

With six minutes left in the half, Danny Mohr, who was in the middle of playing a terrific game, hit three straight turnaround jump shots to pull The Citadel within three points. Taking a pass from Bridges, Tee left his man in the dust and flew through the entire Auburn team to make a beautiful, twisting layup against the glass. His layup narrowed Auburn's lead to one. Then Auburn got serious, and Bobby Buisson spent the rest of the night teaching me the great secrets of playing point guard. Watching him was like seeing Manolete demonstrate the proper use of the muleta to a Spanish boy maddened by the desire to face the great bulls in his own "suit of lights." In Bobby Buisson, I had found what I had been looking for my whole life.

In the realms of college basketball, the entire concept of the point guard was a new and developing one. I had heard the phrase used in my first summer at Camp Wahoo, but the necessity of having a guard who directed the offense and distributed the ball to the big men and the shooting guard (also a new concept) was gradually spreading around the theorists and innovators who created new wrinkles in offensive patterns and strategies. I could see that the five men on my team now on the court were, by far, the five best athletes The Citadel could field on any given night. Mohr, at center; Bridges and Zinsky at forward; DeBrosse and Hooper at guard—any one of these men was fully capable of scoring twenty points in any given game. Though it would take me four or five games to realize this, my team had one great, transparent flaw in its makeup: it lacked a point guard, a Bobby Buisson. Though John DeBrosse looked like a point guard, he was deficient when it came to possessing the proper temperament of the position. John was a shooter, pure and simple.

All five players on the court for my team were either scorers or shooters. There was not a passer among them. Bobby Buisson would begin to cut our hearts out in the second half. His utter joy in getting the ball to his hustling teammates was a besotted, almost maniacal thing. He was guarding DeBrosse so closely that Johnny was having difficulty establishing his game. Buisson was quicker, faster, and stronger than either me or DeBrosse—Auburn led by seven at the half, 50–43.

In the second half, with me and the rest of the Green Weenies in agonized witness, my Citadel team fell apart. The unraveling began with the opening tip-off. Our defense, never strong, simply collapsed under the full fury of the Auburn fast break. Auburn seemed to score on every possession. My team looked exhausted, spent, and beaten down by forces they did not seem to understand. After ten minutes, Auburn led 81–59. What had been a close and fiercely fought game turned quickly into a rout. It got so bad that Coach Thompson put me back in. Playing a desperate catch-up game, I drove the lane and scored my first 2-pointer of the season. Immediately Tee Hooper came back into the game.

"I told you not to shoot, Conroy," Mel Thompson shouted as I headed for the bench.

"Sorry, Coach," I said, noting that I had made the shot in question.

"That's your problem, Conroy," he said. "You're always sorry."

My team did not congeal as a team for the rest of the evening. Each time one of us made a move with the ball, it seemed individual, selfish, and unrelated to the other four players on the court, while Auburn was assassin-like in its delicious execution of its offense. They were a much better basketball team and much better coached, playing with brio, freshness, and unquenchable zeal.

I studied Buisson, dissecting his game and trying to steal as much as I could from him and graft his talents onto my own. First, I saw how much Buisson wanted to be there for his teammates, the joyfulness he took in delivering a pass to an open player and the gratitude they felt toward him for his childlike magnanimity. I basked in the bracing aura of his indomitable confidence. He flashed like a buccaneer across both ends of the court, brash, swashbuckling, all the elixirs of being fully alive and in control sparking off him as his team finished the joy of taking my team to the cleaners. The final score was an unbelievable 105–83.

But ah! There were bright spots for the Bulldogs. As the *News and Courier* sports editor Evan Bussey would write the next morning, "Danny Mohr, The Citadel pivot man, again proved to be old Mr. Dependable in the scoring column. The 6-6 senior scored 20 points and at one stretch in the first half was about the only one holding the Citadel Bulldogs in the game. Sophomore Bill Zinsky got 16 points in his first varsity game and proved to be the best the Cadets had on the boards. He had nine rebounds.

"Doug Bridges had 15 points, DeBrosse 8, and Tee Hooper in a most impressive debut had 11."

I followed the rest of Bobby Buisson's career closely. He proved to be as good as I thought. His nickname was "Bweets," and Adolph Rupp was quoted as saying that Buisson was "one of the finest defensive players we've ever seen."

I agree.

Bobby Buisson. Wherever you are. I was an eyewitness to your mastery, the tender wizardry you brought to my home gym. I dedicated the rest of my year remaking myself in your image. It was an honor to take the court against you. I was no match for you and for that I apologize. But I took some things from your game that would hold me in good stead.

After showering, I walked in darkness behind the barracks on Plebe Walk, trying to control my shame. A second-stringer and a senior, I said, torturing myself. My season was already slipping away, and it had just started. In agony I made my way across the length of the campus alone, doomed to be a spectator while my life as an athlete went flashing past me on the fly.

Shame, I felt, the purest shame.

Steve Rushin

In his commencement address to Marquette's class of 2007, Steve Rushin (b. 1966) recalled that, at his own graduation from the same school nearly two decades earlier, he and his classmates had heard from Supreme Court Chief Justice William Rehnquist. "Inspired by his example," Rushin said, "I vowed then and there that I too would pursue a career that allowed me to spend all day in a robe." And so he has, writing long and short to equal effect for *Sports Illustrated*, as well as authoring books that include a novel, a memoir, and a travelogue, all marked by a sophisticated wit and childlike joy at getting lost in the language. He was as adept at delivering one-liners as 2,000-liners, and wrote magisterial surveys of sports and American life that took up swaths of *SI*'s fortieth- and sixtieth-anniversary issues. Rushin filed offbeat features on arctic golf and roller coasters, which helps explain his appearances in three different series under the Houghton Mifflin *Best American* writing umbrella—sports, travel, and magazine. But it was also for his consistency and knack for calling out the absurd as a columnist that the National Sports Media Association in 2006 named Rushin its National Sportswriter of the Year. Basketball is an abiding presence in his life, for better or for worse: his wife is the Hall of Famer, NCAA champion, and Olympic gold medalist Rebecca Lobo. In this, one of scores of 800-word *amuse bouches* he filed for *SI*, Rushin boils down to a sweet reduction the argument for the game as belief system.

I Believe in B-ball

HOCKEY PLAYERS, among all athletes, have the coolest way of entering a game, hopping over the boards with one hand, like Steve McQueen getting into a convertible. But basketball is forever, and so players are often made to genuflect in front of the scorer's table for a moment before stepping onto the court, as if entering a house of worship. Which, in a manner of speaking, they are.

For one is baptized into basketball not with water but confetti (conferred on the head by Curly Neal). And one *believes* in basketball, as one believes in the Bible and in all those names that are common to both: Moses and Isiah and Jordan. . . .

Adam and Eve were banished from the Garden and so—eventually—were the Celtics, and sometime in between I became a believer, and this is my profession of faith:

I believe in Artis Gilmore, whose wife is named—as God is my witness—Enola Gay.

I believe in new hightops, always evocative of Christmas morning, for you get to open a large box, remove the crinkly paper stuffed into the toes and—before wearing them for the first time—inhale deeply from each sneaker as if from an airplane oxygen mask. (It's what wine connoisseurs call "nosing the bouquet" and works for Pumas as well as pinot noirs.)

I believe in tearaway warmup suits, which make the wearer feel—when summoned from the bench—like Clark Kent, ripping off his business suit to reveal the *S* on his chest.

I believe a team's fortunes can always be foretold—not from the length of its lifelines but from the integrity of its layup lines.

I believe in God Shammgod and Alaa Abdelnaby and James (Buddha) Edwards (and in Black Jesus, Earl Monroe's nickname long before it was the Pearl).

I believe in accordion-style bleachers that push back to expose, after a game, car keys and quarters and paper cups, which sound like a gunshot when stomped on just right. (And always, stuck to the floor, the forlorn strands of molting pom-poms.)

I believe—now more than ever, in this time of global disharmony—in World B. Free and Majestic Mapp. And that control of the planet's contested regions might be better determined by a simple, alternating possession arrow.

I believe that 300 basketballs dribbled simultaneously by eight-year-old basketball campers sound like buffalo thundering across the plains. And inspire even greater awe.

I believe that two high school janitors pushing twin dust mops at halftime can be every bit as hypnotic as dueling Zambonis.

I believe that any sucker can wear a $40,000 gold necklace as thick as a bridge cable when the only necklace worth wearing in basketball is a nylon net that costs $9.99. (But—and here's the point—it can't be bought.)

I'm a believer in Lafayette Lever and regret never having covered him, for if I had, my first sentence about him would have been, "There must be 50 ways to love your Lever."

I believe that jumping off a trampoline, turning a midair somersault, slam-dunking and sticking the landing—while wearing a gorilla suit that's wearing, in turn, a Phoenix Suns warmup jacket—is enough to qualify you as a first-ballot Hall-of-Famer.

I believe in Harthorne Wingo, and I believe in Zap the dingo, the Detroit Shock mascot whose costume was stolen from the Palace of Auburn Hills by two men who were caught—one in the dingo head, the other in the dingo feet—drinking in a bar across the street.

I believe in former Notre Dame guard Leo (Crystal) Klier and former Providence center Jacek (Zippity) Duda and former Iowa State center (What the) Sam Hill.

I believe in dunking dirty clothes into the hallway hamper and skyhooking—from the shotgun seat—quarters into highway toll baskets. And I believe in finger-rolling heads of lettuce into my shopping cart, even though I have never, in the last 10 years, *eaten* a piece of lettuce at home.

I believe I can still hold, in my right hand, a boom box the size of a Samsonite Streamlite while carrying, in my left, a slick rubber ball whose pebble-grain stubble has long before been dribbled away. And that I can do so while riding a 10-speed bike and steering with my knees.

I believe that the Truth (Drew Gooden) *and* the Answer (Allen Iverson) are out there, if we will simply follow the bouncing ball.

I believe that we, the basketball faithful, speak in tongues: the red, wagging tongue of Michael Jordan and the red, wagging tongues of our unlaced Chuck Taylors.

I believe that Larry Bird's crooked right index finger—which he raised in triumph *before* his winning shot fell in the 1988 All-Star Weekend three-point contest—resembles, almost exactly, God's crooked right index finger, as depicted on the ceiling of the Sistine Chapel.

Which would make sense, if God made man in His image. For I believe, above all, in what G. K. Chesterton wrote, and what Rick Telander echoed in the title of a book: Earth is a task garden. But heaven is a playground.

James McKean

That James McKean (b. 1946) would become an elite athlete seemed fore-ordained. He had the bloodlines—an uncle who played football at Washington, an aunt who medaled in swimming at the 1936 Olympics—as well as the size (6'9"), which helped win him a scholarship to play basketball at Washington State. The Cougars for which he started at center for four years—"a group of stable, conservative young men who could have been plowing the good deep soil of eastern Washington instead of playing ball," he wrote—faced off against UCLA and Lew Alcindor four times over two of those seasons, and Washington State proved to be the second most successful Pac-8 team during the Bruins' dynasty. That McKean would become a teacher, decorated poet, and essayist was perhaps less predictable than his athletic success. But over the next decade, while living in Washington's Tri-Cities area and anchoring an AAU team that at one point won sixty games in a row, he taught at Columbia Basin College. He went on to earn an MFA and an English PhD from Iowa, take a professorship at Mount Mercy College in Cedar Rapids, and, after retirement, remain a regular on the nationwide circuit of writing programs, festivals, and workshops. In this essay from his 2005 collection *Home Stand: Growing Up in Sports*, McKean recalls a freshman season in Pullman playing for his temperamental and physiognomical opposite, Jud Heathcote, who years later would win an NCAA title at Michigan State. It's a portrait of a familiar and colorful figure, to be sure. But it's also an exploration of the player-coach relationship from the inside, overlaid with reconsiderations that the passage of time has a way of inviting. As McKean has put it, "Basketball is easy. Explaining yourself is hard."

Playing for Jud

FROM HIGH in the stands, Jud Heathcote looked tortured, a tragic figure in a grand opera, so self-consumed with sorrow or lamentation or anger that we feared what he might do to himself. His whining was a high tenor screech, and his posture crushed. The stories about him were commonplace enough to approach the mythic—how he slammed a basketball to the floor in anger only to have it bounce straight up and strike him in the nose, hunched over as he was in his half-bear, half-wrestler crouch; how he struck his own head with the heel of his hand in frustration, a kind of audible self-mutilation; how he ripped the top of his socks off in anger, or as some say in the optical illusion of retelling, how he lifted himself off the bench by

335

his socks until the argyle gave way and he fell back into his chair and over. Back and forth, pacing, hands out to plead with the officials, his own players, the very fates themselves. All punctuated by his out-of-tune aria of injustice and bafflement.

Twenty years after playing for Jud, I rediscovered close up his precarious balance of calm and catastrophe. At Iowa's Carver–Hawkeye arena, Jud's Michigan State Spartans, then in first place in the Big Ten, were being overrun by the fast-breaking, seemingly undisciplined hometown Hawkeyes. The noise was at ear-damage level. Managers quickly set out folding chairs for a time-out huddle. Sweating and exhausted, the starters watched Jud pound his fist into his hand, as if it were a gavel calling this game to order. But his voice was exact and even, laying out strategy and offering encouragement, and all those fine players at Michigan State—Steve Smith, Mike Peplowski, Kirk Manns, Eric Snow, Shawn Respert, some all-American, some all–Big Ten—all those players listened.

I listened too. I remember how it felt. In the sixties I played for Jud and Marv Harshman at Washington State University. For more than twenty years, I have replayed those seasons over and over, the violence and pain and discipline and humor and anger, the wins and, of course, the losses. It was a classic education without books, corporal and exhausting. Sometimes I regret being so myopic during those turbulent years from 1964 to 1968. On campus, students protested, breaking from convention and authority and the war. I remember in 1968 feeling defensive about my letterman's jacket. "Establishment," someone sneered. "I'm cold," was my half-hearted response. The memories are complex and ambivalent, and then as simple as the ball in hand, the echo of its bouncing in an empty gym. Years later, as I sat behind the Michigan State bench, the memories drew close. I was family again, and from the first row could speak, with practice now, of family matters.

When I wrote Jud to tell him I was going to school in Iowa City and to ask if I could get tickets to the Michigan State game, he wrote back to say there would be tickets for me as long as I didn't root for those sons-a-bitches. When I picked the tickets up at will-call, they read "row 2, courtside." The usher pointed down the steps. The long descent felt nostalgic. Before sixteen thousand Iowa fans, we found our seats directly behind Jud. Beneath the lights, the game was intimate again, the floor crowded and tense. I had forgotten how much happens in so small a space, and how, Macbeth-like, the hand and mind act as one. I could hear the conversations again between the players themselves, clipped, single-word information—*left, right, switch, mine, my fault*—all directed to honing the moment to a simple edge, your two points and their absolute denial. And audible through the roar, the one voice the players on the floor heard was Jud's song *verismo*, full of signals, melancholy, directions, spleen, admonishments, and finally praise.

It's the praise I remember seeking. If I screwed up, I felt that I had let the coaches down, that this game meant everything to them. Returning to the bench, I knew I would hear about my failure in a mix of analysis and despair. If I did well, the encouragement would be there. Once when our Washington State team played the University of Washington at Hec Edmundson Pavilion, I heard two words spoken clearly in a crowd of ten thousand and the noisy rush of the game. Guarded by Jay Bond, Washington's center, whose strategy was to front me at my low-post position, leaning with his right arm folded against me and his left in front waving in the passing lane, I kept trying to move farther out so that our guard Lenny Allen at the top of the key could pass me the ball. Jay Bond kept inching farther and more aggressively in front. I would move out and so would he. Finally, I made a sudden move toward the ball, Lenny Allen pump-faked, Jay Bond scrambled to front, and I changed direction with two quick steps toward the basket, leaving Jay Bond all by himself. It was a backdoor, a classic move, though a rare event in my repertoire; Lenny laid the pass in just so, and all I had to do was rise and drop the ball in. All timing and a wonderful pass. As I ran under the basket and back down court, I heard Jud say, "Nice move." Ten thousand voices, and one clear in its weight and authority. The basket was worth two points, and praise I have never forgotten.

It took a long time to earn that praise. Gangly, awkward, and eager to play, I was recruited out of Wilson High School in Tacoma by Marv Harshman, the head basketball coach at Washington State, who explained in his handwritten letters how badly the Cougars needed me. The center position would be mine when I was a sophomore. I could get a fifth-year stipend if needed. They would throw in a pair of contact lenses. They were building the basketball program, and I could play a crucial role. He called me a "student-athlete." My parents were sold, as was I. Signing the letter of intent, I agreed to play for Marv Harshman, a gentleman, an all-American hero at Pacific Lutheran University in Tacoma, and now the head coach at a Pac-8 Division One school. I was ready for the big time.

The next fall, I hadn't been on campus very long when Coach Harshman introduced me to a slightly balding man who looked like Don Rickles. This was the new freshman basketball coach. I don't remember Jud saying much. His tone seemed perfunctory, as if he was unsure about me. He asked something about my being in shape and getting ready for the season. What struck me immediately was that the basketball office in Bohler Gym looked no bigger than my room at home, with no window shades and only two desks, one for Harshman and one for Bobo Brayton, the head baseball coach and substitute assistant basketball coach whose favorite expression was "That's as obvious as a horse turd in a pan of milk." They borrowed the secretary down the hall in the athletic director's office. Jud would be replacing Bobo. I wondered if they would share the desk.

But during the first week of practice, I had larger worries. After the first team meeting, when the coaches explained that basketball was our first priority at Washington State and they weren't going to let us forget it, the haranguing began. Many of us were freshmen, ex–high school stars, and even Pete, the irascible equipment manager, growled at us. Maybe I wasn't as ready for college ball as I thought I was. During the first week, I also discovered that Coach Harshman focused mainly on the varsity. As a freshman, I was really playing for Jud. I had never been treated like this before.

"What the hell is that? Take that damn Wilson High School turn-around stick shot and leave it in your high school drawer," Jud barked. "There's no way you can play at Washington State if . . ." and then followed an infinite number of transgressions to complete the sentence. Technical problems rated eyebrow-raising impatience and a short demonstration. More egregious errors, such as lack of hustle and stupid choices, earned serious upbraiding and questions that have no good answer: "When are you going to learn, son? What does it take? What do I have to do?"

As the year progressed, we learned to take cover. When the whistle shrieked in the middle of a drill, and you heard "No, no, no" or "Please, how many times . . . ," your first wish was that the scolding wasn't for you. In the Midwest, tornado sirens get the same effect. Everyone seems torn, looking up to see what's coming while heading down to the cellar to hide. We would wander to the edge of the court, shuffle, look at our feet, and catch our breath while the chosen one suffered. After a while, we played with a kind of running-scared and *oh-no* demeanor, which I have seen even on Jud's Michigan State teams. It's a *your-father-knows-you-broke-the-neighbor's-window* look; all that's left is the sentence, the long walk back to the bench, or Jud's bear-like shuffle-walk toward you for an explanation. In a *Sports Illustrated* article that celebrates his career, Jud admits that "Like Bobby [Knight] I'm a negative coach. I'm always harping on what's bad rather than praising what's good. Yes, I've hurt some kids, and I've been bad for some kids. But one thing I'm always proud of is that our players get *coached*. And I think most of them get better every year."

For the 1964–65 season, the Jud-coached freshman basketball team at Washington State had twenty-two wins and no losses. We were balanced and deep. The highest individual scoring average on the team was twelve points per game, and the entire team average was eighty-two. Freshman games at Bohler Gym in Pullman had always been the opening act for the varsity, the rookies with their hand-me-down uniforms and bad passes playing to empty stands. As the season progressed, however, interest in our team began to grow, and at the halfway point we were even getting statewide news coverage. The *Tacoma News Tribune* noted that "Washington State's freshmen own the state's longest collegiate winning streak—eleven straight. The Coubabes beat North Idaho JC 102–61 on Friday night, then came back Saturday to upend Columbia Basin 63–59 to snip the Hawks' victory string at thirty-seven in a row. Marv Harshman lauded the Coubabe–CBC game as the finest freshman basketball game he's ever seen. 'It wasn't run and shoot. It was just a real basketball game,' he said." I would add that it was a real game because of Jud's coaching. We played with a mix of desperation and pride. We wanted that clean record, and we wanted to stay in Jud's good graces. By the end of the season, our record and the rumor of the red-faced, hair-tearing, combustible freshman coach named Jud had filled the stands.

Those players who made the transition to the varsity team indeed got better the next year. Out of sixteen freshman players, six made the varsity team, but several of the best players on the freshman team decided not to play at all. Some dropped out of school for academic reasons. Others decided they couldn't survive another year of Jud. "How do you put up with all that yelling at you?" someone asked. I remember saying that I tried to listen to what he had to say but not necessarily how he said it, that he had good things to teach. I was young and deferential. It was 1965, and on campus, ROTC was still a major. Cadets wore their uniforms to class and in the evenings saluted officer upperclassmen at a soda joint called "The Coug," where the Stones and Buffalo Springfield played on the jukebox, and fifty years' worth of names were carved into the wooden booths.

Shawn Respert, who played for Michigan State, has said that Jud is a great shooting coach. Yes, I agree. Many times Jud walked over to me as I was warming up before practice and said, "Go ahead, shoot a couple." I would turn and shoot a jump shot from fifteen feet, and then another and another until he said, "OK, I see." Then he explained what I was doing and where I might change the shot—an adjustment here or there: hand on top of the ball, or elbow in and stop the ball. "This is a shot, not a throw," he would say. Or, "Turn and square up. Use your legs. Follow through." I remember how easily he seemed to analyze what I was doing, spot my problems in rhythm and form, and offer up a solution. A prosodist of the jump shot, he explained what I might look for—how the ball should spin slowly backward, how it should die on the rim when it hits, how a good shot hesitates in the net, falls through, hits the floor, and bounces back to you. "Ready, shoot" is the drill we would run and run. He passed the ball, and I caught it and set up in a shooting position, right hand behind and up on the ball, left hand supporting, elbow in, eyes on the basket, wait, wait, wait . . . "Shoot," he called, never quite when I expected it—shot opportunities and choices never the same twice, the theory goes—but the setup, the shot, the rhythm, the follow-through, these stay the same, practiced over and over until shooting is second nature.

Although his patience was suspect, Jud's motives never seemed in doubt. He wanted to win and he wanted us to be better basketball players. The outcome of the game mattered to him, but the more I played for Jud, the more I realized that how we reached that outcome mattered just as much. "Do what you can do. Leave the freelancing at home! Where in hell did that come from? That's not your shot! Play the game we practiced." Each season I understood more how playing well meant balancing control and enthusiasm, how the discipline in practice showed in the games, and how focus during the game was a learned skill. If we were asleep on the floor, Jud provided a wake-up. Ironically, it's as if his strategy was meant to drive his players away from him and completely into the moment. The choice was either total concentration on the game or a bench-side critique with Jud.

Many factors provide tension in a game—the crowd, the opposing team, the fear of losing—but Jud provided the means, the reason, and the urgency. He was conductor, expert guide, ally, and scold. An event both of character and outcome, each game meant more to him than we could imagine. A national champion handball player who coached high school basketball as vigorously as college, who arranged his married life around a basketball schedule, who never in my recollection missed a practice or a game, this was a man whose life was competition. "Why don't you hang around the gym more?" he asked me one day. I didn't understand then what he was asking. The gym was where he lived. And it wasn't until in the locker room after one home game against California, when he called me a "hot dog" and an "embarrassment" for my mouthing off to the officials, for kicking the ball away, and for my self-righteous prima-donna antics, that I realized what Jud meant by playing well. It didn't seem to matter that their center, Bob Presley, kept barking in my ear that he was going to kick my honky mother-fuckin' ass, or that I scored over thirty points. We won the game, but I had lost something in Jud's eyes. When I was back in my own room with the door locked, alone and fighting back tears, I realized how painful it was not to be in Jud's good graces. He was a father, I think now, or perhaps my very own Orwellian headmaster, "goading, threatening, exhorting, sometimes joking, very occasionally praising, but always prodding away at one's mind to keep it up to the right pitch of concentration, as one might keep a sleepy person awake by sticking pins into him."

My antics that evening had earned Jud's worst criticism: "You're not *thinking.*"

There has always seemed to be a constructive tension between us. Even now. In one letter written a week or so before a 1992 Michigan State–Iowa game, he said, "Again we need all the help we can get in Iowa City; you have four tickets. We'll be staying at the Holiday Inn. Give me a call or drop by practice as we will be practicing 11:00–12:00 on February 6th. I look forward to seeing you. Maybe you can work on Pep's stick shot and the roll hook, or has memory and age dimmed your talents with both?" Sitting behind the Michigan State bench during warm-ups for that game, I tried to field a ball that had bounced off the floor, bobbled it slightly, and threw it back out to the players just as Jud walked up. "You could shoot but still can't catch," he said, shaking his head. I thought, *how typical.*

Ambiguity honed to an art form, his give-and-take language maintained a kind of suspension between reinforcement and criticism, between satisfaction and wanting more. He was pleased, yet hard to please. "So far so good," he seemed to be saying, "All right as far as it goes." I remember an awful shot I took once—too far out, a turnout, the stick shot that Jud despised but begrudgingly allowed by the time I was a junior for want of something better—a shot I had no business taking, having decided ahead of time I was due. I sailed back in my fadeaway, twenty feet out, and hoisted the ball toward the basket, the arc high as I heard from the bench, "No, no, what the hell . . . no business . . ." and "nice shot" as the ball fell through.

No one was immune. "You know better. You're the best jumper [shooter, defender, ball handler, etc.] on our team, so when are you going to play like it?" Such undercurrents. Such riptides. There were no opportunities to float on what he said. I remember his saying before a practice one day, "I want you to be a great basketball player, not just a good one." Was it praise or criticism? I still wonder. When I heard Stanley Kunitz say once that he didn't worry about all the bad poems being written, only about the ones just good enough, I thought of Jud's high standards and pressure to meet them, his urgent and focused poetics of concentration, thought, rhythm, and movement.

It was inevitable, I guess, that such a dynamic tension might find its limits. Coaches and players define each other's roles—a player learns from the coach and plays for him, and the coach sees the results of his work through the performance of his player. Given the pressure and the application of power in such a relationship, the tolerances need to be clearly defined. Some players at Washington State had no tolerance whatsoever for Jud. Others never seemed bothered. When I was a freshman, for example, the seniors of the varsity—Dale Ford, Ted Werner, and a few other players who seemed far older, rougher, and wiser than I—listened more to Harshman and less to Jud, unfazed, it seemed, by his tirades. Green and heedless, I tried to stay out of each coach's line of fire. It was a strategy that worked until my junior year, when the falling-out came.

On the court, the first string was assigned to defend the "gray" squad in a half-court defense drill. The gray squad had been taught the opponent's offense, and we were supposed to stop them with our man-to-man defense. I was guarding Dave Kessler, an all-American high hurdler, who was six-foot-six and constructed entirely of elbows, knees, and angles. Obedient and enthusiastic, Kessler, who played the game at two speeds—fidget-in-place or full-ahead—had the dubious distinction on our team of having shot, during games, air balls on three successive layups, the most infamous of which hit the backboard and bounced twenty feet back onto the court. Though he lacked a delicate touch, he was extremely fast and eager to please, sporting, despite the Sixties, a flattop which stood up on its own.

It was late in the practice. I was tired and needed to sit down. My job was to prevent Kessler, the mock center for the opposing team, from breaking from his low-post position across the key and establishing position on the other side. His movement was predicated on following the ball around the perimeter, forward to point guard to opposite forward. When the ball left the point guard's hand, Kessler was supposed to break. I was supposed to block him high or low, forcing him high toward the free throw line or low toward the out-of-bounds line under the basket. Then I had to front him to spoil the pass in from the forward. All this meant I had to have an idea where he was going and move quickly enough to get in his way.

Jud set the play up. Kessler bounced on his toes as if he were ready for the starting gun. I got into position, anticipating the break. Standing beneath the basket, Jud blew the whistle. The ball went from one forward to the point guard, who caught it, and Kessler was simply gone. I don't remember if he went right or left, but I spun around just in time to hear Jud's whistle, strident and prolonged. "There's no way, son, you're going to stop anybody, standing around flatfooted. Jesus, move your feet." He had taken two steps toward me and then turned back. "Again, please." Most of the team had wandered some, hands on their hips, looking at the floor or the empty stands, trying to stay out of the mix, but Kessler had stayed in position, ready to go. I was the first-string center, the big shot. I was supposed to make this play.

Back now. With the whistle, the ball went from forward to point guard, who passed; Kessler jack-stepped me left—I fell for it—and then bounced right, buzz cut, elbows, and knees zipping by in a blur. I didn't even have time to grab his jersey. Jud's whistle reached a new octave. Here he was, red-faced in front of me. I backed up. Jud followed, hands out, demanding, "What the hell are you doing? Are you going to get this right today?" Out of the side of my eye, I could see Kessler grinning. Everyone else found something else to look at. This was the dreaded inquisition, Jud's auto-da-fé, and I was the heretic, singled out and guilty of slow feet and fatigue and a timid heart.

My final mistake, a response to embarrassment and a bruised ego, was to cheat—Kessler having won the moment and being anxious, I could see, to win the next. "Let's get it right this time," Jud said, and blew the whistle. Forward to point guard, who passed just as Kessler tried to jack-step again; I met him with a forearm shiver just beneath his armpit and punched, driving up and out so his upper body stayed put while his feet kept going up. Horizontal before he landed with a "whump" on his back on the floor, Kessler never got to the other side of the key. Vindicated and stupid, I didn't help him up.

Jud erupted, his whistle boiling over in the middle of a face as red as I had ever seen. He shuffle-trotted out toward me, fists clenched and head down, bull-like. Embarrassed and frustrated before, now I was scared, backing up as he got to me. I don't remember what he said for the ringing in my ears. I do remember my peripheral vision closing down as if his anger had grabbed at my shirt. My mouth was open, but I couldn't breathe. And then, bang, bang, he started with his index finger pounding on my chest, once, twice . . . "Don't you ever—"

At the third bang, I broke ranks.

The telling takes far longer than my blocking his right arm away with my left hand and stepping with my left foot toward him, cocking my right fist so I could deliver the punch with authority. "Keep your fucking hands off me," I said, quicker than the instant, a slur muddled by fear and anger. I was pushed into a corner and snapping. He took two quick steps back and dropped his whistle, and in that moment we both stood on intolerant ground, far beyond any diagram, watching each other.

Until Coach Harshman stepped in.

"Now, now," he said, as if we were boys in a schoolyard. "We have a game to get ready for." The pontiff had spoken. Harshman, the final authority, refocused our energies on the abstract and holy. Jud was pit boss and teacher, but it was Harshman's team.

Jud and I didn't talk for the rest of the practice. That evening and all the next day, I agonized over what had happened. Fairy tales have this as the defining moment. The final breaking away. Conflict leads to self-sufficiency and independence. Jack cuts the beanstalk down. A mythological son strikes down his father when they meet anonymously, face-to-face on the road. I had never been so defiant of nor as violent with an authority figure. I was immediately lonely. Should I quit the team, or was I already off? Independent for a day, I wanted back in the fold. But that seemed impossible.

The next day, in language as sweet as a good play, Jud fixed it. After the boundaries had been overstepped and the tolerances squeezed down to zero, the first thing he said to me was, "Mind if I throw you a few passes?" I heard him behind me as I warmed up early before practice, by myself, at a far-corner basket in Bohler Gym.

"Sure," I said, turning and bouncing the ball to him to get ready for the "ready, shoot" drill.

"That is," he said, "if you don't hit me in the mouth."

"No," I said, "as long as you don't pound me in the chest if I make a mistake."

"Sounds fair to me," was all he said.

I have learned over the years that I am not the only player to have threatened a swing at Jud. Rumor has it that one of Jud's West Valley High players connected with a right cross, and Jud's response after he got up from the floor was, "That's the most heart you've shown all day." It seems in character. That a player-coach relationship would break down and even turn violent is no surprise. Coaches, from high school to professional, pressure their players, set goals, and make demands. Players need a coach to convince them the pain they are going through is worthwhile. There is a fine line here between push and shove. When that line is obliterated, it is the coach's job to redraw it. That's what Jud did. He took charge, and we all moved on.

When I was a senior, Pete the equipment manager finally talked to me. After three years of machinations and trials and seventy-four games, I felt as if I had earned respect from the coaches and my teammates, and could watch at the far end of the court the new freshmen squirm and grimace under their first year with Jud. Despite such seniority, the pressure was always on, though the tolerances had been discovered and respected both ways, coach and player.

Perhaps what tempered Jud's maniacal intensity for the game was that he seemed capable of perspective, whether through humor, self-parody, or simply by looking the other way. *Sports Illustrated* explains that "Heathcote . . . has a warmth about him, an awkward, gruff-uncle charm. He is most comfortable when turning the needle inward, and unlike Knight, he is incapable of taking himself seriously." True, there are many examples of Jud's self-deprecating humor. "Sooner or later, the game makes fools of us all," he has been quoted as saying. "And I guess I'm living proof." And I remember his being able to poke fun at himself—the time on a road trip, for example, he backed the car over his own suitcases. For thirty miles no one dared speak until someone said from the back seat, "They were easier to get in the trunk." Even Jud had to laugh. Or the time we finally beat Oregon State at Corvallis in the season's next-to-last game and spent the night in downtown Portland at the Benson Hotel. Dick Vandervoort, the trainer, gave us each five dollars to get something to eat. Then we were on our own in downtown Portland late on a Saturday night. I don't know whose idea it was to spend our five bucks at the topless nightclub three blocks north of the Benson, but six of us, four of whom were starters, headed for the night life, dressed in our crimson blazers with the Cougar insignias. We might as well have been wearing overalls and straw hats, as obvious as we were spread out in the front row, our five dollars spent on the two-drink minimum, the glasses weeping on the miniature tables. In blue light and with fine timing before us on stage, Fatima of the Nile rotated her tassels in opposite directions.

We were near deep hypnosis when the door opened and in walked Dick Vandervoort, Coach Harshman, and Jud. They took pains not to trip over us as they walked back behind us into the dark. No one turned to look. As the tassels slowed and we froze, out the door filed Dick Vandervoort, Coach Harshman, and then Jud, who turned to us, one hand on the door, and said, "This isn't the place we thought it was." The next day was a 250-mile trip from Portland to Pullman—a long, silent car ride home.

It's simply not true, however, that Jud is "incapable of taking himself seriously." None of his players worked for Jud's sense of humor. To see the look on his face when the Spartans won the national championship in 1979, or his despair in 1990 when Georgia Tech's Kenny Anderson tied the game on an unwhistled, after-the-buzzer shot, a game Georgia Tech then won in overtime, is to see a coach for whom the game means everything. Lear couldn't have looked more tragic. Basketball was always first. Opinions, one-liners, wit, green blazers, and a bad hairstyle notwithstanding, the forty minutes on the court is serious business indeed.

Watching Michigan State practice on one of their visits to Iowa City, I realized that Jud's teams have always been a reflection of his character—serious, playful, and urgent. There was Jud on the floor at the end of practice, trying to face guard Shawn Respert, who moved left and right and called for the ball. "Mismatch, mismatch," Respert yelled, laughing. How true, both ways. Jud was sixty-four with a bad knee, but Respert played Jud's game.

So did we all. I would like to think I took from my four years a sense of form and rhythm, of creative tension, the ability to concentrate, the need to get things right, and a friendship that has lasted years beyond my eligibility. In 1986 when *Headlong*, my first book of poems, was published, I sent a copy to Jud. He wrote back, "Thanks so much for your book of poems. This is the first of many you will be famous for some day and I will be able to say 'I knew him when.' I do hope sooner or later you will be able to figure out one that rhymes. Remember, you can always start, 'Roses are red, Violets are Blue' and go from there. I do plan to study them all and maybe sooner or later it will make me a smarter basketball coach." He ended his letter by saying, "I am looking forward to seeing you February 6. Count on four tickets as usual as we need all the support we can get."

I wrote back to thank him for the tickets and to say I wasn't sure if my poems would make him a smarter basketball coach, but I knew playing basketball for him had certainly made me a better poet. My legs are gone, but my memory hasn't dimmed. Michigan State won by a point that evening on a three-point shot at the buzzer, picked up their water bottles and towels, and escaped to East Lansing before the Iowa crowd had a chance to sit back down. As the gym emptied out, I sat and waited, thinking of my divided loyalties. An Iowa alum now, I live in Iowa City and follow the Hawkeye basketball team, but here I was sitting all evening in a row of green sweaters, rooting for Michigan State. No, I was rooting for Jud. Ever since I left Washington State University, left home in effect, I have been loyal to Marv Harshman and Jud. They helped me grow up. And even though I don't play basketball much anymore, preferring the humility of tennis after a day of words, I still hear their voices. They have left me something parental, a kind of conscience that speaks from courtside, saying in reference to whatever I do or make, "Too much here or not enough there," or "Effort, please, effort," or "Terrific"—followed always by "try again."

FreeDarko

During its six-year run as an idiosyncratic NBA website, FreeDarko.com (2006–2011) attracted enough of a following to give birth to two books, *The Macrophenomenal Pro Basketball Almanac* (2008), in which this study of Tim Duncan appeared, and *The Undisputed Guide to Pro Basketball History* (2010). Both volumes came larded with illustrations, charts, and boxes, including a sidebar to the Duncan essay that showed how the lifetime stats of the San Antonio Spurs' center track the Fibonacci Sequence, the numerical pattern found in seashells, pinecones, and other representations of the natural world. Adam Waytz (b. 1980), a University of Chicago grad student in social psychology who would go on to become a professor at Northwestern, contributed the Duncan piece under the *nom de blog* Dr. Lawyer IndianChief. It's typical of most FreeDarko posts in that it features no reporting to speak of; as counterpoint to Duncan's opacity, it lets analysis and allusion rush into the void. But that was the point of the site. As regular contributor Jason Johnson said, FreeDarko served up "music criticism from a bizarre universe where basketball actually is jazz." Waytz stays true to the site's founding tenet of valuing player above team, overlooking how Duncan tortured his beloved hometown Minnesota Timberwolves so he might appreciate the impassive Spur *an sich*. As with many FreeDarko contributions, there's a determination not only to connect the spectator to the player, but also the game to the wider world. Co-founder Nathaniel Friedman, aka Bethlehem Shoals, pulled the plug after realizing that, as he put it, "the comments section was probably a better read than some of the posts"—a sign, if ever there were one, that FreeDarko's work was both inspirational and done.

from

The Macrophenomenal Pro Basketball Almanac

TIM DUNCAN: MECHANICAL GOTHIC

TIM DUNCAN proves that absence of style can be style in and of itself, a paradox that defines his daily actions and decisions. Duncan is a figure seemingly birthed from Mount Rushmore's granite façade, yet his movement is fluid. He faces up to his opponents with the saucer-like eyes of a German shepherd, yet with his empty stare he intimidates all who face him. Duncan hails from the Virgin Islands, a location that should evoke images of relaxation and respite, yet Duncan's citizenship status instead elicits a bothersome uncertainty, as no one actually knows what the Virgin Islands are. Duncan's off-court obsession with video gaming, his apparent introversion, and his Wayne Brady–as– Milhouse vocal tone convey an overall tenor of erudite boredom. Nonetheless, all who have faced him hold unbounded respect for him, because so many have met their fate by his hand.

Throughout his career, Duncan has maintained his role as the NBA's gatekeeper, yet his term is unlike that of others who held the position before him. Michael Jordan halted the likes of Ewing, Malone, Stockton, and Barkley, denying them championships with a hand in their faces and a dagger in their hearts. Shaquille O'Neal, as Jordan's successor, towered over the most competent Kings and Nets teams during his reign. Duncan, by contrast, provides no abrupt reaction to an opponent's push. As Duncan denies scores of aspirants an opportunity at the title, they simply collapse at his feet.

Duncan entered the NBA after four years of college at Wake Forest. The circumstances were suspicious: An already championship-ready San Antonio Spurs team implodes for one single season—just long enough to attain the first overall pick in the draft and net the stoic young power forward. Because winning came so immediately for Duncan—in his first year he led the Spurs to one of the biggest single-season turnarounds in NBA history—aesthetics became an afterthought to success. This suited the dull and routine mastery that would soon become Duncan's calling card.

Duncan has always kept his uniform shorts at an appropriate length. Off the court, he rarely dons a suit and is more likely to be seen in the blandest of Banana Republics or the grayest of sweat suits, giving press conferences unpolluted by slang or foul speech. At his most striking, he resembles an oversized and popular Carnegie Mellon engineering student or a recently bankrupt and divorced stock trader. More often, however, Duncan looks like the most glorious human being ever produced in a factory, pristine and plain faced. He is a monument to bottom lines, permanent but not necessarily memorable.

With a game founded on a geometrically accurate bank shot and simple three-step footwork in the post, he has become the modest Carhartt coat that blankets a league full of precious metals. In making a defensive stop, Duncan is not feverish or quick footed; he is a concrete wall of disregard for a player's intention to score. In completing a powerful dunk, Duncan uses an efficiency of motion, rarely jumping higher than necessary, and in speech never emits any proclamation of greatness or dominance. Duncan is known for his dissatisfaction with foul calls, but he generally expresses such angst in a silent widening of his nostrils and eyelids. He is incapable of histrionics. A scholar of psychology and Chinese literature while in college, he confronts the unbridled emotion of his opponents with circumspect reason.

While other players wind-sprint through the season, Duncan marathons, going deep into the playoffs year after year. While his foes throw their hearts and minds into the thick of competition, Duncan stands at a remove, his every action rich with intent. His brain operates with the dull precision of the TI-83 calculator. Can Duncan feel pain? He has faced his share of knee and foot injuries over the years, yet they have slowed him only as an oil leak slows a robot. Does Duncan love? His wife, Amy, a former Wake Forest cheerleader, conveys a forced plastic smile in public appearances, suggesting that not even she knows. Do the concepts of free will or consciousness mean anything to him? If so, he does not experience these capacities as you and I do. Referee Joey Crawford once issued a technical foul to Duncan simply for laughing while on the bench; Crawford more than anything was probably startled at Timmy's capacity to display human feeling. In his eternal drudgery, Duncan moves forward with a single purpose, as though preprogrammed to achieve the sole end of winning. Cognition, emotion, intention—all are merely incidental to the goal at hand.

A world champion multiple times over, Tim Duncan is a human trophy, not a flighty canvas of mood and invention: not a winner, just someone who wins games. His first two championships with the Spurs were more attributable to the aging torpedo David Robinson, Duncan's frontcourt-mate and mentor, than they were to Duncan himself. Although Robinson's skills were declining at this point, it was his spirit and leadership that carried Duncan and the Spurs unto victory. Duncan's third championship, which occurred after Robinson's retirement, lacked any authoritative moment of self-definition—the clutch shooting of Robert Horry and the unstoppable penetration of Tony Parker were as important as Duncan's geologic whir. The Spurs' unwatchable 2007 championship was aided by circumstance: questionable refereeing, the Warriors' first-round upset of the Mavericks (the Spurs' chief competition), and unwarranted suspensions of players on the Spurs' Western Conference Finals foes, the Phoenix Suns. However, the Spurs' eventual victory was not the product of luck or white-hot destiny. These things came to be because of who Tim Duncan is: an automaton of success.

Duncan has little need to probe his own being or to carol his findings to the world. He is style by default—all that is left when time ends and only judgment remains. He is the holiest of all ghosts, occupying a dimension that is not captured by Newtonian laws or quantum theory, but only by spiritual discourse.

Duncan is a vessel through which a beam of magnificence passes. He is the NBA's designated holder of pure athletic dignity, the kind that danced around the ring with Joe Louis and that ran with Joe DiMaggio around the base paths. Duncan emanates such honor and humility that many members of the media have idealized him, fashioning him as some sort of puritanical savior to the league. And although this status is somewhat overblown, without Duncan, one wonders if the Association would ring hollow to the public, who might view it as merely a noisy shell of celebrity and finesse. Duncan keeps us honest. His righteous and calming presence provides balance—and enables the NBA to unashamedly pursue its primary function as a flabbergasting playground for all to enjoy.

Despite all of Duncan's glory, a restlessness envelops him. We watch a player with infinite talent, with MVP, All-Star, and All-Defensive Team honors, with a loving fan base, and we wonder why he expresses no joy. We rarely cheer for him, because at some point all of us have watched him destroy a player or team we love. And even this distaste for him makes us uncomfortable, because he is not villainous. We watch perhaps the greatest power forward in the history of the NBA go relatively unnoticed among his flashier colleagues and wonder why he does not express frustration. Duncan's mind is just as likely to hold the perversions of a serial killer as it is the rote mechanism of success. It is this vacancy—the potential that Duncan's soul may be composed of *any substance at all*, even the substance of turmoil—that keeps us compelled as he plods through his life on-court.

Michael Lewis

Basketball seems too fluid a game to lend itself to the quantitative examination known as analytics, but that hasn't kept fans and executives from trying to isolate and examine its every byte. And anywhere someone is trying to figure out sports by the numbers, you're likely to find journalist Michael Lewis (b. 1960). He can be counted on to transmute the metrics of our games into engaging prose, teasing out essential trends and sketching out engrossing characters. Lewis is most associated with baseball, the game he played at Isidore Newman School in his native New Orleans and explored with his best-selling book *Moneyball*. But in 2012 he wrote about running full-court in one of Barack Obama's private pickup games while profiling the president for *Vanity Fair*. And for this February 2009 piece for *The New York Times Magazine*, Lewis spent time with Shane Battier, then of the Houston Rockets, as well as Rockets general manager Daryl Morey, to explore how someone who scarcely registers in the box score can still be a team's most valuable player. Lewis delves into relevant statistics, to be sure, but he also holds Battier up as a lens, refracting through him cultural themes pertinent to the game during the 1990s and 2000s—from the polarizing profile of Duke, Battier's alma mater, to the tastemaking style of Michigan's Fab Five, to the travel-team underworld. As for the story's final paragraphs, there are Hollywood endings, and then there's this one—more powerful, memorable, and faithful to the innumeracy of real life.

The No-Stats All-Star

OUT OF Duke University. . . . A 6-foot-8-inch forward. . . .
He had more or less admitted to me that this part of his job left him cold. "It's the same thing every day," he said, as he struggled to explain how a man on the receiving end of the raging love of 18,557 people in a darkened arena could feel nothing. "If you had filet mignon every single night, you'd stop tasting it."

To him the only pleasure in these sounds—the name of his beloved alma mater, the roar of the crowd—was that they marked the end of the worst part of his game day: the 11 minutes between the end of warm-ups and the introductions. Eleven minutes of horsing around and making small talk with players on the other team. All those players making exaggerated gestures of affection toward one another before the game, who don't actually know one another, or even want to. "I hate being out on the floor wasting that time," he said. "I used to try to talk to people, but then I figured out no one actually liked me very much." Instead of engaging in the pretense that these other professional basketball players actually know and like him, he slips away into the locker room.

Shane Battier!

And up Shane Battier popped, to the howl of the largest crowd ever to watch a basketball game at the Toyota Center in Houston, and jumped playfully into Yao Ming (the center "out of China"). Now, finally, came the best part of his day, when he would be, oddly, most scrutinized and least understood.

Seldom are regular-season games in the N.B.A. easy to get worked up for. Yesterday Battier couldn't tell me whom the team played three days before. ("The Knicks!" he exclaimed a minute later. "We played the Knicks!") Tonight, though it was a midweek game in the middle of January, was different. Tonight the Rockets were playing the Los Angeles Lakers, and so Battier would guard Kobe Bryant, the player he says is the most capable of humiliating him. Both Battier and the Rockets' front office were familiar with the story line. "I'm certain that Kobe is ready to just destroy Shane," Daryl Morey, the Rockets' general manager, told me. "Because there's been story after story about how Shane shut Kobe down the last time." Last time was March 16, 2008, when the Houston Rockets beat the Lakers to win their 22nd game in a row—the second-longest streak in N.B.A. history. The game drew a huge national television audience, which followed Bryant for his 47 miserable minutes: he shot 11 of 33 from the field and scored 24 points. "A lot of people watched," Morey said. "Everyone watches Kobe when the Lakers play. And so everyone saw Kobe struggling. And so for the first time they saw what we'd been seeing." Battier has routinely guarded the league's most dangerous offensive players—LeBron James, Chris Paul, Paul Pierce—and has usually managed to render them, if not entirely ineffectual, then a lot less effectual than they normally are. He has done it so quietly that no one really notices what exactly he is up to.

Last season, in a bid to draw some attention to Battier's defense, the Rockets' public-relations department would send a staff member to the opponent's locker room to ask leading questions of whichever super-star Battier had just hamstrung: "Why did you have so much trouble tonight?" "Did he do something to disrupt your game?" According to

Battier: "They usually say they had an off night. They think of me as some chump." He senses that some players actually look forward to being guarded by him. "No one dreads being guarded by me," he said. Morey confirmed as much: "That's actually true. But for two reasons: (a) They don't think anyone can guard them and (b) they really scoff at the notion Shane Battier could guard them. They *all* think his reputation exceeds his ability." Even as Battier was being introduced in the arena, Ahmad Rashad was wrapping up his pregame report on NBA TV and saying, "Shane Battier will try to stop Kobe Bryant." This caused the co-host Gary Payton to laugh and reply, "Ain't gonna happen," and the other co-host, Chris Webber, to add, "I think Kobe will score 50, and they'll win by 19 going away."

Early on, *Hoop Scoop* magazine named Shane Battier the fourth-best seventh grader in the United States. When he graduated from Detroit Country Day School in 1997, he received the Naismith Award as the best high-school basketball player in the nation. When he graduated from Duke in 2001, where he won a record-tying 131 college-basketball games, including that year's N.C.A.A. championship, he received another Naismith Award as the best college basketball player in the nation. He was drafted in the first round by the woeful Memphis Grizzlies, not just a bad basketball team but the one with the worst winning percentage in N.B.A. history—whereupon he was almost instantly dismissed, even by his own franchise, as a lesser talent. The year after Battier joined the Grizzlies, the team's general manager was fired and the N.B.A. legend Jerry West, aka the Logo because his silhouette is the official emblem of the N.B.A., took over the team. "From the minute Jerry West got there he was trying to trade me," Battier says. If West didn't have any takers, it was in part because Battier seemed limited: most of the other players on the court, and some of the players on the bench, too, were more obviously gifted than he is. "He's, at best, a marginal N.B.A. athlete," Morey says.

The Grizzlies went from 23–59 in Battier's rookie year to 50–32 in his third year, when they made the N.B.A. playoffs, as they did in each of his final three seasons with the team. Before the 2006–7 season, Battier was traded to the Houston Rockets, who had just finished 34–48. In his first season with the Rockets, they finished 52–30, and then, last year, went 55–27—including one stretch of 22 wins in a row.

Only the 1971–2 Los Angeles Lakers have won more games consecu- tively in the N.B.A. And because of injuries, the Rockets played 11 of those 22 games without their two acknowledged stars, Tracy McGrady and Yao Ming, on the court at the same time; the Rockets player who spent the most time actually playing for the Rockets during the streak was Shane Battier. This year Battier, recovering from off-season surgery to remove bone spurs from an ankle, has played in just over half of the Rockets' games. That has only highlighted his importance. "This year," Morey says, "we have been a championship team with him and a bubble playoff team without him."

Here we have a basketball mystery: a player is widely regarded inside the N.B.A. as, at best, a replaceable cog in a machine driven by superstars. And yet every team he has ever played on has acquired some magical ability to win.

Solving the mystery is somewhere near the heart of Daryl Morey's job. In 2005, the Houston Rockets' owner, Leslie Alexander, decided to hire new management for his losing team and went looking specifi- cally for someone willing to rethink the game. "We now have all this data," Alexander told me. "And we have computers that can analyze that data. And I wanted to use that data in a progressive way. When I hired Daryl, it was because I wanted somebody that was doing more than just looking at players in the normal way. I mean, I'm not even sure we're playing the game the right way."

The virus that infected professional baseball in the 1990s, the use of statistics to find new and better ways to value players and strate- gies, has found its way into every major sport. Not just basketball and football, but also soccer and cricket and rugby and, for all I know, snooker and darts—each one now supports a subculture of smart people who view it not just as a game to be played but as a problem to be solved. Outcomes that seem, after the fact, all but inevitable—of course LeBron James hit that buzzer beater, of course the Pittsburgh Steelers won the Super Bowl—are instead treated as a set of probabili- ties, even after the fact. The games are games of odds. Like professional card counters, the modern thinkers want to play the odds as efficiently as they can; but of course to play the odds efficiently they must first know the odds. Hence the new statistics, and the quest to acquire new data, and the intense interest in measuring the impact of every little thing a player does on his team's chances of winning. In its spirit of inquiry, this subculture inside professional basketball is no different from the subculture inside baseball or football or darts. The difference in basketball is that it happens to be the sport that is most like life.

When Alexander, a Wall Street investor, bought the Rockets in 1993, the notion that basketball was awaiting some statistical reformation hadn't occurred to anyone. At the time, Daryl Morey was at Northwestern University, trying to figure out how to get a job in professional sports and thinking about applying to business schools. He was tall and had played high-school basketball, but otherwise he gave off a quizzical, geeky aura. "A lot of people who are into the new try to hide it," he says. "With me there was no point." In the third grade he stumbled upon the work of the baseball writer Bill James—the figure most responsible for the current upheaval in professional sports—and decided that what he really wanted to do with his life was put Jamesian principles into practice. He nursed this ambition through a fairly conventional academic career, which eventually took him to M.I.T.'s Sloan School of Management. There he opted for the entrepreneurial track, not because he actually wanted to be an entrepreneur but because he figured that the only way he would ever be allowed to run a pro-sports franchise was to own one, and the only way he could imagine having enough money to buy one was to create some huge business. "This is the 1990s—there's no Theo," Morey says, referring to Theo Epstein, the statistics-minded general manager of the Boston Red Sox. "Sandy Alderson is progressive, but nobody knows it." Sandy Alderson, then the general manager of the Oakland Athletics, had also read Bill James and begun to usher in the new age of statistical analysis in baseball. "So," Morey continues, "I just assumed that getting rich was the only way in." Apart from using it to acquire a pro-sports team, Morey had no exceptional interest in money.

He didn't need great wealth, as it turned out. After graduating from business school, he went to work for a consulting firm in Boston called Parthenon, where he was tapped in 2001 to advise a group trying to buy the Red Sox. The bid failed, but a related group went and bought the Celtics—and hired Morey to help reorganize the business. In addition to figuring out where to set ticket prices, Morey helped to find a new general manager and new people looking for better ways to value basketball players. The Celtics improved. Leslie Alexander heard whispers that Morey, who was 33, was out in front of those trying to rethink the game, so he hired him to remake the Houston Rockets.

When Morey came to the Rockets, a huge chunk of the team's allotted payroll—the N.B.A. caps payrolls and taxes teams that exceed them—was committed, for many years to come, to two superstars: Tracy McGrady and Yao Ming. Morey had to find ways to improve the Rockets without spending money. "We couldn't afford another superstar," he says, "so we went looking for nonsuperstars that we thought were undervalued." He went looking, essentially, for underpaid players. "That's the scarce resource in the N.B.A." he says. "Not the superstar but the undervalued player." Sifting the population of midlevel N.B.A. players, he came up with a list of 15, near the top of which was the Memphis Grizzlies' forward Shane Battier. This perplexed even the man who hired Morey to rethink basketball. "All I knew was Shane's stats," Alexander says, "and obviously they weren't great. He had to sell me. It was hard for me to see it."

Alexander wasn't alone. It was, and is, far easier to spot what Battier doesn't do than what he does. His conventional statistics are unremarkable: he doesn't score many points, snag many rebounds, block many shots, steal many balls or dish out many assists. On top of that, it is easy to see what he can never do: what points he scores tend to come from jump shots taken immediately after receiving a pass. "That's the telltale sign of someone who can't ramp up his offense," Morey says. "Because you can guard that shot with one player. And until you can't guard someone with one player, you really haven't created an offensive situation. Shane can't create an offensive situation. He needs to be open." For fun, Morey shows me video of a few rare instances of Battier scoring when he hasn't exactly been open. Some large percentage of them came when he was being guarded by an inferior defender—whereupon Battier backed him down and tossed in a left jump-hook. "This is probably, to be honest with you, his only offensive move," Morey says. "But look, see how he pump fakes." Battier indeed pump faked, several times, before he shot over a defender. "He does that because he's worried about his shot being blocked." Battier's weaknesses arise from physical limitations. Or, as Morey puts it, "He can't dribble, he's slow and hasn't got much body control."

* * *

Battier's game is a weird combination of obvious weaknesses and nearly invisible strengths. When he is on the court, his teammates get better, often a lot better, and his opponents get worse—often a lot worse. He may not grab huge numbers of rebounds, but he has an uncanny ability to improve his teammates' rebounding. He doesn't shoot much, but when he does, he takes only the most efficient shots. He also has a knack for getting the ball to teammates who are in a position to do the same, and he commits few turnovers. On defense, although he routinely guards the N.B.A.'s most prolific scorers, he significantly reduces their shooting percentages. At the same time he somehow improves the defensive efficiency of his teammates—prob- ably, Morey surmises, by helping them out in all sorts of subtle ways. "I call him Lego," Morey says. "When he's on the court, all the pieces start to fit together. And everything that leads to winning that you can get to through intellect instead of innate ability, Shane excels in. I'll bet he's in the hundredth percentile of every category."

There are other things Morey has noticed too, but declines to dis- cuss as there is right now in pro basketball real value to new informa- tion, and the Rockets feel they have some. What he will say, however, is that the big challenge on any basketball court is to measure the right things. The five players on any basketball team are far more than the sum of their parts; the Rockets devote a lot of energy to untangling subtle interactions among the team's elements. To get at this they need something that basketball hasn't historically supplied: meaningful statistics. For most of its history basketball has measured not so much what is important as what is easy to measure—points, rebounds, assists, steals, blocked shots—and these measurements have warped perceptions of the game. ("Someone created the box score," Morey says, "and he should be shot.") How many points a player scores, for example, is no true indication of how much he has helped his team. Another example: if you want to know a player's value as a rebounder, you need to know not whether he got a rebound but the likelihood of the *team* getting the rebound when a missed shot enters that player's zone.

There is a tension, peculiar to basketball, between the interests of the team and the interests of the individual. The game continually tempts the people who play it to do things that are not in the inter- est of the group. On the baseball field, it would be hard for a player to sacrifice his team's interest for his own. Baseball is an individual sport masquerading as a team one: by doing what's best for himself, the player nearly always also does what is best for his team. "There is no way to selfishly get across home plate," as Morey puts it. "If instead of there being a lineup, I could muscle my way to the plate and hit every single time and damage the efficiency of the team—that would be the analogy. Manny Ramirez can't take at-bats away from David Ortiz. We had a point guard in Boston who refused to pass the ball to a certain guy." In football the coach has so much control over who gets the ball that selfishness winds up being self-defeating. The players most famous for being selfish—the Dallas Cowboys' wide receiver Terrell Owens, for instance—are usually not so much selfish as attention seeking. Their sins tend to occur off the field.

It is in basketball where the problems are most likely to be in the game—where the player, in his play, faces choices between maximizing his own perceived self-interest and winning. The choices are sufficiently complex that there is a fair chance he doesn't fully grasp that he is making them.

Taking a bad shot when you don't need to is only the most obvious example. A point guard might selfishly give up an open shot for an assist. You can see it happen every night, when he's racing down court for an open layup, and instead of taking it, he passes it back to a trailing teammate. The teammate usually finishes with some sensational dunk, but the likelihood of scoring nevertheless declined. "The marginal assist is worth more money to the point guard than the marginal point," Morey says. Blocked shots—they look great, but unless you secure the ball afterward, you haven't helped your team all that much. Players love the spectacle of a ball being swatted into the fifth row, and it becomes a matter of personal indifference that the other team still gets the ball back. Dikembe Mutombo, Houston's 42-year-old backup center, famous for blocking shots, "has always been the best in the league in the recovery of the ball after his block," says Morey, as he begins to make a case for Mutombo's unselfishness before he stops and laughs. "But even to Dikembe there's a selfish component. He made his name by doing the finger wag." The finger wag: Mutombo swats the ball, grabs it, holds it against his hip and wags his finger at the opponent. Not in my house! "And if he doesn't catch the ball," Morey says, "he can't do the finger wag. And he loves the finger wag."

His team of course would be better off if Mutombo didn't hold onto the ball long enough to do his finger wag. "We've had to yell at him: start the break, start the break—then do your finger wag!"

When I ask Morey if he can think of any basketball statistic that can't benefit a player at the expense of his team, he has to think hard. "Offensive rebounding," he says, then reverses himself. "But even that can be counterproductive to the team if your job is to get back on defense." It turns out there is no statistic that a basketball player accumulates that cannot be amassed selfishly. "We think about this deeply whenever we're talking about contractual incentives," he says. "We don't want to incent a guy to do things that hurt the team"—and the amazing thing about basketball is how easy this is to do. "They *all* maximize what they think they're being paid for," he says. He laughs. "It's a tough environment for a player now because you have a lot of teams starting to think differently. They've got to rethink how they're getting paid."

Having watched Battier play for the past two and a half years, Morey has come to think of him as an exception: the most abnormally unselfish basketball player he has ever seen. Or rather, the player who seems one step ahead of the analysts, helping the team in all sorts of subtle, hard-to-measure ways that appear to violate his own personal interests. "Our last coach dragged him into a meeting and told him he needed to shoot more," Morey says. "I'm not sure that that ever happened." Last season when the Rockets played the San Antonio Spurs Battier was assigned to guard their most dangerous scorer, Manu Ginóbili. Ginóbili comes off the bench, however, and his minutes are not in sync with the minutes of a starter like Battier. Battier privately went to Coach Rick Adelman and told him to bench him and bring him in when Ginóbili entered the game. "No one in the N.B.A. does that," Morey says. "No one says put me on the bench so I can guard their best scorer all the time."

One well-known statistic the Rockets' front office pays attention to is plus-minus, which simply measures what happens to the score when any given player is on the court. In its crude form, plus-minus is hardly perfect: a player who finds himself on the same team with the world's four best basketball players, and who plays only when they do, will have a plus-minus that looks pretty good, even if it says little about his play. Morey says that he and his staff can adjust for these potential distortions—though he is coy about how they do it—and render plus-minus a useful measure of a player's effect on a basketball game. A good player might be a plus 3—that is, his team averages 3 points more per game than its opponent when he is on the floor. In his best season, the superstar point guard Steve Nash was a plus 14.5. At the time of the Lakers game, Battier was a plus 10, which put him in the company of Dwight Howard and Kevin Garnett, both perennial All-Stars. For his career he's a plus 6. "Plus 6 is enormous," Morey says. "It's the difference between 41 wins and 60 wins." He names a few other players who were a plus 6 last season: Vince Carter, Carmelo Anthony, Tracy McGrady.

As the game against the Lakers started, Morey took his seat, on the aisle, nine rows behind the Rockets' bench. The odds, on this night, were not good. Houston was playing without its injured superstar, McGrady (who was in the clubhouse watching TV), and its injured best supporting actor, Ron Artest (cheering in street clothes from the bench). The Lakers were staffed by household names. The only Rockets player on the floor with a conspicuous shoe contract was the center Yao Ming—who opened the game by tipping the ball backward. Shane Battier began his game by grabbing it.

Before the Rockets traded for Battier, the front-office analysts obviously studied his value. They knew all sorts of details about his efficiency and his ability to reduce the efficiency of his opponents. They knew, for example, that stars guarded by Battier suddenly lose their shooting touch. What they didn't know was why. Morey recognized Battier's effects, but he didn't know how he achieved them. Two hundred or so basketball games later, he's the world's expert on the subject—which he was studying all over again tonight. He pointed out how, instead of grabbing uncertainly for a rebound, for instance, Battier would tip the ball more certainly to a teammate. Guarding a lesser rebounder, Battier would, when the ball was in the air, leave his own man and block out the other team's best rebounder. "Watch him," a Houston front-office analyst told me before the game. "When the shot goes up, he'll go sit on Gasol's knee." (Pau Gasol often plays center for the Lakers.) On defense, it was as if Battier had set out to maximize the misery Bryant experiences shooting a basketball, without having his presence recorded in any box score. He blocked the ball when Bryant was taking it from his waist to his chin, for instance, rather than when it was far higher and Bryant was in the act of shooting. "When you watch him," Morey says, "you see that his whole thing is to stay in front of guys and try to block the player's vision when he shoots. We didn't even notice what he was doing until he got here. I wish we could say we did, but we didn't."

People often say that Kobe Bryant has no weaknesses to his game, but that's not really true. Before the game, Battier was given his special package of information. "He's the only player we give it to," Morey says. "We can give him this fire hose of data and let him sift. Most players are like golfers. You don't want them swinging while they're thinking." The data essentially broke down the floor into many discrete zones and calculated the odds of Bryant making shots from different places on the court, under different degrees of defensive pressure, in different relationships to other players—how well he scored off screens, off pick-and-rolls, off catch-and-shoots and so on. Battier learns a lot from studying the data on the superstars he is usually assigned to guard. For instance, the numbers show him that Allen Iverson is one of the most efficient scorers in the N.B.A. when he goes to his right; when he goes to his left he kills his team. The Golden State Warriors forward Stephen Jackson is an even stranger case. "Steve Jackson," Battier says, "is statistically better going to his right, but he *loves* to go to his left—and goes to his left almost twice as often." The San Antonio Spurs' Manu Ginóbili is a statistical freak: he has no imbalance whatsoever in his game—there is no one way to play him that is better than another. He is equally efficient both off the dribble and off the pass, going left and right and from any spot on the floor.

Bryant isn't like that. He is better at pretty much everything than everyone else, but there are places on the court, and starting points for his shot, that render him less likely to help his team. When he drives to the basket, he is exactly as likely to go to his left as to his right, but when he goes to his left, he is less effective. When he shoots directly after receiving a pass, he is more efficient than when he shoots after dribbling. He's deadly if he gets into the lane and also if he gets to the baseline; between the two, less so. "The absolute worst thing to do," Battier says, "is to foul him." It isn't that Bryant is an especially good free-throw shooter but that, as Morey puts it, "the foul is the worst result of a defensive play." One way the Rockets can see which teams think about the game as they do is by identifying those that "try dramatically not to foul." The ideal outcome, from the Rockets' statistical point of view, is for Bryant to dribble left and pull up for an 18-foot jump shot; force that to happen often enough and you have to be satisfied with your night. "If he has 40 points on 40 shots, I can live with that," Battier says. "My job is not to keep him from scoring points but to make him as inefficient as possible." The court doesn't have little squares all over it to tell him what percentage Bryant is likely to shoot from any given spot, but it might as well.

The reason the Rockets insist that Battier guard Bryant is his gift for encouraging him into his zones of lowest efficiency. The effect of doing this is astonishing: Bryant doesn't merely help his team less when Battier guards him than when someone else does. When Bryant is in the game and Battier is on him, the Lakers' offense is worse than if the N.B.A.'s best player had taken the night off. "The Lakers' offense should obviously be better with Kobe in," Morey says. "But if Shane is on him, it isn't." A player whom Morey describes as "a marginal N.B.A. athlete" not only guards one of the greatest—and smartest—offensive threats ever to play the game. He renders him a detriment to his team.

And if you knew none of this, you would never guess any of it from watching the game. Bryant was quicker than Battier, so the latter spent much of his time chasing around after him, Keystone Cops–like. Bryant shot early and often, but he looked pretty good from everywhere. On defense, Battier talked to his teammates a lot more than anyone else on the court, but from the stands it was hard to see any point to this. And yet, he swears, there's a reason to almost all of it: when he decides where to be on the court and what angles to take, he is constantly reminding himself of the odds on the stack of papers he read through an hour earlier as his feet soaked in the whirlpool. "The numbers either refute my thinking or support my thinking," he says, "and when there's any question, I trust the numbers. The numbers don't lie." Even when the numbers agree with his intuitions, they have an effect. "It's a subtle difference," Morey says, "but it has big implications. If you have an intuition of something but no hard evidence to back it up, you might kind of *sort of* go about putting that intuition into practice, because there's still some uncertainty if it's right or wrong."

Knowing the odds, Battier can pursue an inherently uncertain strategy with total certainty. He can devote himself to a process and disregard the outcome of any given encounter. This is critical because in basketball, as in everything else, luck plays a role, and Battier cannot afford to let it distract him. Only once during the Lakers game did we glimpse a clean, satisfying comparison of the efficient strategy and the inefficient one—that is, an outcome that reflected the odds. Ten feet from the hoop, Bryant got the ball with his back to the basket; with Battier pressing against him, he fell back and missed a 12-foot shot off the front of the rim. Moments earlier, with Battier reclining in the deep soft chair that masquerades as an N.B.A. bench, his teammate Brent Barry found himself in an analogous position. Bryant leaned into Barry, hit a six-foot shot and drew a foul. But this was the exception; normally you don't get perfect comparisons. You couldn't see the odds shifting subtly away from the Lakers and toward the Rockets as Bryant was forced from 6 feet out to 12 feet from the basket, or when he had Battier's hand in his eyes. All you saw were the statistics on the board, and as the seconds ticked off to halftime, the game tied 54–54, Bryant led all scorers with 16 points.

But he required 20 possessions to get them. And he had started moaning to the referees. Bryant is one of the great jawboners in the history of the N.B.A. A major-league baseball player once showed me a slow-motion replay of the Yankees' third baseman Alex Rodriguez in the batter's box. Glancing back to see where the catcher has set up is not strictly against baseball's rules, but it violates the code. A hitter who does it is likely to find the next pitch aimed in the general direction of his eyes. A-Rod, the best hitter in baseball, mastered the art of glancing back by moving not his head, but his eyes, at just the right time. It was like watching a billionaire find some trivial and dubious deduction to take on his tax returns. Why bother? I thought, and then realized: this is the instinct that separates A-Rod from mere stars. Kobe Bryant has the same instinct. Tonight Bryant complained that Battier was grabbing his jersey, Battier was pushing when no one was looking, Battier was committing crimes against humanity. Just before the half ended, Battier took a referee aside and said: "You and I both know

Kobe does this all the time. I'm playing him honest. Don't fall for his stuff." Moments later, after failing to get a call, Bryant hurled the ball, screamed at the ref and was whistled for a technical foul.

Just after that, the half ended, but not before Battier was tempted by a tiny act of basketball selfishness. The Rockets' front office has picked up a glitch in Battier's philanthropic approach to the game: in the final second of any quarter, finding himself with the ball and on the wrong side of the half-court line, Battier refuses to heave it honestly at the basket, in an improbable but not impossible attempt to score. He heaves it disingenuously, and a millisecond after the buzzer sounds. Daryl Morey could think of only one explanation: a miss lowers Battier's shooting percentage. "I tell him we don't count heaves in our stats," Morey says, "but Shane's smart enough to know that his next team might not be smart enough to take the heaves out."

Tonight, the ball landed in Battier's hands milliseconds before the half finished. He moved just slowly enough for the buzzer to sound, heaved the ball the length of the floor and then sprinted to the locker room—having not taken a single shot.

In 1996 a young writer for *Basketball Times* named Dan Wetzel thought it might be neat to move into the life of a star high-school basketball player and watch up close as big-time basketball colleges recruited him. He picked Shane Battier, and then spent five months trailing him, with growing incredulity. "I'd covered high-school basketball for eight years and talked to hundreds and hundreds and hundreds of kids—really every single prominent high-school basketball player in the country," Wetzel says. "There's this public perception that they're all thugs. But they aren't. A lot of them are really good guys, and some of them are very, very bright. Kobe's very bright. LeBron's very bright. But there's absolutely never been anything like Shane Battier."

Wetzel watched this kid, inundated with offers of every kind, take charge of an unprincipled process. Battier narrowed his choices to six schools—Kentucky, Kansas, North Carolina, Duke, Michigan and Michigan State—and told everyone else, politely, to leave him be. He then set out to minimize the degree to which the chosen schools could interfere with his studies; he had a 3.96 G.P.A. and was poised to claim Detroit Country Day School's headmaster's cup for best all-around student. He granted each head coach a weekly 15-minute window in which to phone him. These men happened to be among the most famous basketball coaches in the world and the most persistent recruiters, but Battier granted no exceptions. When the Kentucky coach Rick Pitino, who had just won a national championship, tried to call Battier outside his assigned time, Battier simply removed Kentucky from his list. "What 17-year-old has the stones to do that?" Wetzel asks. "To just cut off Rick Pitino because he calls outside his window?" Wetzel answers his own question: "It wasn't like, 'This is a really interesting 17-year-old.' It was like, 'This isn't real.'"

Battier, even as a teenager, was as shrewd as he was disciplined. The minute he figured out where he was headed, he called a sensational high-school power forward in Peekskill, N.Y., named Elton Brand—and talked him into joining him at Duke. (Brand now plays for the Philadelphia 76ers.) "I thought he'd be the first black president," Wetzel says. "He was Barack Obama before Barack Obama."

Last July, as we sat in the library of the Detroit Country Day School, watching, or trying to watch, his March 2008 performance against Kobe Bryant, Battier was much happier instead talking about Obama, both of whose books he had read. ("The first was better than the second," he said.) He said he hated watching himself play, then proved it by refusing to watch himself play. My every attempt to draw his attention to the action on the video monitor was met by some distraction.

I pointed to his footwork; he pointed to a gorgeous young woman in the stands wearing a Battier jersey. ("You don't see too many good-looking girls with Battier jerseys on," he said. "It's usually 12 and under or 60 and over. That's my demographic.") I noted the uncanny way in which he got his hand right in front of Bryant's eyes before a shot; he motioned to his old high school library ("I came in here every day before classes"). He took my excessive interest in this one game as proof of a certain lack of imagination, I'm pretty sure. "I've been doing the same thing for seven years," he said, "and this is the only game anyone wants to talk about. It's like, Oh, you can play defense?" It grew clear that one reason he didn't particularly care to watch himself play, apart from the tedium of it, was that he plays the game so self-consciously. Unable to count on the game to properly measure his performance, he learned to do so himself. He had, in some sense, already seen the video. When I finally compelled him to watch, he was knocking the ball out of Bryant's hands as Bryant raised it from his waist to his chin. "If I get to be commissioner, that will count as a blocked shot," Battier said. "But it's nothing. They don't count it as a blocked shot. I do that at least 30 times a season."

In the statistically insignificant sample of professional athletes I've come to know a bit, two patterns have emerged. The first is, they tell you meaningful things only when you talk to them in places other than where they have been trained to answer questions. It's pointless, for instance, to ask a basketball player about himself inside his locker room. For a start, he is naked; for another, he's surrounded by the people he has learned to mistrust, his own teammates. The second pattern is the fact that seemingly trivial events in their childhoods have had huge influence on their careers. A cleanup hitter lives and dies by a swing he perfected when he was 7; a quarterback has a hitch in his throwing motion because he imitated his father. Here, in the Detroit Country Day School library, a few yards from the gym, Battier was back where he became a basketball player. And he was far less interested in what happened between him and Kobe Bryant four months ago than what happened when he was 12.

When he entered Detroit Country Day in seventh grade, he was already conspicuous at 6-foot-4, and a year later he would be 6-foot-7. "Growing up tall was something I got used to," he said. "I was the kid about whom they always said, 'Check his birth certificate.'" He was also the only kid in school with a black father and a white mother. Oddly enough, the school had just graduated a famous black basketball player, Chris Webber. Webber won three state championships and was named national high-school player of the year. "Chris was a man-child," says his high school basketball coach, Kurt Keener. "Everyone wanted Shane to be the next Chris Webber, but Shane wasn't like that." Battier had never heard of Webber and didn't understand why, when he took to the Amateur Athletic Union circuit and played with black inner-city kids, he found himself compared unfavorably with Webber: "I kept hearing 'He's too soft' or 'He's not an athlete.'" His high-school coach was aware of the problems he had when he moved from white high-school games to the black A.A.U. circuit. "I remember trying to add some flair to his game," Keener says, "but it was like teaching a classical dancer to do hip-hop. I came to the conclusion he didn't have the ego for it."

Battier was half-white and half-black, but basketball, it seemed, was either black or white. A small library of Ph.D. theses might usefully be devoted to the reasons for this. For instance, is it a coincidence that many of the things a player does in white basketball to prove his character—take a charge, scramble for a loose ball—are more pleasantly done on a polished wooden floor than they are on inner-city asphalt? Is it easier to "play for the team" when that team is part of some larger institution? At any rate, the inner-city kids with whom he played on the A.A.U. circuit treated Battier like a suburban kid with a white game, and the suburban kids he played with during the regular season treated him like a visitor from the planet where they kept the black people. "On Martin Luther King Day, everyone in class would look at me like I was supposed to know who he was and why he was important," Battier said. "When we had an official school picture, every other kid was given a comb. I was the only one given a pick." He was awkward and shy, or as he put it: "I didn't present well. But I'm in the eighth grade! I'm just trying to fit in!" And yet here he was shuttling between a black world that treated him as white and a white world that treated him as black. "*Everything* I've done since then is because of what I went through with this," he said. "What I did is alienate myself from everybody. I'd eat lunch by myself. I'd study by myself. And I sort of lost myself in the game."

Losing himself in the game meant fitting into the game, and fitting into the game meant meshing so well that he became hard to see. In high school he was almost always the best player on the court, but even then he didn't embrace the starring role. "He had a tendency to defer," Keener says. "He had this incredible ability to make everyone around him better. But I had to tell him to be more assertive. The one game we lost his freshman year, it was because he deferred to the seniors." Even when he was clearly the best player and could have shot the ball at will, he was more interested in his role in the larger unit. But it is a mistake to see in his detachment from self an absence of ego, or ambition, or even desire for attention. When Battier finished telling me the story of this unpleasant period in his life, he said: "Chris Webber won three state championships, the Mr. Basketball Award and the Naismith Award. I won three state championships, Mr. Basketball and the Naismith Awards. All the things they said I wasn't able to do, when I was in the eighth grade."

"Who's they?" I asked.

"Pretty much everyone," he said.

"White people?"

"No," he said. "The street."

As the third quarter began, Battier's face appeared overhead, on the Jumbotron, where he hammed it up and exhorted the crowd. Throughout the game he was up on the thing more than any other player: plugging teeth-whitening formulas, praising local jewelers, making public-service announcements, telling the fans to make noise. When I mentioned to a Rockets' staff member that Battier seemed to have far more than his fair share of big-screen appearances, he said, "Probably because he's the only one who'll do them."

I spent the second half with Sam Hinkie, the vice president of basketball operations and the head of basketball analytics in the Rockets' front office. The game went back and forth. Bryant kept missing more shots than he made. Neither team got much of a lead. More remarkable than the game were Hinkie's reactions—and it soon became clear that while he obviously wanted the Rockets to win, he was responding to different events on the court than the typical Rockets (or N.B.A.) fan was.

"I care a lot more about what ought to have happened than what actually happens," said Hinkie, who has an M.B.A. from Stanford. The routine N.B.A. game, he explained, is decided by a tiny percentage of the total points scored. A team scores on average about 100 points a game, but two out of three N.B.A. games are decided by fewer than 6 points—two or three possessions. The effect of this, in his mind, was to raise significantly the importance of every little thing that happened. The Lakers' Trevor Ariza, who makes 29 percent of his 3-point shots, hit a crazy 3-pointer, and as the crowd moaned, Hinkie was almost distraught. "That Ariza shot, that is really painful," he said. "Because it's a near-random event. And it's a 3-point swing." When Bryant drove to the basket, instead of being forced to take a jump shot, he said: "That's three-eighths of a point. These things accumulate."

In this probabilistic spirit we watched the battle between Battier and Bryant. From Hinkie's standpoint, it was going extremely well: "With most guys, Shane can kick them from their good zone to bad zone, but with Kobe you're just picking your poison. It's the epitome of, Which way do you want to die?" Only the Rockets weren't dying. Battier had once again turned Bryant into a less-efficient machine of death. Even when the shots dropped, they came from the places on the court where the Rockets' front office didn't mind seeing them drop. "That's all you can do," Hinkie said, after Bryant sank an 18-footer. "Get him to an inefficient spot and contest." And then all of a sudden it was 97–95, Lakers, with a bit more than three minutes to play, and someone called timeout. "We're in it," Hinkie said, happily. "And some of what happens from here on will be randomness."

The team with the N.B.A.'s best record was being taken to the wire by Yao Ming and a collection of widely unesteemed players. Moments later, I looked up at the scoreboard:

Bryant: 30.

Battier: 0.

Hinkie followed my gaze and smiled. "I know that doesn't look good," he said, referring to the players' respective point totals. But if Battier wasn't in there, he went on to say: "we lose by 12. No matter what happens now, none of our coaches will say, 'If only we could have gotten a little more out of Battier.'"

One statistical rule of thumb in basketball is that a team leading by more points than there are minutes left near the end of the game has an 80 percent chance of winning. If your team is down by more than 6 points halfway through the final quarter, and you're anxious to beat the traffic, you can leave knowing that there is slightly less than a 20 percent chance you'll miss a victory; on the other hand, if you miss a victory, it will have been an improbable and therefore sensational one. At no point on this night has either team had enough of a lead to set fans, or even Rockets management, to calculating their confidence intervals—but then, with 2:27 to play, the Lakers went up by 4: 99–95. Then they got the ball back. The ball went to Bryant, and Battier shaded him left—into Yao Ming. Bryant dribbled and took the best shot he could, from Battier's perspective: a long 2-point jump shot, off the dribble, while moving left. He missed, the Rockets ran back the other way, Rafer Alston drove the lane and hit a floater: 99–97, and 1:13 on the clock. The Lakers missed another shot. Alston grabbed the rebound and called timeout with 59 seconds left.

Whatever the Rockets planned went instantly wrong, when the inbound pass, as soon as it was caught by the Rockets' Carl Landry, was swatted away by the Lakers. The ball was loose, bodies flew everywhere.

55 . . . 54 . . . 53 . . .

On the side of the court opposite the melee, Battier froze. The moment he saw that the loose ball was likely to be secured by a team-mate—but before it was secured—he sprinted to the corner.

50 . . . 49 . . . 48 . . .

The 3-point shot from the corner is the single most efficient shot in the N.B.A. One way the Rockets can tell if their opponents have taken to analyzing basketball in similar ways as they do is their atti-tude to the corner 3: the smart teams take a lot of them and seek to prevent their opponents from taking them. In basketball there is only so much you can plan, however, especially at a street-ball moment like this. As it happened, Houston's Rafer Alston was among the most legendary street-ball players of all time—known as Skip 2 My Lou, a nickname he received after a single spectacular move at Rucker Park, in Harlem. "Shane wouldn't last in street ball because in street ball no one wants to see" his game, Alston told me earlier. "You better give us something to ooh and ahh about. No one cares about someone who took a charge."

The Rockets' offense had broken down, and there was no usual place for Alston, still back near the half-court line, to go with the ball. The Lakers' defense had also broken down; no player was where he was meant to be. The only person exactly where he should have been—wide open, standing at the most efficient spot on the floor from which to shoot—was Shane Battier. When Daryl Morey spoke of basketball intelligence, a phrase slipped out: "the I.Q. of where to be." Fitting in on a basketball court, in the way Battier fits in, requires the I.Q. of where to be. Bang: Alston hit Battier with a long pass. Bang: Battier shot the 3, guiltlessly. Nothing but net.

Rockets 100, Lakers 99.

43 . . . 42 . . . 41 . . .

At this moment, the Rockets' front office would later calculate, the team's chances of winning rose from 19.2 percent to 72.6 percent. One day some smart person will study the correlation between shifts in probabilities and levels of noise, but for now the crowd was ignorantly berserk: it sounded indeed like the largest crowd in the history of Houston's Toyota Center. Bryant got the ball at half-court and dribbled idly, searching for his opening. This was his moment, the one great players are said to live for, when everyone knows he's going to take the shot, and he takes it anyway. On the other end of the floor it wasn't the shooter who mattered but the shot. Now the shot was nothing, the shooter everything.

33 . . . 32 . . . 31 . . .

Bryant—12 for 31 on the night—took off and drove to the right, his strength, in the middle of the lane. Battier cut him off. Bryant tossed the ball back out to Derek Fisher, out of shooting range.

30 . . . 29 . . .

Like everyone else in the place, Battier assumed that the game was still in Bryant's hands. If he gave the ball up, it was only so that he might get it back. Bryant popped out. He was now a good four feet beyond the 3-point line, or nearly 30 feet from the basket.

28 . . .

Bryant caught the ball and, 27.4 feet from the basket, the Rockets' front office would later determine, leapt. Instantly his view of that basket was blocked by Battier's hand. This was not an original situation. Since the 2002–3 season, Bryant had taken 51 3-pointers at the very end of close games from farther than 26.75 feet from the basket. He had missed 86.3 percent of them. A little over a year ago the Lakers lost to the Cleveland Cavaliers after Bryant missed a 3 from 28.4 feet. Three nights from now the Lakers would lose to the Orlando Magic after Bryant missed a shot from 27.5 feet that would have tied the game. It was a shot Battier could live with, even if it turned out to be good.

Battier looked back to see the ball drop through the basket and hit the floor. In that brief moment he was the picture of detachment, less a party to a traffic accident than a curious passer-by. And then he laughed. The process had gone just as he hoped. The outcome he never could control.

George Dohrmann

For generations, young sportswriters got their start on the high school beat, hoping to advance, like the athletes they covered, to the colleges, perhaps the pros, and, for the anointed few, enshrinement as columnists, with names and faces chiseled plaque-like above their musings. George Dohrmann (b. 1973) began in just that way upon graduating from Notre Dame in 1995, covering preps for the *Los Angeles Times*. Yet even after winning a Pulitzer Prize at the *St. Paul Pioneer-Press* in 2000 for exposing academic fraud in the basketball program at Minnesota, and landing at *Sports Illustrated* as a senior writer, Dohrmann couldn't let grassroots sports go. He had been fascinated by something he saw up close at the outset of his career: the unregulated youth basketball scene that sprawls across Southern California, and the college recruiters, shoe company reps, and travel-team coaches angling for a piece of the action. Impressed by the deep, longitudinal work of Adrian Nicole LeBlanc in the book *Random Family*, Dohrmann decided to apply her approach. He spent nearly nine years following a youth coach in San Bernardino County named Joe Keller, as well as Demetrius Walker, the player Keller served as Svengali and impresario after identifying him as a prospect at age ten. The book that resulted, *Play Their Hearts Out* (2010), won the 2011 PEN/ESPN Award for Literary Sportswriting. Few people in its pages could be described as "household names," including many of those once believed to be "can't miss." But that's where the importance and very point of Dohrmann's work lies. This chapter from late in the book recounts the dissolution of the relationship between Walker and Keller, who by now has gained influence in youth basketball to rival that of Reebok executive Sonny Vaccaro. And, near the end, the author drops a hint that another twist awaits—that even without Keller, Walker will ultimately find his way to Division I basketball.

from

Play Their Hearts Out

"HE'S HIDING in the bathroom, Joe," Dave Taylor said into his cell phone. "Did you hear me? He's hiding in the fucking bathroom, in a stall."

On the other end of the line, Keller sighed.

Taylor looked around. A few yards from where he stood in the gym at the Suwanee Sports Academy were more than 100 of the best young basketball players in the country, and he didn't want them to overhear his remarks. He wasn't shouting, but his statements were firm. He had been around Keller long enough to know that he didn't respond to subtleties.

"Do you understand what I am saying, Joe? He's in the bathroom. Right now. Hiding."

Keller was across the country, in his home in Moreno Valley, but the distance did not lessen the gravity of the situation. Demetrius Walker, the prodigy *Sports Illustrated* had labeled the next LeBron, the young soul Keller often bragged was "like my son," was hiding in a bathroom on the third day of the 2006 Adidas Superstar Camp, the most important event of his grassroots season. College recruiters lined the walls of the gym, and many had circled Demetrius's name in their programs, anxious to see if he'd improved from the previous summer. Now, with his future hanging in the air like a ball on the rim, he cowered in a bathroom stall.

"I don't know if he can ever come back from this, Joe," Taylor said into his phone. "Do you understand, Joe? Do you hear what I am saying? This is it for him. This is it! It's the bottom. Demetrius has hit the fucking bottom."

The bottom came during a July week of overcast days, the air thick with the promise of rain and a wisp of southern wind. It reminded me of the week of Nationals in Memphis, when on the last day a storm knocked out the power and it looked as if the finals against the War Eagles would never be played. That day ended with Demetrius asleep on the plane, the glass-bowl trophy in his lap, Keller next to him sipping a beer and reveling in how far they had come together.

Joe and D.

Their partnership had taken them to wondrous heights, but in Memphis greater achievements seemed certain. There was Keller, his shoe deal in place but his Jr. Phenom Camp riches yet to come, his financial fate still moored to his young star. And there was D, the number-1 player in the country, as hard a worker as any of the boys, fearless and full of himself in that way that great athletes have to be.

There had always been something worrisome about their bond—a coach who'd been no father to his own son, Joey, leaping into that role for one of his players—and a happy ending was never preordained. But the broader strokes of Demetrius's failure couldn't have been

predicted. It came so soon—two months before he turned sixteen—
and Keller was so utterly absent, so unwilling to do anything but let
their partnership dissolve. Even in the grassroots game, where trag-
edies outnumbered successes, this one was epic.

In the months leading up to the Superstar Camp, Demetrius sensed
that his great undressing was afoot. "I really don't want to go," he said.
"[But] I know Adidas wants me there, so I guess I just gotta suck it up
and play. But, you know, I haven't been playing a lot lately."

Roberto, Justin, Andrew, Jordan, and the other Team Cal kids played
a packed schedule with their new grassroots teams in the spring and
early summer when Demetrius had played only sparingly and once
again Keller was to blame. Keller realized his contract with Adidas stip-
ulated that he operate a grassroots team and enter it into the top tournaments. He created a shell of a team and hired Dave Taylor to coach
it. Taylor lived in Sacramento and naturally recruited players from that
area and held practices there, few of which Demetrius attended. Keller
also operated the team with an eye on keeping costs down; he entered
it into the minimum number of events.

If you saw Demetrius walking the street, he appeared as fit as ever.
He was sinewy and his biceps were bigger, as he'd recently begun lifting weights. But inactivity had left him in such poor shape that he got
fatigued early in games, making it impossible to sustain solid play. He
would make a few stellar plays in a game's opening minutes but then
grab at his shorts or put his hands on his knees during stoppages. That
was the signal that his energy was gone, and he would do nothing of
consequence the rest of the game.

Contrasted with the year before, when Keller considered the Superstar Camp the ultimate judgment on himself and his star player, his
disinterest in even attending the event bespoke the change in his
goals. His financial interests were no longer tied to Demetrius, and
thus he couldn't be bothered to get him physically ready for the
challenge.

Demetrius was not without friends at the Superstar Camp. Rome
and Rome, Sr., were there, G.J. and Gerry as well. Dave Taylor also
kept an eye on him. Compared to a year earlier, however, when Keller
had watched his every move, Demetrius felt alone. On Wednesday,
when the players learned what teams they were on and scrimmaged
together, he looked around the gym at the many coaches—Mats, the

Pumps, Jimmy Salmon—and said, "Everybody's got somebody here but me. It's like I got nobody in my corner anymore."

In his two games on Thursday, Demetrius attempted a total of twelve shots. Most players were so eager to get the attention of the college coaches that they gunned without even thinking. Demetrius acted as if shooting was a risk he couldn't afford.

"He's hiding on the court," Taylor said. "He's not doing anything that will draw attention to his game."

Taylor gave him a brief pep talk on Thursday night, during which Demetrius made a statement that alarmed him. "You know, D.T., I don't know if I want to do this anymore," he said.

"What do you mean?"

"This camp. I don't know that I want to come back next year. I just don't see the point anymore."

There was no guarantee that there would be a Superstar Camp the following summer. Adidas's purchase of Reebok eleven months earlier had shaken up the grassroots landscape, and the joint company talked of reconfiguring how they went after elite players. The camp model, where hundreds of kids were invited to one place, was inefficient.

"Don't worry about next year, worry about right now," Taylor told Demetrius. "People are wanting to see if you've improved from last time you were here, and you need to show them that you've gotten better."

The next morning was key, Taylor knew, as the coaches would watch the individual drills closely; they were better gauges of a player's abilities as a ballhandler, shooter, and defender than the games. Already a coach from Xavier had mentioned to Taylor that he was eager to scout Demetrius.

On Friday morning, just before the start of the day's first drill, Taylor scanned the gym. His gaze moved from one hopeful basketball player to the next as they stood two-deep around one side of a court, dressed in identical black-and-orange uniforms. Across the court were the college coaches they hoped to impress—Ben Howland, Bill Self, Bruce Pearl—so many that they almost outnumbered the players. In a few minutes, the instructor running the drill would yell out the names of two players, and they would be the first to be judged. Being called out first could be a blessing or a curse. Everyone remembered the opening duel, and it set the tone for the rest of the session.

Taylor had arranged for Armon Johnson, a guard he knew from Sacramento, to be one of the first two players selected. Taylor was awarding him prime placement to show his abilities, and now he had to decide who to match him against. Taylor's eyes moved down the sideline, finding some of the best talent in the country—Eric Gordon, Nolan Smith, Jerime Anderson—before finally stopping on a six-foot-three kid so eager to get under way that he jumped in place. Lance Stephenson's presence at the Superstar Camp was one of the most anticipated developments of the summer. He was a Reebok kid, one of Sonny's boys, but at the last minute he switched from the ABCD Camp to the Superstar. (Vaccaro claimed that Adidas cut a sponsorship deal with his AAU coach and high school that exceeded $100,000.) It was a major get for Adidas, and Stephenson arrived with a camera crew in tow, as his every move was being filmed for a documentary. The full wattage of the New York spotlight had found him, but it hadn't changed the way he played, at least not yet. In a game the previous day, Stephenson picked up a loose ball and broke down the court, and the fans rose in anticipation of a thunderous dunk. But Oscar Bellfield, Justin's teammate on Taft, caught up with Stephenson and blocked his shot from behind, sending it out of bounds. The players, fans, and even a few of the college coaches hooted in delight. It was the most talked-about play of the day. What Taylor thought of as he considered pairing Stephenson with Armon was how Stephenson had reacted after being embarrassed. He immediately demanded the ball and used a screen to isolate Bellfield. He faked as if he were going to drive on him but then shot a 3-pointer over him. As the ball fell through the net, Stephenson got into Bellfield's face, jarring at him, and then he checked Bellfield with his shoulder as he ran back on defense. His instinct after being showed up was to go right back at Bellfield, to erase a humiliating moment with a spectacular play of his own.

Taylor saw a probing look in Stephenson's eyes, as if he were searching the gym for the next challenger to his throne. *It's tempting*, Taylor thought. If Armon showed him up, that would get the attention of the coaches. But then a better choice came to mind.

Demetrius.

Pitting him against Armon could boost Demetrius's stock and his confidence. They were about the same height and weight, and although Armon was a better shooter, Demetrius was more explosive and a little stronger. Most significantly, Demetrius had played with Armon. He knew his game, his strengths. He couldn't possibly fear a challenge from Armon.

Taylor looked around the gym for Demetrius. He knew he was there; he had noticed him when he got off the bus, because Demetrius wore different shoes—blue Promodels—from the rest of the campers. That had annoyed Taylor at the time, but it would now make Demetrius easier to find.

Taylor moved his focus to the players' feet, hunting for those blue shoes. He was still searching minutes later when the coach leading the drill called out Armon and then, after getting no indication from Taylor of who else to pick, selected a player at random.

Where the fuck is Demetrius? Taylor thought. There was no way for him to go back to the hotel, and the trainer's table was visible from where he stood. If he wasn't at one of those two places, that left only one possibility.

Taylor strode across the gym and pushed open the door to the bathroom, stopping just inside. No one was at the sink or at the urinals, and it looked as if all the stalls were empty. Then something caught Taylor's eye, something in the second-to-last stall. He took a step closer and leaned down, and then he saw them: the blue shoes. The accessory Demetrius had chosen to stand out had given him away.

Taylor quickly left the bathroom and sat in a chair near the door, positioned so Demetrius couldn't rejoin the group of players without passing him. He looked at the time on his cell phone. There were fifty minutes left in the two-hour session of individual drills, and he guessed Demetrius had been in there since the start.

The minutes passed and Taylor assumed Demetrius would emerge only after the final drill was complete, when he could blend in with the rest of the campers as if he'd never been gone and catch the bus back to the hotel. At the thought of this, Taylor dialed Keller's number.

Prior to the start of the camp, Keller predicted that Demetrius would feign injury or sickness to avoid competing. On Friday morning, when Taylor called Keller while sitting outside the bathroom waiting for Demetrius, Keller reminded him of his earlier comments.

"So you were right, Joe. So what now?"

Keller didn't say anything.

"Joe, kids like Demetrius are why people say all these bad things about AAU basketball. What has happened to him makes everyone look bad. He shouldn't even be here. He's afraid to compete."

Keller remained silent.

Demetrius emerged forty-five minutes later, just as the individual drills were breaking up, as players headed to the exit and the waiting buses. Had Taylor not been sitting there, Demetrius would have joined the rest of the campers, and his absence might have gone unnoticed.

"You been in there the whole time?" Taylor said.

"Yeah, my stomach is messed up, D.T." Demetrius put his hand to his belly.

Taylor led him to the bus and told him to get some rest back at the hotel.

"He's quitting, Joe," Taylor told Keller in a later phone call. "He's not even a sophomore in high school and he's giving up."

Keller offered another "I told you so" and called Demetrius "soft" and "weak."

"That's not good enough, Joe. Tell me what you are going to do about it. Saying D is fucked-up is not enough. You are responsible for him. Don't just tell me how fucked-up he is, tell me how you are going to fix him."

Taylor pushed hard enough that Keller made hollow-sounding pledges. *I promise I am going to take D back under my belt. I'm going to refocus him and get him back on track. I promise you that*, he wrote in one text message. *I love that kid like my own son.*

The final game Demetrius played at the Superstar Camp came Friday afternoon. There were games scheduled for Friday night and another round Saturday, but he would skip those, citing a stomach illness. The final impression he would make would come against Rome's team, and at the start he walked to the center of the court and playfully stuck a finger in Rome's chest and said, "I got this guy."

"I thought he would go right at me," Rome would say later. "He knows he can get by me."

He did drive past Rome on a few possessions, but he refused to continue toward the rim. He either dished to a teammate or pulled the ball out to the perimeter. He attempted only three shots, missing all of them, and allowed Rome to score 13 points, mostly on little pull-up jumpers and hustle play that took advantage of Demetrius's poor conditioning.

"It's sad seeing Demetrius play without any intensity," Rome, Sr., said before the game was even over. "It's like he is a different person."

Added Gerry: "It used to be that when Demetrius was playing, you almost didn't notice anyone else. Now you hardly notice *him*."

The college coaches at the camp didn't expect Demetrius or any of the young players to exhibit a completely refined game. When scouting kids entering their sophomore year in high school, they looked only for small signs that a prospect could make the jump to the next level. A little burst of speed, an athletic finish on a drive to the rim, or a signature skill, such as G.J.'s passing or Justin's defense, was all they needed to see in order for their interest in that player to continue. The mental side of it was also important. Lance Stephenson's competitiveness, even if it made a mess of games as he attempted crazy shot after crazy shot, was something the coaches wanted to see from Demetrius. They didn't expect him to dominate as he had as a middle schooler, but they wanted to see him try.

Demetrius gave them nothing. Even worse, he planted a poisonous seed in their minds: *Was Demetrius afraid to compete?* There was no room for fear in big-time basketball. A coach could teach a player to be a better ball handler or shooter or defender, but he couldn't teach courage. Even if Demetrius was indeed sick—the college coaches did not know that he was faking—they wanted to see him fight through it. Even if he got his shot blocked five times in a row, they wanted him to attack the rim again. That was what Lance Stephenson did.

The recruiters talked to Taylor, and he knew the extent of the damage Demetrius had done. They questioned his basketball ability and his mental toughness. Most said flatly that they weren't interested in him.

"I don't know if he is a [Division I] prospect anymore," Taylor said. "Maybe some low-major like Loyola Marymount or Long Beach [State] might get interested, but no big programs."

On Saturday afternoon, Phil Bryant, the director of the camp, gave a closing address. He stood at the center of the middle court, the players in a circle around him. Demetrius was on the outer edge of that circle and paid no attention to Bryant as he read off the names of the campers who had been selected for one of the two all-star games.

"Will D come back from this? That is the question," Taylor said. He stood with his arms folded a few yards outside the circle, looking out over the hopeful kids. "He can. There is time. But if you are asking me if I think he will, well . . ."

His voice trailed off as Bryant ended his talk by telling the players: "Whoever it is who is responsible for you being here, say thank you." He then urged the players to give a round of applause to their AAU coaches. Demetrius's head shot up as the players around him applauded, and he clapped lightly three times, a nearly silent salute to the man responsible for his state.

Once Demetrius was back in California, Keller didn't begin working him out again as he had promised. He barely spoke to him, and when they did communicate, it was usually through text messages.

One of the few phone conversations they had came after the start of school, in September, when Demetrius heard that *The Hoop Scoop* had dropped him to number 215 in its rankings of prospects in the class of 2009. There was something fishy about Demetrius's placement. More than a dozen players who'd once played for Keller were ranked ahead of him, including Craig Payne, even though he had recently decided to focus on football, believing that was his best chance at a college scholarship.

"How could they have me so low?" Demetrius asked Keller. "That's bull."

"I told Clark to drop you that far," Keller confessed.

"Why would you do that?"

"I feel like you aren't working as hard as you can and that I need to motivate you."

"You think that by embarrassing me that is going to motivate me?"

"I don't know what else to do. You've already got everything you want—shoes and stuff—so there is nothing I can give you to motivate you."

"That is bull. You are trashing my name. That's like the biggest slap in the face ever. People are seeing that ranking and laughing at me."

That conversation triggered weeks of introspection as Demetrius focused on how Keller treated him in the present rather than what he had done for him in the past. Meeting the bottom brought Demetrius clarity, most of all about Keller.

"You know, me and my mom have started talking a lot lately about Coach Joe, and, I mean, I start thinking to myself, like, is it 'cuz of me that Coach Joe is now living like he is? It eats me up sometimes, because I don't really know the whole truth, but if it wasn't for me, if I had joined another team, would Coach Joe be rich like he is now? Would his name be as big as it is? My mom says that what Coach Joe has probably has a lot to do with me, and I think she is right. 'Cuz, see, it went like this: Adidas wanted a younger kid coming up that's gonna be good, that's gonna be marketable. So whatever they had to do to get a kid like that, they were going to do. And at the time Coach Joe had me. Which means he got paid for it, for me. He got the Adidas shoe contract, with the Adidas money, and everything else, and now he's got everything he wants and it's, like, you know, I'm down here and he has no time for me."

He felt betrayed, used, suddenly aware that the man who often claimed to love him like a son had only exploited him to get rich. Over the next several weeks, Demetrius composed a letter to Keller on his Sidekick. During class or alone in his room, he pecked out the words with his thumbs, and he labored to get across how he felt. He was still coming to terms with his feelings, and it was natural that the finished email centered less on how Keller made him feel and more on what Demetrius felt he was owed.

> I don't understand how you say I'm like your son, but you aren't there for me anymore. You came out of retirement and you found me and I made you who you are. If it wasn't for me being good you would have nothing. You got money from me being successful. You bought a house and Violet a car and you got wood floors all through your house and a big pool and what do I have?
>
> How come when I ask for shoes you take so long to get them for me or you don't get them at all? How come when I ask you for a ride or to come take me to work out you say you are going to come but then I just sit here and wait and you never show?

It was not a "Dear John" email. At no point did he express a desire to sever all ties with Coach Joe. There was anger behind his words but also fear. He had hit bottom, and he was scared. Keller had to know that even though Demetrius wrote of what he was owed, what he really coveted was for Coach Joe to be part of his life again. Yet

Keller focused on the anger, on Demetrius's veiled demands to be compensated.

"When he started talking about the money I owed him, I knew that was it," Keller would say later. As he would do with anyone staking a claim to his hard-earned fortune, Keller cut Demetrius out of his life.

It's a shame we can't continue our relationship. I guess we have to go our separate ways, Keller wrote in response to Demetrius's email.

Demetrius replied immediately: *I don't want that.*

Keller wrote: *I wish we could solve all our issues but I guess we will have to go our separate ways.*

Demetrius reached out to Keller a few times after that—when he was looking for a new grassroots team, when he was deciding whether to stay at FoHi, after he and his mom got into a fight. He sent Keller text messages, and sometimes Keller responded, but most often he did not. Eventually Demetrius stopped trying, and Keller was out of his life forever.

"Man, I'm not gonna lie, it does hurt. I mean, I looked at stuff like . . . like he was my pops, you know. I didn't have a pops and he was like my pops and, you know, okay, I'll just say it: I loved him like he was my pops."

Early in 2007, I traveled to Moreno Valley to say goodbye to Joe Keller.

We would still keep in contact, of course, and I gave updates on Demetrius and his other former players even after he stopped asking for them, but his journey was over. He had gone from a punch line, the guy who lost Tyson Chandler, to one of the most important figures in basketball, the Sonny of middle schoolers. The ending he had long sought had arrived, and he didn't see the advantage in letting me remain inside his world. Phone calls had begun to go unanswered, messages unreturned. When I did reach him, he was annoyed by my inquiries.

Keller greeted me at the door of his home with a hug and asked that I not tease him about the weight he'd gained. He was pleased to be able to show off his house and led me from room to room. The kitchen had been completely redone, with dark cabinets, stainless-steel appliances, and an extra refrigerator with a glass front, full of the Gatorades and soft drinks Keller preferred. New wood floors covered the kitchen, den, and dining and living rooms. The house looked as if it had recently undergone a makeover. There was an overabundance of candles, vases, lamps, and pillows, and ornate place settings were arranged perfectly in front of every seat at the dining table.

The most obvious sign of Keller's prosperity was his backyard. His bean-shaped pool had a waterfall along the far side that was so large you had to raise your voice to be heard over the rush of water. There was a circular spa attached to the pool and a thatched-roof cabana nearby. "My pool's better than Sonny's, don't you think?" Keller said as we took seats at a tall bar table. "Sonny's house is probably still nicer than mine, but my pool is better."

Keller knew I wanted to talk about Demetrius, and he tried to avoid it by rattling off the projects he had in the works, including the purchase of a sports bar, the renovation of the guest bathroom, and the redecorating of his downstairs office. "I also think I am going to buy the house next door," he said. "That's right, Joe Keller is not done buying houses. We are going to buy the one next door and then another one at the end [of the cul-de-sac]. Violet's sister is going to move into one and her parents into the other one. I told them, 'Just keep it as an investment.' All they have to do is pay the taxes on it, which is like three thousand a year."

Business had never been better, he said. He was starting another camp, Phenom Elite, which he said would resemble Sonny's ABCD Camp, and he had recently partnered with former NBA player Antonio Davis. They'd visited with Adidas officials in Portland a few months earlier, and Keller claimed that the three-day summit had changed his perspective on developing young phenoms.

"I'm telling you, we're going to change basketball. Kids now, they think everything should just be given to them. And then when they don't make it, they don't know anything and aren't educated about how to live. We are going to change that by doing all this educational stuff at our camps. We are going to have these assessments for kids, and we are going to have educational stuff for the parents. We're going to do more of that stuff than the basketball stuff. . . . You know what, I know what you are going to say, and I'm at fault for a lot of it because I didn't do it the right way. But Antonio and me, we are going to end that. It took Antonio and me getting together and figuring things out for me to see what is best for kids."

Without being provoked, Keller brought up Demetrius, although he put him at a distance. He was just one of those kids who didn't learn how to manage life.

"D's gotta make some choices in life. I don't think he knows what he is going to do, and, see, that is what I am talking about. That is the problem. Everyone did everything for him. Everyone makes excuses for him. . . . Kisha, she doesn't help. She sent me a letter the other day. She was saying, 'It's your fault,' or some shit like that. Everything she talks about is so negative. . . . She wrote, 'I never thought you were the kind of person that was gonna just leave. Why would you leave him? Why wouldn't you be there for him every minute of his life?' I didn't respond, but I was thinking, *Lady, you want me to forget my whole family for you and your son?* And the thing is, all the money I used to spend on the team, on D and Aaron and all the kids, I now spend on *my* family. And Violet's so much happier, and Jordan and Alyssa are happier, and *I'm* happier.

"With D—and I know what you are going to say: There are some things that I could help him with, like finding a new school and a new [AAU] team—I *could* help him, but, fuck it, you know, with Kisha involved now, and her attitude, fuck it, I'm done. I'm not going to hold his hand anymore. People holding his hand was what fucked him up in the first place."

Keller's attitude reminded me of something playwright Arthur Miller once said about one of his characters, a patriarch named, coincidentally, Joe Keller. Miller described the Joe Keller in *All My Sons* as having "a crazy quilt of motivations and contradictions in his head." The real-life Keller had his own crazy quilt, among several similarities between him and Miller's character. The fictitious Joe Keller was a self-made businessman who, despite no education, rose to great heights, driven by the desire to provide for his family and achieve the American Dream. But in his greed, he knowingly shipped airplane parts that were defective, resulting in the deaths of several pilots, including his son. He lied about his culpability, letting his partner take the blame.

The salient difference between the two Joe Kellers was in the endings to their stories. The structure of *All My Sons* was intended "to bring a man into the direct path of the consequences he wrought,"

Miller said. At the end of the play, Keller kills himself offstage, proving the existence of social justice.

The grassroots-basketball society was not a just one, and the real Joe Keller would never face the consequences of what he wrought. His camps would remain full; parents would still dial his number, hoping to land a spot for their children; his business would expand to the point that he estimated he could sell it for $10 million. The American Dream was alive and well in his Moreno Valley home, and the demise of Demetrius would never threaten that.

Before leaving Moreno Valley, I asked Keller for some photos of the team that he had promised me. We went into his office and he searched for a long time, going through a file cabinet and a dozen boxes piled up in his closet. He got frustrated and repeatedly called out to Violet to help him. She shouted directions, but he still couldn't find his "Team Cal box." She finally came into the room and helped him locate an unlabeled medium-sized brown box at the very bottom of the closet. Keller pulled out programs and pictures and a manila folder that contained the birth certificates of the players. He had once needed them to prove that his amazing collection of phenoms were indeed as young as he said. He tossed them to me unceremoniously and asked that I return them to the players or their parents.

As I prepared to leave, a pile of pictures and birth certificates in my arms, I noticed the glass-bowl trophy given to the team at the 2004 Nationals. It occupied an inconspicuous spot in his office, atop a file cabinet in the corner. Keller had begun purchasing signed sports memorabilia that he intended to place around the room, and it was easy to imagine the trophy from Nationals getting supplanted by a bat signed by Derek Jeter or a football helmet autographed by Terrell Owens. In time, it would likely find its way into that box at the bottom of the closet, shoved in with what few memories he had yet to purge.

I pointed to the trophy and asked Keller what he planned to do with it.

"What do you mean?"

Would it still have a place in his office after the remodel? If not, did he want me to take it, to give it to Demetrius or Rome or Aaron? They would surely display it proudly; nothing they had accomplished had meant more.

"Hell no!" Keller said. "Are you crazy? I'm not giving it to *them*. That is mine. I earned that."

A few weeks later, Kisha found Demetrius alone in his room, sitting on his bed. After his struggles during his freshman season and at the Adidas Superstar Camp, *ESPN The Magazine* wrote a brief story about him titled "Didn't you used to be?" The *Riverside Press-Enterprise* wrote its own obituary of his career, quoting Clark Francis as saying: "The question is, how bad does Demetrius want it? I don't think he has the burning desire to be great." Demetrius didn't tack those articles to the wall above his bed, where the *Sports Illustrated* article labeling him the "next LeBron" still hung, along with other clippings from his glory days.

Kisha sat next to him and, after a moment, Demetrius looked at her and asked, "Mom, am I going to end up like Schea Cotton?" Without pause, she jumped into a lengthy explanation for why that would not be his fate, how he wouldn't be just another touted young player who never lived up to the hype. But Demetrius had succinctly stated what was now the great question. Whereas the debate had once been how good he could be—whether he was the next LeBron James or just a future NBA player—it was now where he would rank on the list of the greatest flops.

The grassroots machine rarely allowed for a player's ending to be rewritten; it was easier to just shift focus to the next junior phenom. So when you mentioned Demetrius's name to prominent AAU coaches like Mats or the Pumps, they spoke as if the case on him was closed, his career dead. "It's sad how he ended up," one of the Pumps said at a tournament in Arizona.

It never occurred to them that a sixteen-year-old might rediscover that "burning desire"—that a great success story might start at the bottom.

Bryan Curtis

Wherever the gate between sports and its many adjacencies swings, you're likely to find Bryan Curtis (b. 1977), who may be the perfect sportswriter for an era when the games we play touch so many facets of the world we live in. He has contributed to generalist outlets that dip into sports (*Texas Monthly*, *The Daily Beast*, *Slate*, *The New Republic*) and sports outlets that consider the wider world part of their purview (*Sports Illustrated* and the short-lived *Play*, the standalone sports magazine of *The New York Times*). Eventually he landed at places that simply let the two bleed into each other, *Grantland* and *The Ringer*. If there's a common thread to Curtis's work, it's that he considers a broad range of things—pop culture, race, the media, politics, science—fodder for what's nominally a sports story. It's a beat he defines as "everything they let me get away with. That's the dream for me, rather than sitting in some press box." A graduate of the University of Texas at Austin who logged time under such titanic editors as Michael Kinsley, Mark Bryant, Tina Brown, and Bill Simmons, Curtis spent years nursing the idea for this piece. With every trip back to Texas to visit his mother, he'd see the fiberglass backboard of his youth still standing in the driveway and be reminded of his story waiting to be told. But he could never quite envision the right place for it until he landed at *Grantland*, where Simmons was coaxing highly personal pieces from his staff during the site's brief run. After this reminiscence went live, Curtis said, "I remember walking away from my computer for a long time. Then I called my mom."

The Fiberglass Backboard

W HEN I was 11 years old, my dad died—killed himself, in fact, while sitting in a van in our driveway. Our home in Texas filled with sympathy gifts. Mom got flowers and a new microwave. A few months later, an uncle arrived from Albuquerque and built me a basketball hoop on the opposite end of the driveway. The hoop's backboard was made of fiberglass. There was an NBA logo in the lower left-hand corner. Over the next five years, that fiberglass backboard and I became fabulous teammates, like Ro Blackman and Derek Harper, and partners in a fierce existential struggle. If I'm picking a sports hero from childhood who deserves a profile . . . Jim Jackson . . . Alvin Harper . . . nope, I'll go with the backboard.

The first thing you could say about my backboard is that it was beautiful. When my uncle installed it, it was the most absurdly white thing I'd seen besides my own legs. It glowed against a backyard tableau of monkey grass, rose bushes, a mulberry tree, crepe myrtles, and a sagging garage apartment. The second key thing about the backboard was its placement: on the long side of a narrow cement rectangle. Picture a court, then, that was wider sideline-to-sideline than an NBA court but not even as deep as a free throw line. There was no top of the key. No elbow. My game was forged deep in the corners. My court was like the factory where Bruce Bowen was created.

Brrrrryyyyyan Curtis, a 5-foot-3 only child, strolls onto this court for the first time. He throws the ball against the backboard. The backboard answers, *Thungggg*. Which was weird. I'd watched Mavs games at Reunion Arena and noted squeaky shoes and (much later) miked rims. The backboards didn't make a sound. Yet here, on fiberglass, every bank shot sounded like I was firing artillery shells into the neighborhood. *Thunggg. Thunggg. Thunggg.*

"Going fiberglass" can do magical things for your Player Efficiency Rating. To bank shots off a glass backboard, you have to have Tim Duncan–quality arc and touch. For the rock-hard backboards on school playgrounds, you need double-Duncan. A fiberglass backboard requires no talent at all. When a basketball hits fiberglass, it instantly loses all its velocity. If you get the angle right, the ball plops down into the cylinder, like a duck being shot out of mid-air. It's a beautifully corrupt form of the sport, akin to bumper bowling, and best appreciated by kids the same age.

When I discovered the secret of fiberglass it was like Naismith discovering the peach basket. I shot a layup off the backboard— *thunggg*—and the ball dropped into the cylinder. I backed up to nearly 20 feet—pretty far out on the prairie for an 11-year-old—and heaved the ball toward the backboard. It bounced into the cup again. I picked one shot on the court I liked best, a 20-footer from the left-hand side— my "3." I used to go to that spot around six o'clock and shoot 100 thunderous bank shots in a row. I bet I hit 90 percent. On a bad day.

Bank shots took the form of therapy. I was angry about my dad dying—even if I didn't show it—and I needed to hurl the ball against the backboard. But I was in a tender enough emotional state that I needed to be good at something, too. The fiberglass backboard came through on both counts. It was like shooting a silky Rabbit Angstrom jumper and committing a flagrant foul in the same motion. My mom looked out the kitchen window and probably thought this was how you were supposed to play basketball.

A frequent trope of sports writing is the athlete who uses sports to escape trauma: dead dads, rough neighborhoods. This—minus the talent—was me. My dad, Dan, didn't know anything about team sports. Though he was a 6'4" runner who chewed up marathons on weekends, he broke out in a cold sweat when his guy friends brought up the Cowboys' draft. (In North Texas, knowing the width of Jason Witten's jock strap is more socially valuable than being able to run a marathon.) When I was five or six, I'm pretty sure I taught him which way to run around the bases. My mom noticed all this and, in a subtle but sly move, steered my play dates toward kids who *did* have sports-crazy dads. Long before my dad died, I got the basics from outside the house.

There were some assists along the way, sure. My grandfather taught me the fine points of softball. My uncles planned a vacation to Cowboys' training camp. Mom took me on shuttle runs to Action Baseball Cards on West 7th Street. That's where we were going one June afternoon, racing to get there before it closed, when we happened to glance inside the windshield of Dad's van.

Bloody pictures like those creep into your head when you play H-O-R-S-E alone. Call it the Loneliness of the Long-Distance Shooter. So I started dragging a radio out to the backyard. Skip Bayless was in his prime as a Dallas drive-time radio host, and I shot baskets to the vocal stylings of "Dr. Bay." When the *Dallas Times Herald* shut down in 1991, Dr. Bay faxed his sports column to interested parties for $99 a year. I was very interested. I didn't have a fax machine, so I arranged to get Bayless' *Insider* by regular mail, and I didn't mind if the game he was writing about had occurred two days before.

Skip's voice—reedy and beseeching, the voice of a needy honors student—changed the atmosphere of the court. Here was a man who knew *a lot* about sports. And wasn't this the kind of guy my mom wanted me hanging out with? Moreover, the opinions Skip was slinging into the night air were . . . *counterintuitive.* He wondered if Steve Beuerlein might beat out Troy Aikman, and, if I remember correctly, called Nolan Ryan a wimp. Skip was a master of setting calculated bonfires in the local media. I might have called him the Christopher

Hitchens of North Texas, if only I'd known who Christopher Hitchens was.

With Skip turned up to an uncomfortably high volume—how else was I going to hear him over the *thunggg*?—the court became a theater of the mind. I started placing calls to *The Skip Bayless Show* from the phone just inside the back door. I had my own counterintuitive ideas: Should the Cowboys draft Notre Dame's Rick Mirer and make him Aikman's backup? Even Skip wouldn't quite endorse that but—this was huge—he said *he liked how I was thinking*. I ran back onto the court and heard him say it again, over the air, thanks to the tape delay.

One of the few days I didn't visit my backboard is when Mom took me to Skip's remote broadcast at a local restaurant. During a commercial, I told Skip how much I liked his show. What I really wanted, it seems clear now, was to thank him for providing the substitute-dad soundtrack to my life. The fiberglass backboard and Dr. Bay and I formed a blended family. There was an athletic regimen to be followed, there were ideas to be debated, and there was a nice, unthorny subject—sports—that knitted everything together. I wouldn't forget what had happened down the driveway, but on those nights I built a sort of mental fire escape that I used to avoid it. When I walked off the court a few years later, there was no way I wasn't going to be a sportswriter.

Now a semigrown writer, I'm 100 percent opposed to cheesy sports metaphors. They're lame; they're boring; they're shortcuts. But here goes one. Before the Mavericks play Game 5 of the Finals, I go home to see my mom in the same Fort Worth house. I walk down the driveway, past the spot where my dad died and up to the basketball hoop. The backboard looks worse for the pounding. There is now a long and vicious crack through it, yet it's still standing. And—forgive the metaphor—I look at my old pal and think, That fiberglass backboard is *me*.

Jack McCallum

Before an NBA All-Star Game during the 1990s, someone had told Joe Dumars of the Detroit Pistons that he was the pregame pick of Jack McCallum (b. 1949) in a reporters' pool to be named MVP. So, after chucking up an errant three-point shot, Dumars ran back down court past press row and stage whispered at McCallum, "Hey man, I'm trying." That story illustrates how McCallum, *Sports Illustrated*'s primary NBA voice for more than two decades, became the closest thing sportswriting has had to an embed. He followed Larry Bird's Celtics and Steve Nash's Suns for books on each, with his sanctioned infiltrations winning the trust of players and coaches alike. McCallum joined the *SI* staff in 1981 after working at four different newspapers. "I killed off three of them," he said, referring to the *Bethlehem Globe-Times* in Pennsylvania, the *Baltimore News-American*, and the *Philadelphia Bulletin*, all now defunct. Along the way he picked up a master's in English from Lehigh, and there's felicity in his dissertation topic, Ernest Hemingway, given the demotic style and reportorial chops McCallum brought to the beat, as well as the setting for the magnum opus of his embeddings, the 2012 book *Dream Team*. In it he revisits his time with the U.S. Olympians who cut a swath through Hemingway's expatriate haunts of France and Spain before and during the 1992 Games in Barcelona. In this excerpt, about the team's intrasquad scrimmage in a Monte Carlo gym shortly before the Olympics began, McCallum conveys the essence of the captains who faced each other that day, Michael Jordan and Magic Johnson.

from

Dream Team

"**Y**OU HAVE a tape?" Michael Jordan asks. "Of that game?"

"I do," I say.

"Man, everybody asks me about that game," he says. "It was the most fun I ever had on a basketball court."

It befits the enduring legend of the Dream Team, arguably the most dominant squad ever assembled in any sport, that we're referring not to a real game but to an intrasquad scrimmage in Monaco three days before the start of the 1992 Olympics. The Dreamers played 14 games that summer two decades gone, and their smallest victory margin was 32 points, over a fine Croatia team in the Olympic final. The common matrices of statistical comparison, you see, are simply not relevant in the case of the Dream Team, whose members could be evaluated only when they played each other. The video of that scrimmage, therefore, is the holy grail of basketball.

A perfect storm hit Barcelona in the summer of the Dream Team. Its members were almost exclusively NBA veterans at or near the apex of their individual fame. The world, having been offered only bite-sized nuggets of NBA games, was waiting for them, since Barcelona was the first Olympics in which professional basketball players were allowed to compete. The Dreamers were a star-spangled export from a country that still held primacy around the world.

This debut couldn't have been scripted any better, and when the Dream Team finally released all that star power in a collective effort, the show was better than everyone had thought it would be . . . and everyone had thought it would be pretty damn good. The Dreamers were Johnny Cash at Folsom Prison, the Allman Brothers at the Fillmore East, Santana at Woodstock.

Most of the 12 names (Michael Jordan, Magic Johnson, Larry Bird, Charles Barkley, Scottie Pippen, Karl Malone, Patrick Ewing, David Robinson, John Stockton, Chris Mullin, Clyde Drexler and Christian Laettner) remain familiar to fans two decades later, their cultural relevance still high. It's not just that Danger Mouse and Cee Lo Green christened their hip-hop duo Gnarls Barkley, or that other artists have sung about Johnson (Red Hot Chili Peppers, Kanye West), Pippen (Jay-Z), Malone (the Transplants) and Jordan (impossible to count). Consider this: The name of Stockton, a buttoned-down point guard, is on a 2011 track by Brooklyn rapper Nemo Achida, and the popular video game *NBA 2K12* features Jordan, Magic and Bird on the box cover—not LeBron, Dirk and Derrick.

Yet the written record of that team during the summer of '92 is not particularly large. The Dreamers, like the dinosaurs, walked the earth in a pre-social-media age. Beyond newspaper stories, there are no detailed daily logs of their basketball activities (*Bird shot around today, but his back is sore*) and no enduring exclamations of chance meetings around Barcelona (*OMG, jst met ChazBark at bar & he KISSED me on cheek; hez not rlly fat LOL*). Much of the story is yet to be told, and the scrimmage in Monte Carlo may be the most tantalizing episode of all.

Negotiating for the team to train in the world's most exclusive gambling enclave started, believe it or not, with commissioner David

Stern, who at the time was understood to be fervently antigambling and terrified of betting lines. But he also recognized that a training camp in, say, Fort Wayne, Ind., was not an inducement for players such as Jordan and Magic to buy in. So he began talking to a friend, New York Giants co-owner Robert Tisch, who also owned the showpiece Loews Hotel in Monaco. From there, NBA deputy commissioner Russ Granik and Loews chairman Robert Hausman reached a deal with the principality.

Players, coaches and schlub journalists like me said bravo to the decision. The Dream Team did get in some work during its six days in Monaco, but on balance it was more like a minivacation. The team's daily schedule called for two hours of basketball followed by 22 hours of golf, gambling and gaping at the sights. Nude beaches and models were a three-point shot away, sometimes closer. "I'm not putting in a curfew because I'd have to adhere to it," said coach Chuck Daly, "and Jimmy'z [a noted Monte Carlo nightclub] doesn't open until midnight."

The Dream Team flew into Nice at midnight on July 18 and made a crash landing at the Loews, or Jet Set Central, about 20 miles away. During a security meeting before the team arrived, Henri Lorenzi, the legendary hotel manager, had complained about the number and the aggressiveness of the NBA's security people. "Do you realize who is gambling in my casino right now?" Lorenzi said to the NBA's international liaison, Kim Bohuny. Lorenzi ticked off the names of politicians, movie stars and even tennis immortal Björn Borg. "No one will care that much about this team," he said.

"Well, we'll see," replied Bohuny.

When the team bus pulled up, there was such a rush of fans to see the players that some fans crashed through the glass doors at the entrance. "I get your point," said Lorenzi.

The Loews casino was located in the middle of the hotel, thereby serving as kind of theater-in-the-round when the Dream Teamers were there, the regulars being Jordan, Magic, Barkley, Pippen and Ewing, the same group that had started playing a card game called tonk back at the team's first training camp, in La Jolla, Calif., and would play right through the last night in Barcelona. On one occasion Barkley, feeling like the luckiest blackjack player in the world, hit on a 19; it would be a better ending to the story to say he drew a deuce, but he busted. From time to time Jordan even reserved his own blackjack table and played all five hands.

Each afternoon, after their workout and lunch, a gaggle of players trod through the foot-thick casino carpets in golf shoes, sticks on their backs, bound for the Monte Carlo Golf Club, a 25-minute ride away. The course wasn't a jewel, but it was hilly and commanded wonderful views of the Riviera. One day, after practice, *Newsday* writer Jan Hubbard arranged a foursome with Barkley, Drexler and me. Barkley was at that time unencumbered by the neuropathic-psychosomatic disorder that has come to plague his golf game, which at this writing remains a wretched smorgasbord of tics and stops and twists and turns. He hit the ball far and had a decent short game, though he was subject to lapses in concentration. Drexler, whom Barkley called Long and Wrong, was just learning the game. With a full, aggressive, coiled swing, he routinely hit 300-yard drives, usually 150 out and 150 to the left or right.

Our merry group played nine, then picked up Robinson at the turn. He was fairly new to the game and, in the fashion of a Naval officer who had built televisions with his father as an adolescent, was working on it with consummate dedication. Robinson was as enthusiastic as anyone about being a Dreamer; as the sole returning member of the 1988 U.S. Olympic team, which won only the bronze medal, he was on a redemptive journey. But Robinson was, to a large extent, a loner. "He wasn't driven like myself and most of the other players," Jordan says. And years after Barcelona, Robinson still seemed unable to fully comprehend the thirst-for-blood competitiveness of his teammates. He told me a Jordan story from the first time they met, at a 1988 exhibition game. "I go back to meet Michael because, like everybody else, I'm a big fan, and you know the first thing he says to me? 'I'm going to dunk on you, big fella. I dunked on all the other big fellas, and you're next.'

"And he said it almost every time we played. I'd go back at him: 'Don't even think about it. I will take you out of the air.' And Michael would always promise to get me."

And did he? "Eventually," Robinson said. "It was a two-on-one with him and Scottie. Michael took the shot and I went up to block it, but I didn't get there, and he dunked it and the crowd went crazy. 'Told you I was going to get you one day,' he said. Man, what a competitor. He never forgot anything, never let you get away with *anything*."

By Dream Team time, Robinson had, as he puts it, "been born again in Christ." He didn't drink or swear and was finding it uncomfortable to be around those who did. But a golf course—certainly one with Charles Barkley on it—is a very tough place for a true believer. Our fivesome played on, insults and four-letter words flying. At one point Robinson complained to Hubbard about Drexler's cussing and also wanted Barkley to tone it down. Charles seemed to comply, but then— I believe around the 14th hole—he let loose with another barrage, all of it in good humor but salty. So Robinson shook his head, smiled, picked up his bag and left.

In my mind's eye, I still see Robinson walking off the course on that day. Most athletic teams and most athletic relationships are built on sophomoric humor, insults and d— jokes, all wrapped in testosterone. To stand with your team yet somehow to have the guts to stand alone from time to time . . . now, that takes a particular kind of man.

If the gentleman from Italy—whose name nobody remembers—had it all to do over again, I'm sure he would toss the ball to his fellow referee, assistant coach P. J. Carlesimo, and proceed rapidly to the nearest exit of Stade Louis II, the all-purpose arena in the Fontvieille ward of Monaco. For soon he will become the unluckiest person in town, and that includes all those who are surrendering vast quantities of French francs at the tables.

He tosses the ball up between Ewing and Robinson, and Robinson taps it—on the way up, illegally—toward his own basket. Robinson's teammate on the Blue Team, Duke's Laettner, the only collegiate Dreamer, races the White Team's Pippen for the ball. Take note, for this is the first and last time in history that this sentence will be written: *Laettner beats Pippen to the ball*. Laettner sweeps it behind his back to his Blue teammate Barkley, who catches it, takes a couple of dribbles and knifes between the White Team's Jordan and Bird. Jordan grabs Barkley's wrist, the whistle blows, and Barkley makes the layup.

"Shoot the fouls, shoot the fouls," Chuck Daly yells, sounding like that character in *Goodfellas*, Jimmy Two Times. It's morning and almost no one is in the stands, but Daly is trying to install gamelike conditions because even the best of the best need a kick in the ass from time to time. As Jordan calls for a towel—it is extremely humid in the arena, and almost everyone is sweating off a little alcohol—Barkley makes the free throw.

Magic Johnson's Blue Team 3, Michael Jordan's White Team 0.

And so the Greatest Game Nobody Ever Saw gets under way.

About 12 hours earlier the U.S. had finished an exhibition game against France. It was awful. The players were still getting used to local conditions—meaning the steep fairways at the Monte Carlo Golf Club and the nocturnal bass beat at Jimmy'z—and even the seemingly inexhaustible Jordan was tired after walking 18 holes and arriving back at the Loews not long before the 8:30 p.m. tip-off. The Dream Team was sloppy and allowed France leads of 8–2 and 16–13 before it woke up and went on to win 111–71.

It didn't matter to the fans, though, who had gobbled up the 3,500 available tickets in a 15-minute box-office frenzy. The opposing team's guys, at least half a dozen of whom had brought cameras to the bench, were deemed heroic by dint of being slain. Happiest of all was the French coach, Francis Jordane. "He was very excited because he figured that his last name would give him special entrée to Michael," recalls Terry Lyons, the NBA's head of international public relations. "We took a photo, and sure enough, there is Jordane right next to Jordan, with his arm around him."

By breakfast this morning Daly had decided that his team had better beat itself up a little bit. The Dream Team had scrimmaged several times before this fateful day, a couple of the games ending in a diplomatic tie as Daly refused to allow overtime. He normally tried to divvy up the teams by conference, but on this day Drexler was nursing a minor injury and Stockton was still recovering from a fractured right fibula he had suffered in the Olympic qualifying tournament. Lord only knows how this morning would've gone had Drexler been available. Jordan had already taken it upon himself to torture the Glide in scrimmages, conjuring up the just-completed NBA Finals—in which Jordan's Bulls had beaten Drexler's Trail Blazers in six games—and taunting Drexler, "Stop me this time!"

So with two fewer Western players than Eastern players, and only two true guards (Magic and Jordan), Daly went with Magic, Barkley,

Robinson, Chris Mullin and Laettner on the Blue Team against Jordan, Malone, Ewing, Pippen and Bird on the White.

The gym was all but locked down. The media were allowed in for only the last part of practice. A single cameraman, Pete Skorich, who was Chuck Daly's guy with the Pistons, videotaped the day. It was a closed universe, a secret little world: 10 of the best basketball players in the world going at each other. Daly had a message for them: "All you got now. All you got."

The absence of Drexler means that Magic and Jordan are matched up. "Those two going against each other," Dream Team assistant coach Mike Krzyzewski told me in 2011, "was the pimple being popped."

Jordan dribbles upcourt, and Magic yells, "Let's go, Blue. Pick it up now." This is what Magic has missed since he retired because of his HIV diagnosis in November 1991: the juice he got from leading a team, being the conductor, the voice box, the man from whom all energy flows. A half hour earlier, during leisurely full-court layup drills, Magic had suddenly stopped and flung the ball into the empty seats. "We're here to *practice!*" he yelled. That was his signal that the players were half-assing it, and the day turned on that moment. Magic had promised Daly back in the U.S., "I will see to it that there will be no bad practices."

Bird gets the ball on the right side, guarded by Laettner. With an almost theatrical flourish Bird swings his torso as if to pass to Jordan in the corner. Bird made better use of body fakes than anyone who ever lived, his remedy for a relative lack of quickness. Laettner bites, and Bird is free to drive left into the lane, where he passes to Malone on the left baseline. Malone misses a jumper, Ewing misses an easy tip, and Laettner grabs the rebound.

Magic dribbles upcourt and goes into his Toscanini act, waving both Laettner and Mullin away from the right side and motioning for Barkley to isolate on the block. Bird has him on a switch. "Go to work, CB!" Magic instructs. "Go to work!" Barkley up-fakes Bird but air balls a jumper. Laettner is there for the rebound and lays it in.

Johnson's Blue Team 5, Jordan's White Team 0.

Playing tit for tat at the other end, Malone posts up Barkley on the left side. But the Mailman misses an easy jumper, and

Laettner—player of the game so far—gets the rebound. At the other end Laettner drives baseline on Ewing, who shoulders him out-of-bounds. "Don't force it if we don't have it," says Magic, directing the comment at Laettner.

After the inbounds pass, Magic dribbles into the lane and spins between Jordan and Pippen, a forced drive if there ever was one. (It is incumbent upon Magic's followers to do as he says, not as he does.) The gentleman from Italy blows his whistle, and no one is sure what the call is, including the gentleman from Italy. Bird, a veteran pickup-game strategist, turns to go upcourt, figuring that will sell the call as a travel, but Magic is already demanding a foul. He wins.

"That's a foul?" Jordan asks in his deep baritone.

(Years later I will watch Magic in a pickup game at UCLA, this one without referees, and he will win the foul battle virtually every time, standing around incredulously until he is awarded the ball, and on defense pointedly playing through his own fouls and acting like a petulant child when an infraction is called on him.)

A minute later Barkley bats away Pippen's shovel pass to Ewing and storms pell-mell to the other end. Bird is ahead of him but overruns the play, and Barkley puts in a layup.

Johnson's Blue Team 7, Jordan's White Team 0.

Jordan is now getting serious and calls out, "One, one!" Pippen gets the ball on the right wing, fakes Mullin off his feet and cans a jumper to break the drought for White.

Johnson's Blue Team 7, Jordan's White Team 2.

Mullin, always sneaky, taps the ball away from a driving Jordan, and Barkley again steamrollers downcourt, this time going between Malone and Ewing for another full-court layup, taking his two steps from just inside the foul line with that sixth sense all great players have about exactly when to pick up the dribble. "Foul! Foul!" Barkley hollers, but he doesn't get the call.

Johnson's Blue Team 9, Jordan's White Team 2.

Malone misses another open jumper; Magic rebounds, heads downcourt and yells, "I see you, baby" to an open Mullin. Mullin misses but Barkley rebounds and finds a cutting Laettner, whose shot is swatted away by Ewing. Laettner spreads his arms, looking for the call, soon to be joined by his more influential teammate.

"That's good!" Magic yells, demanding a goaltending violation.

"He didn't call it," says Jordan.

"It's good," Magic says again.

"He didn't call it," says Jordan.

Magic wins again. Goaltending.

Johnson's Blue Team 11, Jordan's White Team 2.

Bird goes right by Laettner and takes an awkward lefthanded shot in the lane that misses. His back is hurting. Laettner has a layup opportunity at the other end off a quick feed by Magic, but Ewing blocks it, a small moment that presages Laettner's NBA career. He isn't springy enough to dunk or physical enough to draw a foul.

"Dunk that s—, Chris," Jordan says. "Dunk that s—." (Years later Jordan will tell me, coldly and matter-of-factly, "Anybody who had Laettner on the team lost. He was the weak link, and everybody went at him.")

Bird misses an open jumper, and Magic goes over Pippen's back to knock the ball out-of-bounds; nevertheless Magic flashes a look of disbelief when the ball is awarded to White. Ewing swishes a jumper.

Johnson's Blue Team 11, Jordan's White Team 4.

Magic drives, a foul is called on Ewing, and Malone, no fan of this Magic-dominated show, is starting to get irritated. "*Sheet!*" he yells at the gentleman from Italy. "Everything ain't a foul!"

His mood is no better seconds later when he gets caught in a Barkley screen, and Mullin is able to backdoor Pippen, get a perfect feed from Magic and score a layup. "Whoo!" Magic yells as he heads back upcourt.

Johnson's Blue Team 13, Jordan's White Team 4.

(Years later Pippen will go on a nice little riff about Mullin's ability to read the game. "Mullie just killed me on backdoors," Pippen says, watching the tape with me. "He wasn't that fast, but he knew just when to make his cut.")

Jordan is now looking to score. He forces a switch off a Ewing screen, takes Robinson outside and launches a three-pointer that bounces off the backboard and into the basket. A lucky shot. Magic calls for the ball immediately—tit for tat—and Jordan retreats, fearing a drive. But Magic stops, launches a jump shot from just outside the three-point line and yells, "Right back at you!" even before it reaches the basket. It goes in.

Johnson's Blue Team 16, Jordan's White Team 7.

There is little doubt that if Jordan played Magic one-on-one, he would drill him, because Magic simply has no way to defend MJ. Magic is bigger but not stronger; he can't jump as high; he's nowhere near as quick; and Jordan's predaceous instincts are unmatched in one-on-one challenges. But this morning it's Magic's one-on-one game against Jordan's. Going one-on-one against Jordan, however, not only is a flawed strategy but also goes against Magic's basketball nature. Johnson is a conciliator. *I'll bring everybody together* is his mantra, just as it was back at Everett High in Lansing, Mich., where the principal used to call upon Magic to settle racial disputes among his fellow students. "You understand the respect I have for Michael," Krzyzewski will say years later, "but one thing about him—he cannot be kind."

Jordan, with the surety of an IRS accountant, is starting to get into the game. He initiates a play from the point, goes through the lane and out to the left corner, gets a pass from Ewing and hits a jumper as Magic arrives too late to stop him. At the other end Magic waits until Barkley sets up on the left low block, and then Magic passes him the ball. Barkley turns around and hits a jumper.

"Take him, Charles, all day," says Magic.

Jordan dribbles slowly downcourt and motions Malone to the right block. Jordan makes the entry pass, and Malone turns and quick shoots over Barkley. Good. Tit for tat.

Johnson's Blue Team 17, Jordan's White Team 11.

Bird air balls a wide-open jumper. He looks 100 years old. White gets the ball back, and Jordan signals that the left side should be cleared for Malone to go against Barkley. The entry pass comes in, and Malone clears space by slapping away Barkley's hand. He turns toward the baseline and, legs splayed, releases a jumper. Good.

"Right back at you," Jordan yells.

Johnson's Blue Team 18, Jordan's White Team 13.

After a couple of futile exchanges, Magic races downcourt and throws a pass ahead to Robinson. "Keep going, David," he hollers, and Robinson obligingly drives to the basket, drawing a foul on Ewing.

"All day long," Magic hollers. "All day long." Then he gets personal. He yells, "The Jordanaires are down."

Jordan is not amused. About halfway through the Greatest Game Nobody Ever Saw, Magic may have sealed his own doom. "Hold the clock!" Jordan hollers, clearly irritated, making sure there is enough time to strike back. Robinson makes one of two.

Johnson's Blue Team 19, Jordan's White Team 13.

A minute later Barkley spins away from Malone on the right block, and Malone is called for a foul. "Called this same f— s— last night," Malone says to the gentleman from Italy, referring to the game against France. "This is *bulls---*!" To add to Malone's frustration, Daly hollers that the White team is over the foul limit.

"One-and-one," says Daly.

"*Yeah!*" Magic yells. "I love it. I *love* it! We ain't in Chicago Stadium anymore." He punctuates the insult with loud clapping.

Throughout his career Jordan has heard complaints that the referees favor him. At a Michael-Magic-Larry photo session, Magic quipped, "You can't get too close to Michael. It's a foul." Jordan is tired of hearing about it, particularly from Magic.

Barkley makes one of two.

Johnson's Blue Team 20, Jordan's White Team 13.

Now amped up, Jordan goes through four defenders for a flying layup, then Pippen steals Mullin's inbounds pass. Jordan misses a jumper, but Pippen rebounds, draws a foul on Mullin and gets an enthusiastic palm slap from Jordan. As Barkley towels himself off from head to toe, Pippen makes both. Perhaps they *are* in Chicago Stadium.

Johnson's Blue Team 20, Jordan's White Team 17.

Bird grabs the rebound off a missed Robinson shot, and Jordan cans a jumper to bring White within one. Magic, still determined to make this a one-on-one contest, spins into the lane and misses badly. Barkley is starting to get irritated at Magic's one-on-one play and will later complain to Jordan and Pippen about it. Jordan races downcourt with Pippen to the left and Ewing to the right. You know where this is headed. Pippen catches the ball and throws down a ferocious lefthanded dunk.

Jordan's White Team 21, Johnson's Blue Team 20.

Mullin drives and draws a reach-in foul on Pippen. "Wasn't that all ball?" says Jordan. Mullin makes one free throw, misses the next.

Jordan drives the lane, and Magic, now visibly tired, gets picked off. Robinson, the help defender, is whistled for a foul. After Jordan misses the first, Magic knocks the ball high in the air—a technical in the NBA, but who cares?—and keeps jawing. "Let's concentrate," hollers Daly, trying to keep everyone's mind on the business at hand.

Jordan makes the second.

Jordan's White Team 22, Johnson's Blue Team 21.

Malone comes down hard on his right ankle after making a layup off an assist from Jordan. His bad mood has grown worse. Malone walks it off—a normal man would've gone for ice—as Pippen and Bird come over to slap palms and Jordan yells, "Way to go, Karl."

Jordan's White Team 24, Johnson's Blue Team 21.

In March 1992, a few months before the Dream Team got together, I asked coaches and general managers around the league this question: If you were starting a team and could take either Malone or Barkley, which one would you select? Malone-Barkley had the ingredients of a Magic-or-Larry debate. Mr. Olympia vs. the Round Mound of Rebound. Mr. Reliable vs. Mr. We Hope He Isn't in a Bar Sending a Drunk Through a Window.

Malone won the poll 15–7. His supporters invariably mentioned his loyal-soldier quality and contrasted it with Barkley's penchant for controversy; Barkley's backers felt there was no substitute for talent and that Charles achieved more with less, having no Stockton in Philadelphia to deliver him the ball. Even considering the full flush of their careers, it's a difficult call. Malone, the second-leading scorer in NBA history, behind Kareem Abdul-Jabbar, averaged 25 points per game, compared with Barkley's 22.1. Barkley outrebounded Malone by 11.7 to 10.1. Both have been accused of folding under pressure, but the big picture reveals that each was an outstanding postseason player with numbers almost identical to his regular-season metrics. Bill Simmons, in *The Book of Basketball*, has Malone and Barkley together in his pantheon of best players, at 18th and 19th respectively.

But there is always the root question in sports: Who was *better*? You have that moment when you can give only one person the ball, and whom would you choose? I'm sure that if players spoke honestly, Jordan would always get the ball. And I'm equally certain that the Barkley-or-Malone nod would go to Barkley. Charles had that ineffable something that Malone didn't have. He wasn't more important to a franchise, he wasn't as dependable, and he wasn't as good over the long haul. He was just . . . *better.*

Of all the Dreamers, though, Laettner came closest to paying Barkley the ultimate compliment. When I casually commented that everyone believed Jordan was the best, Laettner pursed his lips and considered. "I guess," he said, "but by a very, very small margin over Charles."

Now, at the morning game in Monaco, Jordan and Pippen walk up the court together. "He's tired," Jordan says of Barkley. As if to disprove him, Barkley plows into the lane, and Malone is called for a block. Taking a cue from Magic, the Mailman bats the ball high into the air. Seeing a profusely perspiring Barkley at the line, Jordan moves in for the kill. "A man is tired, he usually misses free throws," says Jordan. This is a recurring theme for His Airness. "One-and-one now," says Jordan, wiggling two fingers at Barkley.

Barkley makes the first—"Yeah, Charles, you gonna get your two anyway," sings Magic—but Ewing bats the second off the rim before it has a chance (maybe) to go in.

Bird misses another open jumper but decides to make something of this personal nightmare. As Magic yo-yo dribbles on the left side, Bird suddenly comes off Laettner and steals the ball. He bumps Magic slightly, but even the gentleman from Italy is not going to call that one. As Magic tumbles to the ground, Bird takes off, Barkley in pursuit, *pursuit* used lightly in this case. In fact, *takes off* is used lightly too. Bird fakes a behind-the-back pass to a trailing Jordan, and Barkley takes a man-sized bite at it, his jock now somewhere inside the free throw line. Bird makes the layup. "Way to go, Larry!" Jordan yells. "Way to take him to the hole. I know you got some life in you."

(Years later I watch some of the game with Mullin. When Bird makes this turn-back-the-clock play, Mullin calls to his wife, Liz, "Honey, come here and watch this. Watch what Larry does here." And we run it back a couple of times, Mullin and his wife smiling, delighted by the sight of the Bird they love. A couple of months after that, I remind Jordan of the play. He grows animated. "That's Larry, man, that's Larry," he says. "Making a great play like that. That's Larry Bird.")

Jordan's White Team 26, Johnson's Blue Team 22.

Laettner makes two free throws, and at the other end Jordan feeds Malone for a jumper. Barkley misses a jumper, but Robinson, an aerial acrobat, a giant with a past as a gymnast, leaps high over Ewing and taps the ball in off the board.

Jordan's White Team 28, Johnson's Blue Team 26.

Jordan launches a jumper from the top of the key, outside the three-point line, as Mullin flies out to guard him. "Too late!" Jordan yells.

Jordan's White Team 31, Johnson's Blue Team 26.

Now mostly what you hear is Jordan exhorting his team, sensing the kill. Magic backs into the lane, Malone guarding him on a switch. The gentleman from Italy blows his whistle . . . and the Mailman blows his top. "Oh, come on, man," he yells. "Stop calling this f—— *bullsheet.*" Jordan comes over and steps between Malone and the ref. "Forget it, Karl," says Jordan. "Don't scare him. We might need him."

Magic shoots the first, which rolls around as Jordan, hands on shorts, yells to Ewing, "Knock it out!" Too late. Magic swishes the second.

Jordan's White Team 31, Johnson's Blue Team 28.

Pippen pops out from behind a Ewing screen and swishes a jumper. At the other end, Mullin loses the grip on a Magic pass, and Bird recovers. Jordan begins a break, motions Ewing to join him on the left side and watches in delight as Patrick takes a few pitty-pat steps and makes a jumper.

Jordan's White Team 35, Johnson's Blue Team 28.

Ewing is whistled for a foul on Robinson, who makes both. At the other end Jordan feeds Malone, who draws a foul on Barkley.

"One-and-one?" the Blue team asks.

"Two shots," says Jordan, who has taken over the whistle from Magic. Malone misses both. Robinson grabs the second miss and gives it to Barkley, who steams downcourt and passes to Laettner, who goes up and fails to connect but is fouled by Jordan. *Dunk that s——, Chris.*

"Every time!" yells Magic from the backcourt, desperately trying to regain the verbal momentum. "Every time!"

Laettner, who has been and will remain silent throughout the game, makes both free throws.

Jordan's White Team 35, Johnson's Blue Team 32.

Magic is called for a reach-in, and now he goes after the gentleman from Italy, trailing him across the lane. Magic lines up next to Ewing and pushes his arm away as Ewing leans in to box out on Jordan's free throws. Jordan makes both. Magic is steaming.

At the other end the gentleman from Italy calls an inexplicable moving screen on Robinson, which delights Jordan. "My man," he yells, clapping his hands. "My man, my man, my man." *We might need him.*

"Chicago Stadium," Magic yells. Malone backs Barkley down, and the whistle blows, and now it's Barkley attacking the gentleman from Italy. "Come on, man!" he yells. "That was clean!" For a moment it appears as if Barkley might strike him. Malone makes one of two.

Jordan's White Team 38, Johnson's Blue Team 32.

Laettner makes a weird twisting layup. On the sideline Daly is beginning to pace, hoping this thing will come to an end before a fistfight breaks out or one of his players assaults the gentleman from Italy. As Robinson lines up to shoot a free throw, Jordan and Magic begin jawing again. "All they did was move Bulls Stadium right here," Magic says. "That's all they did. That's *all* they did."

"Hey, it is the '90s," Jordan says, reaching for a towel.

Robinson makes both.

Jordan's White Team 38, Johnson's Blue Team 36.

Jordan dribbles out front, running down the shot clock, pissing off Magic all the while. Finally he drives left, goes up for a jumper and draws a foul on Laettner. Before Jordan shoots, Magic moves in for a few words. They are not altogether pleasant. Jordan makes the first. Magic keeps jawing. Jordan takes the ball from the gentleman from Italy, slaps him on the rump and says, "Good man." He makes the second.

Daly watches in relief as the clock hits 0:00. He waves his hands in a shooting motion at both baskets, the sign for players to do their postpractice routine, ending the Greatest Game Nobody Ever Saw.

Jordan's White Team 40, Johnson's Blue Team 36.

Except that it isn't over. Not really.

"Way to work, White," Jordan yells, rubbing it in. He paces up and down, wiping himself with a towel, emperor of all he sees, as Magic, Barkley and Laettner disconsolately shoot free throws.

"It was all about Michael Jordan," says Magic. "That's all it was."
It's no joke. Magic is angry.

Jordan continues to pace the sideline. He grabs a cup of Gatorade and sings, "Sometimes I dream. . . ." Jordan has recently signed a multimillion-dollar deal to endorse Gatorade, and the ads feature a song inspired by "I Wan'na Be like You," the Monkey Song in the animated film *The Jungle Book*. The Gatorade version's lyrics are:

Sometimes I dream / That he is me / You've got to see that's how I dream to be / I dream I move, I dream I groove / Like Mike / If I could be like Mike.

As Magic looks on in this sticky-hot gym, sweat pouring off his body, towel around his neck, there is Jordan, captain of the winning team, singing a song written just for him, drinking a drink that's raking in millions, rubbing it in as only Jordan can do. And on the bus back to the hotel? Jordan keeps singing, *Be like Mike. . . . Be like Mike. . . .*

The game would have reverberations in Barcelona as Michael and Magic relentlessly continued to try to get the verbal edge on each other. And in the years that followed, this intrasquad game became a part of basketball lore, "kind of like an urban legend," as Laettner describes it.

And not everybody loved it. "You have to look at who relishes that kind of thing," says Malone. "As they say, it's their *geeeg*." By *their* he means Jordan's and Magic's. (Last year I asked Malone if he wanted to watch a few minutes of the video. "No," he said. "Doesn't interest me.")

But Krzyzewski, no fan of trash talk, looks back on the game fondly, remembering almost every detail. "Every once in a while I'll be doing something and a line from that game will just flash into my head," he says. "*They just moved Chicago Stadium to Monte Carlo.*" It just makes me smile.

"A lot of players talk trash because the TV cameras are on. But the doors on that day were *closed*. This was just you against me. *This is what I got—whatta you got?* It taught me a lot about accepting personal challenges. You know, if somebody could've taped the sound track of the game, not necessarily recorded the basketball but just the sounds, it would be priceless."

Well, I got the original VHS tape, converted it to DVD and even got a specialist to make a CD of the sound track. It picked up almost everything. The Greatest Game Nobody Ever Saw was not about the hoops. It was about the passion those guys put into playing, the importance they placed on winning and on personal pride.

Years later Jordan brought up the game before I had a chance to ask him about it. "In many ways," he said, "it was the best game I was ever in. Because the gym was locked and it was just about basketball. You saw a lot about players' DNA, how much some guys want to win. Magic was mad about it for two days."

Magic, for his part, estimates that his anger lasted only a few hours. "Let me tell you something—it would've been worse for everybody if he lost," says Johnson. "Because I could let something go after a while. But Michael? He'd never let it go. He never let *anything* go."

Brian Doyle

The work of Oregon-based writer Brian Doyle (1956–2017) can be found in award-winning fiction, essays, and poetry, and has appeared in anthologies he edited as well as in the pages of *Portland*, the magazine of the University of Portland, which under his direction won a Sibley Award in 2005 as the best college publication in the U.S. In all that he did, Doyle faithfully paid tribute to the liege lord of story. "Stories swim by the millions," he said, "and most of being a writer is listening and seeing and then madly scribbling." Drawing on compassion, humor, gratitude, and a valent spirituality, Doyle connected with a legion of faithful readers, many of whom contributed to a crowdfunding account to cover medical expenses after he was diagnosed with the brain tumor that led to his death. In 2012 he wrote about driving his older brother Kevin around the Chicago suburb where Kevin then taught college, "to tell a story that sings of my brother and all brothers and grace and courage and hoops and pain and laughter and attentiveness and love and loss," Doyle said, after this account of that afternoon, "His Last Game," was chosen for the 2013 edition of *The Best American Essays*. Doyle's piece features insights that anyone who has played pickup basketball will recognize. But the filmmaker Avery Rimer, who turned "His Last Game" into a ten-minute short of the same name, used her director's statement to point out how the author also nests in just a few pages much larger truths—"about the teasingly feisty and protectively tender ways that men express deep love; about how splendid life is if you can develop . . . the capacity to see what is sacred and magical in the day-to-day 'little things'; and about how our own memories can live on in those who really love us."

His Last Game

W E WERE supposed to be driving to the pharmacy for his prescriptions, but he said just drive around for a while, my prescriptions aren't going anywhere without me, so we just drove around. We drove around the edges of the college where he had worked and we saw a blue heron in a field of stubble, which is not something you see every day, and we stopped for a while to see if the heron was fishing for mice or snakes, on which we bet a dollar, me taking mice and him taking snakes, but the heron glared at us and refused to work under scrutiny, so we drove on.

We drove through the arboretum checking on the groves of ash and oak and willow trees, which were still where they were last time we looked, and then we checked on the wood duck boxes in the pond, which still seemed sturdy and did not feature ravenous weasels that we noticed, and then we saw a kestrel hanging in the crisp air like a tiny helicopter, but as soon as we bet mouse or snake the kestrel vanished, probably for religious reasons, said my brother, probably a *lot* of kestrels are adamant that gambling is immoral, but we are just *not* as informed as we should be about kestrels.

We drove deeper into the city and I asked him why we were driving this direction, and he said I am looking for something that when I see it you will know what I am looking for, which made me grin, because he knew and I knew that I would indeed know, because we have been brothers for 50 years, and brothers have many languages, some of which are physical, like broken noses and fingers and teeth and punching each other when you want to say I love you but don't know how to say that right, and some of them are laughter, and some of them are roaring and spitting, and some of them are weeping in the bathroom, and some of them we don't have words for yet.

By now it was almost evening, and just as I turned on the car's running lights I saw what it was he was looking for, which was a basketball game in a park. I laughed and he laughed and I parked the car. There were six guys on the court, and to their credit they were playing full court. Five of the guys looked to be in their twenties, and they were fit and muscled, and one of them wore a porkpie hat. The sixth guy was much older, but he was that kind of older ballplayer who is comfortable with his age and he knew where to be and what not to try.

We watched for a while and didn't say anything but both of us noticed that one of the young guys was not as good as he thought he was, and one was better than he knew he was, and one was flashy but essentially useless, and the guy with the porkpie hat was a worker, setting picks, boxing out, whipping outlet passes, banging the boards not only on defense but on offense, which is much harder. The fifth young guy was one of those guys who ran up and down yelling and waving for the ball, which he never got. This guy was supposed to be covering the older guy but he didn't bother, and the older guy gently made him pay for his inattention, scoring occasionally on backdoor cuts and shots from the corners on which he was so alone he could have opened a circus and sold tickets, as my brother said.

The older man grew visibly weary as we watched, and my brother said he's got one last basket in him, and I said I bet a dollar it's a shot from the corner, and my brother said no, he doesn't even have the gas for that, he'll snake the kid somehow, you watch, and just then the older man, who was bent over holding the hems of his shorts like he was exhausted, suddenly cut to the basket, caught a bounce pass, and scored, and the game ended, maybe because the park lights didn't go on even though the street lights did.

On the way home my brother and I passed the heron in the field of stubble again, and the heron stopped work again and glared at us until we turned the corner.

That is one *withering* glare, said my brother. That's a ballplayer glare if ever I saw one. That's the glare a guy gives another guy when the guy you were supposed to be covering scores on a backdoor cut and you thought your guy was ancient and near death but it turns out he snaked you good and you are an idiot. *I* know that glare. You owe me a dollar. We better go get my prescriptions. They are not going to do any good but we better get them anyway so they don't go to waste. One less thing for my family to do afterwards. That game was good but the heron was even better. I think the prescriptions are pointless now but we already paid for them so we might as well get them. They'll just get thrown out if we don't pick them up. That was a good last game, though. I'll remember the old guy, sure, but the kid with the hat banging the boards, that was cool. You hardly ever see a guy with a porkpie hat hammering the boards.

There's so much to love, my brother added. All the little things. Remember shooting baskets at night and the only way you could tell if the shot went in was the sound of the net? Remember the time we cut the fingertips off our gloves so we could shoot on icy days and dad was so angry he lost his voice and he was supposed to give a speech and had to gargle and mom laughed so hard we thought she was going to pee? Remember that? I remember that. What happens to what I remember? You remember it for me, okay? You remember the way that heron glared at us like he would kick our ass except he was working. And you remember that old man snaking that kid. *Stupid kid*, you could say, but that's the obvious thing. The *beautiful* thing is the little thing that the old guy knew full well he wasn't going to cut around picks and drift out into the corner again, that would burn his last gallon of gas, not to mention he would have to hoist up a shot from way out there, so he snakes the kid beautiful, he knows the kid thinks he's old, and the guy with the hat sees him cut, and gets him the ball on a dime, that's a beautiful thing because it's little, and we saw it and we knew what it meant. You remember that for me. You owe me a dollar.

Lee Jenkins

Through the 1980s, as the NBA started to pull itself out of a lengthy funk, Commissioner David Stern made a habit of namechecking the players responsible for the league's turnaround. If he didn't specifically mention Magic Johnson, Larry Bird, and Michael Jordan, he usually took care to refer to "the NBA and its players" with such fastidiousness that the phrase all but spawned an acronym in its own right—the NBAAIP. Soon enough, fans began to see the league as a collection of those personalities, which in turn led reporters to lash themselves to the names featured on marquees and in shoe commercials. No one brought this approach into the twenty-first century more stylishly than *Sports Illustrated*'s Lee Jenkins (b. 1977). A graduate of Vanderbilt, where he studied on a Grantland Rice Sportswriting Scholarship, he left *The New York Times* in 2007 to join *SI*. There he cultivated relationships with top players and, critically, several orbitals' worth of people around them. When it came time to file—be it a straight profile, a trend story, or a forensic inquiry into a critical moment in some playoff game—Jenkins would deliver a piece as exhaustively reported as it was gracefully told, conveying the burdens and glories of being an NBA star without voyeurism or fawning. Steph Curry, Russell Westbrook, and Kevin Durant are among the players he attached himself to, but he plumbed no one deeper than LeBron James, whose selection as the magazine's 2012 Sportsman of the Year occasioned this piece. It includes a striking opening scene in which Jenkins captures the polar emotions James experienced as he made his way from Cleveland to Miami and his first NBA title.

The King:
LeBron James, Sportsman of the Year 2012

P AT RILEY stood in the mouth of the tunnel at Boston's TD Garden, between the court and the locker room, and waited for the Boat. That's what he calls LeBron James—"You know," Riley explains, "best of all time"—an acronym he conjured to remind the planet's preeminent basketball player of frontiers still to be conquered. "Hey, Boat," Riley will say. "How is the Boat doing today?" James will reflexively laugh and shake his head because he is not the Boat, at least not yet. But on that sweaty night at the Garden, in Game 6 of the Eastern Conference finals, facing yet another summer cast as the villain foiled, he delivered one of the Boat performances in NBA history.

The image of James throughout the game, bent at the waist, staring skyward with pupils pushed to his eyelids, recalled predators of different breeds. "He was primal," Riley says. "He was a cobra, a leopard, a tiger hunched over his kill."

After James had unleashed 45 points, snatched 15 rebounds and sucked all the juice from an expectant crowd, he marched toward Riley, the Heat president who lured him to South Beach two years ago with his six sparkling rings. He was just a few steps from Riley when a 20-something man perched above the tunnel poured what remained of his beer through a net canopy, dousing James's head and jersey. While a national television audience recoiled, Riley was transported back to the 1980s, when he coached the Lakers and rabble-rousers at the old Garden rocked their buses, spit in their faces and once shoved his mother-in-law over a railing.

"I'm a Catholic, and I was an altar boy, so I say my prayers at night and I believe someone up there is taking care of us," Riley begins. "From where I was standing, there was a backlight on LeBron from the arena, and as the [beer] pellets sprayed up in the air, they looked like they were forming a halo over him. This is what I saw: The good Lord was saying, 'LeBron, I'm going to help you through this night because you're a nice person, and I'm going to give you 45 and 15. But as you walk off, I'm going to humble the heck out of you.' And, you know what, that's the best thing that could have happened."

It was the story of his life. James could log 47 flawless minutes, or win 60 regular-season games, or spend seven years as a one-man stimulus package for a hard-bitten Rust Belt city and still end up with a beer in the face. We forgive our favorite athletes many imperfections and foibles, but James was held to a higher standard. He was too strong, too fast, too blessed to stumble, especially in the fourth quarter of a playoff game. "I'm in a different place than other people," he says. "That's O.K. I understand. I was chosen for this. It's my gift. It's my responsibility."

When James was nine, he played running back for a Pop Warner team in his hometown of Akron called the East Dragons, and he scored 18 touchdowns in six games. "That's when I first knew I had talent," he says. When he was a freshman at St. Vincent–St. Mary High, a basketball coach confided in friends that the best player of all time was on his roster. When he was a sophomore, a local newspaper dubbed him King James, and never again did he play in front of a gym that wasn't jammed.

James is a sucker for underdogs—"I love Arian Foster, from the Houston Texans," he says, "because he didn't get drafted, he played on the practice squad, and now he's probably the best running back in the NFL"—knowing full well he will never be one himself. He will never win in an upset, never know what it feels like to overachieve. He assumes the most unsustainable position in sports, the eternal front-runner, and he kept coming up short at the finish. But after each colossal disappointment, while the talking heads returned their attention to Tim Tebow or whatever topic du jour gooses the ratings, James wiped the beer from his chin and resumed his discovery. "In every adversity there is a seed of equivalent benefit," Riley says, and the Boat finds it. When James lost in the Finals in 2007, with the Cavaliers, he remade his jump shot. When he fell again in 2011, with the Heat, he built a post game. James was born with supernatural ability, but he lets none of it lie dormant. He extracts every ounce, through a distillation process created and refined by failure.

"The game is a house, and some players only have one or two windows in their house because they can't absorb any more light," says Mike Krzyzewski, head coach of Team USA. "When I met LeBron, he only had a few windows, but then he learned how beautiful the game can be, so he put more windows in. Now he sees the damn game so well, it's like he lives in a glass building. He has entered a state of mastery. There's nothing he can't do. God gave him a lot but he is using everything. He's one of the unique sports figures of all time, really, and he's right in that area where it's all come together." A voracious mind has caught up with a supreme body. The marriage is a marvel.

"It gets no better for a basketball player," says Heat guard Dwyane Wade of the year James just completed: NBA champion, NBA MVP, Finals MVP, Olympic gold medalist, hardwood revolutionary. Call him the best point guard in the league, or the best power forward, or both, or neither. "He has no position," says an NBA scout. "His position is to do whatever he wants. There's never been anything like it. You just give him the ball and you win the game." Defend James with bigger players and he pulls them out to the three-point line so he can breeze past them. Try smaller, more nimble players and he backs them all the way into the basket stanchion. The formula sounds simple, for a Mack truck with a Ferrari engine, but only now has it come into focus.

And so, less than 29 months after he sat on a stage at a Boys & Girls Club in Greenwich, Conn., and incurred a nation's wrath, LeBron James is the Sportsman of the Year. He is not the Sportsman of 2010, when he announced his decision to leave Cleveland in a misguided television special, or 2011, when he paid dearly for his lapse in judgment. He is the Sportsman of 2012. "Did I think an award like this was possible two years ago?" James says. "No, I did not. I thought I would be helping a lot of kids and raise $3 million by going on TV and saying, 'Hey, I want to play for the Miami Heat.' But it affected far more people than I imagined. I know it wasn't on the level of an injury or an addiction, but it was something I had to recover from. I had to become a better person, a better player, a better father, a better friend, a better mentor and a better leader. I've changed, and I think people have started to understand who I really am."

He muted his on-court celebrations. He cut the jokes in film sessions. He threw heaps of dirt over the tired notion that he froze in the clutch. "He got rid of the bulls—," says one of his former coaches, and he quietly hoped the public would notice. When James strides into an opposing arena, he takes in the crowd, gazes up at the expressions on the faces. "I can tell the difference between 2010 and 2012," he says. Anger has turned to appreciation, perhaps grudging, but appreciation nonetheless. James has become an entry on a bucket list, a spectacle you have to see at least once, whether you crave the violence of sports or the grace, the force or the finesse. He attracts the casual fan with his ferocious dunks and the junkie with his sublime pocket passes. He is a Hollywood blockbuster with art-house appeal.

In this, the 28th and best year of his life, James came to peace with his power. He still considers himself the spindly guard bounding into the gym at St. Vincent–St. Mary for his first practice—"a 6-foot, 170-pound skinny-ass kid who played like a wizard," remembers his friend, business manager and former high school teammate, Maverick Carter—which is hard to believe when sitting next to him. James fills every room, even a 20,000-seat palace, not only with his size but also his presence. Like a classic heavyweight, his might makes him seem larger than his 6'8", 250-pound frame.

"People tell me how big I am, but I don't see it," James insists. "I just remember that little freshman, taking the ball off the backboard and running. I'm a perimeter guy." Moving into the paint represented more than a new role. It demanded a new identity. "Imagine you have studied your whole life to be something, and you wake up one day and say, 'I have to change,'" James says. "You never forget what you studied. It's embedded in you. But now it's time to study something else. It's like reading two books at the same time."

He has morphed from the most imposing small forward in the league to the most dynamic all-around threat in the history of the league. The switch is both psychological and strategic, and he did not make it alone. The day after the Heat lost to Dallas in the 2011 Finals, coach Erik Spoelstra gathered his assistants at American Airlines Arena and told them, "We have to open our minds and develop a system where LeBron James is the best player in the world every single night."

Dating back almost to the inception of the franchise, Miami constructed its offense around a dominant big man because Riley had always seemed to have one: Kareem Abdul-Jabbar with the Lakers, Patrick Ewing with the Knicks, Alonzo Mourning and Shaquille O'Neal with the Heat. When the club signed James, coaches treated him as a premier wing within a traditional offense. "We tried to put an unconventional player in a conventional system," Spoelstra says. He scolds himself for it.

But in the summer of 2011, Spoelstra and his staff designed an attack as unique as the megastar it features. "Whether LeBron is inside or outside, everything revolves around him," says Heat assistant coach David Fizdale. "He can be the power big or the power guard. It doesn't matter. He's positionless." James is the sun, with sharpshooters spread around him like planets, providing space to post up or drive and dish. Spoelstra rarely has to call a play. In close games James brings the ball up the floor, hands it off, races to the block and gets it right back, simultaneously the point guard and the power forward. He could probably score 50 points a night, but he still can't bring himself to shoot over double teams, so he feeds whoever has been left alone.

Fizdale sighs as he discusses the 2011 Finals, when the Heat clogged the paint with two traditional big men, forcing James to the perimeter. "All those jumpers he missed were as much our fault as his," Fizdale says. "He had to be great in spite of what we were doing. Now he has an avenue to be great because of what we're doing."

Shortly after James completed that first Pop Warner football season with the East Dragons, when he scored those 18 touchdowns, he went to the library at Harris Elementary School in Akron and started checking out books on famous athletes. "How amazing would it be if I made it into one of these?" he told himself. He watched ESPN Classic and grew mesmerized by Oscar Robertson, who saw the floor as if it were in another dimension. By the time James reached St. Vincent–St. Mary, he was uncorking no-look passes and sensing plays before they happened.

Peers often describe James as "a beast," and even though they mean to flatter him, the label dismisses the depths to which he comprehends the game. He can deconstruct the top eight players on every NBA team and many college teams. He can run every set in the Heat playbook from all five positions. In film sessions he sometimes completes Spoelstra's sentences, and at the Olympics, many of Team USA's defensive strategies were suggestions from James in practice. "He's not smart," says Krzyzewski. "He's brilliant. And I don't like to use that word."

In Cleveland, James would crack jokes during meetings because he already knew what the coaches were trying to teach. "It was like the kid in school who can doodle and throw spitballs but still get A's," Jent says. Because James was the Cavaliers' best player, others followed his example, though they did not grasp the material as easily. James couldn't understand, when games began, why they kept blowing assignments. "I expect everyone to be on the same wavelength, and that's a problem I'm still working on," he says. "If I see something and it doesn't happen the way I envision, I can get frustrated."

When James is grabbing a rare rest on the Heat bench, he usually sits next to second-year guard Terrel Harris, narrating the action so a young player can see the game through his eyes. During a mid-November game in Denver, Ray Allen was dribbling upcourt and Rashard Lewis was streaking down the left side. James inched forward in his seat and started yelling, "Rashard, it's coming to you! Get ready to shoot!" Allen raced around a pick-and-roll with Bosh and threw the ball to the corner, where an expectant Lewis caught it and drilled the three-pointer. "How did you know that was going to happen?" Harris asked.

The standard scouting report given to Heat players before games is two pages. The one James receives is four, filled with the kind of advanced stats reserved for coaches, bloggers and Shane Battier. "I want to know that this guy drives left 70% of the time, or pulls up when he drives right, or likes to cross over after two dribbles," James says. Even when he is with friends, he'll geek out in the middle of casual conversation: "Remember when I drove and kicked to Ray at the four-minute mark in the second quarter. If he'd have drifted into the corner, we'd have had a better shot." Then, after a pause: "So what are you guys getting into tonight?"

"He'll be talking about a player and tell you, 'If you post up on the left side and drive middle, he'll foul you every time,'" Carter says. "Everybody sees the dunks and the 35 points, but it's no accident. Carmelo Anthony is the same size. J.R. Smith can jump just as high. Dwight Howard is as good an athlete. It's his thought process that separates him."

The Heat stages intricate shooting games after practice, with as many as eight participants, and James keeps all the scores in his head. One of the games is a free throw contest called 21, in which a player receives one point for a make, gets two for a swish and subtracts one for a miss. When James wins, which is rare, he rejoices before the others have even calculated the outcome. "It's a little like *A Beautiful Mind*," says Battier, a Miami forward. "He has a quasiphotographic memory that allows him to process data very quickly. Usually, the überathletic guys who are so much more physically gifted than everybody else don't give much credence to the mental side of the game. Dwyane, for instance, has no time for this. He couldn't care less about numbers. He goes out, imposes his will, and that's great. It's made him a Hall of Famer. But LeBron is looking for every edge."

James grew up on Galley Boy burgers at Swensons Drive In, an Akron staple, but he no longer eats red meat or pork. He naps for two hours on game days. He arrives at the arena early, just after Allen, and takes the court with Fizdale. He has to make five three-pointers from the right corner, the right wing, the top of the circle, the left wing and the left corner. Then he must sink 10 long jumpers from the same spots inside the arc, and six more off the dribble, three going right and three left. Afterward, James heads into the post, and Fizdale feeds him until he has drained 10 face-up jumpers and 10 baby hooks or fadeaways. Finally, Fizdale positions himself as a defender, and James lets loose his entire repertoire.

Only then does he retreat to his meticulously organized locker and clear his mind of the details running through it. Many players function at the same speed all the time. James, constantly searching for mismatches, shifts back and forth from reading to reacting. His brain can bog him down. "Sometimes I overanalyze things, overthink things," he says. "It can get in my way." He slips on his headphones, turns up the hip-hop and finds his attack mode.

Harris Elemetary School, the three-story brick building in North Hill where James used to play basketball with custodians before class, has been shuttered. SWAT teams use the halls for practice, and bullet casings litter the hardwood floors. James went to third grade at Harris and stayed for fourth, but he missed 80 days that year because he and his mother kept moving. Akron is filled with children growing up just as James did. Eighty-four percent of the city's public elementary school students live in poverty. James tried to help with his annual Bikeathon. Once a summer, for five years, he passed out AK-Rowdy bikes to 300 underprivileged kids and then rode with them through the streets. He even established a bike kitchen downtown where the kids could go for free repairs. "But that was it," says Michele Campbell, executive director of the LeBron James Family Foundation. "It was one and done."

As a spokesman for State Farm's 26 Second Initiative, James learned that a student drops out of high school every 26 seconds, and he asked Campbell what they could do. Studies show that children come to the first major fork in their educational road around third grade. "There is a lot of research that tells us where kids are at third grade in terms of reading level [indicates] where they will be at 30," says David James, superintendent of Akron public schools. In April 2011, LeBron introduced Wheels for Education, and his foundation contacted every incoming third-grader in the Akron public school system deemed at-risk. They all received an invitation from "Mr. LeBron" to join his new program. "I was the same as them," James says. "I could have gone either way."

Last year 300 third-graders across 30 elementary schools signed up. This year 216 followed. To become Wheels for Education members, the students must complete a two-week "fall camp," and at the end James returns to Akron and gives each of them an AK-Rowdy bike. He also makes them recite "The Promise," which they shout in high-pitched voices as if it were the Pledge of Allegiance. "I promise: To go to school. To do all of my homework. To listen to my teachers because they will help me learn. To ask questions and find answers. To never give up, no matter what. To always try my best. To be helpful and respectful to others. To live a healthy life by eating right and being active. To make good choices for myself. To have fun. And above all else, to finish school!" In return James promises to be a positive role model and help where he can.

Every student in the Akron public schools is required to wear a collared shirt. James's students wear shirts emblazoned with a crown over the words THE LEBRON JAMES FAMILY FOUNDATION. "I PROMISE." They wear socks with a crown logo. If they stay home for a few days, they may wake up to this voice-mail message: "Hi, it's LeBron. Your teachers and friends are missing you at school. As soon as you feel better, get back in school and get back in the game." If they ace a few assignments, they may hear this: "Hey, it's LeBron. I heard you were a superstar at school this week. You are keeping our promise, and I am so proud of you. Keep up the great work at school."

In addition to the six recorded messages, James posts weekly on a Wheels for Education website and sends letters to the kids every month or so. "I read a lot of books this summer," he wrote in August. "I love to read. Reading is important because it helps us learn new things. Even though I am not in school anymore, I still read books." He shares book recommendations from his fiancée, Savannah, and their sons, LeBron Jr. and Bryce. Last spring James flew six standouts from Rankin Elementary School to Miami for the presentation of his MVP Award.

James's students attend their regular schools during the day and are then encouraged to participate in Akron After School, which runs from 2:30 to 5:30 p.m. at their respective campuses and includes one hour of reading or math instruction with a second hour of an elective: Theater, ballet, poetry, ceramics and journalism are a few of the options. Desiree Bolden, who runs Akron After School, recalls the first time she met with Campbell about Wheels for Education. "She asked if I had a wish list," Bolden says, "and I've never been asked that before." Bolden lamented the lack of technology in her classrooms. Three months later James donated 1,000 Hewlett-Packard laptops.

On the Monday before Thanksgiving, 14 of James's students were sitting on the floor in the library at Mason Community Learning Center, reading with Austin Qualls. A senior at Akron's Firestone High, Qualls plans to enlist in the Navy next summer, but first he is serving as one of 19 Wheels for Education ambassadors. "I'm not doing this because LeBron is a basketball player," Qualls says. "I don't even watch a lot of basketball. I recognize him more for his fatherly side."

Of the 14 Wheels for Education students at Mason, only a handful come from homes with both biological parents, according to the school principal, Stephanie Churn. "These are children who are not used to having anyone in their corner," Churn says. "A lot of them have nothing to look forward to. Some of them come here for food. But they know they're LeBron's kids. That colors every single day of their lives. I realize he's a basketball hero to a lot of people, but to them he's a guardian angel. They understand what he expects of them, and they're not about to let him down." As Mason third-grader Amyah Hodoh puts it: "LeBron wants us to get to college someday, so that's what we're trying to do."

The preliminary report of Kent State researchers, who are tracking the group's progress, found that James's students averaged 14.7 absences last year, compared with 18.9 for their peers in the district. Even after the Wheels for Education kids pass third grade, they remain in the program. They will be monitored by James and his staff until they graduate from high school. The first commencement ceremony will be in 2021.

James spends his free time like a typical 27-year-old American male. He watches League Pass and Sunday Ticket, mid-major basketball games and small-college football games, all on the big-screen TV in his den in Miami or the 30 big-screen TVs that are fused together in his basement in Akron. He grins when *SportsCenter* comes on and he is part of the championship montage that precedes the show.

If James is impressed by a player, no matter the level, he fires off a tweet. "The next thing you know," says Mims, "we'll go into the city

where the kid lives, and he'll be there. LeBron just took care of it."
James never had an NBA mentor, so he is counseling a generation.
He holds annual basketball camps, and four years ago at the LeBron
James King's Academy in Akron, he was struck by a fourth-grader with
a wicked crossover named Amelia Motz. "I think it's because I was a
pretty good white girl," Motz says, "and I didn't ask him for anything."
She kept returning to the camp, and two summers ago James told her
to keep in touch. She texted him when she received her first college
letter, from Pitt, and he showed up last season to one of her games at
Canton's Jackson Middle School.

At the time, Motz was deciding whether to stay at Jackson for high
school or go to St. Vincent–St. Mary, LeBron's alma mater, and James
shot with her the next day. "People were pulling me in a thousand
directions, and he just told me to do what felt best for me," Motz says.
"It's not about who he is but what he has to offer as a friend. He's like
a big brother." When she turned 14 in July, James took her and her
mother to Red Lobster for dinner. Motz is now a freshman guard at St.
Vincent–St. Mary, 5′9″ with a long brown ponytail, and feeling guilty
because she recently won a starting spot after the regular point guard
tore her ACL. "Last week I talked to LeBron about it," Motz says. "I
want to earn everything I get, and I was worried I didn't deserve it.
He told me someone had to step in, and I put myself in position to
do that."

James is a natural leader, but it is one area in which he can still
grow. He provides support and encouragement, but the greats push
lesser teammates to higher places, without ever losing faith in them
when they fall short. "If you want to be the Boat, you have to continue
to win, and to do that you have to bring other players with you," Riley
says. "He's a leader vocally and by example, but I see his frustration
when we lose to good competition. Sometimes the players who helped
win a championship one year aren't the same the next year. He has to
make sure those guys are in it mentally all the time. He has to be the
leader they trust and whatever he says goes."

James listens to linebacker Ray Lewis exhort the Ravens before
games. He ignores the fire and brimstone, focusing on the message.
"There's always a message," James says. "He's never just yelling."
Miami has appeared disengaged defensively so far this season, ranking
20th in points allowed after finishing fourth in the same category last

year. During a game against the Clippers in November, James stood on the right wing between Chris Paul and Blake Griffin. As they passed the ball back and forth, James shuffled from Griffin to Paul and back again, arms flailing by his sides. He chirped, "Ball! Ball! Ball!" the way coaches ask players to do in practice. He was demonstrating the energy and activity needed from his teammates. When Griffin finally made a move to the basket, James rushed over and blocked his shot with both hands.

Everyone told him he would feel unchained this season, the championship burden lifted, but he is still waiting for that sensation to take hold. "I know there is someone, somewhere, trying to take my spot," James says. "And I know where he is too. He's in Oklahoma. He's my inspiration because I see the direction he's headed, and it's the same direction I'm headed. I know his mind-set, and he knows mine. It's a collision course. We're driving one another." He is referring, of course, to Kevin Durant. They talk on the phone every week, friends and enemies, Magic Johnson and Larry Bird for a new era. "What's important to LeBron is what happens when he is facing KD again, or whoever it is in the Finals," Riley says. "[LeBron] needs that player to look back at him and think, This son of a bitch is too big, too strong, and his will is too great."

On the ninth day of a 10-day pre-Thanksgiving road trip, James sat by the pool on the second floor of the Ritz-Carlton in Phoenix, feeling ill. The Heat had arrived at the hotel that morning at three, and on the flight from Denver, James and Wade killed time watching a video from their rookie season, called *Dunks! Vol. 2*. They marveled at how young they looked nine years ago and how high they jumped. "It seemed like a whole life ago," Wade says. "LeBron was more athletic then, but he's a way better player now. He's another person."

As veterans age, they find it more difficult to recover from travel. James was queasy. He didn't know if he could play the next night against the Suns. As he sipped chamomile tea, he was asked what drives him in the middle of November, at the end of a long trip, against a forgotten team in a faraway city. The Finals, and a potential rematch with Durant, were more than six months away.

James tugged on his Heat cap. In 28 hours he would take the court with a nasty flu. Up by four in the final minute, he would grab a rebound, push the ball down the right wing and dribble once between his legs and again behind his back. Using a screen from Bosh, he would drive to his left and spin back to his right before feathering a layup just over the outstretched hand of 6'11" center Marcin Gortat. The Heat would win, and James would score 20 points or more for the 32nd consecutive game. Even some Suns fans would applaud.

But at the pool he craved a day off. "I've been fortunate to have packed houses every night I go on the floor," James said. "I understand they're coming to watch the Suns tomorrow, but they're also coming to watch us and watch me, and I want people to appreciate how I play. I don't want them to leave disappointed. No matter if you've got a Suns jersey or a Heat jersey, I feel like you're here to see me. So once the lights turn on and the fans come in and the popcorn starts popping, I'll be ready to go. However much I have, I'll use it. I just think about that one guy, coming to one game, who called the radio station, and he was the fifth caller and they said, 'Number 5 caller, you've won two tickets to see the Miami Heat! Go crazy!'

"I'll be damned if I'm going to let him down."

Zach Lowe

A typical dispatch from ESPN.com's Zach Lowe (b. 1977) comes with illuminating graphs, GIFs, and YouTube clips. But Lowe will add much more to those bells and whistles, thanks to a sophisticated understanding of strategy and advanced statistics, and a willingness to set his laptop aside and actually speak with NBA players, coaches, and executives. All this he mixes and serves in a conversational blogger's voice. "Lowe's prose is clear, but it isn't dry," wrote Josh Levin of *Slate* in a 2016 piece making the case for Lowe as America's best sportswriter. "His writing crackles with a kind of conspiratorial glee, like he can't wait to share all the cool stuff he's just figured out." A longtime follower of such numbers-friendly digital journalists as Rob Neyer on baseball and John Hollinger on the NBA, Lowe left a staff job at *The American Lawyer* in 2009 for gigs first with *Celtics Hub* of ESPN's True Hoop network and then with SI.com. At *Grantland* he found his multimediated stride, with duties that included a lively podcasting voice; after ESPN folded the site and parted ways with founder Bill Simmons, the mothership enthusiastically took him in. Before all that, Lowe had spent four years on the police beat at the *Stamford Advocate* in Connecticut, practicing the kind of shoe-leather reporting that served him well around the NBA. Once you've dealt with the families of murder suspects and talked to drug dealers, he said, "NBA players or Gregg Popovich aren't really that scary to talk to." What follows isn't a typical Zach Lowe piece. For that, these pages would have to be web-enabled and made of pixels. But this account of the dissolution of bonds to his favorite team does help explain the evolution in sensibility that led Lowe to become an honest broker on the beat—the writer devoted to conveying what the numbers, the videotape, and his sources all had to say.

The Life and Death of Fandom

A SURPRISING thing happened in the Lowe household Sunday night—something exciting, unnerving, and that served as a useful reminder about the nature of bias and sports.

The boss of this site calls me Spock sometimes. It's intended, I hope, as praise for my ability to dispassionately analyze NBA basketball—to search for the root of what happened on the court without being distracted by the emotion of "liking" or "hating" either of the teams involved. A wise man once told me that an NBA game, separated from the noise and the shouting narratives, is a public text waiting for deconstruction. The truth is in there.

But there is something sad about the Spock nickname, which, thankfully, has not caught on. (Spock is boring, right? I've never seen an episode of *Star Trek*.) It is Bill Simmons's way of lamenting the loss of my fandom, and all the joy and heartache fandom brings. Fandom is a tricky thing. It raises the emotional ceiling, and lowers the emotional floor, in the experience of any sporting event. A sportswriter would never experience Game 6 of last year's Finals the same way a Heat fan would, provided said Heat fan actually stuck with the game until the end. To us, the 30 NBA teams are just large corporations consisting of lots of people performing various jobs. Many of those people will move from one corporation to the other, blurring the lines between the 30 teams.

Different organizations prioritize different things, and behave in different ways, but they're all made up of people who enjoy NBA basketball. You get along with some of those people, and have less in common with others—just like life outside the NBA bubble.

Funny thing: I grew up a Boston fan, just like the boss of this site. And that's not hard to find out, either. It's not a secret. But somewhere in the course of transitioning into the life of an NBA writer, my fandom died. I can't pinpoint the exact date, but I know it happened between the 2010 Finals and the start of the 2011 season—the period in which I made that professional shift.

I cared deeply about the 2010 Finals, when the Lakers beat the Celtics in an ugly and brutal Game 7. My then-girlfriend intentionally left New York City the morning of Game 7, ostensibly to visit her sister in Philadelphia, but really, I think, to vacate the premises in case of an emotional crisis. I watched the game alone, the best way to watch a game about which you care deeply. It's better if no one is around to see the pacing, or hear the expletives fly. The degree of caring is embarrassing. The one exception I made during that playoff run: Game 6 of the conference finals against Orlando, which I watched at a famous Boston-backing New York bar with a few friends. The Celtics had lost two consecutive games after opening a 3–0 lead in the series, and with a potential Game 7 in Orlando, I figured alcohol would have to be involved either way—celebration in case of a win, wallowing if the game ended with Boston on the precipice of the worst collapse in NBA history.

My sister texted me at halftime of Game 7 of the Finals, when the wheezing Celtics were up by six, saying that I must have been so happy they were about to win the championship. I didn't respond. I am still angry about that text. How could she not understand how much time was left in the game, and the way the basketball gods would react to such hubris?

Flash-forward a year: The new Heat, allegedly the most hateable team in the league, was wiping out the Celtics in the conference semi-finals, and I didn't care. It was my job by that point to analyze what was happening, and that job is all-encompassing. There is no moral outrage when Dwyane Wade gets tangled up with Rajon Rondo, injuring Rondo's elbow and affecting a series Boston wasn't going to win anyway. There is just a search for truth: Did Wade really do anything on purpose? Did the refs miss a call? What is the trickle-down effect of any Rondo injury? What do the numbers say?

Last year's playoffs represented the finality of fandom's death within me. Five or 10 years ago, a Boston–New York series would have overwhelmed every other aspect of my life. I grew up in Fairfield County, Connecticut, right next to New York City, and in my formative sporting years, the Celtics entered the post-Bird decline phase, while the Pat Riley–era Knicks were ascendant. All my friends were Knicks fans.

It was unbearable. I bet my eighth-grade English teacher on the outcome of the 1990 first-round series between the two teams, a best-of-five series Boston lost after going up 2–0. I think we bet $5. I'm not sure he accepted my money, but I was angry at him for weeks after that series, and generally for several consecutive years as the Celtics transformed into one of the league's most depressing franchises. The Knicks were really good. All I could do was take pleasure in the fact that they never won the title. I won a lot of money betting on Chicago against my Knicks fan friends in the 1993 Eastern Conference finals, and I got years of mileage out of "Smith stuffed!" 2-for-18, and the Reggie Miller choke sign.

I hated the Knicks. And yet last season, during the first round, I almost found myself rooting for them out of selfish journalistic reasons. I had been high on those Knicks all season, often referring to them as the second-best team in the Eastern Conference in writing and on podcasts with Simmons. I loved the way they played, jacking 3s around Carmelo Anthony at power forward, and the matchup with the always-big Pacers in the next round would be far more intriguing than watching Indiana grind a punchless Boston offense to dust. I also live in New York City, and being able to attend playoff games without traveling is a nice perk.

I caught myself several times during that series: The Knicks were playing the Celtics, and zero emotion registered in my body. I wasn't happy about it, or sad. It was just part of life now. Every NBA writer has his or her favorite teams, and some writers are quite public about their present and past loyalties. But fandom, for me, was just an artifact of a past life. And if I'm being honest, it was almost something I'd come to attach a negative meaning to. Hard-core fans were the ones calling me nasty names on Twitter, or proposing crazy, cap-violating trades in which their favorite team gave up nothing of meaning and received a superstar player. Growing detached from the fan experience is healthy for an objective writer, but it's also dangerous. It creates barriers.

And then this Sunday happened. I realized around 5:30 p.m. that I was planning my entire day, all the errands and game-watching, around the absolute necessity of being in front of the television by 6:30. The Boston–Brooklyn game was starting then, and the Celtics were going to honor Kevin Garnett and Paul Pierce.

Garnett wasn't super-relevant. I love his game, and genuinely believe that in his prime, Garnett might have been the greatest defender ever to play in the modern NBA. I learned a ton just from watching how he moved around the floor; he was my Twitter avatar for years. But he's an ornery, unknowable sort, and while he was the best player on the only Boston championship team since 1986, he was a Celtic for just a half-decade.

Pierce, apparently, is the only thing in existence that can rekindle my fandom. Boston and Miami played a shockingly competitive conference finals in 2012, the sort of series that hooks any fan: An aging underdog with no apparent chance of actually winning summons the extra little bit of guts, or magic, or moxie, or whatever makes a champion, and comes within one game of an impossible Finals appearance. (Let's ignore the fact that Chris Bosh was injured for the first half of that series, or that Oklahoma City's athleticism would have drowned Boston in the Finals.)

And yet, there was only one moment in that seven-game bloodbath that snapped me out of "cold journalist" mode and forced an involuntary yip and fist-pump from my body.

That was it. The rest didn't move me out of Spock mode. I broke down the tape to analyze just how a bad Boston offense was blowing away a good Miami defense, and as LeBron blew past Brandon Bass for basket after basket late in Game 7, I logged on to Synergy to start watching film of regular-season games between Miami and Oklahoma City. Garnett and Ray Allen were heading into free agency, and as the game ended, Doc Rivers hugged all his star players and fought back tears. It was the end of an era, it appeared, but it no longer had any emotional pull on me. But there is something different about Pierce. Paul Pierce apparently means something to me, which is ridiculous. He's just a taller person who plays basketball—a complete stranger.

We are almost the exact same age, which explains some of how this kind of fandom works. You watch him grow as a player, coming to know all his little quirks, but also tracking his progress as a professional human being. He, at first, provided some hope for a franchise that went too long without any real progress, peaking in 2002, when Pierce and Antoine Walker dragged a mediocre team into the conference finals against New Jersey. That series included the defining moment of the Pierce/Walker era—the massive comeback at home in Game 3. He even survived a horrific nightclub attack.

The development sort of stalled out after that. The next half-decade featured some highs, including a couple of memorable Pierce playoff moments against Indiana, but the team never won more than 45 games until the arrival of Garnett and Allen. Pierce became a bit ballhoggy and arrogant as the team around him deteriorated. He looked like a petulant child getting tossed at the end of an undecided elimination game in 2005 against Indiana, and even more petulant after the game, when he appeared at the podium wearing medical tape to treat a phony jaw injury.

He allegedly flashed gang signs. He became the symbol of American basketball decay during the 2002 World Championships, when Pierce scored a ton but alienated the coaching staff with selfish play, poor defense, and a negative attitude. He was just sort of lost there for a while. So are a lot of twentysomethings, which is why I found Pierce's journey relatable. I've always been drawn to imperfect athletes. Every athlete is imperfect, obviously. But some are "perfect" in the ways we crave from warriors standing upon the pedestals we create. They are selfless and team-first, fearless in crunch time, willing to play through any injury without complaining. They'll miss some big shots and make some big mistakes, but they will neither show nor admit weakness.

Those guys are boring. You can't see yourself in them. I grew attached to guys who had flaws by that standard, and owned up to them. It made me like Tracy McGrady more when he admitted how much pain he was in due to a gazillion injuries, and that the pain affected his play. It should be OK to say, "I'm scared." Chris Webber had me the moment he called that infamous timeout and wept afterward. Pedro Martinez could be amazingly immature when a team roughed him up, even throwing at Jorge Posada in the 2003 playoffs simply because the Yankees were hitting him. He threw a tantrum, and safety issues aside, I enjoyed it. Ditto for his declaration that the Yankees were his "daddy," a stunning admission of vulnerability for a star athlete.

Pierce was struggling to find himself, and that was cool. I was too. I was a wannabe journalist who didn't have the guts to pursue the career path, so I hopped around in random directions—from teaching high school, to chasing a PhD in history, to covering high school football in Virginia just to see how it felt.

Pierce eventually grew up, a process that started the year before Danny Ainge snared Garnett and Allen. He became a very good defender, rounded out his game, and won the Finals MVP in 2008. The results were impressive, but they were more rewarding because of the journey he had taken to get there. It somehow felt as if we had shared that journey.

I honestly don't feel anything whether the Celtics win or lose. They are just another NBA team. That's in part because my dad has lost touch with the NBA these days. He's from New Hampshire, a life-long Boston fan, and the reason I picked the team in the first place. You can never really sever that connection. I mean, I imitated Kevin McHale's post moves, minus the hairy armpits, in my backyard, and was such a nervous little fan that I felt relief when Houston upset the Lakers in the 1986 conference finals. I didn't know anything about those cracked-out Rockets. I just knew the Lakers scared me, and that

I wanted Boston to win. I'll always feel some generalized affection for the green team. But that's not the same as being a fan.

Pierce is a different story. It's wild seeing him at Nets games now, warming up two feet away from me, greeting the Brooklyn executives on the sideline as I chat them up. HOLY CRAP, THAT'S PAUL PIERCE, SORT OF SMILING IN MY VAGUE DIRECTION.

It's a useful reminder: There is some fandom in all of us, even if it's dead or dormant. You have to work to check your biases, while also remembering that regular people aren't working to check their own. They're just having fun. Part of me misses being able to do that, and feel that.

Which is why I really cherished, in a way that surprised me, the Pierce tribute on Sunday night. I wanted that thing to last half an hour. It was fun to be a fan again, even for just 90 seconds.

Rowan Ricardo Phillips

Rowan Ricardo Phillips (b. 1974) grew up in New York City in a family of Antiguan immigrants. In addition to writing poetry, for which he has been widely honored, he served as a Guggenheim Fellow; worked as a translator, literary essayist, and art critic; and taught at Princeton, Harvard, Columbia, NYU, and Stony Brook. Along the way he also began to write about sports: soccer for publications ranging from *The New Republic* to *Howler*, and regularly about basketball for the website of *The Paris Review*, where this 2015 piece about the Golden State Warriors and Steph Curry appeared. "I don't have to write about basketball, but I want to write about it," Phillips shared with readers upon introducing himself as the man on *TPR*'s most unlikely beat. "I'm magnetized by something irreducibly pure at the core of the game." Along with a grasp of strategy and tactics that allows him to form sophisticated judgments about basketball, he has a New Yorker's willingness to advance them with confidence. Full-time sportswriters struggled to describe what Curry and the Warriors achieved during their sublime run through the late 2010s. In this lean and allusive piece, Phillips draws on the powers of a poet to make sense of the sensibility of the Dubs and the Everyman who led them.

Days of Wine and Curry

For Jake Leland

WHEN NINA SIMONE first sings the title of "Feeling Good," her voice has been alone for thirty-nine seconds. The solitary singer: there's always something fiat lux about it. Resolute, the individual moves through the void. You know the accompaniment is coming, but the voice, all by itself, makes you care about it: form turns into feeling.

This is how the artist passes on her exuberance. You're affected by her immediate present, implicated in her future, and interested in her past. This is how the strut between you two starts: "and I'm feeling good."

The instruments come to life right after Simone sings those words, as though her voice has just confirmed that the coast is clear—a new dawn, a new day, a new life—the brass begins with those gravel-and-booze notes down low, the piano like morning birdsong, light and constant, up top. The world is being made, and you feel good enough to sing as if you yourself were making it. And maybe you are: the experience heats up, the experience becomes porous, and you don't know anymore where you end and it begins. Is she feeling good? Am I feeling good? Am I being told to feel good? We're feeling good.

And this is where we are with the Golden State Warriors—feeling good. They're 23–0, the best start to a season in NBA history; they're seven wins away from the longest streak the league has ever seen; they're the reigning champions. We've seen phenomena like this before—the 1969–1970 Knicks, the 1971–1972 Lakers, the 1995–1996 Bulls, the 2012–2013 Miami Heat—but these were teams that engaged in different ways, using templates that were widely understood to bring success: a stifling defense, a dominant big man, a stockpiling of superstar players. Those Bulls and Heat, in particular, were when-the-going-gets-tough-the-tough-crushes-your-soul teams. The Bulls were an aging, bitter collection of legends who cut through the league like Sherman cut through the South; the Heat of a few years ago wasted their time trying to figure out if they wanted to be the heroes or the villains of the league.

But the Warriors—they play like, well, like they're feeling good. There's a refreshing absence of internal struggle, a looseness that pundits would condemn as unpreparedness if the Warriors hadn't just won a championship. When you watch this team play, you're watching something that's broken from its tether. It makes no sense. Yes, the high pick-and-roll pace-and-space elements from Mike D'Antoni's offense are there. But the Warriors play elite defense; D'Antoni's teams played little defense at all. And where D'Antoni's offense put the point guard at the center of its universe, the Warriors run something like a dark-matter offense: Curry may be the main ball handler, but anyone can initiate the attack. The center of the universe is wherever the ball is. They run inverted stuff, like ball screens for their center set by their MVP point guard. And while it's in vogue to deploy a deep shooting power forward, the "stretch four," the Warriors have abandoned that notion in favor of a playmaking four. They keep Draymond Green constantly moving, constantly altering his responsibilities in the offense—instead of merely stretching defenses, the Warriors implode them. The rest of the league has yet to catch on; they still extol the stretch four like priests extolling Ptolemy. You see the gob-smacked faces of the Warriors' opponents, of those opponents' coaches and fans. They haven't seen this before. They don't know what to do.

When you watch Steph Curry play these days, it's pretty obvious that he's feeling good. If you played basketball growing up, you learn the importance of follow-through when you shoot: forming the goose-neck, waving good-bye to the ball, reaching into the far off hoop like it's a cookie jar—think Michael Jordan's last shot as a Bull. Curry's way, and I mean *way*, past that. He's to the point where he's putting the ball up like he's getting rid of a bomb. He sometimes looks like he's just throwing the ball up. Then there are the finger rolls, scoop shots and teardrops with either hand. He's rising up from twenty-five feet out and skedaddling back to the other end of the court as soon as the ball leaves his hand. And I wasn't trying to dig into the word-crate when I wrote *skedaddle*: it's the only word that captures what he does as soon as the ball leaves his hand. You can't give him any space at all to shoot, but if you don't give him any space to shoot he'll absolutely embarrass you off the bounce . . . no matter who you are. He's given up on simply blowing past defenders who crowd him—he likes to lead them quick around the court in small figure eights, giving them the impression that they're sticking with him until the rug gets pulled out from under them. The guy is beyond on fire. He's gone full on Super Saiyan.

The NBA is a league of peacocking strutters with their signature celebrations for when a shot goes in. Curry is no stranger to celebra-tion, but his looks unintended, as if some other body has taken over his own, which is exactly what happens when you're feeling good on the court. You become muscle memory from head to toe. It barely lasts. You feel like you can't miss, and this is where the infamous "heat check" comes in. You can't miss. So you start taking shots you know should miss. You test the limits of being hot, of feeling good. Twenty-five feet out. Thirty feet out. Without looking at the rim. Quick-firing after dribbling between the legs four times. The heat check. The search for the end of the streak. No one really wants to be hot forever.

Steph Curry, at the moment, is on an endless heat check. Some-where within the euphoria of his feats is a trace of sadness. He's in a strange quantum all his own, where time and space barely obtain. Any shooter can tell you, things aren't supposed to be this way. Not for the pros. Jimmer Fredette played like Steph Curry in college just a few years ago and he isn't even in the NBA. Plenty of players have been Steph Curry in a high school game or messing around at Rucker Park. But shooters always get found out, always emerge as types: the spot shooter who waits for an opening, the gunner who comes off the bench for an offensive spark, the pick-and-roll point guard who knows just when to let his deadly shot fly, the blacktop legend who just couldn't break through. These limits define the game—and shooters, especially, are supposed to be bound by the ruthlessness of space-time. But Curry has decided to ignore it all. It's not that he's breaking the system, it's that he's a broken system. You can see it in how he loosens his neck and shoulders constantly, how he chews on his mouth guard, the mellow glaze in his gaze during a stoppage of play. It's as though he's missing something. You know how he feels. You don't know how he feels. I know how you feel.

David Shields

An essayist and humorist, but as much as anything an ironist, University of Washington professor David Shields (b. 1956) is known in the world of literary criticism for his provocations, including a belief that barriers between genres should be torn down. Over the years he has also ducked in and out of sports, particularly basketball. The book from which this essay comes, *Other People: Takes and Mistakes*, is one of twenty to Shields's name, a body of work that includes *Black Planet: Facing Race During an NBA Season* (1999); *Body Politic: The Great American Sports Machine* (2004); and his first, the 1984 novel *Heroes*, about the relationship between a middle-aged sportswriter and a basketball star in a midwestern college town. Early in that book, the first-person narrator recalls shooting hoops as a third-grader: "I remember dusk and macadam combining into the sensation that the world was dying, but I was indestructible." Twenty books later Shields reprises that very sentence— first uttered by his fictional Al Biederman of the *River City Register*—for the opening paragraph of this essay, "Life Is Not a Playground." Shields has been noodling with his material for a long time; another theme at play here, mortality, was the subject of his 2008 *New York Times* best seller *The Thing About Life Is That One Day You'll Be Dead*. This piece by a wannabe Warrior might be regarded as a corrective to the can-you-top-this conjurings of Steph Curry, the Bay Area star celebrated in the previous selection. (Curry seemed to fire the world not with death, but with life, and did so where bright lights and hardwood combine.) But as bittersweet as this meditation is, Shields lets the reader down gently. Perhaps it's his way of reminding us that what we call an essay is based on the French word *essai*, or attempt, and that life is much the same thing—that is, a shot taken.

Life Is Not a Playground

THERE HAS always been some strange connection for me between basketball and the dark. I started shooting hoops after school in fourth grade, and I remember dusk and macadam combining into the sensation that the world was dying, but I was indestructible.

One afternoon I played H-O-R-S-E with a third grader, Renée Hahn, who threw the ball over the fence and said, "I don't want to play with you anymore. You're too good. I'll bet one day you're going to be a San Francisco Warrior."

Renée had a way of moving her body like a boy but still like a girl, too, and that game of H-O-R-S-E is one of the happiest memories of my childhood: dribbling around in the dark but knowing by instinct where the basket was; not being able to see her but smelling her sweat; keeping close to her voice, in which I could hear her love for me and my future life as a Warrior opening up into the night. I remember the sloped half-court at the far end of the playground, its orange pole, orange rim, and wooden green backboard, the chain net clanging in the wind, the sand on the court, the overhanging eucalyptus trees, the fence the ball bounced over into the street, and the bench the girls sat on, watching, trying to look bored.

The first two weeks of summer Renée and I went steady, but we broke up when I didn't risk rescuing her in a game of Capture the Flag, so she wasn't around for my tenth birthday. I begged my parents to let Ethan Saunders, Jim Morrow, Bradley Gamble, and me shoot baskets by ourselves all night at the court across the street. My mother and father reluctantly agreed, and my father swung by every few hours to make sure we were safe and bring more Coke, more birthday cake, more candy.

Near midnight, Bradley and I were playing two-on-two against Jim and Ethan. The moon was falling. We had a lot of sugar in our blood, and all of us were totally zonked and totally wired. With the score tied at eighteen in a game to twenty, I took a very long shot from the deepest corner. Before the ball had even left my hand, Bradley said, "Way to hit."

I was a good shooter because it was the only thing I ever did and I did it all the time, but even for me such a shot was doubtful. Still, Bradley knew and I knew and Jim and Ethan knew, too, and we knew the way we knew our own names or the batting averages of the Giants' starting lineup or the lifelines in our palms. I felt it in my legs and up my spine, which arched as I fell back. My fingers tingled and my hand squeezed the night in joyful follow-through. We knew the shot was perfect, and when we heard the ball (a birthday present from my parents) whip through the net, we heard it as something we had already known for at least a second. What happened in that second during which we knew? Did the world stop? Did my soul ascend a couple of notches? What happens to ESP, to such keen eyesight? What did we have then, anyway, radar? When did we have to start working so hard to hear our own hearts?

As members of the Borel Junior High Bobcats, we worked out in a tiny gym with loose buckets and slippery linoleum and butcher-paper posters exhorting us on. I remember late practices full of wind sprints and tipping drills. One day the coach said, "Okay, gang, let me show you how we're gonna run picks for Dave."

My friends ran around the court, passing, cutting, and screening for me. All for me. Set plays for me to shoot from the top of the circle or the left corner—my favorite spots. It felt as if the whole world were weaving to protect me, then release me, and the only thing I had to do was pop my jumper. Afterward, we went to a little market down the street. I bought paper bags of penny candy for everybody, to make sure they didn't think I was going to get conceited.

The junior varsity played immediately after the varsity. At the end of the third quarter of the varsity game, all of us on the JV, wearing our good sweaters, good shoes, and only ties, would leave the gym to go change for our game. I loved leaving right when the varsity game was getting interesting; I loved everyone seeing us as a group, me belonging to that group, and everyone wishing us luck; I loved being part of the crowd and breaking away from the crowd to go play. And then when I was playing, I knew the spectators were out there, but they slid into the distance like the overhead lights.

As a freshman I was the JV's designated shooter, our gunner whenever we faced a zone. Long-distance shooting was a way for me to perform the most immaculate feat in basketball, to stay outside where no one could hurt me. I'd hit two or three in a row, force the other team out of its zone, and then sit down. I wasn't a creator. I couldn't beat anyone off the dribble, but I could shoot. Give me a step, some space, and a screen—a lot to ask for—and I was money in the bank.

The JV coach told me I had to learn to take the ball to the basket and mix it up with the big guys underneath. I didn't want to because I knew I couldn't. I already feared I was a full step slow.

That summer I played basketball. I don't mean that I got in some games when I wasn't working at A&W or that I tried to play a couple of hours every afternoon. I mean the summer of 1971 I played basketball. Period. Nothing else. Nothing else even close to something else. All day long that summer, all summer, all night until at least ten.

The high school court was protected by a bank of ice plants and the walls of the school. Kelly-green rims, with chain nets, were attached to half-moon boards that were kind only to real shooters. The court was on a grassy hill overlooking the street; when I envision Eden, I think of that court during that summer—shirts against skins, five-on-five, running the break.

Alone, I did drills outlined in an instructional book. A certain number of free throws and lay-ins from both sides and with each hand, hook shots, set shots from all over, turnaround jumpers, jumpers off the move and off the pass, tip-ins. Everything endlessly repeated. I wanted my shoulders to become as high hung as Warriors star Nate Thurmond's, my wrists as taut, my glare as merciless. After a while I'd feel as if my head were the rim and my body were the ball. I was trying to put my body completely inside my head. The basketball was shot by itself. At that point I'd call it quits, keeping the feeling.

My father would tell me, "Basketball isn't just shooting. You've got to learn the rest of the game." He set up garbage cans around the court that I had to shuffle-step through, then backpedal through, then dribble through with my right hand, left hand, between my legs, behind my back. On the dead run I had to throw the ball off a banked gutter so that it came back to me as a perfect pass for a layup—the rest of the game, or so I gathered.

Toward the end of my sophomore year—Mother's Day, actually—I went to the beach with my mother. After a while she dozed off, so I walked along the shore until I was invited to join a game of Tackle the Guy with the Ball. After I scored three times, several of the other guys ganged up to tackle the guy with the ball (me) and down I went. Suddenly my left leg was tickling my right ear, the water was lapping at my legs, and a crowd of a hundred people gathered around me to speculate as to whether I was permanently paralyzed.

The summer between my junior and senior years of high school, my father tried to work with me to get back my wind and speed after the long layoff due to my broken leg, but he gave up when it became obvious my heart wasn't in it. I realized I was now better at describing basketball and analyzing it than playing it. To my father's deep disappointment, I not only was not going to become a professional athlete; I was becoming, as he had been on and off throughout his life and always quite happily, a sportswriter. I was pitiless on our mediocre team and the coach called me *Ace*, as in "ace reporter," since I certainly wasn't his star ballhawk. I could still shoot when left open but couldn't guard anyone quick or shake someone who hounded me tough. I fell into the role of the guy with all the answers and explanations, the well-informed benchwarmer who knew how zones were supposed to work but had nothing to contribute on the floor himself.

That same summer, I went to the San Mateo County Fair with Renée Hahn, who had finally forgiven me for not rescuing her in Capture the Flag. Her knowledge of basketball hadn't increased greatly over the years, but she did know she wanted a pink panda hanging from a hook near the basketball toss.

The free-throw line was eighteen rather than fifteen feet away, and the ball must have been pumped to double its pressure, hard as a bike tire. My shot had to be dead on or it would bounce way off. I wasn't going to get any soft rolls out of this carnival. The rim was rickety, bent upward, and was probably closer to ten feet six inches than the regulation ten feet. A canopy overhung both sides of the rim, so I wasn't able to put any arc on my shot. With people elbowing me in back, I could hardly take a dribble to get in rhythm.

I won seven pandas. I got into a groove, and sometimes when I got into a groove from eighteen feet straighatway, I couldn't come out of it. Standing among spilled paper cups and September heat and ice and screaming barkers and glass bottles and darts and bumper cars, Renée and I handed out panda bears to the next half-dozen kids who walked by. This struck me then, as it does now, as pretty much the culmination of existence: doing something well and having someone admire it, then getting to give away prizes together. Renée wound up working with me on the school paper that fall; I don't think I ever saw her happier than she was that afternoon.

I still like to roam new neighborhoods, checking out the courts. In Cranston, Rhode Island, there's a metal ring that looks like hanging equipment for your worst enemy. In Amherst, Virginia, a huge washtub is nailed to a tree at the edge of a farm. Rims without nets, without backboards, without courts, with just gravel and grass underfoot. One basket in West Branch, Iowa, has a white net blowing in the breeze and an orange shooter's square on the half-moon board. Backboards are made from every possible material and tacked to anything that stands still in a storm. Rims are set at every height, at the most cockeyed angles, and draped with nets woven out of everything from wire to lingerie. From Port Jervis, New York, to Medford, Oregon, every type and shape of post, court, board, and hoop.

I once felt joy in being alive and I felt this mainly when I was playing basketball and I rarely if ever feel that joy anymore and it's my own damn fault and that's life. Too bad.

Sources and Acknowledgments

Great care has been taken to locate and acknowledge all owners of copyrighted material included in this book. If any such owner has inadvertently been omitted, acknowledgment will gladly be made in future printings.

The editor would like to thank the following people for their assistance in preparing this volume: Henry Abbott, Bruce Anderson, Alex Belth, Flinder Boyd, Karen Carpenter, Santiago Colas, Aram Goudsouzian, Jack Hamilton, Mark Heisler, Jan Hubbard, Jay Jennings, Richard Johnson, Stefanie Kaufman, Michael MacCambridge, William Meiners, Joe Mitch, Josh Robbins, Sam Smith, Glenn Stout, and Matt Zeysing.

Kareem Abdul-Jabbar, from *A Season on the Reservation*, Kareem Abdul-Jabbar and Stephen Singular, *A Season on the Reservation* (New York: William Morrow, 2000). Copyright © 2000 by Kareem Abdul-Jabbar and Stephen Singular. Reprinted by permission of HarperCollins Publishers.

Pete Axthelm, from *The City Game* (New York: Harper's Magazine Press, 1970). Copyright © 1970 by Pete Axthelm. Reprinted by permission of SLL/Sterling Lord Literistic, Inc.

Douglas Bauer, Girls Win, Boys Lose. *Sports Illustrated*, March 6, 1978. Copyright © 1978 by Douglas Bauer. Reprinted by permission of the author.

Roy Blount, Jr., 47 Years a Shot-Freak. *Sports Illustrated*, April 20, 1970. Copyright © 1970 by Roy Blount, Jr. Reprinted by permission of *Sports Illustrated*.

David Bradley, The Autumn of the Age of Jabbar. *Esquire*, March 1984. Copyright © 1984 by David Bradley. Reprinted by permission of the author.

Jimmy Breslin, The Coach Who Couldn't Shoot Straight. *Sport*, December 1972. Copyright © 1972 by Jimmy Breslin. Reprinted by permission of the Estate of Jimmy Breslin.

Stanley Cohen, from *The Game They Played* (New York: Farrar, Straus and Giroux, 1977). Copyright © 1977 by Stanley Cohen. Reprinted by permission of the author.

Pat Conroy, from *My Losing Season* (New York: Nan A. Talese, 2002). Copyright © 2002 by Pat Conroy. Reprinted by permission of Doubleday, an imprint of the Knopf Doubleday Publishing Group, a division of Penguin Random House LLC, and the Random House Group Ltd. All rights reserved.

Bryan Curtis, The Fiberglass Backboard. *Grantland*, June 29, 2011. Copyright © 2011 by Bryan Curtis. Reprinted by permission of ESPN, Inc. and the author.

Frank Deford, The Rabbit Hunter. *I'm Just Getting Started: The Best of Frank Deford* (Chicago: Triumph Books, 2000). Originally published in *Sports Illustrated*, January 26, 1981. Copyright © 1981 by Frank Deford. Reprinted by permission of *Sports Illustrated*.

George Dohrmann, from *Play Their Hearts Out: A Coach, His Star Recruit, and the Youth Basketball Machine* (New York: Ballantine, 2010). Copyright © 2010 by George Dohrmann. Reprinted by permission of Ballantine Books, an imprint of Random House, a division of Penguin Random House LLC. All rights reserved.

Brian Doyle, His Last Game. *Notre Dame Magazine*, Autumn 2012. Copyright © 2012 by Brian Doyle. Reprinted by permission of the author.

FreeDarko, from *The Macrophenomenal Basketball Almanac* (New York: Bloomsbury, 2008). Copyright © 2008 by FreeDarko High Council. Reprinted by permission of Bloomsbury Publishing, Inc.

Darcy Frey, from *The Last Shot* (Boston: Houghton Mifflin, 1994). Copyright © 1994 by Darcy Frey. Reprinted by permission of Houghton Mifflin Harcourt Publishing Company. All rights reserved.

Peter Goldman, Requiem for a Globetrotter. *Sport*, November 1977. Copyright © 1977 by Peter Goldman. Reprinted by permission of the author.

David Halberstam, from *The Breaks of the Game* (New York: Knopf, 1981). Copyright © 1981 by David Halberstam. Reprinted by permission of the Estate of David Halberstam. All rights reserved.

Donald Hall, Basketball: The Purest Sport of Bodies. *Fathers Playing Catch with Sons* (San Francisco: Farrar, North Point Press, 1985). Copyright © 1985 by Donald Hall. Reprinted by permission of Farrar, Straus and Giroux.

Mark Jacobson, The Passion of Doctor J. *Teenage Hipster in the Modern World* (New York: Black Cat, 2005). Copyright © 2005 by Mark Jacobson. Reprinted by permission of Grove/Atlantic, Inc. Any third party use of this material, outside of this publication, is prohibited.

Lee Jenkins, The King: LeBron James, Sportsman of the Year 2012. *Sports Illustrated*, December 10, 2012. Copyright © 2012 by Lee Jenkins. Reprinted by permission of *Sports Illustrated*.

Dave Kindred, Pete Maravich. *Heroes, Fools & Other Dreamers* (Atlanta: Longstreet Press, 1988). Copyright © 1988 by Dave Kindred. Reprinted by permission of the author.

Melissa King, It's All in the Game. *Chicago Reader*, September 10, 1998. Copyright © 1998 by Melissa King. Reprinted by permission of the author.

Curry Kirkpatrick, Memories. *Sports Illustrated*, March 31, 1986. Copyright © 1986 by Curry Kirkpatrick. Reprinted by permission of *Sports Illustrated*.

Bill Russell and Taylor Branch, from *Second Wind* (New York: Random House, 1979). Copyright © 1979 by Bill Russell and Taylor Branch. Reprinted by permission of the author.

Bob Ryan and Terry Pluto, from *Forty-Eight Minutes: A Night in the Life of the NBA* (New York: Macmillan, 1987). Copyright © 1987 by Bob Ryan and Terry Pluto. Reprinted by permission of Scribner, a division of Simon & Schuster, Inc. All rights reserved.

David Shields, Life Is Not a Playground, from *Other People: Takes and Mistakes* (New York: Knopf, 2017). Copyright © 2017 by David Shields. Reprinted by permission of Alfred A. Knopf, an imprint of the Knopf Doubleday Publishing Group, a division of Penguin Random House LLC, and by the Frances Goldin Literary Agency, Inc. All rights reserved.

Gary Smith, Eyes of the Storm. *Beyond the Game: The Collected Sportswriting of Gary Smith* (New York: Atlantic Monthly Press, 2000). Copyright © 1998, 2000 by Gary Smith. Reprinted by permission of Grove/Atlantic, Inc. Any third party use of this material, outside of this publication, is prohibited.

Red Smith, A Case of Malnutrition. *Out of the Red* (New York: Knopf, 1950). Copyright © 1950 by Red Smith. Reprinted by permission of the Literary Estate of Walter W. "Red" Smith.

Rick Telander, from *Heaven Is a Playground*, 4th edition (New York: Skyhorse Publishing, 2013). Copyright © 1976 by Rick Telander. Reprinted by permission of Skyhorse Publishing, Inc.

John Edgar Wideman, from *Hoop Roots* (Boston: Houghton Mifflin, 2001). Copyright © 2001 by John Edgar Wideman. Reprinted by permission of Houghton Mifflin Harcourt Publishing Company. All rights reserved.

Herbert Warren Wind, Farewell to Cousy. *The New Yorker*, March 23, 1963. Copyright © 1963 by Herbert Warren Wind. Reprinted by permission of the Herbert Warren Wind Trust.

Alexander Wolff, The Coach and His Champion. *Sports Illustrated*, March 6, 1989. Copyright © 1989 by Alexander Wolff. Reprinted by permission of *Sports Illustrated*.

Index

This book is set in 9.5 point ITC Stone Serif, a face designed for digital composition by Sumner Stone in 1987 as part of the ITC Stone font family, an endeavor undertaken in response to the difficulty of mixing different type styles on one page or in one design. The paper is acid-free lightweight opaque and meets the requirements for permanence of the American National Standards Institute. The binding material is Brillianta, a woven rayon cloth made by Van Heek–Scholco Textielfabrieken, Holland. Design and composition by Publishers' Design and Production Services, Inc. Printing and binding by Edwards Brothers Malloy, Ann Arbor.